ROUTLEDGE LIBRARY EDITIONS:
POLITICS OF ISLAM

ARABIC THOUGHT AND ISLAMIC SOCIETIES

ARABIC THOUGHT AND ISLAMIC SOCIETIES

AZIZ AL-AZMEH

Volume 1

Routledge
Taylor & Francis Group
LONDON AND NEW YORK

First published in 1986

This edition first published in 2013
by Routledge
2 Park Square, Milton Park, Abingdon, Oxfordshire OX14 4RN

Simultaneously published in the USA and Canada
by Routledge
711 Third Avenue, New York, NY 10017

First issued in paperback 2014

Routledge is an imprint of the Taylor and Francis Group, an informa business

British Library Cataloguing in Publication Data
A catalogue record for this book is available from the British Library

ISBN 978-0-415-64437-2 (Set)
eISBN 978-0-203-07906-5 (Set)
ISBN 978-0-415-83072-0 (hbk) (Volume 1)
ISBN 978-1-138-91253-3 (pbk) (Volume 1)
ISBN 978-0-203-38146-5 (ebk) (Volume 1)

Publisher's Note
The publisher has gone to great lengths to ensure the quality of this reprint but points out that some imperfections in the original copies may be apparent.

Disclaimer
The publisher has made every effort to trace copyright holders and would welcome correspondence from those they have been unable to trace.

Arabic Thought and Islamic Societies

EXETER ARABIC AND ISLAMIC SERIES

Arabic Thought and Islamic Societies
Aziz Al-Azmeh

ARABIC THOUGHT and ISLAMIC SOCIETIES

AZIZ AL-AZMEH

CROOM HELM
London • Sydney • Dover, New Hampshire

Croom Helm Ltd, Provident House, Burrell Row,
Beckenham, Kent BR3 1AT

Croom Helm Australia Pty Ltd, Suite 4, 6th Floor,
64–76 Kippax Street, Surry Hills, NSW 2010, Australia

British Library Cataloguing in Publication Data

Al-Azmeh, Aziz
Arabic thought and Islamic societies.
1. Arab countries — Intellectual life
I. Title
181′.9 DS36.85

ISBN 0-7099-0584-X

Croom Helm, 51 Washington Street, Dover,
New Hampshire 03820, USA

Library of Congress Cataloging in Publication Data

Al-Azmeh, Aziz
Arabic thought and Islamic societies.

Bibliography: p.
Includes Index.
1. Islamic empire — intellectual life. 2. Islam — doctrines. I. Title.
DS36.855.A96 1986 909′.097671 86-6229
ISBN 0-7099-0584-X

Filmset by Mayhew Typesetting, Bristol, England

Printed and bound in Great Britain by
Biddles Ltd, Guildford and King's Lynn

Contents

Preface
Abbreviations

1. **Metaphysical Foundations of Arabic Thought, 1: Hierarchy, Substance and Combination** 1
   The Great Chain of Being 2
   The Constitution of Composite Beings 13
   Elemental and Somatic Composites 22
   Composition, Justice and the Social Order 31
2. **Metaphysical Foundations, 2: Relations of Creation, Sympathy and Analogy** 55
   Humanity and Spirituality 55
   God and Man 64
   Occult Sympathies 69
   Divine Will and Human Acts 81
3. **A Special Relation: Signification** 106
   Knowledge and its Object 106
   Knowledge and the Arabic Language 114
   Interpretation and Symbolism 123
4. **The Constitution of Islamic and Foreign Sciences** 146
   The Structure of Scientific Formations 146
   Authority and the Classification of Sciences 155
   The Content and Form of Islamic and Foreign Sciences 166
5. **The Institution and Continuity of Scientific Formations** 198
   Criteria of Illicit Knowledge 201
   The Formation of Dogmatic and Legal Schools 211
   The Institutionalisation of Learning 223
   Pedagogic Authority and the Formation of Traditions 228

6. Concluding Notes: Scientific Knowledge and the Social Order 250
The Social and Utopian Being of the *'Ulamā'* 251
Official Knowledge and Social Catholicity 260
Exemplarism, Authority and the Best of All Possible Worlds 268

Arabic Sources 279
Index 287

Preface

It would clearly have been impossible to immerse oneself fully in the medium of Arabic scientific discourse in the Middle Ages. In a book on Arabic libraries quoted elsewhere, Youssef Eche estimated the number of works written in Arabic until the beginning of the fourteenth century A.D. to have been not less than 900,000. Most of these were ephemeral, and of the few that outlived their moment and were of epochal significance, I have had the privilege of sampling works, both major and minor, which cover almost the entire range of scientific activity conducted in the medium of Arabic. But though this sampling may not have been exhaustive, it was deliberately intended to be conceptually comprehensive, especially as one of the assumptions on which this book rests is one of historical closure and internal integration, in which it would not be theoretically impossible to start from virtually any one point and arrive at the others, on the condition that the structural features of the ensemble had been made manifest. The present work is an exploratory synthesis of material based on these samples, and is, by the very nature of things, a synthetic survey, one that is deliberately designed to detect openings, delimit conceptions, identify problems and orient further research.

The book opens with an attempt to identify and describe a number of distinctive features which compose the elementary principles of Arabic thought in the Middle Ages. From these distinctive features are generated, by various permutations, the various positions, theses, ideas, polemic thrusts and other ideational units whose ensemble is Arabic thought in the Middle Ages. These distinctive features are also the technical conditions of possibility of these individual ideas, their conformation in schools and tendencies of thought and of the over-all historical and intellectual order which is their ultimate historical outcome.

Not unnaturally, these distinctive features are of the nature of primary metaphysical principles in the widest sense of the term, and constitute the rough equivalent of, say, the metaphysical foundations of modern natural science as investigated by scholars such as Burtt and Koyré. They provide profiles according to which things are described and related. Thus hierarchy, opposition, sympathy, potency and their correlatives are principles investigated *in situ*, and an attempt is made to show how they and their associated notions underlie conceptualisations of all fields of investigation to which the attention of medieval Arabic thought was directed. To arrive at these distinctive features, scientific discourse from a variety of fields was decomposed and then reconstituted in terms of these implicitly or explicitly structuring elements. Metaphysical and natural-scientific texts were of paramount importance here. It is in such texts that these general distinctive features were articulated in their most explicit forms, not to speak of their most accentuated and pronounced expression, which renders the metaphysical and natural-scientific redaction of these elementary principles their most widely encompassing of forms, so that the normal and 'average' expression of these same principles could be construed and generated from these encompassing forms. It is this general form, in accentuated expression, which unravels the conceptual concordances which a purely doctrinal and idea-historical approach would occlude and obfuscate.

Thus it can be shown that there is a fundamental equivalence between, say, philosophical and dogmatic theological conceptions of composition, despite the cat-and-dog antagonism which often related philosophers and dogmatic theologians. Similarly, from the same fund of notions relating to the idea of composition are derived elemental composites and the forms of composition that characterise the political and ethical orders; whereas texts relating to natural composition are primarily used to unravel these fundamental notions, it will be seen that the generation of notions of political composition from these fundamental principles appears almost natural. Not only does this involve extrapolation, for this in itself is inadequate; it involves primarily the re-establishment, or the elicitation, of these underlying principles in political discourse with the heuristic guidance of findings from metaphysics and natural science. These elementary principles, therefore, are established in the discursive context where they are most explicitly developed, and then seen to be valorised in other discursive contexts. It will be observed that an author or a school of thought might employ a certain notion in a particular context, and vehemently deny it in another. A case in point is the rejection of the concept of nature and of the four elements by an Ash'arite physician in metaphysics and dogmatic theology, and his use of the same notion in his professional activity; another would be Ibn Sīnā's rejection of the possibility of alchemy and Ṭughrā'ī's demonstration of its possibility on the basis of Avicennan premisses. Such matters belie neither contradiction nor worse. They simply indicate that concepts are distinct from doctrines, and that contradiction is not a particularly relevant point of investigation, but is one which finds its bearings in wider, extra-discursive contexts.

The book then tackles the question of signification in Chapter 3. It sees this as a particular relation among others that had been studied earlier, not as a notion with particular privileges which makes it anything over and above being a relation. The modes of signification are studied with the aim of describing the manners in which knowledge is elicited and constructed, and the discursive and extra-discursive principles underlying this elicitation and construction. In this, as in previous discussions, emphasis is placed on the isolation of elementary conceptual parameters, and then on aspects of their valorisation in varying contexts.

After the elementary principles have been described, the book moves on to another, historical, plane, that of the paradigmatic configurations which are the sciences of Arabic thought. It must be stressed here that 'science' is employed in the most general of terms, the equivalent perhaps of *Wissenschaft*, to indicate any historically-recognised and self-perpetuating body of investigation concerning a particular object. Arabic paradigmatic formations, which utilised the elementary principles described in the first half of the book, are briefly described and then directed towards their doctrinal being, that is to say their institution in society and polity through the educational and pedagogic systems. It is these which are seen as the repositories and guarantors of continuity and tradition, provided tradition is regarded not as an inert being, but as a continuous elaboration of themes and ideas which are only putatively original. Finally, an attempt is made to weave together the conceptual, doctrinal and social aspects of the previous investigation in a way which suggests the manner in which they were correlative and integrated into an historico-cultural unity.

The historical epoch which is regarded, for the purposes of this book, as closed — i.e. as complete and self-impelling — is roughly that beginning in the fourth/tenth century and ending with the work of Suyūṭī, who died in 911/1505. Use has occasionally been made of work antedating or following this roughly delimited period, but such work is seen to be conceptually integral to works in our period. It would be pointless pedantry to set definite dates that might serve the main purpose of this book, which is the description of Arabic thought in its finished and consummated form. Any such attempt would have to decide what body of statements it was that represented the first consummate instance of, say, theology or law; the proposition is absurd. The works employed here are integrated according to the manners suggested in the body of this book, and it is the modes of their integration, not their beginning in calendar time, that guarantees their integration, realised for us today by virtue of the very fact that it could viably be taken for the unitary object of analysis. It goes without saying that the elements integrated could viably, if singly, be integrated in other contexts: medieval Christian, pagan or other contexts, and indeed, the similarities between many topical and conceptual features of Arabic and other contexts of thought are striking. But the mode of integration and realisation studied here is specific to the closed system of Arabic thought in the Middle Ages.

The integration across the epoch indicated extends geographically to encompass societies which had an officially Islamic polity in the period under review. The book treats of thought expressed in Arabic, much as one writes on Latin culture in the European Middle Ages and in late antiquity. Arabic was the sole or at least the principal language of learning. It is in this sense that the thought studied in this book is Arabic thought, and in this sense it incorporates work generated by Christians, Jews and Sabeans, to which reference is made. One might also surmise that Syriac thought in the Middle Ages could not have been conceptually distinct from that described here. Not only did they share a common patrimony which goes very far beyond the ostensible Qur'ānic and other scriptural 'origins' of Arabic thought, but they were both part of a common cultural experience. It is not by hazard or by a freak of a circumstance that the metrical structures, for instance, of Hebrew and of Persian poetry in the epoch under review were closely modelled on that of Arabic. All these languages, and the religions to which they were sometimes correlated, formed part of one unified culture, and the description of societies in this book as 'Islamic' is a political one and, equally important, carries a macro-cultural sense indicating an essential high-cultural, categorical and structural scholarly unity. Another matter of related relevance is that, as the reader will note, only scant attention is given to Shī'ite works, with the exception of Ismā'īlī works, which have a particular distinctiveness. The reason for this is that it carried out separate and independent careers before it cohered under the Safavid aegis, and was not generically different from Sunnite thought.

* * *

Studies of Arabic thought in the Middle Ages have generally borne the full burden of the orientalist tradition. Two primary elements constituted this tradition in its original form and ethos, both of which have shown a strange resistance to advances in the human sciences and to changing circumstances in the past one and a half centuries. The orientalist tradition was fashioned from the confluence of a positivist philology on the one hand, and a field to which this philology was applied, a field to which the oriental philologist was related by various cadences, grades and forms of antipathy, ultimately reducible to political and cultural antagonism shared by the oriental philologist and his wider milieu. Implicit or (less so nowadays) explicit antagonism was articulated in terms of tropes and *topoi* in terms of which oriental societies, histories and matters generally were expressed, analysed, typified, thought and identified, and which infirmed matters oriental within the bounds of a fantastic specificity and otherness. It is perhaps this very conception of impermeable otherness which prevented oriental philology from deriving benefit or advancement from refinements and conceptual developments achieved in the philological study of rather more normal languages and histories, as in the context of classical and romance studies, not to speak of historical, sociological and linguistic sciences in general. The present work intends to revise the present state of scholarship on medieval Arabic thought by tackling both components: it proposes to incorporate what has become the common stock of historical and other social and human sciences into the field, and to shed the topical repertoire of orientalism.

Positivist philology rests on a number of simple assumptions which are as misleading as they appear self-evident. It is assumed that a text — any text — is endowed, almost by force of nature herself, with an intrinsic and finite objectivity of meaning. It is, moreover, assumed that this meaning is immediately accessible with simple reference to the lexicon and to the immediate and identifiable historical origin in which the reality of this lexicon is thought to reside, so that the intellectual effort expended in this search for reality is one for which the scholar is deemed prepared and duly qualified with his or her acquisition of the standard techniques of library use. Underlying this matter is the assumption that 'reality' and discourse are in direct and immediate communion, with words being the direct transcript of discrete things. Correlatively, a rather elementary form of historicism operates as the diachronic context of such investigations, a historicism expressed in terms of the categories of origin, influence, originality and decline. Historicism normally rests on a teleology, and the teleology animating orientalist historicism has two termini. The first is the normal terminus of historical development, the bourgeois-capitalist epoch which is employed as the yardstick of normalcy so that other societies are regarded as its mirror image, the antonym of its components. This oriental societies, in orientalist discourse, have in common with other societies, such as those of medieval Europe or of 'aboriginal' peoples, and leads to the construal of these societies in terms of contrastive pairs relative to modern Western societies; thus if normal societies are characterised by reason, then oriental societies should be bound to irrational belief, and if normal societies be distinguished by order, oriental societies fail to find a mean between disorder and tyranny. To this ideological terminus of orientalist historicism, from which the topics according to which the orient is apprehended are derived, is added one derived from an inverted historicism. The second terminus, which is the methodological component of orientalist philology, locates the essence of things oriental not at the end, but in the beginning, the most accomplished state of these things oriental whose history is one of decline and of a betrayal of this beginning. Thus the Qur'ān, for instance, becomes not only the ostensible fount of all things Islamic, but also their explanatory principle. Things are thus, as a matter of principle and of methodological inevitability, reduced to their origins, either to explain them, or to measure their degree of authenticity, or both. 'Inauthentic' matters are then attributed to extra-Islamic influences which involve a greater degree of spirituality or rationality, and this constitutes their 'explanation'.

By contrast, this book does not seek originality, nor does it chase wild hares in the search for lines of filiation and charters of authenticity binding one text or statement to another. Neither does this book seek doctrines as such, nor does it, as philological historians of Arabic thought have generally done, seek to commune exclusively with genius. The authenticity of a particular view is not a concern of this study, neither are singular statements the primary units of the present investigation. What are being sought are matters which, in important ways, are antithetical to the topical and other concerns of traditional orientalist philology. While philological groundwork is undoubtedly essential, it is so in the same sense as common literacy is essential to intellectual endeavour in general, and is by no means the end of the affair nor the accomplishment of scholarly work. What discussions this book offers of discrete historical-philological matters, usually in footnotes, such as the discussion of the connection between Arabic thought and Stoicism or Hermeticism, are intended to contribute to the philological wherewithall of the field, not to underline the intrinsic importance of such matters nor to service an eccentric antiquarianism.

Instead of seeking originality, matters such as regularity have been investigated. Instead of influence, continuity according to principles underlying both antecedent and consequent, a continuity of which the events in ostensible filiation are instances. Instead of the ultimately ethical conception of authenticity which relates an event to an ostensible origin, this book seeks historicity and discursive reality. In other words, the universe of scientific ideas is regarded as a field of regularity, of constant motifs, categories and relations which describe a unified epochal unit — Arabic thought in the Middle Ages — and of which particular ideas are instances generated from the particular transformation of this anterior field of possibilities. In terms of the history of ideas, which only truly exists in terms of the history of scientific formations as in this book, or of ideological and cultural structures, these unified epochal units represent the logical and scientific integration of an epoch, a correlative of the cultural and historical unity of an historical period.

An historical period does not manifest what it takes for normalcy, and therefore for regularity and 'authenticity', in its outstanding examples. Genius is therefore not the true expression of the historical unity of an epochal phenomenon, but is rather the tolerably anomalous elaboration of its motifs and categories. Epochal tendencies are rather manifested in the common run of ideas, the primary grey matter which carries it, just as oriental philology is manifested less by its outstanding examples and advances than by the oral instruction which carries over its normalcy from generation to generation in university faculties. This is why an attempt has been made in this book to seek out lesser writers in addition to the more celebrated ones; the former may have a less proprietory claim to current ideas, but they are in fact their medium, the occasion for their daily occurrence and are therefore the truer indices of the vitality and of the scientific and cultural relevance of such ideas and categories.

In conceptual terms, only the common patrimony of contemporary human sciences has been brought to bear. There has been, for instance, no thorough employment of what is commonly termed 'deconstruction', although this is not absent. Most of the analytical procedures employed will be familiar to readers acquainted with historical and philological research outside the bounds of orientalism, particularly in the history of sciences and discursive formations, in the political and social aspects of knowledge, in the theory of discourse and in the vast fields of intellectual history in the widest of senses. One very important impulse derived from the sciences of man is the refusal to impute to Arabic thought in the Middle Ages divisions that correspond to the current departmental specialisations in European universities. Thus there has been no urge to see an economic science, for instance, in Arabic thought; phenomena which correspond to what is today termed 'economics' are treated in their own context — in this case, theological and metaphysical. Correlatively, there has been no reservation about treating matters which may be anathema today as conceptually central. Such for instance was alchemy; it was not an insinuation on the part of irrationality, but a location where a number of very central concepts were developed. Arabic thought in the Middle Ages, like medieval European thought or Greek thought properly studied, and indeed like the conceptual systems of 'aboriginal' peoples, is utterly other and foreign today. It is this difference which is underlined, not the continuity of a mythological Islamic essence, for history is the domain of discontinuity in addition to harbouring regularities. This assumption is a cardinal precondition for studying our object as one which is self-sufficient, independent of us and our presumptions of an apocalyptic objectivity, and thus one which can be made to yield itself to us without us having to conjure it up to ourselves in the form of our antithesis or our incomplete self. Only then will it be possible to conceive of Arabic thought as something other than the series of absences and inadequacies which much modern scholarship makes of it: absence of reason except under seige, absence of form, absence of creativity, absence of spirituality. The difference between medieval Arabic and modern thought is a real and determinate difference; Arabic thought in the Middle Ages is not simply the domain of utter or simply antithetical otherness, but of an otherness which is comprehensible in terms of the social and human sciences, whose proper task it is to unravel social and human topics, wherever they may be. It is indeed the generality which modern historical sciences can generate which permits the scholar to study fields on which no sufficient monographic work exists, as is the case with many topics addressed in the present work. Given this situation, it is perhaps not surprising that the conceptual tools used are not as finely tuned and as thoroughly employed as the author would have wished; but such is the hazard of all exploratory work, that it cannot be as consummated as it ought to be, and that it provokes sanctimonious territorialist instincts especially as the field has so far been fragmentarily studied and researched.

* * *

I owe a debt of gratitude to libraries which particularly facilitated research on this book over many years: that of the American University of Beirut, the British Library, the Exeter University Library, the Institut Français des Etudes Arabes in Damascus, the Orient-Institut der Deutschen Morgenländischen Gesellschaft in Beirut and the Library of the School of Oriental and African Studies in the University of London. The Librarian and staff of the Faculty of Letters Library at Kuwait University treated me as an honoured guest and accorded me such privileges and unfailing help as are unique, and I am particularly grateful to them. I should also like to thank M.A. Cook for reading the typescript of this book and for making helpful suggestions. I.R. Netton has been an exemplary colleague, having read the various chapters of this book as they emerged with sympathy and encouragment. M.A. Shaban availed me of his constant friendship, which made possible the writing of this book in very difficult circumstances. The contribution of K. Sen to the fashioning of this book has been inimitable, at once unique and in no need for public announcement. D. Croom is unique amongst publishers for his good sense and energy, both of which qualities, along with the staff of Croom Helm, gave the present work smooth passage. I should also like to thank R. Fry for preparing the map, and P. Auchterlonie for the preparation of the index.

Abbreviations

BEO	Bulletin d'Etudes Orientales
BSOAS	Bulletin of the School of Oriental and African Studies
DA	Dirāsāt 'Arabiyya
EI	Encyclopedia of Islam, new edn, (Leiden-London, 1960 ff. (in progress))
IBLA	Institut des belles lettres arabes
IJMES	International Journal of Middle Eastern Studies
JESHO	Journal of the Economic and Social History of the Orient
JRAS	Journal of the Royal Asiatic Society
MIDEO	Mémoires de l'Institut Dominicain d'Etudes Orientales
REI	Revue d'Etudes Islamiques
SI	Studia Islamica
ZDMG	Zeitschrift der Deutschen Morgenländischen Gesellschaft

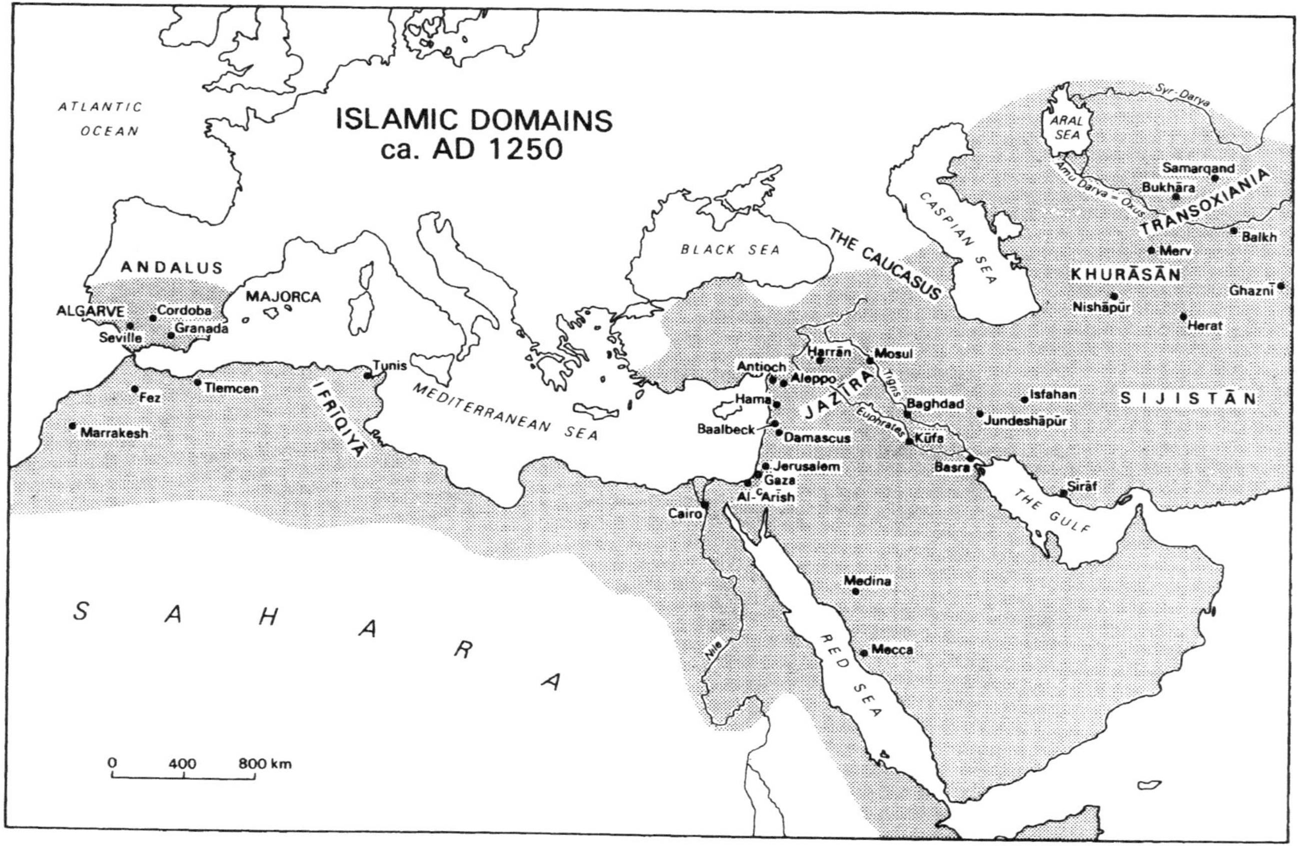
ISLAMIC DOMAINS
ca. AD 1250
ATLANTIC OCEAN
ANDALUS
ALGARVE
Cordoba
Seville
Granada
MAJORCA
Tunis
Fez
Tlemcen
Marrakesh
IFRĪQIYĀ
MEDITERRANEAN SEA
BLACK SEA
THE CAUCASUS
CASPIAN SEA
ARAL SEA
Syr-Darya
Amu Darya = Oxus
Samarqand
Bukhāra
TRANSOXIANIA
Balkh
Merv
KHURĀSĀN
Ghaznī
Nishāpūr
Herat
Harrān
Mosul
Antioch
Aleppo
Tigris
Hama
JAZĪRA
Baghdad
Isfahan
SIJISTĀN
Baalbeck
Euphrates
Jundeshāpūr
Damascus
Kūfa
Jerusalem
Basra
Gaza
Al-ᶜArīsh
Sīrāf
Cairo
THE GULF
Medina
Nile
Mecca
RED SEA
SAHARA
0
400
800 km

Chapter One

Metaphysical Foundations of Arabic Thought, 1: Hierarchy, Substance and Combination

Arabic thought in the Middle Ages reclaimed a very ancient metaphysical repertoire in its conception of both terrestrial and extraterrestrial beings. This repertoire is rehearsed explicitly in works of metaphysics, in pronouncements of metaphysical whimsy scattered throughout Arabic *Schrifttum*, in speculative and sagely reflections of a literary and scientific type as well as in political and social writings, concerned as they are with notions of order and rectitude. We also find it implicit in several other textual locations which will become explicit in the course of the following pages. At the heart of the conception of order that derives from this ancient repertoire is the idea of hierarchy, for the world of men, along with that of inanimate substances and that of incorporeal beings, is bound to the location to which it is assigned in an hierarchical order of things within which everything has its station. Just as there seems to be a natural priority of foodstuffs over one another, one reflected in the order in which food is served to guests (fruit first, followed by meat and ending with water),[1] there is a sytem of hierarchical precedence by means of which all things are con-joined in a system of order. Things descend along this chain of being[2] from God down through the heavenly spheres and other incorporeals to the human soul, where they meet an ascendant hierarchy which takes things from the four elements through inanimate minerals, plants, animals and humankind. And within each of these stations, things are again arranged in an hierarchy of excellence, worth and honour constituting, as it were, the imprint of macrocosmic hierarchy in microcosm. Thus foods are so arranged, as are the elements of language in which nouns precede verbs and particles,[3] while the forms of the syllogism are arranged not only in a deductive order, but correlatively in an order of honour[4] where simpler forms precede inferior and more mediate ones.

The Great Chain of Being

The chain of being assembles all beings in a comprehensive association which specifies every particular being with the attribution of a relative, at once and indifferently ethical and ontological, position with respect to other beings. This assembly is a scale bounded by its extremities, the topmost of which is endowed with absolute value and the lowest of which is somewhat like the obverse of the first and its mirror image. The topmost point of the scale, which is occupied by God, is the one in possession of normative positivity in its absolute fullness, positively as ethical norm and as ontological value. All that is not God is regarded according to the neo-Platonic scheme of things: as degrees of privation. Full existence, absolute goodness and eternity (as distinct from sempiternity), are attributable solely to God; apart from Him, existence and value are relative matters. This is the meaning of the saying which Abū Ḥayyān al-Tawḥīdī (d. after 400/1009) attributes to Abū Sulaimān al-Sijistānī (d. after 391/1001), that 'evil is nothingness . . . while good is being',[5] a saying that seems to duplicate many others of the same import. Evil, according to another, is 'the privation of essence, or rather, the imperfection of essence'[6] — for at issue here is not, as Fakhr al-Dīn al-Rāzī (d. 606/1210) pointed out, a simple opposition between good and evil, but one in which 'good is the realisation of perfection . . . while evil is the lack of such perfection'.[7] Similarly, things that exist either exist utterly and absolutely ('al-wujūd al-ḥaqq'), or else exist relatively and merely by virtue of perfect existence.[8] The hierarchy binding the eternal God with sempiternal and corruptible, perishable creation is a pyramid constituted by its apex, at once its metaphysical and political generator.

The apex of the chain of being dictates its very primacy as the condition of all that does not belong to its essence, so that other things are not only derivative in the normative sense, but are so in a demiurgical sense, regardless of whether this involved creation in time. Things are ranged along the chain of being in a manner that is purely linear, the distance from the apex being the determinant factor in allocating the value of the thing in question. Things are thus ranged on a sliding scale of ontological and ethical value along which are placed things of a decreasing value and reality and an increasing degeneration, ending with a moral indifference, absurdity and depravity of existence. Throughout, the arrangement of things in this cosmic assembly is along the lines of primacy, ontological and normative primacy implying potency, just as terrestrial political assembly starts with the head who is also the most perfect, in addition to being the most puissant, and slides down the line of imperfection and dependence until we reach creatures whose entire being and actions are dependent upon, and in the service of, superior beings.[9] The political and cosmic orders are recapitulated in, among other locations, the faculties of the human soul and their arrangement whereby the baser ones, the appetitive and reproductive, are in the service of the higher faculties, the intellectual, with their multifarious functions which are themselves hierarchically arranged.[10] That which is primary is antecedent and relatively perfect in relation to that which is baser, just as the heart is the primary organ in the body, ruling its functions and coming into existence first in the process of embryo formation, thus effectively causing the body to be.[11]

Thus things constitute two fundamental classes, that of created and that of uncreated beings, both being relative matters, for angels or celestial spheres can be said to be less created than corruptible things, being closer in essence, in being and in value to the creator. To this distinction corresponds the classification of things between eternal and non-eternal, between that which is *sui generis* and that which is not so, between the simple and composite.[12] In all cases, hierarchy is a system of metonymic correspondences between various articulations of value, ontological, ethical, temporal. But such a system was imperfect. Thus Ibn Rushd (d. 595/1198) found it difficult to decide precisely what order governed the arrangement of the heavenly spheres and why the saturnine sphere should, by common belief, come second, as the heavenly spheres can be normatively arranged according to various criteria involving honour, none of which has a conclusive claim to superiority.[13] Similarly, a bitter critic of Ibn Sīnā (d. 438/1037) charged that the philosopher was proceeding counter to the exigencies of the nature of incorporeals when he maintained that the lowest of the spheres (the lunar) was solely responsible for the emanation of forms destined for the world. This assertion depended on imputing considerations of spatial distance amongst incorporeals, where there is in fact no space and where there should be nothing to stop direct emanations from the First Intellect reaching the world.[14]

The differential potency of members of the chain of being is perhaps the most essential constituent of the chain. Apart from the Active Intellect, the philosopher-king of Fārābī's (d. 339/950) virtuous community is beholden to no one, but is the supreme component of the community[15] just as God is the supreme component of all being. That which is superior is not only more excellent, but is also more potent, fuller of plenitude, self-sufficiency and completeness. After the Philonic moment of Platonism, it seems that providence became, *de rigeur*, creation[16] and the demiurgical providence required by monotheistic divinity[17] recapitulated and absorbed philosophical notions of primacy in its religious purview. For in creation were encapsulated all the senses of anteriority and precedence that were known to Arabic thought: temporal, precedence in rank conceived as relative distance from the apex of the hierarchy, precedence involving honour as the precedence of Abū Bakr over 'Umar, natural precedence as in the precedence of the number one over two and essential precedence as expressed in causal anteriority and differential plenitude.[18] The idea of dramatic creation by a creator-preserver, essential to myths of creation as those philosophically or narratively expressed in Arabic thought, is never, and could not have been, eschewed, as can be seen for instance in Ibn Sīnā's importation of temporal elements into the philosophy of perpetual creativity.[19] The assertions of an Ibn Rushd, for instance, on the eternity of the world, are philosophical assertions concerning the sempeternity of the world, not implying it to be coeval with God, for time does not figure in the realm of the philosophical language of causality and is irrelevant to, and does not necessarily contradict, creation *ex nihilo* and in time.[20] Both the philosophical and the more explicitly mythical tales of creation involve the five types of primacy that we have just seen; and all but time are relevant to the chain of being and its hierarchical order: rank, honour, nature, causality. In addition to time, these matters not only distinguish lower things from higher ones, but also contribute to the sense of absolute priority, of the higher being the absolute ground for the lower, both according to the nature of the mind, which sees essential priority as that which conjoins natural and causal priority.[21] Thus the chain of being is an hierarchy of grounds, stretching from the sublimity of the ground of all grounds to the most abject creatures as exist wholly on account of others.

Self-sufficiency in an hierarchy of grounds is the criterion according to which the station of everything is determined, from that of plants to that of nouns in the hierarchy of parts of speech (noun, verb, particle) — this, according to the grammarian Ibn Jinnī (d. 392/1002), is headed by nouns because of their independence of the other two, for a noun can convey a meaning without recourse to verbs or to particles, which particles and verbs cannot accomplish.[22] Anteriority, in an hierarchical world, is the correlative of self-sufficiency,[23] and dependence in such a world is wholly unilateral, with the higher transmitting down to the baser whatever is under scrutiny: existence, goodness or wealth as in Ibn Khaldūn's (d. 808/1406) characterisation of the relation between social estates, which he shared with his culture.[24] In all cases, the superior is the purer, the less adulterated with external causality, with participation in another essence, with contingency.[25] The apex of this scale, the creator, according to a theologian. 'is self-subsistent, that is, by virtue of His existence, He dispenses with a creator to Create Him, and with a subtrate to occupy'.[26] Similarly, the number one is the principle, origin and ground of all numbers in that they would all vanish if it were removed, whereas the one will never cease to be with the absence of other numbers[27] — or beings.[28]

The superior terminus of the chain of being is therefore the ground, at various removes of immediacy, of all its members. It is their causal and normative ground. Equally, it is their final cause, to use an Aristotelian term which well conveys the sense with which the anteriority of this beginning is infused, but which not all discourse on the chain of being would deem doctrinally fit to utilise. This superior terminus is not only the generative cause of all being, but the ultimate purpose for which creation took place. It is the beginning and the end; it is the *telos* of all creation. This much flows directly from the structure of superordination and subordination which constitutes the chain of being. For that which is sublime cannot have existed for the sake of baser stuff, otherwise the order of things will have been confounded; rather, things work in the opposite sense, so that it is not possible to conceive of that which was caused as the cause of its cause, or as the final cause of the efficient cause.[29] Indeed, all causes are of a fuller grade of being than that which they cause to be,[30] and this applies not only to ontological fullness, but to its parallel normative fullness as well. Truth, according to Fārābī, runs parallel to existence, and actuality may run parallel to it as well. For the truth of something is the existence appropriate to it.[31] This appropriateness is fully relative and utterly dependent on the only value which truly structures all other values and acts as their absolute measure, that of the ultimate superordinate which dictates the ontological and other values of all creatures in accordance with the distance from this ultimate apex established by their position on the chain of being. No creature is intrinsically necessary, for all but the creator is contingent; its existence is fully dictated and comprehended by its dependence upon, and subordination to, the creator, which is the sole, and the absolute, value. The created is an auxiliary constituted by its privation in comparison with an absolute fullness. And indeed, all beings are, correlatively with other classifications, divisible into the necessary, and therefore ultimately self-generating, and the contingent, and therefore ontologically dependent on an external and prior creative act.[32] Contingency itself has been construed as a privative nature,[33] although the question of necessity and contingency was a highly complex one.[34]

It is this hierarchical dependence which dictates the appurtenance of things and their very nature, which flows from their appurtenance. It is a unilaterally prescriptive hierarchy of this type which, among other things, animates the recursive conception of all things, from genealogies to beliefs, stripping them of all that is not directly imparted by their ground and origin, and maintains that any doubts concerning the ground of things is one cast about those things themselves.[35] Yet this continuity between absolute perfection and absolute imperfection is not, except for the advocates of pantheistic monism, the continuity of an invariant essence. It is not the continuity of a substrate inhabited by the multifarious avatars of a continuous substance, but is truly structured by a duality. At issue is not only metaphysical discourse, but a matter that is firmly allied with religion, and no thought connected with religion, except pantheistic monism, can feel comfortable with the absence of irreligion. No religious outlook can sustain itself in a situation where evil, the devil or privation are not, at least temporarily, a match for God. Evil and privative existence are effectively, if not explicitly in metaphysical and religious discourse, self-subsistent substances. They are even temporarily self-sufficient, active on their own behalf, endowed with a normativeness which can enter into a relation of competition, even of a contrary plenitude and generativeness, with the analogous properties of divinity. Indeed, they act as an effective, if occasional anti-divinity, which infuses and therefore contaminates and possibly corrupts things in close contact with godliness. That is why Subkī (d. 771/1369) counselled his vizier to keep money wrongfully gained in the service of his sovereign apart from that legitimately acquired: apart they each maintain their normative purity; in the same hoard they both become illegitimate.[36] Evil adulterates absolutely.

The chain of being can thus be said to be composed of God and not-God, and the continuity it described can thus be said to be structured by an essential duality, a dyadic concomitance, cleft at the top, or towards the middle, depending on our perspective. We have, in the first place, God and His spiritual domain. This domain was variously conceived and named: God and the angels, associated with the angelical component of humankind (prophetic and saintly souls), according to trustees over religion generically dubbed the '*ulamā*'; the First Intellect from which the heavenly spheres emanate (and their number was the subject of some controversy) along with the fully accomplished and realised human souls, according to the philosophers; or again, the marriage of religious and metaphysical imagery that we witness in the esotericist tradition in general,[37] and in Ismā'īlism in particular,[38] along with the narrative allegorisation of the intellects/spheres/angels conception by means of religious-mythological notions of the Pen that, before Creation, writes the writ of all that is to come, and associated notions.[39] This last tendency often describes the role of man in the kingdom of God either as a final release from the cycles of reincarnation as in Ismā'īli theory, or as his participation in the essence of divinity as is maintained by some mystics.

In the second place we have those components of the chain of being which cannot be included amongst the members of God's immediate kingdom whose members, in varying degrees, partake of His divinity. These compose the corporeal sensuous world, which starts with the four elements — fire, air, water, earth — of which minerals are alloyed, on through the plant kingdom, insects and reptiles, animals and finally, man in so far as he is a corporeal creature. The line of ascendance here is one towards growing autonomy and spirituality:[40] growing animation and growing differentiation in animate faculties, starting with movement, on to appetite of various descriptions, and forward to greater capacities for intellection and the receipt of divine emanations in the widest sense of the term. This line of progression differentiates inanimate substances from plants, plants from animals and ordinary animals from man, the one animal endowed with a soul and intellect. Yet the line is continuous, for each station — the inanimate, the plant and the animal — tends to shade off into the next and participate in its more primitive qualities. Thus plants are intermediate between minerals and animals in the sense that they are not quite as inanimate as the former, but do not possess the perfection of sense and movement appropriate to the latter, and therefore partake of the properties of both.[41] The extremity of each station is contained, potentially, in superior stations, in the sense that superior stations comprehend inferior ones,[42] just as man comprehends the properties of inferior beings and is distinguished from them by what he adds over and above his inferiors. A further naturalistic edge to this growing comprehensiveness is given by the Ikhwān al-Ṣafā': the inferior is to the superior as its matter, as the matter of its form and the raw material of its body, interiorised by feeding.[43]

We thus have, along the chain of being, movement in two senses, from the extremities towards the middle where man is located. The two domains, which some saw as mutually impermeable,[44] start from different premisses, the top half proceeding on a line of descent and the bottom ascending to the station of man.[45] The dyadic character of the chain of being is one which effects a specification and division amongst classes of elements belonging to the chain, but this division is not absolute and does not sunder the essential generative unity, the unity of dependence and hierarchy, which fashions the chain. Man lies at the confluence of these two classes of things. He is body and soul: body in so far as he is the terminal point in the ascension of corporeals to higher stations, and soul in as much as he is the terminal point reached by incorporeal substances in their descent from the more absolute realms of sublimity. The two components of man and his dyadic structure are the edges of the two classes of creation, at the point where they meet and differentiate.

This generative continuity is uneven: for while 'the distinctive character of any divine order travels through all derivative existents and bestows itself upon all the inferior kinds',[46] this continuity traces its course of uneven passage through territory increasingly subject to deterioration, even degeneration. The base thus has no autonomous constitution independent of the sublime: the baser classes are, at one and the same time, the contrary and the result of the sublime. They are a drawing away from them at the same time as being an aspiration towards them, for their mobility is oriented towards the terminal point of the baser class of things, man, which partakes of, and shades into, incorporeal things. Bereft of any self-constitutive principles, the creatures, being creatures of a very particular creator, must derive their metaphysical constitution from whatever is bestowed upon them. And being ranged on an ontological continuum whose values are dictated by the absolute value which structures this continuum — the chain of being — they can find their definition only in terms of those that define the creator: as privation of a variety of properties. Creatures elicit their determinations relatively, with sole reference to the creator; these determinations thus serve, in the first place, to differentiate it from the creator. Creatures therefore subsist within the flow of what looks like a divine polemic, bent on pointing out that which is not Him, but with sole reference to Him and to that which he shares with his immediate entourage of angels, spheres and other spirits, and from which all else differs absolutely, i.e. in so far as it is a negativity.

Despite metaphysical exigency, this negativity is never fully realised, as the foregoing will have indicated. For despite the relation of opposition in which the only self-subsistent value is the positive one attributed to the ceiling of all things which is required by the metaphysics of Arabic thought, we are in fact registering an opposition that is not true to its theoretical requirements and that is not always fully realised. What is at issue in fact is not simply an opposition grounded in and founded upon one value; it is rather a binomial dyad which is displayed, and the creature is not simply the negative of a positivity which is the creator, but is also one which carries a positive opposition to the creator, one in which the creature is a term *sui generis*, for just as there is no effective divinity without the devil, and no creature without a creator, there is no creator deserving of the name without creatures, dogmatic assertions notwithstanding. What holds true of the creator and the creature as positive terms in mutual active opposition also holds for their various differentiae, which meet in man. It is indeed possible to draw up a list of opposite terms which would comprehend the locations and terms in the context of which the conception of divine and profane things is constituted, and the subsequent pages will bring many of these terms into full view: humanity/divinity (*nāsūt/lāhūt*), truth/existence (*ḥaqq/khalq*), soul/matter, mind/sense, life/lifelessness, freedom/servitude, and other terms of opposition without which things cannot be comprehended or conceived. What should be stressed is that these oppositions duplicate the essential normative opposition of sacred and profane, which is likewise duplicated in the opposition between activity and passivity and their concomitants: simplicity/composition, necessity/contingency, and, by implication, the opposition between artifice on the one hand, and character or disposition (*sawiyya*) on the other.

The term *sawiyya*, here indifferently rendered as character and disposition, is used advisedly and in preference to 'nature' (*ṭab'*, *ṭabī'a*). To have used 'nature' would probably have committed some strands of medieval Arabic thought to much more than they would have been prepared to sustain, and would have imputed a number of senses which are absent. Nature, in any case, is not the unambiguous term that it is popularly taken to be; it has a very rich history, both as a term and as a concatenation of intersecting senses, and this state of affairs makes it almost inevitable that shifts of sense occur without the awareness of the user of this term.[47] Additionally, the term 'nature', and occasionally even *sawiyya*, imply a regularity which was strenuously refuted and zealously contested by parties to medieval Arabic thought, mainly Ash'arites bent on denying activity to all but God. Medieval scholars were well aware of this ambiguity. The grammarian Abū Sa'īd al-Sīrāfī (d. after 364/975) declared that 'nature' belonged to the class of 'equivocal nouns' (*al-asmā' al-mashūba*), an equivocation less marked in its analogues like 'norm', 'character', 'disposition' (*ḍarība, salīqa, sajiyya*).[48] Abū Sulaimān al-Sijistānī, the brilliant philosopher and acquaintance of Sīrāfī, saw it as 'a common noun',[49] and many authors have provided us with a wide variety of definitions of 'nature',[50] all of which intersect around the essential sense of an intrinsic character which defines a given object, along with 'the potency immanent in a thing', causing it to unfold in the way it does.[51] Regardless of whether this nature is extrinsic to the thing in possession of it, being for instance a potency proper to the Universal Soul and transmitted to sublunary beings,[52] or thoroughly denied as it was by the Ash'arites, there is no denying the regularity of things and their constancy, without which no form of thought would be possible. It is moreover not necessary to hold to a Peripatetic definition which links nature to the Aristotelian conception of change,[53] nor to subscribe to the prevalent metaphysical conception of nature which was infused with the Stoic vitalistic notion of potency which has been encountered, in order to employ this notion. Regardless of technical senses, nature remained the principle that preserved a thing and endowed it with integrity, and without which the thing would cease to be identifiable and would no longer have a name: to waive nature is to establish nothingness.[54] Nature is simply that which is not artificial, and occurs without the need for instruction of any kind.[55] Ibn Ḥazm (d. 456/1036) and Ibn Taimiyya (d. 728/1327), in their radical rigour and lack of regard for terminologies, are always our best guides in the complex field of terminological proliferation which they are always willing to sort out and defenestrate. To them, the denial of nature by the Ash'arites goes counter to the opinion of 'the majority of reasoning men, both Muslim and non-Muslim, both men of the *Sunna* such as theologians, jurists, traditionists, and mystics, and men not belonging to the *Sunna* such as the Mu'tazilites and others',[56] all of whom subscribed to the affirmation of constant dispositions and definite, ascertainable causalities for things that occur in the world, matters known as disposition, character, norm and the like.[57] Nature and its analogues are matters which the Prophet never denied, they are constants which, if removed, would remove things from existence.[58] Indeed, to deny nature and to affirm an occasionalistic conception of regularity is a denial of the possibility of miracles.[59]

Regularity is not denied by Ikhwān al-Ṣafā' who, while stripping nature of autonomy and refusing to ascribe it to the intrinsic properties of things, nevertheless stressed regularity — denying it, according to the Ikhwān, is tantamount to a denial of immediate evidence and to a lack of awareness of the power of incorporeals.[60] In all cases, 'nature' implies — and does not unambiguously designate — a certain regular disposition, a propensity for a particular thing to behave in a certain ascertainable manner, regardless of whether this propensity is regarded as impelled by an internal, almost pneumatic, quality (such as air being light and thus seeking its natural location upwards), or merely describes a predisposition to receive certain effects from external agencies. Additionally, there is often a teleological component to 'nature', as in the nature of the famous Khaldūnian *'aṣabiyya* which naturally seeks state-formation and consolidation as its teleological consummation, its full accomplishment,[61] its moment of rest, just as a light body comes to rest when it reaches its natural position 'up there'.

Nature and *sawiyya* are thus terms located in the midst of very rich semantic and lexical fields which refer to a multiplicity of senses all of which converge upon the sense of a continuous integrity of being, the identity of the origin and custodian of this continuity and its preserver notwithstanding. It is the description of the *status quo*, regardless of whether this description takes the guise of a vitalist interpretation. When the regulative compulsion is intrinsic to the thing, it would then take on the name of 'nature' without any hesitation. Regardless of this, or of the ultimate control over things and natures by spiritual agencies (and this was affirmed by some of the strongest proponents of the concept of nature),[62] the unvarying constitution of things was not generally open to question, whether intrinsic potency was involved, or whether it was external — in which case nature and the soul were coterminous.[63] That is how it was possible to expand the use of the term 'nature' to sublime locations where it was not strictly appropriate by one of the greatest intellects of the Arab-Islamic Middle Ages: Fakhr al-Dīn al-Rāzī held that the heavenly spheres could be said to have a nature over and above the Four Natures that compose the world (the four elements) — the ground for the circular movement of the spheres, 'although it is not natural, is not yet foreign to them, and is as if it were natural'. Rāzī added that 'every potency causes a movement by means of inclination . . . the mover of the first movement incessantly creates an inclination in the body [that is being moved], and there is no reason why this inclination should not be termed nature, for it is caused neither by compulsion nor by will or election, not by any outside effect, neither can it not move nor be moved in a contrary direction . . . if you therefore chose to call this nature you could say that the sphere only moves by virtue of nature'.[64] We shall therefore proceed without regard to the ultimate metaphysical custodian of regularity in constitution and constancy in potency.[65]

But to dwell upon the inner constitution of things without regard to external determinants would be inadequate. The two notions are in fact correlative. The division of things into the category comprising self-generated and intrinsic potency and that of things which lack such character is one which posits mutually sustaining correlates. This division also corresponds to the division of things into activity and passivity, into self-subsistence and externally-induced position, in short, into nature and artifice. Ibn Rushd classified all things into nature, i.e. as all things that possess within themselves their principles of motion and rest, and artifice, or else things are said to belong to a category which joins the two properties: the realm of contingency.[66] Similarly, Ibn Khaldūn categorises things as natural and intended.[67] Tawḥīdī, for his part, preferred a usage which respects the views that oppose the concept of nature, and grounds knowledge in the mind while grounding art (in the sense of *technē*) in nature[68] — whereas, in another text, he counts nature a part of the divine realm and artifice within the domain of humankind.[69] For Abul-Barakāt al-Baghdādī (d. 547/1152–3), artifice is an act lacking in essential constitution and is ever the result of an act; it is the passive recipient of the act and fully its effect.[70] Nature is everywhere relative to its discourse: it is self-generation, superior to dependence, but is also, in other contexts, the inferior terminus, as in the relation of nature to spirit illustrated in Rāzī's discussion of the 'nature' of the spheres. It is sometimes the synonym of artifice.

The distinction between natural and posited occurrences is the correlate of that between activity and passivity, or passivity and activity, depending on one's preferences regarding 'nature'. This distinction in turn is a moment in the general distinction between spiritual and corporeal entities. This is perhaps best illustrated in Abū Sulaimān al-Sijistānī's urbane reflection on this matter: although artifice, being of baser stuff than nature, always seeks to emulate its more sublime correlate, it does nevertheless come to the aid of nature when this latter is striving to perfect itself with the help of the mind and the soul, which utilise artifice to ameliorate things and conduct them to the perfection and fullness appropriate for them. That is how a dancer can dance to perfection.[71] Artifice is nothing but the result of intention, and that is the meaning of Ibn Khaldūn's enigmatic statement to the effect that action starts where thought ends.[72] The distinction governs Ibn Khaldūn's classification of all being to essences and acts,[73] and his insistence, shared by others, that premeditation is the condition of all acts.[74] Between nature and artifice is therefore an hierarchical opposition, much like the one discussed earlier; for the artificial is opposed to the natural, and this correlative opposition is transcribed into the hierarchical terms of generation. That is why, as we saw, artificial things always emulate nature;[75] they are of a lower rank.[76]

It is perhaps worth pointing out quickly here a matter to be discussed in some detail later: that alchemical action which transforms base metals into gold is based on this very idea of emulating nature. This was the *leitmotiv* of an important line of criticism levelled against this difficult art: that this idea is premised upon the alchemist's absolute knowledge of gold and of the other substances and multifarious processes involved in transmuting metals to it, and that such a presumption should not be questioned, as without such absolute knowledge no exact emulation of the ways of nature in the manufacture of gold would be possible.[77] *Sawiyya*-nature, both as an intrinsic matter and as the result of external causality is the ground and base, and artifice the derivative and dependent. These are the terms in which the anteriority of beduinism over civilisation, in Ibn Khaldūn, is made an anteriority of nature: the Arabs, Ibn Khaldūn declared, are a natural people, and thus indispensable for the unfolding of history,[73] just as objects which satisfy need are natural, and supererogatory objects artificial.[79] In the same way, agriculture is anterior to craftsmanship, and this in turn is anterior to commerce, for it has natural priority.[80] And much along the same line of thought, Ibn Taimiyya criticises Aristotelian logic on the assumption that definitions, being conventional and therefore artificial, do not enter the realm of science, which is reality, and which is open to necessary, almost congenital, 'natural', knowledge.[81]

The Constitution of Composite Beings

Nature-*sawiyya* is thus the decisive term which encodes the division of things into the active and the passive, that which is its own constitutive principle and that which is extrinsically constituted by the action of an agent.[82] *Sawiyya*-nature occupies the realm of necessity, artifice that of contingency; theoretical and practical reason flow from them, respectively.[83] That which links the two realms is the regulative potency inherent in the world of necessity and self-regulation, and such a world cannot but be endowed with consciousness for, as we saw in the previous paragraph, acts must be preceded by thought. Self-regulative and self-impulsive entities, like those which impel movement in others, must therefore be soul-bearing.[84] Artificial creatures are such in so far as they are composed of elementary components which do not naturally form the configuration which is the artificial creature. Simplicity and perfection are metaphysically equivalent.[85] It is hardly surprising that opponents of the idea of nature made use of the same idea — that composition is contrary to nature — to combat the notion of regularity and naturalness of created things.[86] The preservation of a composite which is the body cannot be the act of the body but the effect of the soul;[87] on this assertion there is hardly any disagreement. A creature, as the theologian Bāqillānī (d. 403/1013) asserted according to this logic of activity and passivity, cannot act upon another creature[88] and the composition of things from elemental entities upwards requires a considerable degree of external compulsion. Elementary things are opposites and contradictories as we shall see — such was one proof employed by the Mu'tazilites to demonstrate the existence of a creator[89] and is identical to the manner in which Māturīdī (d. 333/944) proved the creation in time of all bodies.[90] The same thesis — the primacy of simplicity over composition, and that composites are nothing but the association of simpler stuff — lies at the heart of the traditional argument for the externality of all causality, being invariably the act of an agent external to the thing within which the change occurs.[91] It is no accident that the Aristotelian theory of the four causes conceived internal causality (the material cause) to be a passive agency.

This conception of artifice, regardless of its theological admissibility, rests on what might be described as an arithmetical conception of the composite. A composite is simply that which is formed by the association of separate parts; such association is not only one that is foisted upon these separate parts, but is also contrary to nature, for nature is synonymous with purity, integrity, separateness and the lack of adulteration.[92] A composite is the associative sum of simpler components, technically termed *isṭiqs* (pl. *isṭiqsāt*), after the Greek *stoicheion*, such as are stones and bricks to a castle, phonemes to speech, the one to number and the four elements to things.[93] The Baghdadian philosopher Abul-Ḥasan al-'Āmirī (d. 362/973), a member of Sijistānī's circle, declared in an excess of zeal that cooks knew the *isṭiqsāt* of sweets.[94] Simple bodies are not only the starting point of a composite, but are its very principle of composition, forming its essential constitution in addition to being its constituents. A simple body is by definition that which cannot decompose, whereas a composite is ever ready for decomposition[95] and for reverting to the elements of which it is but an assembly.[96] A composite is that which was composed by something apart from itself, and which was separate and was gathered together, such as the components of clothing, food and drugs.[97] This arithmetical conception of the composite applies to logic, where polysyllogisms are readily reversible and lead back to their components.[98] It also applies to the principles of jurisprudence, where a general term is decomposable into its separate referents.[99] It applies equally well to metaphysics; all that is composed of parts is fully conditioned by these parts, and no reciprocal effect obtains, for parts are the cause of their composite,[100] and a whole is nothing but the parts to which it decomposes.[101] This is where Arabic thought located the difference between the general and the whole. It is not only that the general is present only in the mind while the whole is concretely existent, but the whole is merely an account of its parts which precede and constitute it, and this does not hold true of the general, which might, indeed, involve an opposite sense to things.[102] Such is the distinction between the ontological conception of the composite, and the epistemological conception of whole, i.e. the general.[103] Such is also one of the conditions for a primary constitutive notion in Arabic thought, that nothing is uncaused,[104] and that it is impossible to know anything without knowledge of its cause, from whence arise the countless proofs for the existence of a first cause.[105] It follows from this that, as Ibn Khaldūn asserted,[106] the extent of anything is proportional to the extent of its origin,[107] and that consequently the power of a state, its geographical extent and its life-span, are proportional to the numbers of people engaged in its foundation.[108] A similar conception dictates the assertion by Fakhr al-Dīn al-Rāzī that a relation is endowed with a magnitude which is proportional to the relative potency of its terms.[109]

Our arithmetical notion of the composite still holds if we test it by giving consideration to the difference between the notion of combination (*tarkīb*) and mere composition (*ta'līf*), the more obviously 'arithmetical' and the more thoroughly associative. Combination is said to make composition a reality 'naturally, not artificially unified',[110] causing in the composite forms and properties that do not occur in the single elements out of which the composite was fashioned; such, for instance, is the case with flesh, bone or with a horse, all composed of the same elements and humours.[111] In the human body, elements and properties are so fused as not to be singly identifiable.[112] But the use just encountered of the notion of nature to distinguish the human body (as a natural entity) and pharmacological compounds such as *sakanjabīn* (a combination of honey and vinegar) is not one which deploys the metaphysical usages of the term we have been discussing. It refers to a distinction between self-sustaining compounds and readily dissoluble ones, for *sakanjabīn* is not really distinct from honey and vinegar in the same way that flesh is distinct from earth and water. The human body is natural in a conventional sense without regard to the extra-corporeal agency, or at least the agency of extra-corporeal provenance and destination, which makes for the consistency of constitution characterising the human body: the soul.[113] Despite the naturalness of the human body, it does, upon the death that is occasioned by the departure of the soul, revert to the elements from whence it came. Combination does not annihilate the elements combined, nor does it adulterate their integrity. In combination, two (or more) elements adjust in such a way that they mutually produce a formal property distinct from both, although both are present in the common form in efficient proximity, the proof of this being the eminent possibility of separation after combination[114] — a separation perhaps not unlike the dissolubility of numbers into their *stoicheion*, the number one.[115]

The division of all things into simple and compound bodies, into authentic natures and virtual, compound and artificial natures readily decomposable into simple bodies, is the basis of all combination and the secret of all material, corporeal existents. The essence of a composite is located in its components, for the knowledge of a composite is possible only by the knowledge of its elements; that is why it is not possible to know simple bodies in their essence and only by knowing their outward description, their attributes, for they are bereft of components.[116] The combination of simple bodies is the basis of all composition, and such combination is only possible if we assume a sort of affinity between elements combined. In addition, therefore, to the differentiation of elements which alone makes the notion of combination meaningful, there is another condition for the possibility of combination over and above external coercion which releases things from their natural infirmity within singularity and impels them to association. Affinity of various descriptions that will be taken up below can be said to be inscribed in what we may term 'elementary matter', at the risk of offending many strands of Arabic thought. This is the hypothetical continuum within the bounds of which all elements are associated and specified.

Some philosophical schools in Arabic thought explicitly adopted such a notion; some called it, on behalf of themselves and of others who were repelled by the term and its intellectual and historical connotations, a 'primary *hyle*',[117] while others termed it the 'absolute body'[118] and a host of other terms. The unitary character of things was not only the *leitmotiv* of the theology and cosmology of monistic mystics such as Ibn 'Arabī (d. 638/1241)[119] who saw all things to be God and the appearance of diversity and particularity to be nothing but a ruse of divine reason;[120] the unitary character of things, without the concomitant deliberate postulation of continuity with the divine essence, is implicit in Ash'arite theology, as Ibn 'Arabī himself saw when he established the identity of his conception of God with what the Ash'arites called *jawhar*, substance[120] (the Greek *ousia*), which they identified with the atom. The unity of things is also stressed in many a non-technical vein.

Unity, according to the fourth/tenth-century Baghdadian philosopher Nawshajānī, suffuses things and encompasses them; with unity, things are integrated and rendered similar, and with diversity they are differentiated.[122] Distinct things are differentiated moments of a continuum along which things are connected, associated, dissolved back to their components and transmuted into each other.

Such is the protoplasmic *qābil*, the generic substrate and constituent of any thing and all things, that 'in which, and of which, all things are', also termed after its various manifestations: matter, element, *stoicheion*, locus or carrier (*maḥall*) and *hyle*.[123] All these, and other related terms carry the sense of ultimate or proximate materiality, of a generalised substrate in which individualised things subsist.[124] The *hyle* is 'a locus for the acquisition of [real] existence';[125] it is a term for matter in as much as it is the recipient of formal and individualised effects, and *mauḍū'* is a name for matter in as much as it is a substratum.[126] This notion of *qābil* in its manifold of names and fields of sense organises a semantic field which draws together into the definition of matter properties identifed with a passive substratum, ready to receive form in the most general and not only the technical Aristotelian sense, a substratum bereft of all intrinsic properties, whose very 'nature' is to be the recipient of acts by anterior external, and therefore superior, agencies which make for its differentiation and various constitution. The *qābil*, matter in general, *hyle*, all carry the sense of a formless pre-thing which is ready for transformation into formed quiddity.[127] This *hyle* is the carrier of quality and of quantity, and is the primary one amongst all natures which allows their mutual convertibility.[128] It is that which cannot be constituted except through another, and which can receive contradictories and opposites.[129]

Attention to the specific terms used to convey this constellation of associated notions is therefore not very important for the present argument. Essentially uniform in terms of the notion of *qābil*, the different terms identify their users as belonging to specific historical schools of thought, rather than adherents to distinct notions. Matter, *hyle*, substratum, all refer to a substance which is relative in an hierarchical sense, attributing a differential materiality to things, such as the undefined matter of a certain elementary form, which in its turn acts as the matter of a superior form, or of a substratum which can be seen as providing a substrate to something which is itself the substrate of another, or of the nature of a nature. In all cases, emphasis is placed on the relative incompleteness and relative formlessness whose inadequacy is only remedied and whose nature consummated when joined to an externally given form. This is what Ghazālī (d. 505/1111) meant when he declared that matter is every object capable of acquiring an entelechy when associated with something apart from itself.[130] This raw material of all generational processes was termed matter, *hyle*, or other names by the philosophers. The philosophers' adversaries, and mainly Ash'arite theologians, ascribed the same properties to what they conceived to be the original material out of which all things are fashioned: the atom, literally 'individual substance' (*jawhar fard*), or 'indivisible single substance' (*jawhar wāḥid ghair munqasim*), or again and very commonly the 'indivisible part or component' (*al-juz' alladhī lā yatajazza'*).[131] These terms designate an original materiality, a common and general substratum, wherein accidents inhere, endowing this substance with form, quality and modality.[132]

Unlike the Democritan atom, these substances are totally devoid of properties, and are merely a substratum where characteristics, the accidents (*a'rāḍ*), can subsist. Created beings, according to the mainstream of *kalām* (dogmatics) are either composite quiddities, or else they are the elements of which composition was forged, namely, substances (atoms) and accidents.[133] Substances are locations for the inherence of properties and forms, and this basic ontological composition is not really effected by the specific determination of this originary substratum, be it atom, or matter, or some general substance. This matter seems to have been clearer to Ash'arī (d. after 320/932)[134] than to modern students of Arabic thought. Regardless of whether substances be uniform, differing only by their accidents, or they be of two substances such as we encounter in Manichean doctrine, or if they should be the four elements[135] and whether substances be *hyle* or *ousia*,[136] they will belong to the same conceptual profile of a uniform ontological structure composed of the meeting of atom and accident, of matter and form, of a passive recipient and a property or quality, or any of a series of analogues to these terms. As is very often the case, Ibn Ḥazm is a reliable guide to conceptual homologies between terms used by antagonistic schools. He maintains that all creation is of two classes, that which subsists in itself and carries other things, which he calls substance, and that which must subsist in another due to the lack of an internal constitution, and this he calls an accident. Yet his substance is not the atom, but is any body and all bodies.[137] Ibn Ḥazm indeed uses these two terms, substance and body, interchangeably, for whatever can subsist in itself in distinction from what cannot.[138]

Thus there is an essential metaphysical unity of the various terms in which the idea of the substratum was conceived. This holds regardless of whether the accidents were taken, as they were by theologians, for anything that was relatively conceived, or whether these were tabulated in an orderly manner, as the philosophers did when they assimilated them to the Aristotelian categories.[139] And although thinkers susceptible to strict Aristotelian notions tended to view matter in which accidents inhere as already in possession of a form and in which this form is naturally and causally anterior to the accident,[140] the same ontological function obtains for the simple qualities inhering in substances, as it does for accidents and form together. In connection with their role in the constitution of tangible quiddities, they represent their very constitution *qua* quiddities.[141] The *hyle*, although it is a condition for quiddity, is not what endows this quiddity with existence but is merely the location where this existence is acquired.[142] That which supplies concrete and fully realised existence is, for those of a philosophical bent, the form that precedes matter in its essence[143] and constitutes the thing by putting it on the register of its species.[144] For the Ash'arites, substance is even baser material, for it is completely determined by accidents which bring about its quiddity[145] – indeed, a moving body is a substance in which movement inheres,[146] involving a relation in which the priority of the accident is not relative but near to being absolute. This notion of the power relation and of precedence connecting substratum and realised form comes closest to articulating the conception of concrete realisation.

Matter is the stuff of things: it makes possible the individuation of things, whereas form makes possible its realisation, i.e. its appurtenance to a particular species, even the comprehensive 'species' of existents as distinct from intangibles. This is the basis for the explanation that Fārābī, for instance, gave to the existence of the two sexes, both of which he and his contemporaries realised could exist together in certain individual living things. Whereas the female sex provides the matter of a living body, the male provides the form by means of which the species is realised and preserved.[147] This is also at the basis of the Peripatetic definition of the soul as the proximate entelechy of a moving natural body.[148] It is a form which could, as in the Avicennan conception, constitute the *hyle* and link it to the spiritual realms[149] or alternatively, as in the Averroistic conception, be constituted within it.[150] Such is also the connection between the *'aṣabiyya* of the Ibn Khaldūn and kingship, which are related as matter and form, and as a nature and its *telos*.[151] In all cases, we witness a normative relation, binding a donor of reality to a receiver, an activity to a passivity, a superior to an inferior, a 'nature' to a 'spirit', or again a 'nature' to a formless materiality which takes it.

Regardless, therefore, of what is given normative primacy, form, like accidents, constitute the concreteness of things, be this concreteness conceived as a link to a species, or the more sensuous understanding which Ash'arites and Ḥanbalites advocated. The soul, for Ibn Sīnā, was the agency by means of which the body moves, and Ash'arī himself saw it as the accident inherent in the body, which it moves[152] — i.e. which it causes to grow and think. Form and accident without regard to their substratum — and the Mu'tazilite Ibrāhīm b. Sayyār al-Naẓẓām (d. 220–230/835–845) denied the existence of any substratum and affirmed that a body is merely the conjunction of its accidents, such as sourness, whiteness and warmth[153] — constitute the reality of the thing and the source of its activity. Form is therefore, in practice and in terms of the fully realised and constituted thing, nothing but the quality of the body, and the body the carrier of this quality, as Ibn Ḥazm put it in his disregard for doctrinal terminologies.[154] Form is, practically, an accident inhering in the *hyle*: in so far as the body originates in it, it is a form, and in so far as it is inadequate without which it inheres into, it is an accident; a white man has whiteness as form in as much as he is white, and accident in so far as he is a man. Form and accident are relative terms, though form remains 'the mother of all accidents',[155] making a thing what it is.[156]

Every being is, then, the conjunction of a recipient and an inherent — and we except the ultimate actor and the *telos*[157] for the moment, which are directly divine with the Ash'arites, and only mediately so with the philosophers. *Kalām* sensitivities to using the term 'nature' notwithstanding, we can say that everything which comes to pass in the material world, and all knowledge of the world of corporeals, rests on two fundamental notions which transcribe into the immediate realm of visible nature the basic ontological structure of all creatures in Arabic thought: element and quality,[158] into which their sister dyads ultimately collapse, such as substance and accident, form and matter, quality and matter, recipient and inherent. The recipient and substrate receives the inherent form which realises the qualities of the object, i.e. its actions; and this conjunction is the result of action by the nature-artifice we spoke of earlier, the nature that implies no immanent necessity but can only come into effect by the work of any external agency which makes it come to be and preserves it in its integrity. This artificial nature does, however, have an effective regularity and a definite *sawiyya* regardless of the position of the Ash'arites, who felt compelled to deny it because they ascribed all acts directly to God and who consequently insisted that He could always change whatever happened, and regardless of the agnostic position taken by some Mu'tazilites on this issue and their refusal to answer the question of whether God could have created a cold hot thing.[159] Regardless of the ultimate criterion for the presence or lack of continuity, it is phenomenally patent.

This is why despite occasional explicit denial on certain doctrinal grounds, the theory of the four elements was, for all intents and purposes, never challenged in practice, where it underlay medical and other thinking. In accordance with an elementary metaphysical criterion which was discussed above, that every consequent is comprehended in its precedent, and every composite in its constituents, all material things must depend in their qualities on their elements and the qualities of those elements: these are the four elements, nature in its originative sense, fire, air, water and earth. Everything is composed of these four elements, and this is why they are called 'the pillars' (*al-arkān*) without further qualification. They are *arkān* in relation to the world, *stoicheia* in relation to particular things composed of them, and elements in relation to what they result in.[160] All composites are products of these pillars and their concomitant qualities and of the relations of sympathy and antipathy in which these elements and qualities stand to one another. We must stress here another feature of 'nature' as conceived by Arabic thinkers, a feature shared with Greek thought, and most pronouncedly with Stoic natural philosophy.[161]

This conception is a vitalistic, biological conception, based on medical models, which could well be connected an anthropomorphic conception of things. Medicine has normally been associated with natural speculation, and vice versa, and this holds true in a very full sense of the immediate environment in which Arabic thought, and especially natural and philosophical speculation, was first conducted, the schools of Ḥarrān in Mesopotamia and of Antioch, and the Hermetic speculation which infused Arabic thought by obscure albeit overwhelming means.[162] The medical conception of the four elements conferred a highly pronounced concretisation, even personification, on the study of nature,[163] a fact that Ibn Taimiyya himself noted in the course of his reference to the close connection between medicine and natural science in general, and his statement that knowledge of the natures of sentient bodies demonstrates those of others and the principles that govern 'motion and rest' by the body.[164] It is therefore not at all odd that Fārabī and others should link medicine with natural science in general,[165] and that Muḥammad b. Zakariyyā al-Rāzī's (d. ca. 320/932) teacher, Abul-Ḥusain b. Rabban al-Ṭabarī (d. after 237/850), should start his medical treatise, *Firdaws al-Ḥikma*, with an exposition of the theory of elements, qualities, quantity and form. The Ash'arite refusal to countenance admitting the theory of the elements for its incompatibility with the metaphysic of accidents and for the aspertions it might cast on God's absolute omnipotence[166] was localised and confined to metaphysical statements. Our sources name numerous Ash'arite physicians, and a very great number of men of medicine engaged in the religious institutions.[168] We also know of very many Ḥanbalite physicians, including the famous preacher Ibn al-Jawzī[168] (d. 597/1201). The highly conservative Andalusian Traditionist, Ibn 'Abd al-Barr (d. 436/1044–5), moreover stated that medicine is the basis for any understanding of plants, animals, minerals, climates and elements.[169] The notion of elements and their qualities is decidedly medical,[170] and derives much material from alchemy[171] whose fecundity, and the diffusion of whose basic notions and the breadth of whose purview have been discerned by a contemporary scholar.[172] Alchemy was very sharply criticised, as we shall see later, but this left its basic notions untouched. After all, what higher authority can one appeal to in favour of the medical theory of the elements and qualities, but the Prophet himself? The *Prophetic Medicine* of Ibn Qayyim al-Jawziyya (d. 751/1350) put together sayings of a medical nature attributed to the Prophet himself, and these are based on the theory of the elements.[173] And indeed, one prophetic statement had it that the action of contraries is wondrous, and is but another sign of the perfection of God and the consummation of His potency.[175]

Elemental and Somatic Composites

The elements are four, each of which has particular qualities, and they collectively constitute all corporeal things. This holds true for those who add a fifth nature peculiar to the heavenly spheres in the manner sketched above. This merely underscores the distinction of the spheres from all sublunary creatures,[175] as well as for those who, like Suhrawardī (d. 587/1191),[176] thought fire to be the most sublime and the closest to the spheres, without this contention effecting the nature of fire, only its status on the ladder of sublimity. The status is underscored in any case by its natural property as being the lightest of the elements, its natural location is the highest and physically the most elevated. The four elements are thus the four substrata inhabited by bodies they constitute. They are, according to the Stoic definition, the beginning of all things, and the constituents to which they revert when they disintegrate.[177] They are also, according to the Aristotelian definition, the primary components of things which are not divisible to more primary elements.[178] The elements, as pillars, are primary simple bodies formally indivisible, to which composites are divisible.[179]

When elements are qualified by the four primary qualities — heat and coldness (which are active) and humidity and dryness (which are passive) — they become *stoicheia*,[180] that is 'forms wherein simple bodies subsist' and which transform the elements according to a binomial principle, becoming either active or passive.[181] Humidity and dryness, 'the principles of passive quality',[182] qualify water and earth respectively, whereas heat and cold respectively qualify fire and air. And although these four primary qualities do not in their enumeration exhaust all quality, other qualities are equally well binomially arranged[183] and can be seen to originate in the four primary ones: rarity and density (or divisibility and indivisibility), heaviness and lightness, pulverulence and plasticity, and many others.[184] All but the primary pair of opposites do not inhere in the elements as *stoicheia* and are reducible to the two primary qualities of activity and passivity.[185] The recursive nature of these qualities in relation to primary ones is well illustrated in the interpretation Rāzī proffers of Ibn Sīnā's statement in one text that humidity is tangible, and his assertion of its non-tangibility in another. Ibn Sīnā (*al-shaikh*) probably meant by the intangibility of humidity its plasticity, and by its tangibility its adhesive quality.[186] In all cases we have a quality whose activity is brought about in opposition to another,[187] and it is always an opposition of activity and passivity that is involved — i.e. ultimately an hierarchical contrariety which recapitulates the order of the universe.

Every *stoicheion* thus possesses 'an essential form which makes it what it is' in active qualities (heat and cold), and matter in passive qualities (humidity and dryness).[189] This is an obvious assertion given the hierarchical relation linking matter and form discussed in more than one context above. The qualities of the elements dictate the properties of matter: earth confers cohesion upon a thing, while water provides it with plasticity; fire and air calibrate these qualities, with air rarifying the plastic and fire ripening a thickening mixture[189] — ripeness being an impartment of heat to a body containing humidity for the purpose of attaining a particular result and cooking being the process of heating which results in the rarification of a humid essence.[190] Thus the four elements have qualities the proportion of whose combination determines the properties of their products. Earth is cold and dry, and imparts cohesiveness and stability to forms and shapes; water is cold and humid, thus lends itself to multifarious shapes; air is hot and humid, and effects rarefaction; finally, fire is hot and dry: runs, mixes, ripens and thins, inducing air to mitigate the coldness of the two cold elements and push them towards mixing.[191] Each of these elements, along with their qualities and because of them, has natural locations. Earth is absolutely heavy and thus moves naturally towards the centre of the world, 'downwards', whereas fire is absolutely light and consequently moves upwards towards the inner surface of the lunar sphere. As for water, it is relatively heavy, and its natural location is between earth and air, which is naturally located above water and below fire, being relatively light. Such movements and locations are connected with the necessary connection between heat and weight, hot things being light and thin.[192] They are also connected with the proximity of lightness to sphericity wherein the 'nature' of the heavens lies,[193] as well as with the reciprocal and relative connection between the elements[194] and, finally, with the appropriate stations of things, that of the earth being 'the middle'.[195]

Bāqillānī detected a contradiction in the theses proposed by proponents of the elements when they maintained that each element has a natural station where it is at rest, yet also maintaining that these same elements have natural movements.[196] Bāqillānī's criticism would have been far more devastating than it in fact is had the views he criticised been as fully literal and naturalistic as he claimed or assumed. The four elements would indeed have occupied their appropriate locations under free circumstances, as 'matters [properties] ascribed to natural forces and qualities, especially those said of elemental ones, are only valid on condition that no obstruction should intervene'.[197] Artifice, that which is an obstruction to natural movement, is a positive effect deflecting the natural order, for all material things are under the influence of spritual entities. The true mover of things in their concrete reality is the realm of the heavenly spheres; the sublunary world is fully subordinate to the spherical. The four elements are almost never present in their elementary purity, because the powers of the heavenly bodies permeate them and cause heat to mix the coldness of some elements, causing them to be transmuted into smoke and vapour and to mix with fireness and airness, and because the higher elements also receive earthly smoke and watery vapours and mix with them.[198] Elements would only regroup with their own kind and in their natural locations once that which divides their parts is withdrawn.[199]

Yet the effects of heavenly bodies are not wholly arbitrary and they operate, moreover, in keeping with terrestrial and sublunary principles. The condition of possibility for the combination of elements to form minerals and humours is what we may hypothetically take for the essential qualitative continuum and substratum along which all material things exist and along which they might be said to slide when transmuted to each other. There are two primary manifestations of this continuum. The first links together every qualitative dyad which, we saw, consists of a relatively negative and a relatively positive pole connected by a continuum allowing mutual transformability, from negative to positive and vice versa, from cold to hot, from hard to soft. The continuity of things is also manifested in a sense transverse to this first one: the 'material' continuity which was briefly discussed above, the continuity of the passive substratum of things and their primary matter, which allows tranformability and transmutation. Such a conception lends substance to the criticism of Abul-Ma'ālī Imām al-Ḥaramain al-Juwainī (d. 478/1085), Ghazālī's master and the systematiser of Ash'arite theology, who held that the advocacy of the theory of the elements and their combination implies that two things can hold the same substrate, which would lead to the absurd idea that the whole world could be encompassed within a single mustard seed.[200] Things can change into one another because, according to the alchemist Ibn Bishrūn (d. ca. 391/1000), more concerned with concepts in their effective than theoretical modes, 'natures are present in all things',[201] natures being qualities. This same idea is deployed by the archetypal alchemist Jābir b. Ḥayyān, who stated that all things subsist in all things.[202] The elements are transformed or rather transmuted into one another by the changes in quality that overcome them: when air thickens, it turns to water which, when thickening, turns to earth, in a reversible process[203] which is widely demonstrable.[204] And whereas it is difficult to transmute water to fire due to the severity of their incompatibility,[205] they are linked by the elements intermediate between them. It is by considerations such as these that attempts were made to understand the nature of the *jinn* and their uncanny power to transform their appearance.[206]

Of the transformations undergone by the four elements vapours, juices and other constituents are produced, and these constitute what Ikhwān al-Ṣafā' termed 'the *hyle* of corruptible beings'.[207] Minerals are subterranean products of the various qualitative and quantitative combinations into which vapours and smoke enter,[208] and these minerals are divided into those of a tough constitution, comprising malleable and non-malleable metals, and those of a weak constitution, which are classified as salts and fatty substances. Each category of mineral has properties expressed in terms of their liability to combination, their propensity for disintegration and other similar ones. The malleable metals are termed the Seven Bodies comprising gold, silver, zinc, lead, copper, iron and one on whose identity there was no agreement, and they are composed by the thorough admixture of water and earth and a cooking of the earth by the water to a degree where a malleable fatty humidity is produced. Non-malleable metals are either soft such as mercury, or hard, such as jade, but both kinds are strongly constituted. Weakly constituted minerals are either soluble, and these constitute salts, or insoluble, and these are the fatty substances, such as arsenic and sulphur. A relation of hierarchy reigns in the field of minerals. The Seven Bodies are the Olympians of the mineral realm, being formed of the combination of mercury (itself composed of rarefied watery and earthly parts) and sulphur (the product of a thoroughly heated and well-cooked mixture of airy and earthly parts). The king of malleables is undoubtedly gold: it is the result of the perfect and most thorough cooking of pure mercury and pure red sulphur, undertaken over a long time and characterised by perfection of proportions, so that sulphurness absorbs the humidity of mercury and dries its wetness. Should a coldness perchance intervene, perfection will be downgraded and the product will be mere silver, whereas if there is a disproportionate amount of earthliness, iron will be the result.[209] It is the latent relations and possibilities according to which things are connected that make alchemy possible, both in principle, and as a technique involving complicated arithmetical proportions and relations between qualities and quantities which has led one scholar to call Jābirian alchemy 'an exact science',[210] which is a valid and apt description, regardless of whether one accepts its premisses or not.[211]

Cooking, mixing, combining in appropriate proportions and using appropriate degrees of heat, are the stock in trade of alchemy, whose objective is the transmutation of base metals to gold. Such transmutation is based on similarity: the assimilation of bodies to each other, robbing minerals of their original qualities and bringing to them the qualities of gold, in which case they will have been assimilated to this most noble of metals.[212] This matter is very much in keeping with the principles of the continuity of matter and the opposition and connection of opposites that have been discussed in the foregoing paragraphs. Indeed, the alchemist Ṭughrā'ī (d. ca. 515/1121) wrote a treatise refuting Ibn Sīnā's refutation of alchemy using as the main grounds of his argument principles enunciated in the latter's *Shifā'*[213] — it is indeed thought likely by modern scholars that Ibn Sīnā had, in his youth, written two short treatises about the transmutation of elements which are still extant.[214] Ibn Sīnā's primary argument in his refutation of alchemy was his contention that the seven malleable metals were not transmutable because they are utterly distinct from one another, each of which is specifically and individually realised in a distinct species and genus. This ran counter to the bases upon which Ibn Sīnā's natural philosophy rested, and Ṭughrā'ī maintained that even if this assertion of Ibn Sīnā's were to be conceded, alchemical art had the means of so treating the metals that they became ready to receive new specific differences.[215] Rāzī advanced the same objections to Ibn Sīnā's argument, adding that the specific differences of the metals were, in any case, unknown and unknowable, and that they could only be identified by recourse to their visible properties and concomitants, for gold is only known to us as such by means of its qualities and humour, not by its form as Ibn Sīnā's argument would have required[216] — this is why gold is not characterised by recourse to definition (*ḥadd*), but rather to a depictive description (*rasm* — the Greek *epographe*).[217]

Ibn Khaldūn's retort to Ibn Sīnā is as simple as it is radical. He showed no interest in Ibn Sīnā's absolute specification of the metals, but resorted to the essentials of all natural philosophy in Arabic thought (as we could assume Ṭughrā'ī did) that we have discussed, and asserted the theoretical possibility of alchemy on their basis, at the same time denying its practical possibility because this would imply the absolute knowledge of all things that would allow alchemy to run a course parallel to that of nature.[218] The generation of gold entails the realisation of qualities inherent in nature, and art cannot hope to achieve such a realisation; the most it can do is generate what may resemble gold or pass for it.[219]

The foregoing discussion was highly 'naturalistic', and skirted a very important fact which brings alchemy back to the realm of other happenings in the natural world: their inseparability from the will of spiritual beings. These beings deploy what is inherent in nature but unknown to man — utterly unknown to man, according to Jābir b. Ḥayyān himself.[220] Alchemy is only possible with the intervention of an element which analogises minerals and living beings and links them: the Elixir. Unlike the action of leaven in the preparation of bread, which transforms dough to its own nature and prepares it for the corruption brought about by digestion, the elixir of gold merely imparts some of the qualities it carries upon the base metal to be transmuted.[221] These qualities are carried by a multitude of substances which have elixiric effect; substances derived from animals are preferred, such as human hair (considered the best), blood, urine, eggs (seen as the second best), gall bladders, brains and horns, followed by metallic substances, such as gold, silver and mercury.[222] The elixir is composed of a body and a soul,[223] and is ultimately a magical substance, or a substance with magical effect.[224] It is the alchemical analogue of a talisman, for both are possessed of a spiritual potency which operates according to stellar secrets and numerical proportions and spirit-drawing types of incense, the *modus operandi* of which is the analogisation of metallic and occult qualities[225] according to sympathetic relations which will be the subject of a subsequent discussion. That is the reason why the famous philosopher and alchemist Maslama al-Majrīṭī (d. 398/1007) maintained that alchemy and sorcery were correlative: the one brings sublime spirits to play in the realm of corporeal nature, and the other releases spirit from corporeality.[226] There are very pronounced astrological assumptions at work in alchemy: the nether deployment of spiritual potencies takes place according to correspondences between the qualities of particular corporeal bodies and particular spiritual ones; gold corresponds to the sun, and can thus make astrological use of it, while silver corresponds to the moon and iron to Mars. But there is considerable disagreement about what corresponds to what, except for the general concordance of the sun-gold and moon-silver pairs.[227]

With the first glimpse of the concrete and direct intervention of the spiritual realm into the terrestrial world, we start our approach towards the transition from the inanimate world into that of living being, that whose members move by a sort of inner volition of many grades. Precisely as the elixir endows metals with qualities they are desired to adopt for their transmutation to gold, Arabic embryology isolated an agent which operates similarly in engendering generation. Blood flowing in the man's testicles mixes therein with the animal spirits, as well as with a proportion of psychic spirits and produces sperm.[228] The generative faculty of the soul, moreover, takes from the body wherein it dwells a part which is potentially like itself, then operates on it by means of power derived from other bodies, presumably the species, and turns it into an actual likeness of the parent.[229] This elixiric effect of the soul in the process of generation is analogous to natural elixiric action, for a foetus is made in very much the same way as cheese, male semen playing the role of the cheese culture and female semen that of milk.[230] The spontaneous generation of man in the Ḥayy b. Yaqẓān cycle of myth, where a baby is generated by the gestation of natural qualities and their slow maturation under appropriate degrees of heat and humidity, is itself at its crucial stage dependent upon the spirit, which God orders to enter the coagulating mess and turn it into a human being, for the soul is ever emanating from God, who is akin to the sun in His everlasting bounty, and is dominant in the world of matter.[231]

The 'cooking' of substances and qualities to the temper appropriate to human beings does not result, by itself, in a human, a sentient and animate creature, although it is a condition underlying animation; the adoption of the form appropriate to animate beings is a complement and consolidation of such temper.[232] Animal form — soul or psyche — is the entelechy of animal temper, exactly as form is to matter and accidents to substance. And even though 'temper' is a concept specifically counterposed to inanimate matter,[233] it has no autonomous and *sui generis* constitution capable of continuing without the intervention of the soul, but then the animal soul itself which resides in the heart is endowed with apposite qualities which confirm its central position in the organism.[234]

All this is understandable given the metaphysical principle discussed above, according to which a composite is always contrary to nature in its unadulterated elemental form. A temper is defined as a quality resulting from the interaction of opposite qualities.[235] A temper belongs to the same category of things (*min jins*) as the four elementary qualities,[236] but is weak in comparison with pure quality, for in it the purity, and hence original strength, of qualities is adulterated and tempered by other qualities, and according to given proportions. It is temper as composite quality which calibrates the absolute resilience of elementary qualities and prepares them for the acceptance of animal form or soul.[237] And as the elementary qualities constitute two binomial dyads — hot-cold and humid-dry — the immediately resulting tempers constitute four such pairs, each opposed by means of one or two qualities to the other. The bilious or choleric temper is that proper to the bile or choler humour, which is to be found in the spleen; it is hot and dry. The sanguine temper proper to blood, whose place is the liver, is hot and humid and generated of fire. The humour phlegm, located in the lungs, is cold and humid, made of water, and produces a phlegmatic temper consistent with the qualities which compose it. Finally, the splenetic or melancholic temper is the result of atrabile located in the gall bladder and, like its constituent qualities and its earthly material, it is cold and dry. Of the humours and their combinations in various proportions are generated the different parts and organs of the body, the properties of each of which is determined by the precise proportion in which its constituent humours are determined by their own constituents. Digestion and assimilation operate according to these principles. It is blood which carries nourishment around the body, and thus carries humours to their locations, the blood feeding the brain, for instance, being intermixed with a soft phlegmatic material, and that feeding bone tissue would have an admixture of a tough and choleric substance.[238] Humours rise in complexity with the complexity of the constituent, reaching very complex constitutions with certain drugs, and with substances such as milk, which, at many removes from the four basic qualities, combines waterness with cheeseness and fatness.[239] And while assimilation implies the transformation of humours into others, this does not seem to occur directly, for not all humours can turn to all others, and humours are various degrees of cooking which are not reversible.[240]

The entities that result from the combination of qualities are by no means independent of, or distinct from, their constituents to which they revert in any case after the constituent has disintegrated, as the human body does upon death. Nor is the resultant constituent a quality which is absolutely intermediate between its constituents. A temper is constituted and held together by the dominance in it of one of its qualities; without such a welding element in any combination no coherence will be preserved, just as no body politic can cohere without the dominance within it of one element.[241] The equivalence of qualities or of elements in combination is an impossible state of affairs,[242] for such equivalence will simply result in the disintegration of the compound and the reversion of its constituents to their natural places from which, we have seen, they were forcibly removed. Temper and temperate mixtures are the result not of an immanent, but of a teleological balance not unconnected with the concept of entelechy. A temperate compound is the result of a quantitative and qualitative combination in the proportions required by human temper which also happen to be the most just of all proportions[243] — entelechy and justice, be it said in initial form here, register things as they are given and assert the excellence of what is given. Arabic pathology therefore rested on the assumption that illness arises in a situation where the balance of humours in a certain organ is upset. Illness is, simply, distemper; it is the negation of the nature appropriate to a particular organ,[244] so that it becomes, say, hotter or drier than it should be.[245] Illness is a process which runs parallel and opposite to nutrition, therefore, and is akin to toxification whose deleterious effect is carried out by changing the proportions according to which humours combine in the effected organ.[246] Pain registers the intrusion into an organ of a temper incompatible with that natural to the organ, which heats it beyond its natural heat and thus separates its parts, or cools it and therefore thickens it and effects the proper connection between those parts.[247] Upsetting the natural balance of an organ causes it to disintegrate to its components.[248] Pharmaceutical compounds thus turn distemper into a properly constituted temper, so that if the organ's distemper is manifested in its excessive heat, the patient would be given a drug which has a cooling effect.[249]

In all cases, we witness interactions, or rather counteractions, which relate and adjust qualities. Medicinal therapy appears as a reconstitution of an organ, the re-establishment of a previously apposite temper which had been upset by an agent whose antidote is the medicine. The medicament strips the diseased organ of a novel natural state which had intruded upon it, and imposes on it a new, recreated temperance. Just as alchemical action strives for the apex of all inanimate combinations, gold, so does medical action:[250] it strives to restore an excellence, one appropriate to the organ as its generic end, just as gold is the generic end of minerals, we could even say their entelechy. In all cases, what is witnessed is a transmutation of one form into another, of one nature as the specific configuration of qualities into another nature. The body assimilates its nutrients and transmutes them into tempers by 'taking them over' (*istīlā'ahā 'alaihā*).[251] We witness a uniformisation of the stuff of the body (*mujānasa*):[252] a temper extracts from nutrients that which has affinity to itself, exactly as a drug does not only expel its contrary from the distempered organ, but also extracts from the diseased organ qualities consistent with its own nature. Such is the affinity of natures, which requires every diseased organ to yearn for the nature of the medicine which is contrary to that of the disease and, when the medicine arrives in the vicinity of this organ, it is pulled towards the organ by its pulling power and purges by the force of its contrariety the nature of the disease, the excess or paucity of requisite qualities.[253] This therapeutic tug-of-war is well illustrated by a famous therapy attributed to Muḥammad b. Zakariyyā al-Rāzī who, when presented with a man who had accidentally swallowed a leech, proceeded forcibly to stuff mushrooms down his oesophagus until the wretch finally vomited the leech along with the mushrooms — for the leech, presumably a mushroom eater or at least a dweller in mushroom terrain, 'naturally' veered towards the mushrooms and left its previous, deeper location.[254]

Composition, Justice and the Social Order

When Abū Sulaimān al-Sijistānī asserted that there can be no perfect middle in the world of generation and corruption because it is itself an intermediary[255] — an intermediate stage between generation and corruption — he was referring to the lack of stability which marks this world. There is no such thing that is so perfectly equipoised as not to lend itself to change. The world of generation and corruption is that which is neither as perfectly stable and unchanging as the world of divinity and spirituality, nor as perfectly fluid and Heracleitian as pure and formless becoming. What holds true of the intermediary between being and becoming holds equally true of all intermediaries. The heavenly spheres are not subject to becoming because of their innocence of contradictories.[256] This implies that, as we have seen, corporeal things are determined and structured by contradiction and opposition. And indeed things in relation to others are described, according to the expression of certain jurists, as either similar, or coexistent, or else mutually exclusive.[257] As the qualities which constitute the natures of all corporeal bodies are structured in contradictory pairs, such as the cold and the hot, it is the contradictories which coexist. The world is so based upon contradiction and opposition that Ibn Rushd was driven to assert that, had it not been for the contradictories, the world would not have had a stable form.[258]

The constitution of every body occurs in a 'proximate *hyle*' which is simply the location where the purity of opposites is tempered by opposition.[259] Temper is therefore a juxtaposition of opposites whose outward manifestation gives the impression of a qualitative integration, whereas this is in fact no more than a visible aspect which occludes opposites that have come into proportionate relation and which will revert to their purity upon the disintegration of the composite. The heaviness of the heavy in a composite, for instance, does not alter the lightness of the light,[260] and lukewarm water does not acquire lukewarmness as a new nature, for its natures remain the cold and the hot which are attenuating each other.[261] And although there exist qualitative gradations amongst composites of the same qualities, this gradation is directly proportional to the volume of the respective constituents, not to any intrinsic scale of purity or strength.[262] Ibn Sīnā summed up the considerations concerning composition with reference to potencies of the soul in this way:

> acts with differential strength and weakness . . . have their principle in one potency, which is now more, now less consummately active. And if non-consummation required that everything that is less consummate should have a separate potency specific to itself other than that which belongs to the most consummate, then there should be a number of separate powers corresponding to the various grades of consummation and the lack thereof —[263]

each of which would itself have been measure, which is inadmissible. There is thus no conception of 'degree', no truly quantitative measure of differentiation within the bounds of one ladder of measurement, not even in the Jābirian proportions which rest themselves on quantum leaps of proportion according to pre-given measure not linked onto a uniform continuum of measurement. What there is, is purity, consummation and its attenuation by an opposite consummateness; lukewarm water is intermediate between hot and cold water in the exclusive sense of breaking heat and cold simultaneously.[264] And whereas physicians did postulate four degrees of body temperature,[265] these are really of the nature of different qualities of severity, not a measure along a continuum. Quantity, in the context of Arabic thought, is qualitatively conceived. It is a strengthening of a particular quality, or its weakening, so that the quality of a larger mass of things is greater than the quality of a smaller mass, and an infinitesimal quality of a particular quality — say, heat — is closer to the negation and to the contrary of this particular quality.[266] Diminution is not a matter of degree, but is privative, while addition consummates in terms of a metaphysic of entelechies. This is the sense of Ibn Khaldūn's statement that soothsaying is the contrary of prophecy, although they are epistemologically equivalent: the prophet utilises the subliminal senses that soothsayers are incapable of, and this implies a diminution in facility which amounts to contrariety.[267]

Things are constituted by the contrariety of their qualities and their simultaneous juxtaposition within them. This is a primary conception of Arabic thought, and a basic principle according to which simple and composite entities are regarded. Not only was it of 'archaeological' status in Arabic thought, but it is also a principle which preponderated in wide sections of Greek thought in fields such as medicine, philosophy and religion.[268] There is ample anthropological evidence of its preponderance in other cultures as well. Arabic thought classified things and understood them with reference to contrariety and opposition in natural science as we have seen,[269] as well as in the classification of geographical orientations,[270] and often, as we will have occasion to see, looked at opposition and contrariety as a natural antipathy between things, an antipathy occasionally of occult origin, such as that between certain precious stones, or between hyenas and dogs.[271] Everyday life is itself described in terms of contrariety in contemplative writing; all that man does is inevitably beset with opposition or what is very much like opposition: life and death, remembrance and forgetfulness, mendacity and truthfulness, libertinism and uprightness.[272] Opposites not only bring one another in sharper and therefore clearer relief, but they also constitute mutual conditions for the very existence of each other. Had it not been for the sun, shade would have been unknown, and had it not been for rectitude, wrong itself would have remained unknown.[273] Such is the principle upon which is based an intellectual procedure which is extremely common in Arabic thought, especially in *kalām*, namely, the apagogic proof, the paralogical demonstration of a thesis by disproving the opposite thesis. Such is also the principle upon which is based the rhetorical figure known to Arabic critics as 'inversion', *al-qalb*, the designation of a thing by means of its opposite. This figure not only renders the thing inappositely designated in a more pronounced and stronger way, to use the terms of Arabic criticism, but also gestures towards what could have been the ultimate anthropological grounding of the theory of opposites in the realm of magical speculation: Ibn Qutaiba (d. 276/889), no doubt retailing common knowledge, maintained that a result of inversion was optimism and pessimism;[274] that is why Arabs, especially before Islam, gave their children repulsive names to avert the evil eye, such names as *kalb* (dog) and *jaḥsh* (ass). And whereas Ibn Qutaiba referred the famous phenomenon of *aḍdād* in Arabic — use of the same word for opposite meanings, such *ẓann* for certainty and doubt, *qar'* for ritual impurity brought about by menstruation and freedom therefrom, and *ṣarīm* for morning and night[275] — to inversion,[276] we really ought to exclude the *aḍdād* from the sort of contrariety and opposition under review, being a purely lexical phenomenon rather than an ontological or epistemic one.[277]

A composite, we have seen, is a thing in which two qualities, or a series of opposite qualities, are juxtaposed in which one preponderates, thus impressing its own description upon the whole. Before we continue our pursuit of composites, it will be appropriate here to glance at a situation, a very exceptional situation, in which a thing in the world of generation and corruption can aspire to a state where opposites are so perfectly balanced that they are negated simultaneously by that which is absolutely intermediate between them. Contrariety ceases, and where there are no contraries, we are surely approaching the world of permanence and full being, and such is indeed the case with virtue in its philosophical description. Virtue occurs in a realm unbeholden to matter, the realm of the rational soul — literally, the 'speaking soul' — once it has taken full control of the body it inhabits and of the lower, appetitive and other faculties of the soul, and liberates itself from the derogation brought about by contact with materiality,[278] much like the situation obtaining in the famous chariot of Plato's *Phaedrus*. When man achieves virtue, a truly rare occurrence, he would become closer to angels than he is to fellow humans,[279] in keeping with the chain of being that we discussed earlier on in this chapter. In the refinement of character, man seeks the true golden mean wherein all opposites and contraries are abolished by virtue of the absolute intermediacy of this mean. Virtues, after all, are the mean point on the link between two extremities which are vices.[280]

Virtue therefore negates all contraries, and marginalises them as its own contraries. Virtue is composed of four practical virtues: wisdom or knowledge which lies between pretentiousness and stupidity, modesty which is between incontinence and sanctimoniousness, courage which negates cowardice and rashness, and finally, justice itself, which manages other virtues and guards over them, and which, in alliance with the rational soul, assures the dominance of reason over the appetitive and aggressive faculties of the soul. Justice is the agreement of correct knowledge and correct behaviour, and concordance between right and man, and is arrived at by the rational soul which uses the aggressive faculty to discipline the appetitive.[281]

This state of felicity is beset, nevertheless, by the fate of all mortals. For even if a virtue were to become thoroughly free of the vices which bound its field, it is yet nothing without the contradictories it transcends. Virtues, like everything else in the sublunary world, is a mean between two contradictory extremities, albeit the golden mean; this mean is therefore deducible from the extreme vices (*wajaba an tufham minhā*).[282] And although Ghazālī explicitly declared that justice was not opposed to two vices at its extremities but rather to the corresponding vice of injustice,[283] he was doubtless referring to the fourth of the virtues enumerated in the previous paragraph, justice that holds the virtues together,[284] the justice with which reason rules in a state of virtuousness, not to the justice that is the mean between vices.

The equivalence of contraries and opposites in their composite is therefore a very sublime occurrence, when it does come to pass, and almost transports us beyond the boundaries of humanity. Equivalence is the most sublime of proportions, not only in ethics, but also in music, where it never occurs naturally but has to be arrived at by mathematical means where it is expressed by unity and by the proportions to which unity is decomposable.[285] It is possibly only with the intervention of the most rigorous rationality. The conception of money in Arabic thought is very much akin to the idea of a sublime equivalence: the *dīnār* — and there are weights of it, as for its *dirham* subdivisions, canonically prescribed by the Law[286] — establishes equivalences between things until a mean is established between them in the process of exchange.[287] The *dīnār*, like currency in general, evaluates transactions with a view to establishing their just equivalence, and money is a suitable return for suitably proportioned exchange; it is a silent justice not far removed from the loquacious justice, the ruler.[288] Money is the means of evaluating two tasks (*'amalain*) done in exchange for one another with view to doing justice to them both.[289] This just return which money allocates is what is meant by the value of a task (*'amal* is a task, not the abstract labour of classical economics which some commentators are wont to detect). It is a moralising conception which modern commentators have seen as evidence of the contemporaneity of Ibn Khaldūn's economic theory, his alleged discovery of the labour theory of value.[290] Reality lies elsewhere, and Ibn Khaldūn's theory of *kasb* in the realm of economic life[291] falls well within the boundaries of the ideal mean under discussion. In its terminological and partly in its conceptual profile, it is ultimately a conception of theological provenance involving just returns for things produced by more than one individual.[292] It expresses the balance of things in the perfectly proportioned manner, so that they are so proportionally related as to exclude discordance.[293] For discordance is the differentiation of two things normatively related across the same continuum, and it can thus only be a contrariety. That is what makes Maqrīzī (d. 845/1441) ascribe inflation and the rise in the price of gold to adopting coins made of metals other than gold; to these new coins are related the values and equivalences of things, a task which ought to devolve upon gold and silver only, as they are innately just measures of equivalence[294] — the debasement of currency is thus an economic fact only in an incidental sense subordinate to this primary normative conception.

The achievement of virtue in the manner described, or of the perfection of balanced reward in currency over which the Law should be ever watchful and the ruler vigilant, are acts that require the continuous application of the will. If perfect balance is ever achieved, it is nevertheless inherently unstable, as it goes counter to the dissociative nature of composite things. The perfection of temperateness implied by the eradication of contrariety is an aspiration, and remains an aspiration, in the mutable world. It is an aspiration which is activated, and has constantly to be maintained, by compulsion, for it implies a disnature. Justice, in the realm of virtue as in that of monetary value and of the domain of polity of which we shall shortly speak, is compulsive, just as the uneven temperateness according to which qualities are juxtaposed in the bodily organs is the product of compulsion exercised by the soul. Justice is an oppressive custodian which compels separate things to abandon the enjoyment of their pure natures and to enter into configurations that suit that purposes of Justice itself, for it is the potentate whose purpose is exclusively primary. Justice is therefore the teleological state of assembly in which things are combined in such proportions as to achieve a purpose unaccounted for by the components of this assembly. It is composition according to a precise proportion suitable for the constitution of the composite, which is thus not a natural product of its elements but is the brain-child of a transcendent purpose — transcendent being used here in the most general sense, although divine transcendent will and purpose lie at the apex of the ladder of transcendent purposes. This transcendent purpose is what we have often seen, in the foregoing pages, described as 'appropriate', 'apposite' and by cognate terms and which, at one point, we identified with the positivity of things, their givenness being identified with their excellence. Appropriateness and consummateness are synonymous with the way things are, and the way things are is invariably identified in Arabic thought with a theodicy. Every thing is the product of a local teleology according to which the thing itself is constituted of unwilling elements, and it is such an assembly of entelechies which constitutes the world as it fulfills a transcendent purpose which stands for its positivity and divine *status quo*. Perfect balance is indissolubly allied to a transcendent purpose; it is in itself unnatural, but is ultimately premised on a transcendent and subliminal proportionality, a real, i.e. heavenly isonomy to which all proportions — musical, numerical, alchemical — are ultimately reducible, in the sense of being teleologically beholden.[295]

Moral virtue is isomorphous with financial justice, and these are structurally parallel to the even healthy temper and the consummation of natural teleologies. In all cases, things cohere under the influence of a transcendent potency, and the natural disassociation of things is only forcibly turned to their composition. What applies to bodily tempers also applies to the state which, according to Ibn Khaldūn, also has a temper whose constitution varies with its various temporal vicissitudes.[296] Indeed, the association and aggregation of men and the formation of societies is always a process requiring force for its inception as well as for its maintenance. Men are fractious, refractory, aggressive and selfish, and no order would assure their cohesion if it were not a constant sanction involving force. Men need each other, and yet they need to be kept apart from and warded off from each other.[297] Everything that involves multiplicity requires a chief who integrates and preserves each member of the collectivity by assuring mutual complementariness: this applies to the human body, as well as to armies and market exchanges.[298] Nothing is wasted in a collectivity, not even pores on the skin or saliva glands in the mouth, as things are for each other; bodily organs are to each other as the members of a species are to one another or the members of a single generation, or indeed all co-existing things of different species.[299] This anthropomorphic base of a metaphysic of things under discussion is perhaps most eloquently expressed in a Stoic statement to the effect that the universe has a social intelligence, intending low things for the higher, and the higher for one another, thus putting all things in their places.[300] Justice is order; this is why as we saw, justice is not negated by vices, but by the injustice which is its own contrary for, Ghazālī, continued, 'there is no mean between order and disorder'.[301] Any person who has seriously read Ghazālī especially, or so attuned himself in reading the works of other Arabic thinkers, could not fail to be struck by the metaphor of kingship which is used whenever there is talk of order in all domains, metaphysical, cosmological and social. Justice is personified by the invincible chief; that is why the soul is to the body like the governor to the city.[302] And had it not been for the necessary and indissoluble connection between coherence, justice and authority, a man who enjoyed consummate virtue would not have been a natural leader,[303] neither would justice, the order of things, have been a proportion according to appropriate stations of superiority and inferiority.[304] The order of things, the reign of justice within them, is an hierarchy the mechanism of which is a vertical attachment to a leading factor which makes this order and preserves it. This is how the body coheres, it containing master organs, such as the heart, the liver and the brain, and servant organs, all arranged along a definite hierarchy, exactly as people are hierarchically arranged in the city under the sway of a potentate who is by definition the member who is absolutely served and does not serve.[305] This also runs parallel to the classification of faculties of the soul according to their station in the hierarchy of faculties: hierarchy is the expression of difference and difference, we saw, is reducible to contrariety and opposition. Faculties are therefore either *sui generis*, or else they are made for the service of superior faculties, the uppermost of which is that which is intended for itself only.[306] This is how it becomes possible to express the relations between faculties of the soul in terms of analogies with the various offices of state.[307]

The hierarchy according to which components of the social order, of the human body and of the cosmos in general,[308] are arranged, follows a stable and explicit pattern set by the manner in which Arabic thought conceives of the composite in which the individual members are juxtaposed in their integrity and externally associated, and in which coherence is achieved by the compulsion of an element which may be internal, as the heart in the body, or both internal and external, as the soul in the body, or entirely external, as the king to the political order[309] or God to all creation. What has been called Islamic political thought expresses these relations with singular force and clarity. Translating the hierarchical and arithmetical conception of order to the sphere of the political and social order reveals power, and by this is always meant force or potential force personified in a sovereign, as the seal of human collectivities, just as the soul seals together the various organs of the body and at the same time constitutes its cause and its *telos*, or as a quality which dictates itself upon a temper is the seal of this temper. There is no social collectivity without the king, just as there can be no collectivity without a custodian which ensures the reciprocal serviceability of tasks — and it is interesting to note that Miskawaih (d. 421/1030) described money in a manner analogous to the terms in which the role of the sovereign is described in Arabic writings on the political order.[310] No order can reign amongst men were it not for a custodial authority, which Ibn Khaldūn termed the *wāzi'* without whom there would be nothing but *bellum omnium contra omnes*, and divine will as embodied in revealed law would have no means of fulfillment. Indeed, the innate fractiousness of men and the need for a mediating force constitute the standard proof for the necessity not only of kingship and the caliphate,[311] but of prophecy itself.[312] Prophecy is indeed the peculiar property of certain individuals, and in this capacity will be the occasion of a subsequent discussion. But it is also a social and political function, and in this capacity it is, like kingship and the caliphate, the agency by means of which the collectivity of human beings is stripped of its formlessness and disorder and acquires a definite temper,[313] as is required by all composite things, be that temper articulated by the primacy of an element, or by the golden mean, as in philosophical virtue.

That kingship is the seal and necessary condition of every viable human collectivity is clear from historical writing, which conceives of collectivities as states, and dwells upon the impossibility of the existence of a collectivity bereft of kingship, and indeed, makes of kingship the criterion for continuity in time, and its absence the immediate cause for the disintegration of a collectivity.[314] The substance of this collectivity is not germane to this matter; it does not matter if it be a city, a tribe or a collection of nations:[315] the important thing is that power should be held exclusively by the sovereign. A king, according to Abū Sulaimān al-Sijistānī, is a human god.[316] The sovereign is to his subjects what the soul is to the body,[317] or, in the mildest and most benign of expressions, as a *pater familias* to his household.[318] The binary and simultaneously hierarchical order of things — soul and body, patriarch and family, king and city, *telos* and humanity, consummation and temper, virtue and soul — is a binomial dyad which takes the guise of an ontological relationship between a power and powerlessness.[319] Justice does not rest upon equality, but on an exclusive exercise of power which assures order.[320] Indeed, any pollution of this exclusivity by common elements tends to look as if it went against the very nature of things.[321] This is why when the Abbasids allowed their clients to partake of the state, even nominal participation displayed in titles pertaining to the state such as *'Aḍud al-dawla* (Pillar of the State), they tended to share the state with them and eventually lost their state to them.[322] For the same reason, theologians proving the unicity of God often had recourse to the argument that the presence of more than one would deny divinity because sovereignty is exclusive and indivisible, for should there have been more than one god, each would have striven to appropriate the whole of divinity.[323] Finally,

> a father should be honoured in a manner befitting a father, and a king in one befitting a king, and people should honour each other fraternally. Each one of these stations has certain prerogatives . . . and if these were not preserved with justice [unjust] augmentations and diminutions will ensue and these will lead to corruption, and as a result powers will be transferred and upset and things will be inverted, so that the sovereignty of legitimate kingship will turn into a violent sovereignty . . . and things will go into disorder which negates the order arranged by God for His creation and described in the *Sharī'a* and made obligatory with supreme wisdom.[324]

Justice, the ultimate entelechy, is the order of the *status quo* based upon the power of the day.

Such is the hyper-positivism of the theodicy substantially or paradigmatically underlying this conception of justice as consummate isonomy and appositeness, that aesthetic conceptions in Arabic thought were construed along very much the same principles and in the same spirit. Thus beauty is the agreement of the object — sight or sound — with the soul according to proportions (of tones, of shapes) required by the particular matter of this object;[325] it is an object consummated, regardless of the very specific metaphysical overtones of the statement just paraphrased. It is the existence of an object 'as it should be'.[326] Such was the basis of *badī'*, what we may call poetics, as practised by the mainstream which took its inspiration from Ibn al-Mu'tazz (d. 296/905) through 'Āmidī (d. 370/980) and 'Abd al-'Azīz al-Jurjānī (d. 392/1002, not to be confused with the great 'Abd al-Qāhir, d. 471/1078–9), which evaluated the excellence of poetry according to appositeness and correctness of words, of syntax and of figures, as well as appositeness in terms of common sense and common taste.[327] In short, excellence was evaluated according to canons of taste which we may term classicist, and which identify beauty with appositeness of poetry, and appositeness with its prevalent criteria. Excellence of expression is valid only if it is also appropriate for its subject-matter (itself graded from sublimity downwards) and clearly indicating its purpose which goes over and above the object or its representation — otherwise, if one had to stress only the beauty of expression, one would be doing something not very unlike hanging rubies around the necks of swine.[328] The beauty of women in the *Thousand and One Nights* can likewise be described as 'objectivist' and of very definite description,[329] which is according to prevalent tastes that is given the guise of excellence. There is not intrinsic description of aesthetic worth, just as there is no compelling need for things to be as they are apart from that which forces them to be as they are. The consummateness of things, as we have already seen, is not described by intrinsic criteria; man's ability to speak is ascribed to that which is 'for the better', as it is not merely for utilitarian purposes but is also the pillar of theoretical sciences which have no practical value[330] yet are in keeping with the divine propensities of humankind. The famous definition of the soul as the proximate entelechy of a natural body[331] is of the same conceptual domain: the soul is that which preserves the body, exactly as the preponderance of a particular quality holds a composite together.

Similarly, the spontaneous generation of a human being from an accidental natural mixture whose temper is equivalent to that of the human body occurs only because the generosity of God does not deprive the deserving of what they deserve — in this case, a soul which inheres in the temper which is ready to receive it[332] — for indeed, as we saw, God likes regularity and orders things to occur as He predisposed them to come to pass. The coherence of a thing which achieves a purpose — humanity and its purpose known only to divine wisdom, virtue and its purpose in emulating angelicalness, and so forth — is an effect of an external agent, a just effect on what resembles inanimate matter. It is the incorporation of things within the bounds of their purposes, and the elevation of immobility to the domain of teleology. Transcendent purpose is the discursive transcript of the *status quo*, composed of positivities construed as entelechies, perfect because they are. Things that are explainable in terms of themselves, construed as transcendent.[333]

Notes

1. Ṭāshköprüzade, *Miftāḥ*, vol. 3, p. 191.

2. The great work of A.O. Lovejoy, *The Great Chain of Being* (Cambridge, Mass., 1964), traces the history of this notion from Greek thought through to the nineteenth century century, but confines its scope of investigation to philosophical works. It is unfortunate that this chain, despite its importance, has met virtually no interest in studies of Arabic thought, except for a preliminary sketch by M. Arkoun [*Al-Fikr al-'Arabī*, tr. A. 'Awwā (Beirut, 1982), pp. 88–9], and apart from authors intent on proving that the chain of being as sketched by Bīrūnī, Ibn Khaldūn and Ikhwān al-Ṣafā' amounts to a precocious Darwinism: but this does not, as the chain of being does, rest on an atemporal hierarchy of value in which transition from one rung to another, rare as it is, only occurs with the intercession of incorporeals.

3. Zajjājī, *Īḍāḥ*, p. 67.

4. Suhrawardī, *Lamaḥāt*, p. 80.

5. Tawḥīdī, *Muqābasāt*, p. 252.

6. Suhrawardī, *Lamaḥāt*, p. 143.

7. Rāzī, *Mabāḥith*, vol. 1, p. 104.

8. Tawḥīdī, *Muqābasāt*, p. 65 and see Suhrawardī, *Lamaḥāt*, p. 122.

9. Fārābī, *Milla*, paras. 19–20.

10. Avicenna, *De Anima*, pp. 50–51 and see Fārābī, *Milla*, paras. 21 ff.

11. Fārābī, *Madīna* (ed. Dieterici), p. 55.

12. Some theologians took these divisions to be matters innately known to the understanding: Juwainī, *Irshād*, p. 16 and see also Bāqillānī, *Tamhīd*, paras. 7, 26, and see Rāzī, *Mabāḥith*, vol. 1, p. 114 and Ibn Rushd, *Mā ba'd aṭ-ṭabī'a*, p. 149.

13. *Mā ba'd aṭ-ṭabī'a*, pp. 157–8.

14. Shahrastānī, *Muṣāra'a*, p. 126 and see Ibn Sīnā, *Shifā'* (*Ṭabī'īyyāt, 2*), p. 125.

15. Fārābī, *Madīna* (ed. Dieterici), p. 57.

16. See H.A. Wolfson, *Philo: Foundations of Religious Philosophy in Judaism, Christianity, and Islam*, 4th. rev. printing (Cambridge, Mass., 1968), vol. 1, p. 298 and see Lovejoy, *The Great Chain*, pp. 49 ff.

17. Proclus, *Elements of Theology*, tr. E.R. Dodds (Oxford, 1963), proposition 152: 'All that is generative in the gods proceeds in virtue of divine potency, multiplying itself and penetrating all things, and manifesting especially the character of unfailing perpetuity'. Whether plenitude produced a compulsion in God to create the world was the subject of much controversy in Arabic thought. Many philosophers (for instance, Fārābī, *Madīna*, p. 16) saw it as an involuntary act of God emanating from His very existence, a view which pantheistic mystics, in their joyfully blasphemous abandon, exacerbated by seeing creation as an act of divine narcissism (Ibn 'Arabī, *Inshā'*, pp. 36–8 and Ibn al-Khaṭīb, *Rawḍa*, p. 582). But this mystical view also had a providential aspect shared with the Mu'tazilites, who saw creation 'for the sake of the better' — see the review of this matter in Māturīdī, *Tawḥīd*, pp. 96 ff. and Baghdādī, *Uṣūl*, pp. 150 f. — which was a circular view of divine providence fulfilling the aims of divine providence (see Ibn Sīnā, *Najāt*, 2nd edn, p. 284). The standard position was that to impute a motivation to God was to impute a lack and a need to Him (Bāqillānī, *Tamhīd*, paras. 56–7 and Shahrastānī, *Muṣāra'a*, pp. 113–14).

18. Ghazālī, *Maqāsid*, pp. 187–8 and Ibn Rushd, *Mā ba'd aṭ-ṭabī'a*, p. 31.

19. See the comments of L. Gardet, *La pensée religieuse d'Avicenne* (Paris, 1951), p. 43 and see p. 65.

20. Ibn Rushd, *Tahāfut*, pp. 137–9, who also (pp. 121–2) criticises Fārābī and Ibn Sīnā for admitting, after the dialectical fashion of dogmatic theology, temporal considerations in a philosophical context — yet Ibn Sīnā carefully distinguishes the temporal and essential aspects of anteriority (A.-M. Goichon, *Lexique de la langue philosophique d'Ibn*

Sīnā (Paris, 1938), para. 572). The philosopher Yaḥyā b. ʿAdī maintained that causality does not involve time any more than time is involved in the precedence of nouns over verbs (Pseudo-Sijistānī, *Ṣiwān*, p. 327).

21. Tahānawī, *Kashshāf*, p. 1214.

22. Suyūṭī, *Muzhir*, vol. 1, p. 11.

23. Rāzī, *Mabāḥith*, vol. 1, p. 447; Jurjānī, *Taʿrīfat*, pp. 179–80.

24. Ibn Khaldūn, *Prolégomènes*, vol. 2, pp. 290–1.

25. A comprehensive account is given by Ibn Sīnā, *Najāt* 2nd edn. pp. 219 ff and see Proclus, *Elements*, propositions, 7, 9, 24, 36, 40.

26. Isfarāʾīnī, *Tabṣīr*, p. 138.

27. Ikhwān al-Ṣafāʾ, *Rasāʾil*, vol. 1, p. 57.

28. Oneness is also the attribute of the one (*ibid.*, p. 49), and this is correlative with the ground of all grounds being one and only one, for along with the division into eternity and contingency, all being is classified into that which is one and that which is not, one aspect of which is the division of being between God and His alterity — see Suhrawardī, *Lamaḥāt*, pp. 125–6; Ibn Rushd, *Mā baʿd aṭ-ṭabīʿa*, pp. 116–18 and Ghazālī, *Maqāṣid*, pp. 183–4.

29. Abul-Barakāt b. Malkā al-Baghdādī, *Muʿtabar*, vol. 2, p. 145.

30. *Ibid.*, p. 388.

31. Fārābī, *Madīna*, pp. 10–11. The fullest description of the transmission of existence into essence in its various grades, and the origin of these in Being and its origin, can be found in A.-M. Goichon, *La distinction de l'essence et de l'existence d'après Ibn Sīnā* (Paris, 1937).

32. For instance, Ghazālī, *Maqāṣid*, pp. 203–4 and Rāzī, *Mabāḥith*, vol. 1, pp. 125 ff. who (*ibid.*, p. 348) saw this division as, again, one innately given to the understanding. On the distinctions between this matter and similar Aristotelian topics, see P. Duhem, *Le système du monde. Histoire des doctrines cosmologiques de Platon à Copernic* (Paris, 1916), vol. 4, p. 495.

33. Ibn Rushd, *Tahāfut*, p. 328 and Shahrastānī, *Muṣāraʿa*, p. 121.

34. See Ibn Sīnā, *Najāt*, 2nd edn, pp. 18–19, along with the comments of Ibn Rushd, *Tahāfut*, pp. 602–3; Rāzī, *Mabāḥith*, vol. 1, p. 113 and Gardet, *Avicenne*, pp. 46–7, 67–8, 200–1.

35. Ibn Taimiyya, *Muwāfaqa*, vol. 1, p. 1.

36. Subkī, *Muʿīd*, p. 41.

37. See, for instance, Būnī, *Uṣūl*, pp. 13–14.

38. See Ikhwān al-Ṣafāʾ, *Rasāʾil*, vol. 1, p. 145. The characterisation of the Ikhwān as Ismāʿīlīs is the subject of controversy in modern scholarship and the present author favours this characterisation. See the review of the question in S.H. Nasr, *An Introduction to Islamic Cosmological Doctrines* (London, 1978), pp. 26–36. The reader is referred to the recent research of A. Hamdani ('An Early Fāṭimīd Source on the Time and Authorship of the *Rasāʾil Ihwān al-Ṣafāʾ*, in *Arabica*, 26 (1979), pp. 62–75) which supports the Ikhwān's Ismāʿīlism and of I. Netton, *Muslim Neoplatonists. An Introduction to the Thought of the Brethren of Purity* (London, 1982), pp. 95 ff., which questions the connection. Indications concerning the authors of the *Rasāʾil* by Pseudo Sijistānī (*Ṣiwān*, p. 361), Tawḥīdī (*Imtāʿ*, vol. 2, p. 5) and Qifṭī (*Tārīkh*, p. 82), have been studied by S.M. Stern, 'New Information about the Authors of the "Epistles of the Sincere Brethren" ', in *Islamic Studies*, 4 (1964), pp. 405–28.

39. The confusing Qurʾānic account of creation is well organised and sketched by E. Beck, 'Iblis und Mensch, Satan und Adam. Der Werdegang einer Koranischen Erzählung', in *Le Muséon*, 89 (1976), pp. 195–244 and see the detailed account of Ṭabarī, *Tārīkh*, vol. 1, pp. 29 ff., 135–7.

40. See the succinct account of the Ibn Sīnā, *Nubuwwāt* (ed. Marmūra), paras. 13–15 and the detailed accounts of Ibn Khaldūn, *Prolégomènes*, vol. 1, pp. 173 ff. and Miskawaih, *Tahdhīb*, pp. 64 ff. The most complete and comprehensive statement is Qazwīnī's *ʿAjāʾib*, a natural history of all creatures.

41. Qazwīnī, *'Ajā'ib*, p. 282.
42. This is the sense in Ibn Khaldūn's interpretation: *Prolégomènes*, vol. 1, pp. 174–5.
43. Ikhwan al-Ṣafā', *Rasā'il*, vol. 2, pp. 180 ff.
44. Such was the view of the great alchemist Ibn Bishrūn in a text recensed in Ibn Khaldūn, *Prolégomènes*, vol. 3, p. 201.
45. See the various expressions of this in Fārābī, *Madīna*, pp. 20ff.; Ibn al-Khaṭīb, *Rawḍa*, p. 575; Ibn Sab'īn, *Budd*, p. 112 and Pseudo-Sijistānī, 'Al Muḥarrik al-awwal', p. 375.
46. Proclus, *Elements*, proposition 145.
47. On the multitude of senses connected with 'nature' see G. Boas and A.O. Lovejoy in Boas and Lovejoy (eds.), *Primitivism and Related Ideas in Antiquity* (Baltimore, 1935), pp. 447–56 and see the incisive comments on difficulties met in dealing with this term in A.O. Lovejoy, *Essays in the History of Ideas* (Baltimore, 1948), p. 67 and in A. Lalande, *Vocabulaire technique et critique de la philosophie*, 8th edn (Paris, 1960), p. 671.
48. Tawḥīdī, *Muqābasāt*, p. 129.
49. *Ibid.*, p. 311.
50. The most comprehensive and useful accounts are in Baghdādī, *Mu'tabar*, vol. 2, pp. 4–6 and Tahānawī, *Kashshāf*, pp. 908–10.
51. Ibn Ḥazm, *Fiṣal*, vol. 1, p. 15.
52. This is the view of Ikhwān al-Ṣafā' (*Rasā'il*, vol. 2, p. 63), who identify this potency with the guardian angels, and see a similar view held by the Peripatetic Sijistānī (Tawḥīdī, *Muqābasāt*, p. 312).
53. For instance: Goichon, *Lexique*, para. 394.3 and Ibn Rushd, *Mā ba'd aṭ-ṭabī'a*, pp. 34–5.
54. Ibn Rushd, *Tahāfut*, pp. 782–3 and see Ibn Sīnā, *Shifā (Ṭabī'iyyāt, 2)*, p. 132.
55. Baghdādī, *Mu'tabar*, vol. 2, p. 5.
56. Ibn Taimiyya, *Radd*, p. 94.
57. *Ibid.*, pp. 94, 310–11.
58. Ibn Ḥazm, *Fiṣal*, vol. 5, pp. 15–16.
59. *Ibid.*, p. 15. One modern commentator (M. Fakhry, *Islamic Occasionalism and its Critique by Averroes and Aquinas* (London, 1958), p. 110) declares that the Ash'arites, instead of considering miracles to be truly unique events, considered all events as if they were miracles. For the substance of the refutation of nature, see M. Bernard, 'La critique de la notion de nature (*ṭab'*) par le kalām', in *SI*, 51 (1980), pp. 59 ff.
60. Ikhwān al-Ṣafā', *Rasā'il*, vol. 1, pp. 145–7 and *passim*.
61. See A. Al-Azmeh, *Ibn Khaldūn: An Essay in Reinterpretation* (London, 1982), pp. 52 ff.
62. Ibn Rushd, *Manāhij* (ed. Qāsim), p. 170 and Ibn Rushd, *Mā ba'd aṭ-ṭabī'a*, pp. 50–1 and Ikhwān al-Ṣafā, *Rasā'il*, vol. 2, pp. 63, 143 ff.
63. Baghdādī, *Mu'tabar*, vol. 2, p. 298; Ibn Rushd, *Tahāfut*, p. 786 and Ibn Sab'īn, *Budd*, p. 116.
64. Rāzī, *Mabāḥith*, vol. 1, p. 626.
65. In the views on the intrinsic versus extrinsic ground of the nature of things can be detected echoes of the conflict between the Aristotelian conception of nature, which affirms that the ground of movement is essentially external, going back, ultimately, to the Prime Mover (see Aristotle, *Metaphysical*, V, 3, 1014b16–1015a5) and the Stoic conception which emphasises the internal constitution of things according to their *logoi spermatikoi*, without this latter view necessarily denying the idea of an ultimate single ground for all movement (see Diogenes Laertius, *Lives of Eminent Philosophers* (Loeb ed.), vii. 148–9). The strict monistic tendency of some mystics and and Ash'arites belongs to the first tendency, and one modern scholar (H.V.B. Brown, 'Avicenna and the Christian Philosophers in Baghdad', in *Islamic Philosophy and the Classical Tradition*, ed. S.M. Stern, A.H. Hourani and V. Brown (Oxford, 1972), pp. 35–48) saw Avicenna's frequent snide references to Christian philosophers of Baghdad, such as Abū Bishr Mattā, as caused

by their affirmation, and their exclusive interest in causes and natures inherent in things rather than paying regard to the distant ultimate causes and movers, and their ascription of reality (not virtuality) to the visible necessities of nature rather than considering them to be absolutely contingent on distant movers. (A different, and distantly related, interpretation of Avicenna's animosity towards Baghdadian philosophers was proferred by S. Pines, 'La "philosophies orientale" d'Avicenne et sa polémique contre les Bagdadiens', in *Archives d'histoire doctrinale et littéraire du môyen age*, 27 (1952), pp. 5–37). It is not surprising that disagreements between Avicenna and his Baghdadians do not refer to Stoicism or Aristotelianism. Contrary to the Aristotelian tradition (itself filtered through Stoic and neo-Platonic avenues) and its impact on Arabic thought, the presence of Stoicism in Arabic thought is very imperfectly known. Whereas the influence of Stoicism is widely acknowledged — and it should not be forgotten that Stoicism was the philosophy of late antiquity *par excellence* — its precise impact and its avenues are unclear, despite the profundity of this impact (see the remarks of R.M. Wenley, *Stoicism and its Influence* (New York, 1963), pp. 107, 121). This is probably due to the wide proliferation of Stoic notions in all fields of intellectual pursuit. Arab knowledge of formal Stoic philosophy (on which see F. Jadaane, *L'Influence du Stoicisme sur la pensée musulmane* (Beirut, 1968) was full, but not very clear in its contours. Such knowledge was probably indirect in any case, not acquired through formal philosophy (see the very pertinent comments of O. Amine, 'La Stoicisme et la pensée islamique', in *Rev. Thomiste*, 59 (67e. anné, 1959), pp. 83 ff., 97), nor mainly through Aristotelian commentators nor medical and ethical writings of the Galenic school. It also found its way through, among other things, Roman rhetoric (see J. Schacht, *The Origins of Muhammadan Jurisprudence* (Oxford, 1953), pp. 99–100), from whence it found its way to Islamic law (on Islamic law and Stoic logic, see N. Shehaby, 'The Influence of Stoic Logic on Al-Jaṣṣaṣ's Legal Theory', in *The Cultural Context of Medieval Learning*, ed. J.E. Murdoch and E.D. Sylla (Boston, 1973), pp. 61–85, and compare with the findings of D. Daube, 'Rabbinic Methods of Interpretation and Hellenistic Rhetoric', in *Hebrew Union College Annual*, 22 (1949), pp. 244 ff.). For Arabic theological literature, see the footnotes to J. Van Ess, 'The Logical Structure of Islamic Theology', in *Logic in Classical Islamic Culture*, ed. G.E. von Grunebaum (Wiesbaden, 1970), pp. 21–50. But Stoic influence is much more than its textual instances described by Van Ess and Jadaane and is more advisedly studied in manners suggested by H. Lewy, *Chaldean Oracles and Theurgy. Mysticism, Magic, and Platonism in the Late Roman Empire*, tr. M. Tardieu (Paris, 1978), p. 430 and 430n.–431 n.

66. Ibn Rushd, *Samā'*, p. 12.

67. Ibn Khaldūn, *Prolégomènes*, vol. 2, p. 366.

68. Tawḥīdī, *Imtā'*, vol. 1, p. 144.

69. *Ibid.*, vol. 2, p. 39.

70. Baghdādī, *Mu'tabar*, vol. 2, p. 15.

71. Pseudo-Sijistānī, *Ṣiwān*, p. 314.

72. Ibn Khaldūn, *Prolégomènes*, vol. 2, p. 366.

73. *Ibid.*, p. 365.

74. *Ibid.*, vol. 3, p. 28.

75. See, for instance, Ibn Rushd, *Athār*, p. 85.

76. Pseudo-Sijistānī, *Ṣiwān*, p. 314.

77. This is the thrust of the refutation of alchemy in Tawḥīdī, *Imtā'*, vol. 2, pp. 39–40; Rāzī, *Mabāḥith*, vol. 2, p. 215 and Ibn Khaldūn, *Prolégomènes*, vol. 3, p. 239.

78. Ibn Khaldūn, *Prolégomènes*, ch. 2, sec. 2 and Ibn Khaldūn, *Muqaddima*, p. 121.

79. Ibn Khaldūn, *Prolégomènes*, vol. 1, pp. 224 and *passim*.

80. *Ibid.*, vol. 2, pp. 250 and *passim*.

81. Ibn Taimiyya, *Radd*, p. 26.

82. Compare the Stoic division of cosmic principles into the active and the passive, the mind-God and unformed matter, an active principle and inert matter (Diogenes Laertius, *Lives*, vii.134–9).

83. Ibn Rushd, *Nafs*, p. 64.
84. See the statement by Aristotle, *Physics*, 255a7–12.
85. Circular movement, that of the heavenly spheres, is the simplest therefore most perfect: *ibid.*, pp. 144 ff.; Rāzī, *Mabḥith*, vol. 1, p. 627; Ibn Rushd, *Samā'*, pp. 43–4 and Ibn Sīnā, *Shifā' (Ṭabī'iyyāt, 2)*, p. 9. See the criticism of Ibn Ḥazm, *Fiṣal*, vol. 5, pp. 36 ff.
86. For instance: Ibn al-Jawzī, *Talbīs*, p. 43.
87. Avicenna, *De Anima*, pp. 28, 31–2.
88. Bāqillānī, *Bayān*, para. 104–6 and see Sukūnī, *'Uyūn*, para. 226.
89. Khayyāṭ, *Intiṣār*, pp. 40–41.
90. Māturīdī, *Tawḥīd*, pp. 12, 17 ff.
91. *Ibid.*, pp. 18–19 and Ash'arī, *Luma'*, pp. 18–19.
92. This is a very ancient idea. For a particularly lucid exposition (and an eloquent refutation), see Philo Judaeus, *On the Eternity of the World* (Loeb Classical Library, 363), vi.28–vii.34.
93. Khwārizmī, *Mafātīḥ*, p. 137.
94. Tawḥīdī, *Imtā'*, vol. 2, p. 85.
95. Baghdādī, *Mu'tabar*, vol. 2, p. 195.
96. One scholar (S. Sambursky, *The Physical World of the Greeks*, tr. M. Dagut (London, 1963), pp. 141–2) contrasts the Aristotelian notion of the continuum, which he described as topographical, with the Stoic notion which rests on the idea of interpretation.
97. Ibn Taimiyya, *Muwāfaqa*, vol. 1, p. 170 and see Jurjānī, *Ta'rīfat*, p. 59.
98. Goichon, *Lexique*, para. 611.8.
99. Ibn al-Ḥājib, *Mukhtaṣar*, pp. 5–6 and Shawkānī, *Irshād*, p. 3.
100. Ghazālī, *Maqaṣid*, p. 189.
101. Ibn Ḥazm, *Fiṣal*, vol. 1, p. 15.
102. See, for instance, Rāzī, *Mabāḥith*, vol. 1, p. 451 and Tawḥīdī, *Muqābasāt*, p. 323.
103. Baghdādī, *Mu'tabar*, vol. 1, p. 55.
104. Sukūnī, *'Uyūn*, para. 208.
105. Ibn Rushd, *Tahāfut*, p. 785.
106. Ibn Khaldūn, *Prolégomènes*, vol. 1, p. 327.
107. *Ibid.*, p. 293.
108. *Ibid.*, p. 294.
109. Rāzī, *Mabāḥith*, vol. 1, p. 443.
110. *Ibid.*, vol. 1, p. 347.
111. Avicenna, *De Anima*, pp. 24–5.
112. Baghdādī, *Mu'tabar*, vol. 1, p. 55. But these not being identifiable does not imply that the composite now has a *sui generis* form and matter, as Ibn Sīnā cautioned (*Shifā' (Ṭabī'iyāt, 2)*, p. 132). Ibn Rushd rightly criticised the Ash'arites for treating the composite as dissociable, thus confusing discrete and continuous quantity (*Manāhij*, p. 35). But this motif remained polemical, and was never conceptually active otherwise.
113. Arabic thought conceived of the soul (*pneuma*) and pysche, *rūḥ* and *nafs*, in different manners, but the soul was normally seen as a material entity, variously located in the heart (Ibn Sīnā, *Qānūn*, vol. 1, pp. 66–7) after the Aristotelian fashion (Aristotle, *De Anima*, II.1, 412a6–21) or in the cavities and pores of the body (Abū Ya'lā, *Mu'tamad*, paras. 172, 176), and rarely assimilated to the immortal psyche of rational nature (as in Miskawaih, 'Nafs', text, pp. 30–1) — for thorough accounts of this matter, see Ibn Khaldūn, *Shifā'*, pp. 18–19 and Baghdādī, *Mu'tabar*, vol. 2, pp. 303–4. Ibn Sīnā's displeasure with the Baghdadian philosophers was also related to controversy over this matter (S. Pines, 'La "philosophie orientale" d'Avicenne'), and to his reaction to a treatise on this issue by Quṣta b. Lūqā, on which see L. Thorndike, *A History of Magic and Experimental Science* (New York, 1923), vol. 1, pp. 658 ff.
114. Ibn Rushd, *Kawn*, pp. 12–13.
115. Ikhwān al-Ṣafā', *Rasā'il*, vol. 1, p. 50.

116. Rāzī, *Mabāhith*, vol. 1, p. 376 and Ibn Sab'īn, *Budd*, p. 32.

117. Muhammad b. Zakariyyā al-Rāzī and Abul 'Alā' al-Ma'arrī should be singled out in this context as the ones who, along with others, subscribed to the thesis of the eternity of *hyle* and of matter. See Rāzī, *Rasā'il*, p. 197 and Rāzī, *Muhassal*, p. 203. S. Pines, *Madhhab adh-dharra 'ind al-Muslimīn*, tr. M.'A. Abū Rīda (Cairo, 1946), pp. 60 ff., and T. Husain, *Tajdīd dhikrā Abil-'Alā*, in T. Husain, *Al-Majmū'a al-kāmila li Mu'allafāt al-Duktūr Tāha Husain* (Beirut, 1974), vol. 10, pp. 268 ff. It is perhaps appropriate here to mention that the general matter, contrary to Aristotle's *hyle*, is in actual, not just in potential existence (cf. Pines, *Madhhab adh-dharra*, pp. 41–2). It is also appropriate to compare these notions of a general substrate to the Stoic *hypokeimenon*, the *hyle* in which forms subsist as in a substance susceptible to all forms. See Zeller, *The Stoics, Epicureans, and Sceptics*, tr. O.J. Reichel [1879] (New York, 1962), pp. 100–1.

118. Ikhwān al-Safā', *Rasā'il*, vol. 2, pp. 6–7.

119. On the pantheistic cosmology of Ibn 'Arabī, the reader is referred to the only comprehensive study of this thinker and the scholar's sure guide to his enormously complex and rich thought: A.E. Affifi, *The Mystical Philosophy of Muhyid Din-Ibnul Arabi* (1939) (Lahore, 1964), pp. 11 ff. and *passim*.

120. Such was the view of extremist pantheists such as Ibn Sab'īn. See Ibn al-Khatīb, *Rawda*, pp. 604, 602 ff.

121. Affifi, *The Mystical Philosophy*, p. 59. This close similarity between Asha'rism and pantheism is also brought out in connection with the illuminationist emanationism of Suhrawardī by M.'A. Abū Rayyān, *Usūl al-falsafa al-'ishrāqiyya 'inda Shihāb al-Dīn al-Suhrawardī* (Cairo, 1959), pp. 124 ff., 176. For an explicit Ash'arite statement on the essential unity of all things in the substratum that subsumes them and makes them mutually convertible see 'Abd al-Qāhir al-Baghdādī, *Usūl*, p. 54.

122. Tawhīdī, *Muqābasāt*, p. 162.

123. Baghdādī, *Mu'tabar*, vol. 2, p. 8.

124. See, for instance, the enumeration of Ghazālī, *Mi'yār*, p. 298.

125. Ibn Sīnā, *Najāt*, 2nd edn, p. 208.

126. Rāzī, *Mabāhith*,. vol. 1, p. 522.

127. Baghdādī (*Mu'tabar*, vol. 2, pp. 10–11) defined *hyle* and *maudū'* as

> that which is a locus of subsistence for changing conditions and the various accidents of generation and corruption . . . that which is waning is the one undergoing corruption, and that which is undergoing creation is the generated, while that which is renouncing that on the wane and substituting the newly generated for it is *mahall, maudū'*, *hyle*. That which is analogous to what the writing board is to writing is called *mahall* and *maudū'*, and that which is analogous to what wood is to a bed or what sperm is to the foetus or the egg to the chick is called *hyle* . . . If we consider the substratum in relation to what occurs to it, such as the body to whiteness, we call it *maudū'*; in relation to what results from their association in 'the white thing', we call it *hyle*.'

Thus wheat is a *hyle* for flour, bread a *hyle* to the humours of the body, and these humours *hyle* to the various parts of the body. A *hyle* is thus proximate or ultimate, and a look at the formation of bodily parts from humours, and humours from nutrients, and nutrients from plants, would reveal that 'every consequent one is a *hyle* for it precedent, being formed of it and undergoing transformation into it'. Ibn Sīnā, for his part, declares (*Najāt*, 2nd edn, p. 200) that a *mahall* is self-subsistent, being considered *maudū'* if it were taken as independent of what subsists in it, and *hyle* if it were not seen as being so independent. As for the absolute *hyle* Ibn Sīnā defines it in the same text as a simple essence which is *mahall* in itself. See Baghdādī (*Mu'tabar*, vol. 2, p. 14):

> A body, by virtue of its very bodiness in so far as it is a receptor of the forms of things, we call a first *hyle*; we call a proximate or intermediate *hyle* the body in virtue of

the readiness it has to receive some forms by virtue of the prior presence in it of others. We call a body a *mauḍū'* in so far as it is the actual carrier of a form, and we call it matter or stuff (*ṭīna*) in so far as it is held in common by forms.

128. Ṭabarī, *Firdaws*, p. 9.

129. *Ibid.*, pp. 10–11. If one were to attribute an historical antecedence to these views of the activity of form and passivity of matter, one would surely have to seek a Stoic apparantage, not an Aristotelian one such as that represented by the position of Ibn Sīnā quoted in n. 5 above. See the very pertinent discussion of P. Kraus, *Jābir Ibn Ḥayyān*, Cairo, 1942–3 (Mémoires presentés à l'Institut d'Egypte, vols. 44, 45), vol. 2, pp. 168–72 and 171n2. This undifferentiated substratum in Stoic natural philosophy assures the continuity displayed by all beings in the universe. See S. Sambursky, *Physics of the Stoics* (London, 1971), p. 17.

130. Ghazālī, *Mi'yār*, p. 298.

131. In the early stages in the development of *kalām* theology, the term *jawhar* alone was used to designate the atom, but this changed with Bāqillānī, who placed *jawhar* in counterposition to 'body'. See the comments of Pines, *Madhhab adh-dharra*, p. 4. It is perhaps worth pointing out that, of the Mu'tazilites, Ibrāhīm b. Sayyār al-Naẓẓam (d. 220–230/835-845), one of the pillars of that school, rejected the concept of the atom (Shahrastānī, *Milal*, p. 25).

132. On this and related matters, see the rigorous analysis of R.M. Frank, *Beings and their Attributes. The Teaching of the Basrian School of the Mu'tazila in the Classical Period* (Albany, 1978), ch. 2.

133. Bāqillānī, *Tamhīd*, para. 27.

134. Ash'arī, *Maqālāt*, vol. 2, pp. 4 ff.

135. *Ibid.*, p. 9 and see Baghdādī, *Uṣūl*, pp. 52 ff.

136. See Fakhry, *Islamic Occasionalism*, p. 35.

137. Ibn Ḥazm, *Manṭiq*, pp. 16–17.

138. Ibn Ḥazm, *Fiṣal*, vol. 5, pp. 66–7. See Ibn Ḥazm's criticism of atomistic theory (*ibid.*, pp. 69–70, 92 ff.), where he argues that the atomists' assumption that their substances are self-subsistent yet ready for the inherence of contrary qualities, and that they do not occupy space or have dimensions, is contrary to the evidence of the senses as well as going counter to the requirements of the intellect.

139. See, for instance, Ibn Sīnā, *Najāt*, p. 160 and Ibn Khaldūn, *Lubāb*, pp. 41–2.

140. Ibn Sīnā, *Najāt*, pp. 160–1.

141. See Pines, *Madhhab adh-dharra*, p. 8.

142. Ibn Sīnā, *Najāt*, 2nd edn, p. 208.

143. Baghdādī, *Mu'tabar*, vol. 2, p. 123.

144. Ghazālī, *Mi'yar*, p. 297.

145. See R.M. Frank, 'The Structure of Created Causality According to al-Aš'ārī', in *SI*, 25 (1966), pp. 20–1.

146. Ash'arī, *Luma'*, p. 73.

147. Fārābī, *Madīna*, pp. 40–41. In this Fārābī follows the Aristotelian view of female passivity in preference to the Galenic-Hippocratic view, in keeping with the mainstream of Muslim thinkers. It is noteworthy that Ibn Sīnā attempted a reconciliation of the two views by holding that, while women do contribute semen and hence an active principle, yet this is purely material and is not a principle of movement, i.e. a soul. See B. Musallam, *Sex and Society in Islam* (Cambridge, 1983), pp. 40, 43 ff., 47 f.

148. Ibn Sīnā, *Najāt*, p. 258.

149. See the view of Sijistānī in Tawḥīdī, *Imtā'*, vol. 3, p. 110.

150. Ibn Rushd, *Nafs*, pp. 6–7.

151. Ibn Khaldūn, *Prolégomènes*, vol. 2, pp. 92, 96, 259.

152. Ash'arī, *Maqālāt*, vol. 1, pp. 27–9.

153. *Ibid.*, vol. 2, p. 9.

154. Ibn Ḥazm, *Fiṣal*, vol. 5, pp. 71, 73.

155. Baghdādī, *Mu'tabar*, vol. 2, pp. 121–2.

156. *Ibid.*, p. 122.

157. For definitions of things, see, for instance, Ibn Khaldūn, *Prolégomènes*, vol. 3, p. 221 and Fārābī, *Iḥṣā'* (ed. Amīn), p. 116.

158. R. Arnaldez and L. Massignon, 'Arabic Science', in *Ancient and Medieval Science*, ed. R. Taton (London, 1967), p. 412, maintain rightly that these two notions constitute the core of Arabic natural science.

159. For instance, Khayyāt, *Intiṣār*, p. 41. It has been said that the Ash'arites' denial of nature and regularity, and their occasionalism, are animated by their denial of any effectivity to anyone but God, so that, like Ibn 'Arabī (Affifi, *The Mystical Philosophy*, pp. 25–6), they saw causality as immanent, not transitive, relating things directly to God. It is well here to refer to the excellent study of J.-C. Vadet, 'Le primat de l'Action sur l'Etre et l'Essence, fil conducteur de la logique d'al-Aš'arī?', in *SI*, 44 (1976), pp. 25–60, which draws out the inner logic of Ash'arite thinking as based not on the principle of being, but of the existent, not of predication, but enunciation, so that the thorough creationism galvanising this theological system becomes an active principle of reasoning rather than a simple article of belief. The predicative relation of things, whether causal or propositional, is defenestrated for the benefit of inherence, and this itself is based on a number of principles developed in the context of Arabic grammar.

160. Ghazālī, *Mi'yār*, p. 298.

161. See Sambursky, *Physics of the Stoics*, pp. 22 ff.

162. On these schools and the confluence of medicine and philosophy in them, see M. Meyerhof, 'Von Alexandrien nach Baghdad. Ein Beitrag zur Geschichte des philosophischen und medizinischen Unterrichts bei den Arabern', in *Sitzungsberichte der preussischen Akademie der Wissenschaften; Philosophisch-Historische Klasse*, 1930, pp. 409 ff. Extant texts on Sabeanism (published in D. Chwolsohn, *Die Sabier und der Ssabismus* (St. Petersburg, 1856), vol. 2) show this mix.

163. See the valuable comments on a similar situation by R. McKeon, 'Medicine and Philosophy in the Eleventh and Twelfth Centuries: The Problem of Elements', in *The Thomist*, 24 (1961), pp. 211–56.

164. Ibn Taimiyya, *Naqḍ*, p. 167.

165. Fārābī, *Ḥurūf*, para. 113 and see Ibn Khaldūn, *Prolégomènes*, vol. 2, p. 316.

166. For instance: Bāqillānī, *Tamhīd*, para. 59 ff. and Māturīdī, *Tawhīd*, pp. 141–2.

167. For instance: Ibn Abī Uṣaibi'a, *'Uyūn*, pp. 647, 648; Nu'aimī, *Dāris*, vol. 1, pp. 172–3 and vol. 2, pp. 129–31 and Ibn Taghrī Birdī, *Manhal*, vol. 1, p. 20.

168. Ibn Rajab, *Dhail*, vol. 1, p. 412 and vol. 2, p. 349.

169. Ibn 'Abd al-Barr, *Jāmi'*, vol. 2, p. 39.

170. The basic concepts are sketched in brief and useful compass by M. Ullman, *Islamic Medicine* (Edinburgh, 1978).

171. A comprehensive account can, of course, be found in Kraus, *Jābir Ibn Ḥayyān*. A short general account is that of G. Heym, 'Al-Rāzī and Alchemy', in *Ambix*, 1 (1938), pp. 184–91. For an historical discussion, though not a full one, see J. Ruska, *Arabische Alchimisten* (2 vols., Heidelberg, 1924).

172. M. Ullmann, *Die Natur- und Geheimwissenschafen im Islam* (Leiden, 1972) (*Handbuch der Orientalistik*, 1. Abt., Ergänzungsbd. VI, 2. Abschnitt), p. 145.

173. Ibn Qayyim al-Jawziyya, *Ṭibb*, pp. 5 and *passim*.

174. *Ibid.*, p. 10.

175. Al-Kindī subscribed to this view (Qiftī, *Tārīkh*, p. 371), of which an exceptionally good account is given by Sijistānī, 'Ajrām', esp. pp. 367, ff.

176. Abū Rayyān, *Suhrawardī*, pp. 225–6.

177. Diogenes Laertius, *Lives*, vii.136.

178. Aristotle, *Metaphysics*, V.3.1014a26.

179. Ibn Sīnā, *Qānūn*, vol. 1, p. 5.

180. Ibn Sīnā, *Shifā' (Ṭabī'īyyāt, 2)*, pp. 154–5 and Jābir b. Ḥayyān, *Ikhrāj*, p. 16.
181. Ibn Rushd, *Kawn*, pp. 16–17.
182. Ibn Rushd, *Āthār*, p. 86.
183. See, for instance, Ibn Rushd, *Kawn*, pp. 15–16.
184. A detailed account of these pairs can be found in Ibn Sīnā, *Shifā' (Ṭabī'īyyāt, 2)*, pp. 150–1 and see Rāzī, *Mabāḥith*, vol. 1, p. 269.
185. Ibn Rushd, *Āthār*, pp. 16–17.
186. Rāzī, *Mabāḥith*, vol. 1, p. 280. It should be indicated that Kraus (*Jābir Ibn Ḥayyān*, vol. 2, p. 165) maintained there was a distinct difference between the Jabirian view of the elementary qualities as concrete and separable, and the Aristotelian view of them as logical abstractions. Yet such differences do not effect the active qualities and their roles in combination, only their theoretical status.
187. See Rāzī, *Mabāḥith*, vol. 1, pp. 272–3, where a refutation is given of the position that cold, for instance, is the mere privation of heat and its absence, a refutation built upon the assumption that reactions of contraries require that the contraries each be positive in itself, and only negative in relation to the other.
188. Ibn Sīnā, *Shifā' (Ṭabī'īyyāt, 2)*, p. 129.
189. *Ibid.*, p. 189.
190. *Ibid.*, pp. 223, 228.
191. A thorough summary of these processes is given by Ibn Sīnā, *Qānūn*, vol. 1, pp. 5–6.
192. For instance: Ibn Sīnā, *Shifā' (Ṭabī'īyyāt, 2)*, pp. 14–15 and Baghdādī, *Mu'tabar*, vol. 2, p. 127.
193. For instance: Ibn Rushd, *Tahāfut*, pp. 110–11.
194. For instance: Qazwīnī, *'Ajā'ib*, p. 134. One Baghdadian philosopher of the Sabean persuasion believed that the movement of light bodies upwards is caused not by the search for their natural loci, but for communion with parts of the same element. This being impossible, parts of elements seek equidistance — hence the sphericity of the earth originating in the inclination towards the common centre of things. See S. Pines, 'Quelques tendances antipéripateticiennes de la pensée scientifique islamique', in *Thalès*, 4 (1940), p. 216 and see p. 217.
195. Ikhwān al-Safā, *Rasā'il*, vol. 1, p. 162. The complexity of the whole question of 'influences' on Arabic thought, and the probable impossibility of any attempt to locate discrete and direct influence, is well brought up in Bāqillānī's contention (*Tamhīd*, para. 110) that the idea of rising light bodies and falling heavy ones derives from the Manichean identification of rising things with light, and heavy falling things with darkness.
196. Bāqillānī, *Tamhīd*, para. 84.
197. Ibn Sīnā, , *Shifā' (Ṭabī'īyyāt, 2)*, p. 170 and see Qazwīnī, *'Ajā'ib*, p. 134.
198. Ibn Sīnā, *Shifā' (Ṭabī'īyyāt, 2)*, pp. 202–3. Ibn Sīnā does not explicitly state in this passage what it is that agitates the elements in their elemental connection and separates them and produces vapours, but is clear from other passages which will be cited later that the heavenly spheres (and not some autonomous heavenly body, like fire) are the ultimate causes.
199. Baghdādī, *Mu'tabar*, vol. 2, pp. 153–4.
200. Juwainī, *Irshād*, p. 336. The mustard seed argument was very common among Ash'arites, and of Mu'tazilite origin.
201. Ibn Khaldūn, *Prolégomènes*, vol. 3, p. 200.
202. Jābir b. Ḥayyān, *Ikhrāj*, pp. 6–7.
203. For instance: Ikhwān al-Ṣafā', *Rasā'il*, vol. 2, pp. 57–8. This series of transformations is imputed to Heraclitus: Marcus Aurelius, *Communings with Himself of Marcus Aurelius Antoninus* (vol. 58 of the *Loeb Classical Library*), iv.46.
204. Suhrawardī, *Lamaḥāt*, p. 109.
205. Ibn Sīnā, *Shifā' (Ṭabī'īyyāt, 2)*, p. 123.
206. Qazwīnī, *'Ajā'ib*, p. 387.

207. Ikhwān al-Safā', *Rasā'il*, vol. 2, p. 58.

208. Qazwīnī, *'Ajā'ib*, p. 242.

209. For instance, *ibid.*, pp. 242–4; Rāzī, *Mabāḥith*, vol. 2, pp. 211–13 and Ikhwān al-Ṣafa', *Rasā'il*, vol. 1, pp. 106–7; a slightly different classification of minerals was adopted by Jābirian alchemy. See Kraus, *Jābir Ibn Ḥayyān*, vol. 2, pp. 18–19.

210. Kraus, *Jābir Ibn Ḥayyān*, vol. 2, p. 187. See *ibid.*, pp. 224–7 for an indication of the proportions involved and tables thereof, and see p. 173.

211. One such operational premiss, for instance, is that the number 17 is the base of all balance, and the degrees of nature are organised according to the series 1:3:5:8, which itself deforms the series 4:6:8. See *ibid.*, p. 207, 227 ff., and pp. 94–5 for the notion of 'balance'.

212. A concise and comprehensive *exposé* of the principles of alchemy is given by Ḥajjī Khalīfa, *Kashf*, col. 1526–33. For details on some essential operations, and on the all-important conception of assimilation, see Jābir b. Ḥayyān, *Ikhrāj*, pp. 77–8.

213. Ḥajjī Khalifa, *Kashf*, col. 672.

214. H.E. Stapleton *et al.*, 'Two Alchemical Treatises attributed to Avicenna', in *Ambix*, 10 (1962), pp. 43–4.

215. Ibn Khaldūn, *Prolégomènes*, vol. 3, pp. 233–4.

216. Rāzi, *Mabāḥith*, vol. 2, pp. 214–15, 216.

217. *Ibid.*, p. 212.

218. Ibn Khaldūn, *Prolégomènes*, vol. 3, pp. 237–8.

219. Tawḥīdī, *Imtā'*, vol. 2, pp. 39–40.

220. Kraus, *Jābir Ibn Ḥayyān*, vol. 2, p. 235n11.

221. Ibn Khaldūn, *Prolégomènes*, vol. 3, p. 230.

222. Khwārizmī, *Mafātīḥ*, p. 266 and Ibn Khaldūn, *Prolégomènes*, vol. 3, p. 191, who adds to this list bones, feathers and excrement.

223. Khwārizmī, *Mafātīḥ*, p. 266.

224. Ibn Khaldūn, *Prolégomènes*, vol. 3, p. 239.

225. Jābir b. Ḥayyān, *Ikhrāj*, pp. 80 and *passim* and Ibn Khaldūn, *Shifā'* (ed. Khalifé), p. 54.

226. Ḥajjī Khalīfa, *Kashf*, col. 833.

227. Jābir b. Ḥayyān, *Ikhrāj*, p. 62; Būnī, *Uṣūl*, p. 10 and Khwārizmī, *Mafātīḥ*, p. 258.

228. Baghdādī, *Mu'tabar*, vol. 2, p. 267.

229. Avicenna, *De Anima*, p. 41.

230. Ibn Sīnā, *Qānūn*, vol. 1, p. 22.

231. Ibn Tufail, *Ḥayy*, pp. 69–70. It is noteworthy that Arabic entomology conceived of the generation of worms and other 'insects' as a process of spontaneous generation from elements, qualities and humours that exist in the soil, and the generation of such creatures, as of plants, is brought about by celestial emanations — see for instance, Ibn Rushd, *Mā ba'd aṭ-ṭabī'a*, p. 50.

232. Rāzī, *Mabāḥith*, vol. 1, p. 519.

233. Avicenna, *De Anima*, p. 28.

234. Ibn Ṭufail, *Ḥayy*, pp. 105–6.

235. Ibn Sīnā, *Qānūn*, vol. 1, p. 6.

236. Rāzī, *Mabāḥith*, vol. 1, p. 382.

237. *Ibid.*, p. 519.

238. On the constitution of organs and parts of the body, see Ibn Sīnā, *Qānūn*, vol. 1, pp. 13–18.

239. *Ibid.*, p. 223.

240. See the discussion of Ullmann, *Islamic Medicine*, p. 59.

241. Ibn Khaldūn, *Muqaddima*, pp. 131–2.

242. Ibn Sīnā, *Qānūn*, vol. 1, p. 6. Baghdādī (*Mu'tabar*, vol. 2, p. 174) judges such a combination as 'highly improbable'.

243. Ibn Sīnā, *Qānūn*, vol. 1, p. 6.

244. Rāzī, *Mabāḥith*, vol. 1, p. 395.
245. Ibn Sīnā, *Qānūn*, vol. 1, pp. 8–9.
246. See A. Siggel, *Das Buch der Gifte des Ǧābir Ibn Ḥayyān* (Wiesbaden, 1958) (Veröffentlichungen der Orientalischen Kommission der Akademie der Wissenschaften und der Literatur, Bd. XII), p. 41.
247. Ibn Sīnā, *Qānūn*, vol. 1, p. 108 and Rāzī, *Mabāḥith*, vol. 1, pp. 390 ff.
248. See Baghdādī, *Mu'tabar*, vol. 2, p. 172.
249. On the principles of therapy, see Ibn Sīnā, *Qānūn*, vol. 1, pp. 187–90, and the useful remarks of J.-P. Charnay, 'Nature et principe des contraries dans la médicine d'Avicenne', in *L'Ambivalance dans la culture arabe*, ed. J. Berque, J.-P. Charnay *et al.* (Paris, 1967), pp. 104–7.
250. Rāzī, *Mabāḥith*, vol. 2, p. 218.
251. Baghdādī, *Mu'tabar*, vol. 1, p. 180.
252. Ikhwān al-Ṣafā, *Rasā'il*, vol. 2, p. 111.
253. Tawḥīdī, *Imtā'*, vol. 2, p. 109.
254. Ibn Abī Uṣaibi'a, *'Uyūn*, p. 417.
255. Tawḥīdī, *Muqābasāt*, p. 250.
256. Baghdādī, *Mu'tabar*, vol. 2, p. 164.
257. Shawkānī, *Irshād*, p. 102.
258. Ibn Rushd, *Samā'*, p. 5 and cf. 59. See the remarks on the lack of a conception of an intermediary, and the primacy of identity and opposition, in G.E.R. Lloyd, *Polarity and Analogy. Two Types of Argumentation in Early Greek Thought* (Cambridge, 1966), p. 8.
259. Ibn Rushd, *Kawn*, p. 14.
260. Rāzī, *Mabāḥith*, vol. 1, p. 280.
261. Tawḥīdī, *Muqābasāt*, p. 283.
262. Baghdādī, *Mu'tabar*, vol. 2, p. 173. The author (*ibid.*, p. 168) maintains a graphic conception of tempers, according to which the parts of the composite are so small and intermingled that they are not visible.
263. Avicenna, *De Anima*, pp. 33–4.
264. See Rāzī, *Mabāḥith*, vol. 1, p. 104 and Ibn Rushd, *Ma ba'd aṭ-ṭabī'a*, pp. 111–12.
265. Ṭāshköprüzade, *Miftāḥ*, vol. 3, p. 220.
266. Ibn Sīnā, *Shifā' (Ṭabī'īyyāt, 2)*, pp. 215 and 215 ff.
267. Ibn Khaldūn, *Prolégomènes*, vol. 1, p. 181.
268. See the remarks of Lloyd, *Polarity and Analogy*, pp. 56 ff.
269. See the diagram of elemental, temperamental and geographical contraries deployed by Ibn Sīnā in Charnay, 'Nature et principe des contraires', p. 103 and see Nasr, *Cosmological Doctrines*, p. 224.
270. See J. Chelhod, 'A Contribution to the Problem of the Pre-Eminence of the Right, Based on Arabic Evidence', in *Right and Left*, ed. R. Needham (London, 1973), pp. 239 ff.
271. Kraus, *Jābir Ibn Ḥayyān*, vol. 2, pp. 65 ff.
272. Tawḥīdī, *Imtā'*, vol. 1, pp. 149–50.
273. Ibn Qutaiba, *Ta'wīl*, p. 242.
274. *Ibid.*, p. 142.
275. On this phenomenon in general, see Suyūṭī, *Muzhir*, vol. 1, p. 387.
276. Ibn Qutaiba, *Ta'wīl*, p. 144.
277. We must therefore be in agreement with the view of D. Reig ('Antynomie des semblables et corrélation des opposés en Arabe', in *BEO*, 24 (1971) pp. 136, 141) that, in themselves as well as for Arabic linguists, these did not constitute a veritable 'problem', neither did they occupy a privileged analytical position, and any attempt to privilege them would therefore have to be forced.
278. Avicenna, *De Anima*, pp. 46–7 and Ghazālī, *Mīzān*, p. 204.
279. Yaḥyā b. 'Adī, *Tahdhīb*, p. 122 and see Miskawaih, *Tahdhīb*, p. 82.
280. Miskawaih, *Tahdhīb*, pp. 24–5.

281. See the detailed discussion of this topic, and the minor differences, in Miskawaih, *Tahdhīb*, pp. 16–28, 112 ff.; Ghazālī, *Mīzan*, pp. 264 ff. and Yaḥyā b. 'Adī, *Tahdhīb*, pp. 127 ff.

282. Miskawaih, *Tahdhīb*, p. 250.

283. Ghazalī, *Mīzān*, p. 273.

284. Miskawaih, *Tahdhīb*, pp. 113 ff.

285. Miskawaih, *Tahdhīb*, p. 113 and see Ikhwān al-Ṣafā', *Rasā'il*, vol. 1, p. 195.

286. Ibn Khaldūn, *Prolégomènes*, vol. 2, pp. 51–3.

287. Miskawaih, *Tahdhīb*, p. 116.

288. *Ibid.*, p. 115.

289. *Ibid.*

290. See the discussion of this matter in A. Al-Azmeh, *Ibn Khaldūn in Modern Scholarship* (London, 1981), pp. 165 ff., and the references therein.

291. Ibn Khaldūn, *Prolégomènes*, vol. 2, pp. 144–6.

292. On conceptions of livelihood, reward, return and kindered notions, see *ibid.*, pp. 273–4, Baghdādī, *Uṣūl*, pp. 144–6 and Miskawaih, *Hawāmil*, p. 102.

293. Juwainī, *Irshād*, p. 367 and Maqrīzī, *Ighātha*, p. 84.

294. Maqrīzī, *Sulūk*, vol. 3, pp. 1131–2, and see Ibn Khaldūn, *Prolégomènes*, vol. 3, p. 238. See the general account of D. Gimaret, 'Les theologiens musulmans devant la hausse des prix', in *JESHO*, 22 (1979), pp. 333–4.

295. See the discussion of Jābir b. Ḥayyān in Kraus, *Jābir Ibn Ḥayyan*, vol. 2, p. 235 n. 11 and of Miskawaih, *Tahdhīb*, pp. 113, 113–15. Compare Greek conceptions of even and uneven proportions in A.G. Vlastos, 'Isonomia', in *American Journal of Philology*, 74 (1953), pp. 345–6 and *passim*.

296. Ibn Khaldūn, *Prolégomènes*, vol. 1, p. 314 and see the comments of Al-Azmeh, *Ibn Khaldūn. An Essay*, p. 59.

297. Ibn Khaldūn, *Prolégomènes*, vol. 1, pp. 71–2.

298. Baghdādī, *Mu'tabar*, vol. 1, p. 286.

299. *Ibid.*, p. 288.

300. Marcus Aurelius, *Communings*, v.30.

301. Ghazāli, *Mīzān*, p. 273. We are reminded (Abū Ya'lā, *Mu'tabar*, para. 195), that the lexical sense of injustice (*ẓulm*) indicates the misplacement of things, and that injustice means the action of an agent in a domain that is not his.

302. Ghazālī, *Mīzān*, pp. 235–6.

303. Yaḥyā b. 'Adī, *Tahdhīb*, p. 139.

304. Ghazālī, *Mīzān*, p. 272.

305. The hierarchy of bodily organs is explained in Ibn Sīnā, *Qānūn*, vol. 1, pp. 20–21, and their analogy with the political order was drawn by Fārābī, *Madīna* (ed. Dieterici), p. 55. Similarly, Arabic literature construes society as divisible into free men and slaves, and free men are divided into majors and minors, majors then being divided into men and women, men into rulers and ruled, and so forth, all categories based on the degree of unaccountability they possess in practical life. See the comments of 'A. 'Arwī, *Mafhūm al-ḥurriyya* (Casablanca, 1981), p. 15.

306. Ghazālī, *Mīzān*, p. 209.

307. *Ibid.*, p. 211.

308. Fārābī, *Milla*, paras. 21–2, 27.

309. On the externality of the king with respect to the social order, see the incisive comments of W. Sharārā, 'Al-Malik/al-'āmma, aṭ-ṭabī'a, al-mawt', in *DA*, 16/12 (1980), pp. 19 ff., and see 'A. Al-'Aẓma, 'Al-Siyāsa wa al-lā-siyāsa fil-fikr al-'arabī al-islāmī', in *Al-Fikr al-'Arabī*, 3/22 (1981), pp. 286 ff.

310. Miskawaih, *Hawāmil*, p. 347.

311. For instance: Ghazālī, *Iqtiṣād*, pp. 234–7; Rāzī, *Muḥaṣṣal*, p. 176 (and see A.S. Tritton, 'Al-Muḥaṣṣal by . . . ar-Rāzī (Cairo, 1323)', in *Oriens*, 18–19 (1967), *ad. loc.*, ll. 11–14) and Ṭurṭūshī, *Sirāj*, pp. 41–2.

312. See the particularly good expression of this in Māturīdī, *Tawḥīd*, pp. 182–3.

313. W. Sharārā, *Ḥaula ba'ḍ mushkilāt al-daula fil-thaqāfa wal-mujtama' al-'arabiyyain* (Beirut, 1980), p. 33.

314. See A. Al-'Aẓma, *Al-Kitāba at-tārīkhiyya wal-ma'rifa at-tārīkhiyya* (Beirut, 1983), pp. 76 ff., and Al-'Aẓma, 'Al-Siyāsa', pp. 284 f. The lack of sovereignty amongst a people classifies them as barbarian: see Al-Azmeh, *Ibn Khaldūn in Modern Scholarship*, pp. 134 f.

315. Fārābī, *Milla*, para. 1.

316. Tawḥīdī, *Imtā'*, vol. 3, p. 99 and see *ibid.*, pp. 86–91.

317. Ṭurṭūshī, *Sirāj*, p. 43 and see *ibid.*, p. 39.

318. Yaḥyā b. 'Adī, *Tahdhīb*, p. 135.

319. On this duality, see Sharāra, *Mushkilāt*, pp. 25–6.

320. This was noted with reference to Fārābī by 'A. Bin'Abd al-'Ālī, *Al-Falsafa al-siyāsiyya 'ind al-Fārābī* (Beirut, 1979), p. 82.

321. See the remarks of Sharārā, *Mushkilāt*, pp. 31–3, 41.

322. Bīrūnī, *Āthār*, p. 132.

323. For instance: Ash'arī, *Luma'*, pp. 20–1; Māturīdī, *Tawḥīd*, p. 20 and Ibn Rushd, *Muqaddimāt*, p. 8.

324. Miskawaih, *Tahdhīb*, p. 147.

325. Ibn Khaldūn, *Prolégomènes*, vol. 2, p. 355.

326. Ibn Sīnā, *Najāt*, 2nd edn, p. 245.

327. M. Mandūr, *Al-Naqd al-manhajī 'ind al-'Arab* (Cairo, n.d.), pp. 382 ff.

328. Ḥajjī Khalīfa, *Kashf*, col. 232.

329. B. Yāsīn, 'Ṣūrat al-mar'a fī ḥikāyāt Shahrazād' in *DA*, 18/7 (1982), pp. 81–5. Similarly, excellent musical composition achieves an 'apposite' combination of melody and rhythm — see, for instance, Ḥajjī Khalīfa, *Kashf*, col. 1902.

330. Ibn Rushd, *Nafs*, p. 64.

331. Avicenna, *De Anima*, pp. 39–40.

332. Ibn al-Nafīs, *Risāla*, p. 5.

333. A study of the causality immanent in Arabic historical writing reveals the same mode of explaining things in terms of themselves, so that the event is explained pseudo-causally in terms of its positive inception — see 'Aẓma, *Al-Kitāba aṭ-ṭārīkhiyya*, pp. 95 ff.

Chapter Two

Metaphysical Foundations, 2: Relations of Creation, Sympathy and Analogy

The previous chapter noted that the tempers of the body transform nutrients into matter of a similar and identical nature; that the soul preserves the body and realises humanity; that God creates the world and preserves it and that kingship gathers fractious individuals and creates society. The relations between the heavenly spheres and the elements, and the indissoluble connection between spiritual and terrestrial matters were brought into view. These and other such matters are but instances of the manner in which things are associated with each other, exercise influence upon one another or receive influence from others. In all these instances, two elements were detected which were always present: juxtaposition as a fundamental anatomical quality, and the action/reaction relation as the primary motor and potency that brings this juxtaposition into existence and guarantees its continuity, endowing it with a 'nature'. It is now incumbent upon us to look into the conditions of these two elements that were isolated and identified, and into the reasons why — the external conditions *asbāb* and *shurūṭ*[1] — beings are constituted in the manner investigated in the previous chapter and not after some other fashion. The location of these conditions lies in the structure of created being and the nature of the relations that bind its components to each other, at the head of which is God.

Humanity and Spirituality

We have already noted that the arrangement of creatures along the great chain of being is one of juxtaposition and normative differentiation. The different grades of being arranged along this chain are juxtaposed with particular density in humankind, which is an abundance of being and the field of contestation between sublimity and meanness. Humankind is the knot of creation; it articulates the world which ascends from the elements and descends from God; it is the link between mutable materiality and immutable spirituality. Humankind, according to the eloquent statement of Sijistānī, is the concatenation of potencies or natures distributed amongst creation, and is the form in which everything is consummated.[2] Humankind is the gist of creation; it is a plant in so far as it feeds and grows, animal in so far as it moves and senses and angel in so far as it possesses reason.[3] Humanity exists for the sake of the rational soul; the rational soul exists for the sake of a finalist teleology, *al-afḍal*, and humanity therefore occupies an intermediate position between sensuous and rational existence.[4] Humanity itself is therefore hierarchically organised in a manner which reproduces the chain of being according to the faculties of the soul that predominate in each category of humanity. Some people are closer to animals than they are to humanity, such as the inhabitants of the intemperate climatic zones of the world whose material culture is rudimentary and who lack laws, currencies and may even lack language and cannibalise one another.[5] All of these matters are due essentially to the effect of their climate.[6] Equally closer to apes than to the common run of humanity are 'the louts amongst Arabs and Turks, the animal herders amongst them'.[7] Just as animals have differential capacities for learning, so humans differ in their readiness and ability to accept rationality and spirituality.[8] The relative stations of human beings are determined by their closeness and distance from the inconsistency and wildness that marks the behaviour of animals.[9] Nations that are the most temperate are also the most civilised and the ones with the loftiest laws; they are, also, the only nations capable of engendering prophethood. Such are the inhabitants of North Africa, of Syria, Iraq, Spain, China, the Sind and whatever Europeans as live in the proximity of these territories.[10]

In addition to a social and cultural ladder along which nations are differentiated, individuals are also placed in relations of normative subordination and superordination with regard to the spirit and the mind in the contentious opinions of the philosophers and mystics. The more endowed a person be with the capacity to grasp rational entities and abstractions, the greater would be his affinity to these entities themselves. When the human species is consummated by the full acquisition of the emanations of rationality and the emulation of the principles of all being by the human soul,[11] a person may even attain the station of the spirituality termed *al-'aql al-qudsī* which allows for the direct apprehension of rational principles and the direct reception of the forms emitted by the active intellect. This is the consummate degree of prophecy, and the highest station of humanity and of human potency.[12] Indeed, the attainment of this station merges humanity with angelicalness, for an angel is nothing but 'a simple immortal substance endowed with life and rationality [*nuṭq 'aqli*], and is an intermediary between God and earthly bodies. Some of it is rational, part spiritual, and part corporeal'.[13] Some even went so far as to maintain that man, in his capacity as the substance of sainthood, is parallel to the creator and to creation, the being before whom angels fall prostrate, with the power of whose soul the heavens move, and for whose sake the whole world is conceived.[14]

The departure of men from ordinary humanity and their participation, however momentary, in the spiritual realm, is manifested in many spheres of life. Intuition itself, according to Sijistānī, arises from a divine power, soothsaying, which men possess by virtue of the intermediate position they occupy between nature and divinity, and which is pronounced amongst many people, even common people.[15] And whereas it was commonly assumed that soothsaying is an evil power inspired by the devil in contrast to the divinatory power inspired by God (prophecy), both are, fundamentally, of the same operational nature. This is so despite the infallibility of prophecy and the fallibility of soothsaying, which is due to the lack of total liberation from matter of the soothsayer's soul.[16] In both cases, the soul tears itself away from humanity and peers into angelicalness by moving over into the station immediately superior to humanity in the chain of being.[17] It should not be forgotten that Satan himself was, to some at least, an angel, albeit a fallen one, a matter which alters his normative status, but should not alter his spiritual (or, to those who believed he was a *jinni*, fiery) substance. Prophecy in this context is the entry of the human soul to a realm transcending the mind, a realm which opens 'another eye' capable of beholding the future.[18] This is the most sublime knowledge where facts and realities are apprehended intuitively and by inspiration, without having to be acquired[19] by the senses or the mind. In addition to this gnostic capacity, the prophet is endowed with the mastery over matter which allows him to perform miracles and according to Suhrawardī 'to tame the *hyle*'.[20] Ibn Sīnā expressed this in the following manner:

> it pertains to the soul to effect a change of temper without this being caused by a bodily action or reaction, so that heat can be induced without something hot, and cold without something cold. Indeed, if the soul were to imagine some thing or some power, the bodily element will readily receive a form or a quality appropriate to that which was imagined, and this is because the soul is of the same substance as certain principles which themselves provide matter with its

> constitutive forms . . . The form that dwells in the soul is the principle of that which comes to pass in the element, just as the healthy form in the mind of the physician is the principle of remission of diseases . . . It often happens, if forms be firmly grounded in the soul, and if it is believed that they should materialise, that matter will react to this . . . so if this were to occur in the Universal Soul which is that of the sky and the earth, it would then effect the nature of all, whereas if it were to occur in a particular soul, then the effect would be exercised on a particular nature. It also often happens that a soul influences a body other than the one which pertains to itself . . . And indeed, if the soul be strong and sublime, similar to principles [of form], it will be obeyed by the element which is in the world, which will react to it

— it is thus that healing, rain-making, pestilence, eclipses and fertility occur.[21] However rare this state of affairs may be, it is by no means strange; it could be accounted for by the continuity of all things, and the division of everything into matter and spirit with definite relations, some of which were discussed in the previous chapter. The matter of the four elements, after all,

> is common among them and a receptor of all their forms. And as it is manifest that imaginings of the soul may become principles for the occurrence of events without the involvement of bodily agents, it is possible that these imaginings could become the principles of extraordinary occurrences. . . . The Master [Ibn Sīnā] put it well when he said that sublime active potencies and lowly reactive potentialities have extraordinary conjunctions.[22]

This interpretation of prophecy and allied phenomena was, as indicated earlier, confined to philosophical, mystical and esoteric discourse, and its conceptual content strenuously denied by mainstream theological and religious opinion,[23] although it does offer an explanation for the otherwise unexplained (except by reference to special divine endowment), though uniformly accepted, Signs of Prophecy: capacity to divine the future and to perform miracles. But such discourse on prophecy was religious, pietistic and dogmatic, not involving components of philosophical discourse.

Be that as it may, sainthood, *wilāya*, runs epistemologically parallel to prophethood, though it is, for the majority, doctrinally distinct. Such is the case with gnostic intuition which, according to a very common expression, God interjects into the heart of the prophet or the saint. Such is also the case with miracles performed by the sheer act of the will, notwithstanding the difference in status between a prophet and a saint which some mystics expressed by saying that whereas a prophet partook directly of divine light, a saint had to do, in his access to the realm of divinity, with the leftovers.[24] Yet in both cases, knowledge is immediate,[25] and knowledge and being are not differentiated, so that knowledge of occult matters results in the actualisation of the fruits of gnosis. With the deployment of the kinship between humanity and angelicalness a miracle is effected, i.e. an act which breaks the familiar course of things and achieves wondrous results. And although prophetic miracles and saintly wonders are designated by different terms — *mu'jiza* and *karāma*, respectively — the kinship between them is manifest and makes their difference one of status, one which pertains to the realm of dogmatics and to devotional etiquette, not to the science of the miraculous. Some mystics, and mystics were the party most directly concerned with sainthood, differentiated the two by saying that whereas prophethood was exoteric and involved the direct public delivery of divine ordinance, sainthood was esoteric.[26] This distinction also developed into the statement of historical import, that although the two are, in essence, identical, they constitute a general and a particular instance of prophethood, sainthood being a general prophecy, not necessarily bound to legislation.[27] It may have been in response to such a supererogation of mystical sainthood that many persons of conformist piety attempted to refute the existence of saints and their miracles, but such attempts were fairly early pre-empted by moderate mystics with traditionalist demonstrations making abundant use of standard sacred texts.[28] They proposed that, whereas a prophet is under an obligation to reveal the miracle he works, a saint is under no such obligation,[29] which ultimately amounts to the same assertion of identity. Some mystics, in the same apologetic mode, went so far as to claim that saints were in fact ignorant of their own felicity, or that their sainthood was only recognisable to others with the same sort of endowment.[30] Yet in mystical devotions, as in common religiosity to this very day, Muḥammad has been the subject of his own cult which does not differ in essence from hagiolatrous cults, in which prophetology is constructed around hagiological models.

Despite differences brought about by doctrinal officiousness on the part of a more orthodox disposition, there is nothing to arrest the attempt to compare saintly with prophetic miracles, nor the comparison of these with magic. A miracle and a magical act both have this essential characteristic in common, that they are effected by means of a spiritual agency external to the nature of the substrate where the act takes effect, the difference being that whereas overall the purpose of the miracle is benign, that of magic is malign and positively evil.[31] This property common to both was evident, and Bāqillānī, in a treatise devoted specifically to this topic, could do no better than to mitigate the similarity by stating that some acts brought about by magicians are not really akin to miracles, although they are of the same type (*min jins*),[32] and that the real distinction resided in divine will: as acts which break the familiar order of things are possible for God only,[33] God would certainly refrain from aiding a sorcerer in his magical act if He knew that the sorcerer intended to use this act to claim prophethood,[34] for it is miracles that differentiate authentic from presumed prophecy.[35] The possibility of magic not involving the presumption of prophecy is thus preserved, and indeed, it is admissible both rationally and in terms of its not contradicting sacred texts, although the consensus was that magic is only manifested in an evil personality, while a saintly miracle is impossible for such a person.[36]

Outright denial of saintly miracle, accompanied with an assertion of the rational inadmissibility of miracles along with acceptance of those prophetic miracles attested by sound traditions, as was the rigorous position of Ibn Ḥazm premised upon the necessity of natural regularity,[37] was very rare and went counter to the impulse of practical religiosity. The usual differentiation, along with statements on value and sublimity, normally involved the historical criterion of challenge, *taḥaddī*, whereby a prophet, for the sake of his credibility as such, challenged his contemporaries to a particular act, a sort of trial by magical ordeal, and won the day.[38] Such were the exhibitionistic contests of magical efficacy, of biblical origin, which we find in the Qur'ān and in exegetical literature, involving encounters between Moses and Pharaoh's sorcerers, or between Abraham and those of Nimrod. And indeed, a perceptive historian related a statement to the effect that God equipped His prophets with a superabundance of the skills prevalent among people to whom they are sent: thus Moses was sent to people distinguished by magic (hence his stave), Solomon to people skilled in talismanic magic (hence his control over the *jinn* and the winds) and Muḥammad to people of a particularly eloquent and loquacious disposition, hence the Qur'ān.[39] Indeed, the famous miraculous inimitability (*i'jāz*) of the Qur'ān is a topic which finds its bearings in this very context; it is a demonstration of Muḥammad's prophethood. The greatest of the later Mu'tazilites, the Qāḍī 'Abd al-Jabbār (d. 415/1024), believed that the miracle is the best demonstration of prophethood because it is totally unambiguous: unlike speech, it is univocal.[40] But the greatness and uniqueness of the Muḥammadan demonstration lay precisely there: that it was undertaken through the medium of language. There is a general concordance about the components of this miraculous inimitability:[41] that the Qur'ān prophesised, that it contained the register of sacred history as delivered by a prophet unlettered in historical and prophetic lore (*ummī*), and that it was so eloquent that no verbal composition could be its equal.[42]

Whatever the content of miracle might be, it belongs to a wider class of psycho-epistemological phenomena which are intuitive and automatic and without bearing on the normal course of intellection which involves the act of reason and the evidence of the senses. The psycho-epistemological underpinnings of this, explicitly described by Ibn Sīnā, are the same as those obtaining in truthful dreams and other instances when the soul peers into the future or otherwise behaves in an extraordinary fashion.[43] A truthful dream is, indeed, akin to a *karāma*.[44] For dreams are divided into true visions, *ru'yā ṣaḥīḥa*, and mere dreamy illusions, *aḍghāth aḥlām*. These are ultimately reducible, according to a modern scholar, to the distinction between matter and spirit which animates Islamic thought.[45] The bulk of illusions seen during sleep are caused by the tempers which predominate in the body, those with a choleric temperament being prone to seeing frightful dreams involving caves, sanguine individuals tending to dream about light and happiness and redness. Such illusions are also full of dreamers' worries, wishes and the like, or are simply inspired by that great confounder, Satan.[46] Truthful dreams, whose division into those manifestly meaningful and those in need of interpretation need not detain us here,[47] themselves are subject to differential veracity attributable to the body: individuals with the most even tempers dream the truest,[48] dreams of males are truer than those of females and, amongst the latter, dreams of virgins are less truthful than dreams by those with consummate womanhood.[49] As divine grace would not omit to favour those in higher stations in the world, and hence in the cosmos, the dreams of sages and of kings are truer than those of commoners.[50]

In all cases, a dream is the product of a regard by the rational soul into its own spiritual essence, wherein it beholds a glimpse of realities.[51] In oneiromancy, as in prophecy, soothsaying and mystical gnosis, the 'veil of sense' is removed.[52] A true dream foretells the future, for good or ill, and an augury is only possible by transcending the sheer humanity of humanity and passing over into a superior station of being, one which affords readier access to the beyond where absolute knowledge is contained. One Persian illuminationist expressed this well by saying that dreams foretell the future because they reveal the Tablet of Fate, *al-lawḥ al-maḥfūẓ*[53] which, according to Islamic cosmology, contains the register of all posterity and which God caused to be written immediately upon the creation of the Pen, created before the world.[54] And while the human psyche possesses the equipment with which to receive such unfamiliar knowledge,[55] this knowledge can only be partaken of under the influence of divine intervention.[56] It is by virtue of this divinely ordained access into divinity that the soul gains access into the future, and this access is only made possible by the divine potency which, as Ibn Sīnā noted, Greeks termed emanation, the Syriacs the Word, the Manicheans the Good Spirits, the Arabs the Angels, the Persians Light, the Sabeans the Proximate Ruler[57] and Aristotle the Active Intellect,[58] each according to their cosmological scheme, which ran parallel at many junctures. Regardless of the doctrinal expression, the process is recursive, the divine element in man looking inwards, to what Ibn Sīnā gave the Platonic term 'remembrance'.[59] In all cases, the process involves a de-corporealisation of the soul[60] such as that obtaining in sleep, or in the case of divine fools whose souls can even obtain the requisite access during theoleptic waking abstractedness.[61]

There is therefore no doubt that what makes possible the communication between mankind and higher realms, such as that witnessed in oneiromancy, soothsaying, prophecy and sainthood, is an essential connection anterior to, and coexisting with, the severance between humanity and spirituality. The connection of man and the realms of divinity is no more than the realisation of the spiritual component of humanity, that component variously known as an angel, a soul, an intellect, and other terms designating less the concept as such as much as its many users (God, after all, imparted His breath to the clay from whence Adam came). Yet this access of humanity to divinity is not simply a theoretical, psychological or epistemological fact, for the soul itself, the agency of this access, is not wholly corporeal, but partakes of a residual divinity by virtue of its spirituality.[61] This access is not solely attributable to employment of a spatial metaphor which establishes a localised proportionality and suitability between the soul as an extra eye which sees things occluded from the physical eye by the veil of sense, but is grounded in a full mutuality which expresses itself in correspondence and full proportionality. Humanity contains the two universes, the terrestrial and the extra-terrestrial, the corporeal and the spiritual, by being their articulation, their union, the gist of their stuff. And whereas the universe does contain man, this is true of the extreme and local particularity of man, for if the universe were to be regarded as a circle, man would be its centre, the point from which the arc of the circle maintains equidistance. This is what is meant by the saying, very frequently uttered in all manner of contexts, that the universe is a macrocosm, and man a microcosm. Man can be said to be the archetype of the universe, relating to it by the mutual correspondence of all components of both. The mystical conception of the Perfect Man is conceived precisely in these terms.

It is in this spirit that Tawḥīdī declared that, when purified, the reasoning faculty of the soul tends to scrutinise man first, then the world, for 'to know man is to know the microcosm (*al-'ālam al-ṣaghīr*), and to know the world is to know macro-humanity (*al-insān al-kabīr*)'.[63] The relation between the two worlds is not confined to the metaphysical and ontological aspect fully developed by mystics — that the exoteric aspect of humanity is parallel to the world whereas its esoteric aspect runs parallel to divinity,[64] that the world is really a collection of aspects of humanity which is directly reducible to the emanationist reality of Muḥammad as cosmic principle,[65] and that the perfection of humanity expressed in the Perfect Man is the cause of the cosmos in the sense that it is the consummation of its purpose, namely, divine manifestation.[66] The relation between humanity and the rest of the world is one of the correspondence of plastic components, for the chain of being is also seen as a truly conical projection of reality at descending degrees of firmness and association, on which everything is similarly constituted in terms of reversible components. The human brain corresponds to phlegm amongst wet substances, to water amongst elements, to winter amongst the seasons. Testicles similarly correspond to bile, earth and autumn.[67] What we find in humankind we also find in other things, this common existence being an aspect of homology and participation which constitute the mesh of creation. Growth is shared by plants and humans; salt water by the sea and human eyes; and just as the world contains lions, devils and beasts, so humanity harbours oppression, vindictive malevolence and bestiality witnessed in eating and fornication: nothing present in one world is absent in another.[68] It is reflection in this general sense which prompted Fārābī to locate the grounds of dysfunction in human communities in their deviation from the morphological order of the universe in which an hierarchy is organised with a ruler at its apex — ultimately, God — managing things in a manner in which the microcosm and the macrocosm correspond.[69] This philosophical view is distinct from the mystical view of an ontological monism and posits only a metaphorical analogy in which the human soul, suitably purified, can correctly understand the order of things, then try to reproduce it in such a way that the microcosm and the macrocosm morphologically correspond.[70]

God and Man

The correlativity of microcosm and macrocosm intimates the thesis, rejected by some for ideas unconnected with the implicit metaphysic of the two worlds, that God and man are correlative. Humanity, through Adam, is a *khilāfa* of God, according to famous Qur'ānic pronouncements, and the caliphate is an agency of God, which implies both continuity and transferrence, and this in turn implies, and indeed requires, considerations of homology and isomorphy, despite the doctrinal complications that Ash'arites felt acutely when dealing with this matter. The centrality of humanity and its representational relationship to God can be seen as grounded in an ontological community, and this position was held, we saw, by representatives of pantheistic monism which is one possible variant of the chain of being. Continuity in the opposite sense is not very different. Instead of looking at man as homologous to God and metaphysically continuous with Him — the Perfect Man, the Muḥammadan light which emanates to all being, or as with the position adopted by Abul Barakāt al-Baghdādī, alone amongst philosophers, which saw human attributes as analogues of divine ones, with existence engendering existence, and will engendering will, as the prime mode of causality linking God and man[71] — we could well look at anthropomorphism as a correlative, whereby man and God are taken for homologues. The continuity here is not only what we may describe as a seminal one, with God creating man and everything else, physically, and out of nothing, but is also a continuity in analogy. One is the metonym of the other.

Certain anthropomorphists believed God looked like a young man, and others believed he looked like an old man.[72] Yet others, a sect by the name of the Hishāmiyya, believed He had a length equal to His width, and a width equal to His depth.[73] Some groups confounded the normal order of things with reference to the physical characteristics God is said to have. It was maintained for instance that He had a colour which was His taste, and a smell which was His colour.[74] Indeed, anthropomorphic theses are replete with inapposite connections and associations the primary purpose of which seems to be a confirmation of a physicality which is totally other than that which described humanity, so that the result of the attempt to avoid anthropomorphy was the distortion of the physical characteristics of humanity by their redistribution. Yet the pillar of anthropomorphism is not to be found in the detailed descriptions and transferrences of attributes, but in maintaining that both man and God are possessed of quiddity, physical thinghood, and as all physical things share their qualities, analogies between human and divine attributes are readily at hand, without necessarily having to propose theses to the effect that God can actually be touched.[75] But, of necessity, anthropomorphism in the sense we defined leads to one of the important points of contention between the Ash'arite and Ḥanbalite crypto-anthropomorphists on the one hand, and their Mu'tazilite critics, and occasional deadly enemies, on the other, the one concerning Beatific Vision which Ash'arites meant to take literally and physically. According to one of the most important amongst their number, what cannot be seen is like what does not exist, and all that exists admits of being seen.[76] Apologists for Ash'arī maintained that he said, in defence of himself against the charge of anthropomorphism, that what the Prophet meant by the saying 'and you shall see your God with your eyes, as you see the moon' was that other-worldly vision will be like earthly vision, without this implying a comparison between the objects of vision. According to the apologist, Ash'arī's position did not propose a particular organ for vision, nor a definite shape to be seen.[77] This is an evasion of the question in a manner which did not seem to trouble Ash'arī himself when he said that Muslims lift up their hands in supplication because God is sitting on His throne, and His throne is on top of the heavens,[78] and his criticism of those who refused to admit the possession by God of eyes and hands.[79]

There can be little doubt that the fundamental concern of crypto-anthropomorphists is theological and doctrinal and not philosophical. The fundamental impulse is a refusal to be drawn into making any comment whatsoever on verses of the Qur'ān of an explicitly anthropomorphic content, allocating to God not only power and will, but also a throne, along with eyes and hands, an allocation which was very embarrassing given the doctrinal requirement of *tanzīh*, the positing of an absolute break between God and his creation. The simple solution, which the Ash'arites adopted was of Ḥanbalite provenance[80] or possibly a joint Ḥanbilite-Ash'arite provenance; a standard statement of Ḥanbalite theology stated that texts relating to divine attributes are accepted on faith,

> a faith which accords with the letter of the text which is indubitable and whose veracity is incontestable, and whose meaning is known best to Him who uttered it, and in which we believe according to the

> meaning He intended for it . . . and we thus joined the requirement of faith with a refusal to concur with the proscribed anthropomorphism.[81]

The same point is expressed by Ibn Taimiyya, the most rigorous, radical and acute thinker amongst Ḥanbalites, by the simple statement to the effect that the textual meaning is contained in the letter of the text without any further specification or elucidation, and that it is only legitimate to interpret this meaning with recourse to the letter of other, equally canonical, statements.[82]

Deference to the letter of the text in an absolute manner, and the simultaneous insistence that this does not involve anthropomorphism when the Qur'ān speaks of a divine face and of divine speech, is clearly a discursively untenable position. To adopt the thesis that the text is a collection of words knowledge of whose meaning should be deferred and considered to be beyond the competence of the reader of the text, and to adopt this thesis in the face of texts of unambiguous anthropomorphism, is a position which is only administratively tenable, in the sense that it can only be maintained without regard to the thesis itself and with exclusive reference to the authority which enforces dogma. As such, this thesis could not but have a negative place in the scientific discourse of Islamic theology, and subsisted on the fringes between theology and cultic incantation, between science and devotion, between dogmatics and iconolatry, between the affirmation of dogma and its dissertation. The Ḥanbalite Ibn Qudāma (d. 620/1223) himself, despite his refusal to pronounce upon the meaning of Qur'ānic attributes of God, felt there was no avoiding interpreting a Qur'ānic text in which reference is made to God's speech by recourse to the manifest lexical sense of speech, and duly concluded that God has a physical voice.[83] This is a natural outcome not only of the texts themselves, but of the excoriation of the opposite, Mu'tazilite view of *tanzīh* (or *ta'ṭīl*, disqualification, according to their enemies), their view that God and man are in no wise comparable or analogous, and that therefore textual references to an anatomical or other affinity between man and God must be the subject of an interpretation which abrogates their literal sense. Ash'arī maintained that the denial of sensuous qualities to God is not only in contradiction to the text, but derogates God himself, for he who cannot see or hear must be stricken with the infirmities of deafness and blindness, inadmissible of God.[84]

It is this sensuousness to which literalism leads which made of the problem of divine attributes with the Mu'tazilites, according to an exacting modern student, a linguistic and semantic problem premised on rigorous linguistic considerations[85] concerning the existential mode of connection between the divine essence and its attributes and the related connections between nouns and grammatical attributes. It was concern with maintaining an absolute break between God and man which prompted Abū Hashim (d. 321/933) not only to reduce all divine attributes canonically prescribed to two (knowledge and potency), but to consider them as mere modalities,[86] thus avoiding the implication of composition in the divine essence (the standard Ash'arite position was that attributes were inseparable from the divine essence). This position was later adopted by the Ash'arite Juwainī, and seems convincing in terms of the problematic it addresses.[87] A mode is 'a qualification pertaining to an existent, but not in itself qualified by existence nor by nothingness'; it must be stressed that most *mutakallimūn* denied the existence of modes, believing that to maintain their existence would imply they inhered in God, thus rendering him a substrate, which is untenable.[88]

It is this obsession with the literal sense of the text on the one hand, and with denying analogy between God and man on the other, which led to the veritable deluge of sophistical texts attempting to square this circle without facing it directly. The most comprehensive short statement is given by Abul Muẓaffar al-Isfarā'īnī (d. 471/1078–9):

> Of the attributes mentioned and pertaining to Him eternal, it is not admissible to say they are He or other than He, nor that He is they or otherwise, nor yet that they confirm to Him or diverge, or that they are inseparable from Him or distinct from Him . . . not that they are like or unlike Him. What must be said is: they are His attributes which are existent in him, constituted in His essence, particular to Him. We said that they are not He because if these attributes were to be He it would not be admissible for us to say that He is omniscient or that He is omnipotent . . . for knowledge is not omniscient, nor is omnipotence omnipotent . . . and we said that they are not not He because of different things it is admissible that one should exist while the other does not, and as this is impossible with regard to the divine essence and attributes, it results that they cannot be different from Him.[89]

What mattered was obviously the sacerdotal word, dogma in its elocutionary mode, totally without redaction. The Ḥanbalite-Ash'arite slogan of *bilā kaif* exhorting the consideration of Qur'ānic statements on God as fully exhausted by their letter, is not an attitude towards the knowledge pertaining to or conveyed by the text, but is an interdiction of any specification of textual elements beyond those supplied by the text and in terms other than those of the text. What mattered was the word as a devotional element, unattainable to discourse. For the Ash'arites before Juwainī and his Mu'tazilite motifs, what mattered was the word as a semiotic value gesturing towards and standing in for the authority of religion and its experts, not as a function in discourse; theirs was an anti-theological theology.

Ash'arites were therefore primarily animated by the necessity they perceived for affirming the appurtenance to God of attributes of canonical textual provenance, while simultaneously seeking to show that they do not figure as qualities and accidents, for God is one and utterly undifferentiated in conformity with metaphysical requirements of the simplicity of sublime things. They sought to depict the attributes as concomitant with God, yet as not subsisting in Him, for He is not a substrate. That is why they had recourse to a distinction between essential attributes (*ṣifat dhāt*) and attributes of activity (*ṣifat fi'l*), the former eternal and the latter realised in time,[90] for whereas divinity itself is eternal, activity in the world is not, for the world was created in time. Again, the Ash'arites chose not to face the problem consistently and found themselves in difficulty when the matter, as they presented it, inevitably devolved upon executing this idea and choosing what attributes were to be considered as pertaining to the divine essence, and which were of a more perishable stuff.[91] Fideism pertaining to the Names of God as they occur in the Qur'ān was generally concurred upon,[92] although some important Ash'arites insisted that these Names are nothing but the divine essence itself or attributes thereof.[93] The Mu'tazilite contention that attributes and names are nothing but the products of convention, as qualifications and designations performed by mankind, was strongly rejected,[94] as was the charge that the affirmation of attributes and names constitutes anthropomorphism[95] — indeed, the position that names and attributes were matters of convention was seen as entailing that the designation of God with eternal divinity should be subject to the same consideration, and should be rejected as such because of the heretical and ungodly conclusion attendant upon it.[96]

The fully consistent maintenance of God's absolute transcendence can result only in a position not unlike that which Ghazālī attributes to the Ismā'īlīs, that in addition to God not being amenable to an affirmation as to His existence,

> He is neither known nor unknown, and is neither qualified nor unqualified. They claimed that all Names do not pertain to Him, as if

> they were striving to deny the Creator . . . and, when doing so, they sophisticated and called their denial *tanzīh*, and called its contrary anthropomorphism.[97]

Ultimately, it does not matter to the believer what exactly is meant by God's face, any more than it matters to the Calabrian peasant whether cannibalism were implied in eating the *corpus Christi*. The specifically religious and devotional aspect of a statement concerning God lies in the sacerdotal character of the statement itself and the authority on which it is based. The statement is both literal and metaphorical in that God's throne is a throne and is not a throne, and when a religious statement is rationalised, what happens is that (as a recent commentator showed), the metaphor is translated into metonymic language and only in this particular sense is it explained.[98] When a religious statement leaves the devotional mode of signification, it immediately separates itself from the literal sense, even without recourse to allegories, as Ibn Ḥazm showed.[99] It appears always to be the case that fideistic and literalist positions are only articulated at the margins of, and in response to, the theorisation of religious conceptions which are intellectually exigent, as was, for instance, Arianism, whose affinity to the standard Islamic position on *tanzīh* (to which fideists also were beholden) brought Arius the approval of Arabic thinkers.[100]

Occult Sympathies

The discrete homologies between visible aspects of humanity and divinity then, and regardless of doctrinal complications, are the basis for the association of the two. This homological association is indeed unavoidable if we are to regard it within the perspective of the analogy underpinning the conception of *istikhlāf* which, besides being the guarantee of the canonical text, is also vouchsafed by the continuity described by the chain of being along which the analogical affinity between man and God is due, according to an analysis of Ibn Rushd, to man's station in creation, his attributes being so lofty that those of God, *mutantis mutandis*, can be likened to them.[101] This chain of being links stations and personalities of creation according to more invisible and less tangible bases than that encountered with man and God, and there can be little doubt that these other analogies are moments in the relation between God and his creation, as well as being relations between the various created beings. Just as we find analogies, homologies and correspondences between man and the cosmos and between God and man, we find other such relations whose overall concatenation constitutes the order of things and the criterion of its coherence. Such are the relations between numbers, elements, planets and other created things, which we witness in particularly dense texture in alchemy, magic, medicine, natural history and, in a more rarefied form, in metaphysics proper and theology. These have been regarded as Hermetic, but are probably, in strict historical terms, of Sabean provenance,[102] and also suggest a strong Stoic input, some of which are attributed to one (legendary?) Bolus, whose authority in late antiquity equalled that of Aristotle and Theophrastos.[103]

One Mughīra b. Sa'īd (d. during second half of second/eighth century),[104] the founder of the Mughīriyya anthropomorphic sect, believed that God had a body akin in shape to the human body, and that each part of God's body corresponded to a letter of the alphabet, with the *alif* corresponding to the foot. This Mughīra, according to Ash'arī, went on accounting for other letters of the alphabet until he reached the *hāl*, when he adds 'that if you were to see the position it occupied you would behold something prodigious, alluding . . . to genitals and implying he had seen Him, may God curse him'.[105] There can be little doubt that behind this conception lay a primitive system for the classification of things prevalent amongst the folk who embraced (or produced) this sect. Not unlike other such systems, this presupposed a seemingly arbitrary system of correspondences whose origins are buried in remote folk origins of a magical character, but which later took the status of the arbitrary presuppositions upon which science is constructed. Arabic thinkers were not unaware of this. Thābit b. Qurra (d. 288/901), the Sabean thinker, declared that although the wisdom and significance of Pythagorean numerology and the connections it made between numbers and things is unknown, this was probably because Pythagorean science had died out with the passage of time, a situation which makes what is asserted of the Pythagoreans probable, not necessarily impossible.[106] Things are connected by correspondences: thus zodiacal signs, seasons, members of the body, tempers, behaviour during coitus, colour and age are all correlated (see below). The same applies of angels, letters of the alphabet, numbers and cardinal points,[108] as of letters and natures.[109]

Not the least important of the morphological properties of the correspondences between things is their arrangement in fours, or in two pairs as we saw in the previous chapter. Kindī (d. after 252/866) divided everything into fours, and linked by correspondences the four strings of the lute with the four quarters of the sky and of the moon, the four elements, directions and seasons, as with the four humours, the four faculties of the human soul and the Four Ages of Man.[110] God's wisdom, according to the Ikhwān al-Ṣafā', decreed that everything should be divisible into fours, each group comprising both concordance and contrariety: the four seasons, the four elements, the four smells, on the basis of which both medicaments and talismans are conceived.[111] Additionally, the first four cardinal numbers contain the principles of all things, and correspond not only to visible things as the fours mentioned, but to the spiritual principles of being, such as the World Soul and the primary *hyle*.[112] And although the geographer Muqaddasī (d. after 381/991) divided Islamic sects into fours rather than according to the septenary division in common use,[113] this was because, he said, some canonical precedents made this appropriate: the four corners of the Ka'ba and the four canonical books of Tradition.[114] It is as if there resided in some numbers, notably four and seven, one of the secrets of creation which distributes and organises things by virtue of being four and seven.[115] The same fascination lies behind Bāqillānī's wonder at the numerological inimitability of the Qur'ān: the Arabic alphabet comprises 29 letters, and the number of Qur'ānic chapters which opened with the citation of letters is 28, and the letters mentioned at the opening of chapters was half of the total comprised in the alphabet (14).[116]

Behind the belief in the effect of the septenary division of things, and of proportionalities which act as correspondence, lies a prior conviction that the topographical arrangement of things and relations of spatial contiguity and relative proximity are in themselves relations of mutual indication and mutual effect born of a certain essential homogeneity. If a number or letter corresponded to a humour, it would indicate this humour as well as cause, in the phenomenal world, a realisation of this same humour. This is the principle of talismanic action which has already been encountered above, and is an age-old magical idea. By themselves, these correspondences are not, according to a prominent critic, sufficient to show concrete effect, for the correspondence of numbers and letters are entirely conventional, and the venerable antiquity of this convention is not proof enough of its validity.[117] Like things arranged in numerical groups, letters and numbers are related by specific sympathies and antipathies, and they are, moreover, convertible into one another, just as they are convertible to, and represent, other things, such as humours and stars. Each is a microcosm encompassing the things it represents, thus constituting their secret and key, precisely as man represents and holds the key to the rest of creation. Literature on these matters was large, including works by Ghazālī himself.[118]

Some proponents of esoteric letters detected the secret of their action in a 'naturalised' quality, their correspondence to the elements. The 28 letters with which the Tablets were inscribed, according to a great master of this art, 'spell out all that obtains in the universe, singly and in composition. If you scrutinised the secret immanent in these lofty letters you would find that all that there is in the universe is in them and of them':[119] the letters a, h, ṭ, m, f, sh and dh correspond to dry heat, i.e. to fire, whereas water has its counterpart in d, ḥ, l, ', r, kh and gh. Each of these groups is also arranged along a scale of potency, letters being weaker than one another and differing in the degree to which they effect nature.[120] Letters also combine in definite orders which have specific correspondences to composites in nature as well as to the spirits of the heavenly spheres, and the letters that combine to form the formidably potent Beatific Names — God's names, *al-asmā' al-ḥusnā* — and the effects inherent in the letters are activated by the physical alignment of correspondent things: the effect of the moon can be brought to bear upon the citation of its alphabetical correspondent in favourable circumstances, i.e. on Mondays, for Monday too corresponds to the moon, and with the burning of amber incense on that apposite day, as amber is the counterpart of the moon amongst odours.[121] Others saw the secret of letters to reside in numerological correspondences rather than in more immediately naturalistic terms, and there were procedures for aligning letters, numbers, horoscopes and other matters of enormous complexity, one of the best known perhaps being the *zā'irja* of which we have a complete and meticulous description.[122]

Letters, numbers, elements and things correspond and stand for one another according to specific patterns, exactly as do stars and mundane matters.[123] The zodiacal signs of Leo, Sagittarius and Aries, for instance, are fiery, being dry and hot, and are commanded by the sun and Jupiter. And whereas the sun is masculine, fiery and auspicious, Saturn is masculine, cold and augurs ill, and Mercury effects those born under its sign by causing them to have a mercurial temperament, enabling them to achieve great skill in the finer crafts and in the making of talismans.[124] Talismans[125] themselves operate along principles derived from these correspondences, their principle of operation being the intervention of spiritual potencies brought down from heaven by corresponding alphabetical or numerological proportions,[126] and these lie at the basis of particular arrangements of letters which act upon nature in much the same way as medicaments do, by reinforcing a quality and repelling another, an effect which can also be elicited with iconic correspondences rather than numerological or alphabetical ones. For example, the talisman effective in the treatment of scorpion stings which consists of the image of a scorpion deployed at a time when the moon is in the sign of Scorpio.[127] A talisman is a particular realisation of the correspondences — sympathetic and antipathetic — that obtain between the stars and the elements, along with their icons, letters and numbers which contain their secret and their trigger, and operate as medicaments do.[128] If it were desired to bring a lion to a particular place, for instance, one should work a talisman on a day falling under a zodiacal sign appropriate to the temper of lions and containing at that particular time a hot and dry planet (Libra, Leo or Sagittarius visited by the Sun, Mars, Venus or Mercury). If one wished to repel serpents, on the other hand, one would have to choose a stellar configuration opposite in its qualities to the one just mentioned, as serpents are, by nature and temper, the contraries of lions.[129] A talisman is the deliberate mixture of mundane and extra-mundane potencies with a view to effecting a potency which produces an extraordinary effect,[130] its extraordinariness indicating its rarity rather than a judgement on possibility, for it takes place according to the same principles as prevail in medicine, among other things. All that a talisman does is be a component of a process of matching qualities with intent to effect changes of quality in the world of quality.[131] Indeed, so pervasive and deep-seated was this sympathetic mode of causality to Arabic thought in general, that fate itself was seen to act according to its principles: when a Shāfi'ī judge who had destroyed a Mālikite treatise by throwing it into the Nile himself drowned in the Euphrates, this was seen as directly correlated to his treatment of the unfortunate treatise, as punishment and acts punished are homogeneous.[132] Might this sympathetic mode of intellection be particularly relevant to Old Testament, Roman, Islamic and other penal maxims based on the principles of talion?

Knowledge of the secret correspondence of things opens the way to the acquisition of extraordinary spiritual powers which can effect the realm of elements, and it is no doubt universal centrality of this sort that was foretold for Ibn 'Arabī in a dream he had when still a young man and which he related thus:

> I dreamt one night that I had copulated with all the stars of the heavens, and there was not a single star left with which I had not copulated with supreme spiritual pleasure, and when I had finished copulating with the stars I was given the Letters, and I copulated with them.[133]

Such prodigious potency as Ibn 'Arabī and similar mystics claimed for themselves, both as power to work marvels and to have theoretical knowledge of the secrets of things, is based upon gnostic revelation which is not only divinely inspired,[134] but which also corresponds to definite relations between things which divine wisdom occluded and hid away from the minds of men. Knowledge of occult correspondences implies access to knowledge of occult sympathies and antipathies between things which make possible their correspondence and mutual effect in the particular sense that the effect is exercised, as repulsion or as attraction. Correspondence between iron and a magnet is premised upon concordance and attraction — the science dealing with *nairanjāt*, visible attractions and repulsions as those found in magnetism, is a sister science of *ṭilasmāt*, talismanics[135] — whose principles are unknown. The sympathies and correspondences upon which rest the correspondence and action of letters and numbers are the equivalents of soothsaying, oracles and auguries: all these matters rest upon the deduction of future happenings from seemingly unconnected present occurrences, which in fact are connected by occult correspondence.[136] Such correspondences had become a matter of convention into which novices were instructed by their masters, although some believed these correspondences to be evident from practice or to be the result of spiritual gifts, such as those which Muḥammad possessed.[137] Similarly, phrenology does not only depend on knowledge of the tempers of persons under scrutiny, but on the correlation between definite types of physiognomy and corresponding traits of character[138] and these correlations, whose *raison d'être* is obscure, are observable and can be acquired by experience, although there is a deeper insight capable of reading the hearts of its object of scrutiny and which is a divine gift.[139]

Not far removed from the affinity between character and physical form is the association between symbol and signification in the interpretation of dreams. Oneirocriticism, Ibn Khaldūn asserted, is a science which interprets a dream according to general principles,[140] and these principles are, as principles in Arabic thought could only be, a list of correspondences to which elements in the dream are referred. Indeed, oneirocriticism is based on knowledge of the association between imaginings and occult events, so that the former indicate the latter.[141] Oneirocritical associations do not only stand on unilateral and unambiguous signification, but also involve occasionally complex relations of indication, the associations being based on similarity, symbolism, analogy and other modes of signification.[142] A dream might be as clear and unambiguous in its meaning as to be equivalent to the certainty of immediate sense perception,[143] such as that which might occur in times of adversity and emergency, warning its witness of impending calamities.[144] Dreams could also contain implicit rather than explicit signification, where 'wisdom is implanted in the substance of the visible'.[145] Although the particular stellar configuration occurring at the time of the dream might, in the opinion of some, effect the interpretation of a particular dream,[146] and in spite of the fact that the significance of particular items in the manifest content of dreams may vary according to external circumstances, such as mud being auspicious in India and a singularly bad omen elsewhere[147] oneirocriticism ultimately rests on a list of equivalences, which is to be used as a base from which variations according to contextual and other considerations can be derived — and that is why 'Abd al-Ghanī al-Nābulsī's (d. 1143/1731) treatise is so enormously useful, being planned according to the alphabetical order of subjects that might conceivably occur in dreams. The register of symbols is thus not a closed one, for over and above its essential definitiveness, improvements are possible depending on the learning of the oneirocritic, his piety, skill and the degree to which God may choose to enlighten him.[148] Some dream elements might indicate real elements symbolically and rather arbitrarily, although some distant analogies could be drawn. Such is, for instance, the equivalence of combs with kinship, or of honey and the Qur'ān, or again of goldsmiths and mendacity. Dream elements can also indicate their contraries, happiness in a dream indicating weeping for instance. These principles for the extraction of meaning, along with other methods,[149] are all based upon the implantation within the symbol of a real empirical equivalent according to a set convention only rarely troubled by the sort of ecological or astrological noise referred to. There are relations of assonance and implication relating single elements within and without the dream. It is possible, and would be of great anthropological interest, to make an analytical register and concordance of such equivalences and of the possible analogies, counter-analogies, and associations on which they are manifestly based, and to reduce these relations to certain structural and mythological features which they realise and manifest. But this is not likely to give us a key to unravelling the conditions for the association of these equivalences in the context of oneirocritical science in so far as it is a science based on the association and assonance of things, some epistemologically containing the others, just as Ibn 'Arabī's gnostic mastery was prefigured in his carnal domination of the secrets wherein the knowledge of things is deposited.

The assonances and correspondences of things are both existential and epistemological: we have seen how dreams contain reality in being direct or indirect knowledge of it, and how the appropriateness and sympathies of times, stars, odours, elements, numbers and letters constitute an analogical and homological system in which things correspond due to sympathy and antipathy, and how things without tangible quiddity, such as letters and numbers, act in the world of quiddities because of their relations of sympathy and antipathy with it. It is perhaps right to say that the most significant, as well as the most manifest, association is that which directly links mundane events with extra-terrestrial ones, the stars and the heavenly spheres. Just as magical works are the effect of potent spirituality applied, according to psychic premeditation and with the direct intervention of interpellated stellar, alphabetical, numerological or satanic potencies,[150] to the elemental world, so the stars have a manifest and direct effect on mundane things. The effect of the stars is in no wise confined to dictating fortunes and misfortunes as are determined by the horoscopes of individuals, but are of a truly historical scope and significance. The Grand Conjunction of Jupiter and Saturn, which recurs once every 960 years, indicates such major events as the appearance and disappearance of nations, states and religions, while the Middle Conjunction which recurs every 240 years presages the rise of, among other things, upstart powers seeking to appropriate existent states, and the Minor Conjunction, occurring every score years, precedes relatively minor events such as insurrection.[151] Stellar activity is moreover not limited to state-related matters, but determines, according to the Ismā'īlīs, the cycles of the Imāmate and other related events.[152] It also determines the incidence of pestilence[153] and the ages of individuals and states.[154] Not only do the stars seem to account, or at the very least concord with, the amplification of material culture in eastern Islamic lands at the expense of the Western,[155] but is also directly connected with what Ibn Khaldūn saw as the transferrence of the seats of human culture northwards,[156] and turns inhabited parts into waste while transforming wastelands into full bloom.[157] The movement of the sun from northern to southern signs also has the effect of transforming waste into habitation and habitation to wilderness.[158] And lastly, one should not omit to mention that the relations of sympathy and antipathy that exist between individuals are in turn dependent upon the individuals' respective horoscopes and on the relations of proportion, mathematically expressible in the way that mathematics expresses musical assonances and dissonances, which exist between these horoscopes.[159]

There is no doubt about the manifest reality of stellar influence on things terrestrial, despite doubts which are themselves premised upon such influence: the famous astrologers Nawshajānī (who was also a philosopher) and Ghulām Zuḥal (literally, Saturn's Servant), both members of Sijistānī's circle, asserted that the veracity of an astrologer's prediction is itself dependent on his own horoscope.[160] At the other end of the spectrum of opinion on this matter was the position taken by Ibn Rushd, for whom the specific effect of a planet depended on its proximity and position relative to the object of its effect, factors which determine the nature specific to this object and thus determinant of its inception and decrepitude; and, he added,

> although the specific effect of individual planets is hidden from us . . . it yet appears to be true in general that the planets do have an effect on the world of generation and corruption, so that if we were to imagine the lapse of a single planetary movement or the absence of a single planet, then either generation itself would cease, or at least the being of some existents will not be consummated. It also appears that particular planets influence particular existents, and that is why we find those who observed the planets in foregone ages divided all existents amongst the planets, and asserted the correspondence of particular existents with the nature of particular planets.[161]

Ibn Khaldūn is also silent about the specific mode of effectivity deployed by stellar entities in their mundane interventions, for he asserts the correspondence of astrological expectations with mundane realities, and defers to astrologers for a stellar explanation of mundane matters which he himself explained according to mundane criteria.[162] But neither Ibn Khaldūn nor Ibn Rushd proferred explanations, while neither sought to deny stellar influence, and we may take it that both, like all their cultural contemporaries, assumed that the planets have a network of mundane agencies and footholds in the natures of things which carry out their influence. Ibn Khaldūn in the text just quoted did not assert that earthly matters will take their course without planetary influence, and neither did he speak of direct unmediated influence on things that possess no specific natures of their own. Influence is demonstrable, yet ineffable: this position could only have been premised on a correspondence between stellar and mundane matters, without imputing a particular 'material' mode of effectivity. This makes this influence by correspondence between stellar and mundane matters, without imputing a particular 'material' mode of effectivity. This makes this influence by correspondence the result of an assonance which is difficult to distinguish from the anthropomorphic sympathy that Stoics detected between the stars and earthly beings,[163] and which we have seen active amongst mundane things. It is also difficult not to relate this effectivity directly to an important metaphysical premiss of Arabic thought, that the relationship between more sublime and baser things is organised according to two principles: as the mystics expressed it, love, passion and longing linking the lower to the higher, and coercion, disposition and comprehension relating a sublime thing to its inferiors.[164] Like other occult sympathies, these are based on hierarchy, on bountiful activity and acquisitive receptivity.

With this we return to the type of paracausality comprehended in the context of assonance, proportionality and correspondence. All mundane movements, including acts of choice and of will, are asserted by Ibn Sīnā to become after they had not been, and thus entail a cause, which is ultimately movement; whilst all movement is ultimately derived from perfect motion, motion in a circle, so that this is the way that the heavenly spheres move.[165] Ibn Sīnā went on to suggest that the tempers of all things were determined by the movement of the planets, and that if these were to be still, every particular section of the world would have to be confined to the quality of the physically corresponding planet, so that certain parts under the influence of a hot planet would eventually be completely desiccated.[166] Ikhwān al-Ṣafā' in their turn suggested a generally similar explanation based on considerations of planetary azimuths and the relative degrees to which different parts of the world are exposed to 'emissions' from particular planets.[167] Yet such explanations should not be misconstrued in a naturalistic sense. What is at issue is action at a distance on the part of heavenly bodies endowed with pre-given natures, and these natures are figurative and relative to effect on mundanities, for the planets do not have a nature defined by elemental qualities, being spiritual entities which, strictly speaking, can neither be hot nor cold, although they specialise in causing and enhancing particular qualities in the elemental world to which they correspond, but of which they cannot partake. Stellar effect is thus akin to that of strong spirits such as we encounter in magic and talismanic phenomena, which cause things to happen without due cause, altering tempers without corporeal activity, and causing cold to originate without contact with something cold.[168] This can be construed as the only possible explanation given that Ibn Sīnā, like Ibn Rushd and Ibn Khaldūn, preferred to defer knowledge of the means of exercising stellar effect in the world of elements while at the same time stating that such effect is undeniable and cannot be physical or natural, for although heat can travel by radiation, the stars do not emit rays.[169] This places these effects in the same class of phenomena as those to which Ibn Ḥazm ascribes epilepsy which, while being immediately caused by a bilious excitation which sends fumes rushing up to the brain, is still directly caused by the devil, who suggests this change to the bodily temper according to a mode of contact which is unknown to us.[170] The difference, though, is that stellar influences for someone like Ibn Sīnā are premised on a cardinal metaphysical principle, that acts are primarily attributable to qualities emanating from agencies and received by passive material,[171] much like the relationship between matter and form in which the latter, though inducing heat, does not itself have to be hot.[172] Properly, such action is a calque of divine effectivity, regardless of which positions on intermediate demiurgical causality are held, as those by Ikhwān al-Ṣafā' (their World Soul).[173]

Action is therefore the effect of one thing on another, whereby the recipient of effect is subjected to a qualitative change. The recipient of the effect is ready for the receipt of the act, and the effect is mediated by its potentiality.[174] And whereas contiguity and contact, or at least proximity, between the actor and the acted upon is a necessary precondition for every effect,[175] this contact does not have to be material: it could be iconic, as we saw in the case of talismanic propitiation, or isomorphic, homological or simply due to some hidden correspondence which makes the relationship appear arbitrary. In all cases, we are faced with a material or conceptual contiguity and continuity which make things relate sympathetically or antipathetically. Magnetism is perhaps the terrestrial sympathy most akin in its seeming arbitrariness to the sympathetic correspondence between particular stars and particular qualities, and the occult alternative of the tangible mode of sympathy between a medicament and a distempered organ.[176] Iron is as beholden to a magnet as a lover to the beloved and is equally pliant,[177] and Ikhwān al-Ṣafā utilised an olfactory metaphor to explain magnetism, according to which iron veers towards a magnet on sensing its smell, and it veers towards it because it is in sympathetic connection with it, just as the community of temper draws the distempered organ towards its curative agent.[178] And whereas homogeneity links the diseased organ and the humoural agency of its cure, the homogeneity that accounts for the sympathy between iron and the magnet, like that connecting stars and things, is based on occult principles. A proper scientific explanation for this was provided by Ibn Rushd, who proffered a teleological interpretation of magnetism based on the conception of entelechy: he termed the movement of iron towards a magnet one of assonance and appropriateness, like that of matter and form.[179] But such explanations, as we saw in the previous chapter, are ultimately no more than a register of things observed and the endowment of their sheer givenness with a value transcending the terms related, a truly meta-physical value, based on the assumption that things are as they are because this is the best, and most likely the only one, of all possible worlds, in which things are in assonance because they are in correspondence. This is why the teleological explanation proffered by Ibn Rushd remains well within the bounds of interpretations that have been related in the foregoing paragraphs, for he offered no explanation for effectivity, but only a higher purpose. What occult connections govern the demiurgical assonance of God and His creation was a matter that belonged to other topical fields of investigation, which have been taken up at various points in this book.

The effect of an actor, we saw, is that of an external agent in the context of a relationship between activity and passivity, animation and inanimation, loftiness and lowliness. A potency is a principle of change in relation to an external agency of change, and change is invariably inferior to changelessness.[180] Causality is, ultimately, but an instance of hierarchy,[181] for if it were an act of will and volition it presupposes the superiority, in all senses, of the actor over his object, and if it were a natural causality, such as fire causing other things to burn, it indicates the superior potency of the actor.[182] Despite the almost naturalistic conception of act as that which realises a pre-existent naturalistic potency — called the 'matter of the act', although already in possession of qualitative formation — that we find in Jābir b. Ḥayyān,[183] this remains a localised statement and its discursive effect is not generalised to those areas of Jābirian natural philosophy where they would have had the effect of truly founding a naturalism, namely, the numerological, astrological, elixiric and other decisive components of natural operations. And in any case, a naturalistic act realises a nature, i.e. lifts a potentiality into consummation, for every nature ends in an entelechy, and this is the realisation of a purpose. Everything that is caused (with a main exception that will form the subject of the coming paragraphs), is caused either by necessity, or for the sake of *al-afḍal*, or again by coincidence[184] — or alternatively, and more neutrally, things can be caused by nature, by artifice or again by coincidence.[185] Coincidence being a purely residual occurrence of no consequence and is merely a haphazard entelechy,[186] it emerges that the cosmos is one which is strictly governed by a purpose, whether immanent or transcendent, whether knowable or ineffable. Causality is the realisation of a purpose which is ultimately an intention of God; metaphysical formulations and differences do not effect this initial premiss.

Divine Will and Human Acts

Activity and causality as the realisation of purpose and hierarchy receive their clearest impress in the realm of humanity, despite the complexity of human action due to humanity being, at one and the same time, active and passive, rational and self-moving yet elemental and moved. The relation of a human being to his act is that of a free rational being to inanimate nature, and is also the relation of a predetermined creature to another, doubly predetermined and inanimate one. In metaphysical terms, as we have seen, man belongs to the class of receptors as well as to that of agents, and acts are either immediately deliberate, or else the realisations of a nature, which is a striving for consummation and consequently for a mediate purpose, 'wisdom' or 'the optimum'. That man is an actor makes of him an agency for the realisation of a nature, an agency which seeks the realisation of volitions, whereas his being passive makes of him the substrate wherein inhere spiritual volitions and correspondences and the location for the realisation of divine and intermediate spiritual ordinance. Human activity is the realisation of human will applied to pliant nature, or an acquired capacity occasionalistically created by God for particular acts according to the Ash'arite ontology of created beings, or, finally, the realisation of the ultimate divine purpose in creation whose good order and maintenance is guaranteed not only by the grace that infuses and preserves things, but also by divine ordinance realised in the *Sharī'a*, the optimal *modus operandi* of *istikhlāf*. Human activity is thus of two broad types in relation to divine will: it is either the extension of direct divine creative activity, with humanity being the substrate wherein actions inhere as accidents, or else it is a delegated discretion; it is either merely a visible avatar of divinity or a self-sufficient activity whose conditions, but not realisations and instantiations, are created by God who creates the normative archetypes of human activity (the commands of *Sharī'a*) and the actor (humans) and leaves the marriage of reality and archetype to the actor. This last idea was formulated in a brilliant form by the always original and clear-headed jurist Shāṭibī (d. 790/1388), Ibn Khaldūn's older contemporary, who, heedless of Ash'arite considerations and over-riding dogmatic sensitivities, said that the will of God has two senses: *irāda qadariyya*, demiurgical creative will, which accounts for what there is, and *irāda amriyya*, will expressed in the command to do certain things and to refrain from others, this last being the object of *fiqh*.[187]

The Ash'arites saw human activity as merely an instance of the immediate effect of the demiurgical will of God, for God is the sole actor in the sense that the particular act would not have occurred had the capacity to undertake it not been immediately created by God at the moment of its occurrence; that man is an actor is to be understood figuratively, as a manner of speaking.[188] Despite man's special privileges in the rungs of creation, therefore, what applies to creation applies equally to him, for he occupies the same ontological station as the rest of that which is not God, being therefore bereft of any capacity for action, generative or otherwise, for the creator is absolute *qua* creator, and the created is absolute *qua* created, the one active, the other passive. Over and above this ontological equality of created beings, man is privileged only in a very dubious sense: that he is absolutely responsible for his actions despite them being dictated by God, and can therefore justly be sent to hell, a matter which was a main point of thrust in Mu'tazilite attacks on Ash'arite theology and a primary underpinning of the former's doctrine of free will,[189] a criticism to which Ash'arī and his followers invariably retorted that since no link except for demiurgy connected God and man, what is unjust for the latter and in his terms cannot be said of the Creator.[190] To fortify their position, the Ash'arites decreed acts to be acts of God and of man in the sense that God creates the act and simultaneously creates in man the power to carry it out, which makes man capable for whatever he does, for after all, God does predetermine all things, but it is mankind that carries out these things and is therefore in a position of primary responsibility.[191] The Mu'tazilite argument that this position imputes gross injustice to God was dismissed on an administrative, authoritarian ground: that such an imputation is inadmissible impertinence, for one should impute to God neither injustice nor the creation of Satan nor of such matters as ordures, for to do so is merely to display scurrilous intent and a calumniation of the Creator.[192] Moreover, that God predetermined evil does not in any way imply, as the Mu'tazilites claimed, that he commanded evil to take place; evil was created, predicted, necessitated, but not commanded.[193] Whatever God created is an act of bounty, and His choice to make unbelievers disbelieve is equally an act of bounty.[194] God is absolutely free, and He is indeed capable of willing one thing and its opposite at one and the same time, for His will is absolute. This was a standard Ash'arite position, much criticised for absurdity,[195] but which a theologian like Māturīdī, while admitting its difficulty, preferred to the opposite position whose results he considered to be disagreeable and unacceptable.[196]

Thus there is no consistent theoretical, scientific location for the Ash'arite, and to a lesser extent the Mu'tazilite position on human activity, it being bonded to the terms of the theological polemic some of whose features have been expounded. This is a matter which did not go unnoticed; Ibn Rushd spoke of the *mutakallimūn* in general as having put forward their theses 'not because they were arrived at by way of reason, but rather to sustain matters whose truth they presupposed . . . and sought to demonstrate what was consistent with them and refute that which was not'.[197] The Ash'arites saw human acts in terms of their notion of *kasb*, appropriation or acquisition: as an act is composed of an actor and a capability, a substance and an accident, and as God is the sole actor as well as being in sole possession of capability, human action is therefore akin to an occasional mandate. God created all actions with His eternal will, whilst man claims particular acts which he undertakes by means of a capability created by God at the very moment of its actuality.[198] Human capability, therefore, does not transcend the particular act it undertakes and for whose exclusive actuality it is created, but is the mere capability to acquire and to appropriate as its own an act which God created; it is an accident which cannot endure for longer than the occasion for which it is meant.[199] Capability and act are coeval as well as concurrent,[200] without residue or trace. There is no doubt that one could well detect a certain monistic continuum along which human will operates as an indistinct moment in divinity, a notion akin to monistic pantheism, as noted above. One might even say that this notion is what today might be called Spinozistic, eternity and actuality of acts corresponding respectively to *natura naturans* and *natura naturata*. But this would have been intolerable to Ash'arī and his followers, whose 'system' can be likened to a board game where the rules do not permit natural movement between contiguous squares whose contiguity also expresses their correlativity, so that the 'system' consists of patches of assertions, bounded by immediate conclusions that are inadmissible according to criteria external to the assertions. Ash'arī therefore resorted to the distinction between reality and figurativeness, in dealing with this matter:

> If acquisition indicates an actor whose act is really his, it does not have to indicate that the real actor of this act is he who acquired it. Neither does it have to indicate that the real acquirer is the real actor, for an acquirer acquires because he undertakes an action by a created capacity, and it is inadmissible of God that He should act according to a created capacity, and it is therefore inadmissible of Him to have acquired the acquired act, although He be the real actor.[201]

The middle position that Māturīdī attempted remains unconvincing and skirts the question: acquisition is seen as capability in general, which is created by God, and the juristic category of 'intent' (*qaṣd*) is interposed between the act and its acquisition, both specific instances of divine will, as the means of grounding responsibility in a manner which, however, preserves all the ontological essentials of the Ash'arite position except for the most dispensible of components in the context of divine justice: strict occasionalism, which is merely deferred.[202] By making an absolute distinction between predestination and free will the Ash'arites had no way of maintaining the principle that God never commands men to do what is beyond their capability.[203]

Over and above the immediate mode of correspondence between human and divine activity that we witness in Ash'arism, no links are apparent between God and man, at least no direct links between direct commands and particular acts. While the plenitude of divinity endows the cosmos very amply, and is ultimately responsible for the particular effects of stars and other agencies that influence sublunary beings, particular acts of particular men can also be seen as a striving to conformity with a different set of causes, those embodied in the divinely ordained law, *shar'*, expressed in jurisprudence, *fiqh*. This mode of correspondence registers not realities, but commands. It therefore does not belong to the sphere of positivities and is not a register of natural facts and proclivities, but is rather inscribed in the realm of desirable possibilities for, as we have already seen, men are not naturally given to civilised living but have to be brought into it under the sanction and in the custody of an absolute power. Indeed, there are no regularities of a sociological character that govern human assembly, neither is there a body politic which is properly constituted according to naturalistic criteria, despite claims made for Ibn Khaldūn.[204] Political and historical literature reveals a conception of internal societal or historical order[205] which regards the continuity of human societies as a matter guaranteed by a metaphysic of order that was studied in the previous chapter, and which sees human collectivities as being vertically held together as by a hinge, the state, or by a hinge which is equally natural and in conformity with divine wisdom, which is divine legislation whose highest point is Islamic law.[206] The point has already been made, and will again be made, that the political order is in line with the requirements of the best order of humanity, and that societies which do not possess such a formal order are the very quintessence of barbarism.[207] Bereft of the order which is only guaranteed and preserved by kingship, a state of *hubris* prevails, an anti-society, defined by its lack of the political order that is the seal of social life, the political order whose own quintessence is political life in accordance with divine will: the caliphate, the literal as well as substantial result of *istikhlāf*, the retrieval in history of the perfection of the original order of creation, and the consummation and transcendence of all pre-Islamic religions.

Over and above the naturalistic imperfection of social orders not bound to the definitive revelation of Muḥammad is the correspondence of the divine will to all particular events. Such correspondence would achieve the perfection which is only attainable if divine command and human behaviour were to become correlative, so that the conception of *istikhlāf*, humanity as an agency of divinity, might be consummated, and so that harmony in the universe might be definitely established and divine wisdom accomplished in the only area open to *hubris*, that of humanity, and the only area of creation where correspondence, correlativity and assonance do not rule absolutely. But the realisation of what Shāṭibī termed *irāda amriyya* is predicated on the possibility of its accomplishment, that is, on the assumption that what God commands man to do is within man's capacity. In this respect, the insistence of the Ash'arite school that God can order what He wishes without regard to the possibility that this will be carried out, and that He could well expect what He did not demand or command what He does not wish[208] and that this, however, does not go counter to the rational order of things,[209] becomes redundant. For indeed, it is confined to be the realm of dogmatic theological discourse and does not form part of jurisprudential speculation for understandable reasons. Indeed, the author of one major work of jurisprudence, among many others, made sure that he rejected this Ash'arite notion very explicitly[210] and asserted that reason is a precondition for legal majority and culpability (*taklīf*),[211] a position which precludes the Ash'arite position that God could well consign small children to hell-fire for having been born of infidel parents.[212] It is little wonder that, especially amongst Ash'arites, there was a constant insistence that *'ilm*, the knowledge of basic dogmatics at least of catechismal character, is a *farḍ*, obligation, for every adult, a position complemented by the fact that treatises on *kalām* normally contained early sections execrating *taqlīd* and demonstrating the duty to learn.[213] The Ash'arite position is therefore theoretical without discursive interference in jurisprudence, where any consideration favourable to it would have unavoidably had to identify God as the originator of *hubris*, not to speak of this making the whole science of jurisprudence redundant. And indeed, this position seems originally to have been specifically set up in counterposition to the Mu'tazilite notion of *al-aṣlaḥ* or *al-afḍal*, that God creates only that which makes this the best of all possible worlds,[214] and that His will is therefore circumscribed by this concern, making Him incapable of creating things in a way other than he did[215] — to which one Ash'arite retorted that He might, if He wished, not have created anything in the first place, or created nothing but disbelief, without this in any way detracting from His wisdom.[216]

Over and above the question of whether or not mankind can in fact comply with divine commands is that which concerns the means of realising such commands in the imperfect world. Certain procedures are necessary for the translation of divine command into practical usage, a condition the fulfillment of which is a precondition for the realisation of man's privileged position in the cosmos. But as humanity, despite its privileges, is not divinity, man approximates God by means appropriate to mankind: theocracy can never become a realisable project, and the order which is appropriate for the governance of humanity is nomocracy; for in the divine *nomos* are incorporated the commands of God which take the phenomenal form of statements. Theocracy only prevails before and after history, before Adam was ejected from Paradise and after the Apocalypse, when the End recapitulates the Beginning. In between, the best order is that informed by nomothetic prophecy at the apex of which is Muḥammad. But such an order is not theocratic, but is rather thoroughly, though not irretrievably, imperfect. And in the highest order of such imperfection, Islam, the Qur'ān, along with utterings and acts of the infallible Muḥammad and the decisions, infallible to most, of successive generations of nomothetes, concensus (*ijmā'*), form the basis and paradigm of all behaviour that, by being rightful in adhering to the rectitude prescribed and guaranteed by the three founts of the law, result in the realisation of divine will in as much as this is possible in an imperfect world. Yet how is the world, with its manifold of changing particularities, to be comprehended in the divine *logos* expressed in the Qur'ān? How are future eventualities to be considered as having been fully anticipated by divine *logos* and the infallible example set by the acts of the Prophet, by his words and by the consensus of foregone generations of legists? And how are elementals to be conjoined to divine command? In other words, how is a positive association between humanity and divinity to be arrived at? That was the subject of one of the most fertile areas of Arabic thought, the science of *uṣūl al-fiqh*, the principles of jurisprudence or legal theory, these principles being, in descending order of infallibility, the Qur'ān, *ḥadīth* purporting to record the sayings and actions of the Prophet, *ijmā'*, and finally, for the majority who admitted it, *qiyās*, particular legislation arrived at by analogy with the previous three *uṣūl*.

The correspondence of humanity and divinity is thus indirect — it is mediated by a linguistic agency, the text of the Qur'ān and of *ḥadīth*. Human acts and divine will correspond by the correspondence of act to nomothetic discourse, *khiṭāb al-shar'*, an expression preferred by Ghazālī to that of 'text' (*naṣṣ*) because it comprehends linguistic (semantic, syntactic), as well as non-linguistic conceptual components of language.[217] This correspondence is achieved by adherence to the five types of nomothetic command recognised by Islamic law: duty, exhortation or recommendation, permission, disapprobation and interdiction (*wujūb, nadb, ibāḥa, istikrāh, taḥrīm*).[218] Yet the adherence of particularities to the generalities embodied in general commands, and the particularities recorded in particular commands and examples, has to be allowed for in the way in which these textual commands are related and made thereby applicable to changing circumstances. The means of establishing such a relation of applicability relating an *aṣl* which is textually established and a particular observable case which requires relation to a higher textual principle in order to become a legitimately established case, a *far'*, is analogy, *qiyās*, which extends the purview of nomothetic discourse to previously uncharted domains. On the matter of analogy there was an almost total consensus, except for an isolated current which strongly denied its possibility and legitimacy, starting with Ibrāhīm b. Sayyār al-Naẓẓām the Mu'tazilite and some of his followers, through to Dāwūd b. 'Alī al-Ẓahirī (d. 270/884), the founder of the ephemeral Ẓahiriyya anti-analogical school of law immortalised by the prodigious intellect of Ibn Ḥazm.[219] Ibn Ḥazm's vehement denial of the legitimacy and efficacy of analogy, was based on the argument that it constitutes an imputation to divinity of a judgement God did not actually pass[220] and that the similarity of features between *aṣl* and particularity on which analogy is based does not imply a similarity of judgement.[221] In addition, he held that the purely explicit linguistic sense of sacred texts contains all being, with the result that analogy is not even a necessary expedient.[222] This rigorous radicalism notwithstanding, and despite the intrinsic force of its logic given a scripturalist culture, the Ẓāhirite criticism remained inoperative, for it was practically impossible to legislate on the basis of its fundamental premiss that all legislation should proceed exclusively on the basis of the explicit sense of the Qur'ānic text, the text of utterances and acts attributed to Muḥammad and of that rare species of *ijmā'* which was not only affirmed, but the assent of every party to which could be explicitly ascertained.[223] The textualist insistence was answered fairly early on by the assertion that the text of the Qur'ān, being consonant with the tongue of the Arabs, also employs all the semasiological features of Arabic: abbreviation, implication, metaphor, metonymy, occultation of sense and others.[224] And indeed, since texts are finite while events and occurrences are infinite, deniers of analogy could not in effect dispense with it and resorted to analogy under the guise of textuality and incorporated the operations of analogy in their techniques for textualist reduction.[225]

There was a constituency of legal opinion which held that the norms of legal action commanded by divine and other infallible pronouncements were realistically correlated to those matters which are in the interest of human collectivities. As such, law is designed, according to some Mu'tazilites, for the sake of *al-afḍal* or *al-aṣlaḥ*, and matters are judged as good or bad upon such considerations as this and as could be judged as such by the human understanding.[226] Had this not been the case, God would have to be seen in the inadmissible guise of a legislator who charges men with what it is impossible for them to attain (*taklīf bimā lā yuṭāq*): such was the *leitmotiv* of Shāṭibī's attempt, built on Mu'tazilite doctrinal bases and formulated in terms of the Mālikite conception of the common weal, to elevate legal theory to the status of a science built on certainties, not probabilities, with the thorough theoretical incorporation of matters as local usage, expediency and allied matters.[227] But such matters, which were particularly well cultivated in Ḥanafite and Mālikite law (and in Shāfi'ite positive law as well) and which were assimilated to more canonically acceptable criteria of legislation such as analogies and the particularisation of general statements from the Qur'ān and other sources for nomothetic discourse,[228] were the occasion for vehement criticism for inadmissibility on the assumption that the human understanding is not a legislator, and that such matters as expediency are an illegitimate addition to law.[229] Though such objections remained theoretical, they were prevalent, and the public weal, expediency and custom were normally relegated to peripheral corners of legal theory, though they were crucial in positive law, as we shall have occasion to see later on in this book; they were also in conformity with the Ash'arite contention that the will of God is arbitrary, as well as with the general opinion that the wisdom of God is ineffable and that the law is binding because it is law.

Yet even Shāṭibī had to concede that not all laws have a rationality which is accessible to the understanding.[230] Whereas matters with a visible correlation to the common weal could be registered as such, the causes and exigencies behind specific commands and interdictions are not necessarily visible. The correlation between, say, prayer and the specific times of day on which it is prescribed is a case in point. Similarly, while adultery is correlated with the statutory punishment of stoning (not of Qur'ānic sanction and authority, incidentally), there is no intrinsic correlation between the two, only the compelling necessity brought about by a nomothetic command.[231] A nomothetic judgement is not the attribution of an intrinsic correlation, but the prescription of a legal correlation.[232] Matters that are cited as conditions of correlation in law (*'ilal, asbāb*) and which are the cornerstone of analogical connection, are therefore not in themselves the 'causes' of judgements in a naturalistic sense, but are causalities and the grounds for correlation on purely scripturalist grounds. They are, according to an enlightened Ḥanbalite, indices (*amārāt*) which are only metaphorically grounds of judgement for which they are posited by the nomothete[233] — ultimately, God. These matters were well expressed by the Mu'tazilite grammarian Ibn Jinnī in the context of his comparison of grammatical and legal analogies: the analogical connectors, *'ilal*, of law are signs and indices whose wisdom is hidden from us. He wrote,

> Do you not see that the order of pilgrimage rituals, and the prescriptions pertaining to ritual cleanliness and to prayer, divorce and other matters, are rendered obligatory by the command which conveys them, and that the reason why there should be five prayers a day rather than some other number is unknown?[234]

The grounds of legislation are not therefore caused by their correspondence to the predilections and dispositions of men, as some would maintain:[235] Were they to be so, they would have been current before their prescription by the *shar'*: to those who maintain that the penalty for adultery is designed to preserve virtue and the integrity of lineages should be retorted that virtue was preserved before the advent of Islam, and that the preservation of virtue is not a legal but a pragmatic matter[236] — all non-Islamic law is thus legally invalidated.[237]

Even for those who found in some divine commands a palpable cause related to mundane criteria, such a cause is not pronounced to be transitive with respect to the derivatives of this command — such legislation as is derived by analogy from a specific textual command follows from the compulsion of the text, not from sharing a common causality with the matter addressed to the text.[238] It is not the naturalistic causality behind the *aṣl* which prescribes a judgement upon a particularity, nor is the judgement arrived at on the basis of the causality of a legal cause, but for the appropriateness of judgement as posited by the nomothete.[239] Regardless of the proximity or distance between the analogically correlated *aṣl* and *far'* and of the specific effectivity of the former upon the particularity it transforms into a *far'* by means of analogical correlation,[240] the assonance of the one with the other is one which occurs without recourse to an active causality in which one thing engenders another. Analogical relation in the context of legislation is grounded in exemplariness and is based on the abrogation of particularity to the advantage of an absence, that of the nomothetic discourse. Analogy is premised on the 'submission' (*idh'ān*) of a particularity to the premiss of an analogy, to an *aṣl*.[241] The correlation between the textual command which is given the guise of the generality in an analogical relationship, and the particularity for which legislation is sought, is therefore that of the subordination of the one to the requirements of the other and its appropriation by it, without this subordination being caused by anything else than the authoritarian status of the superior as an *aṣl*, or being related to an effective causality. Analogical justification is the transference by fiat of ineffable wisdom, much like the transference of a term from literal to figurative usage.[242] As this ineffable wisdom is exclusive to God, we can only assume that, in practice and 'for us', it does not exist — except for Him. The assonance of particularities and nomothetic discourse, therefore, cannot be distinguished except in subject matter from the assonance of mundane and astral things: it is based on the submission of the one to the other, without this submission being related to the intrinsic constitution of either. The relationship is not one with a logical or discursive justification, but one of power: it is a political relationship.

This is why the epistemological status of analogy and of the premisses employed by it are considered irrelevant. *Fiqh*, according to a leading authority, is knowledge of, and adherence to, legal judgements based upon first principles adumbrated according to a presumption of certainty, and despite the possibility that these judgements may not, in themselves, be certain.[243] What is at issue is definitive belief; not certainty of a rational kind, but one premised upon a surrender to scriptural authority. Analogy is the attribution of a correlative index linking a premiss and a judgement 'according to he who affirms' the correspondence.[244] The epistemic process by which a legal judgement is arrived at is 'a firm belief' which does not admit falsification.[245] Analogy is a form of proof according to the *shar'* only,[246] and compelling certainty is not guaranteed it in terms of other discourse. This is why the efforts of Shāṭibī to ground *shar'* in the context of an epistemological certainty, *ratio legis* or *maqāṣid al-shar'*, were concentrated on the meta-legal domain: certainty in the field of legal judgements is vouched only for general principles, which benefit from the dual guarantee of the confluence of individually uncertain, albeit legally and cumulatively compelling arguments, and the agreement of reason in all nations and religions that law is posited for the preservation of five necessities: religion, life, wealth, progeny and sanity.[247] The constancy and regularity of general legal principles is such, according to Shāṭibī, that they arrive at a degree of certainty comparable with that of rational generalities.[248]

Such analogy as lacks grounds in *ratio legis* which Shāṭibī was attempting to salvage by the imputation of a compelling generality, was the same as the object of Ẓāhirite attack on the precise grounds that it lacked an intrinsic certainty which it could only have if knowledge leading to it were all-encompassing and therefore, after a Popperian manner, certain of the absence of that crucial falsifying textual exception.[249] This analogy, lacking the precision guaranteed by Aristotelian definition and the resulting syllogistic possibility and custodian of certainty,[250] operates by means of considering its particular textual premisses as logical generalities.[251] The assonance between divine command and human behaviour, when this last conforms with divine command, is therefore one mediated by matters uncertain to man but, in all certainty, quite clear to the ineffable intention of God. Nomothetic behaviour is a practical transcript of the divine will; it does not calque its origins in divine intentionality, but puts into effect the visible manifestations of God, the *logos*, delivered in a manner suitable to the utterly inferior being which is man. God commands in a perfectly anthropomorphic manner, and this command is relayed in the form of statements fit for human comprehension, but which do not in themselves, as we saw, encompass everything except in principle. Over and above this approximation, in which divine will is translated into a form comprehensible to humanity, another approximation of a kind we have just seen to be decidedly inconclusive intervenes, namely, that of generalising the particularity embodied in nomothetic discourse and embedding, by an analogical operation, other particularities within its purview, along with the correlative and opposite particularising (*ta'mīn, takhṣīṣ*). What emerges is an assonance of ineffable causality, like stellar and numerological effects, in which an index relates a statement and a situation and assimilates the latter to the former. Having no compelling necessity, the concordance of the one with the other, and the compulsion of the index linking the two in an analogical relation, is a matter which lies beyond rational certainty, but is guaranteed by the authority of the text and its hermeneutician. The final arbiter who decrees the ineffable to be operative is therefore equally the final cause of this decree; and the concordance which assures the assonance of humanity with divinity and thus evades the horrors of infernal eternity is one whose custodian is the authority that decrees it.

If human acts were to be appropriate for divine purpose and in conformity with its commands, they would, therefore, have to be appropriated by it. And the only mode of assimilating one thing to another, utterly dissimilar thing, such as the appropriation of an act by a text or the appropriation of a thing by a statement concerning a different thing, is to override this difference — not 'naturally', but by the primary ruse of discourse and the pillar of all analogy: such is metaphor. Metaphor is the basis of all analogy, and a particularly thorough and generalised metaphor, metonymy, is the form of all analogies. It is in such terms that God and humanity in its ideal and most accomplished standards are related. Analogy is a relation between a text and a particular reality which is based on positing the appropriateness of the one to the other on the basis of an indexical correlation. It might also be based on a more sensuous type of similarity, itself based on a connecting sign which, however, seems to be linked to the two related parties as a constituent — hence the classification of analogies into two basic types, *qiyās al-'illa* and *qiyās al-dalāla* or *qiyās al-shabah*, the difference being not only that the former is indexical while the latter is based upon the similarity of a particular morphological feature but, more importantly in view of the nomothesis under discussion, that the index of correlation (*'illa*) in the former is explicitly indicated in the base text, the nomothetic discourse; but it does not appear that theoreticians of law ever undertook rigorously to apply this distinction in practice in a manner that disallows their confusion.[252]

The assonance of ideal human conduct with the requirements of divinity is effected by the index of correlation, the *'illa*, by means of which particularities and textual enunciations are conjoined. In effect, this amounts to the elimination of all those features of the particularity in question except for that which can be somehow assimilated to this index, which is itself not an index by virtue of any necessary correlation between the terms so related, but is decreed to be such by the will of the nomothete. This nomothete, ultimately and ideally, is God whose discourse is translated in the sacred texts; but he could also be a prophet or legist who scrutinises texts for indices of correlation which can be rationally extracted from them. The grounds of judgement have been very liberally described as comprising (in descending order), sacred discourse, that which can be rationally isolated as an index of correlation contained within this discourse (*ma'qūl al-'aṣl*) and expediency.[253] Analogical judgement itself was described as the deployment of that which is rational in a text[254] — and therefore generalisable. Indeed, correlation in analogy can be indicated by nomothetic discourse, by the implication of that discourse, by *ijmāʿ*, no less than by the similarity between the terms of analogy, the linguistic or conceptual inclusion of the particular within the sense of the base text, the concomitance of a property, and similar considerations.[255] Yet all these and other indicators of correlation are ranged hierarchically: for an *ʿilla* to be effective of the degree of certainty required by the law, this effectivity should be concomitant with the most sublime and potent characteristic of any *ʿilla*: that its appropriateness for the analogy in question and transitiveness (*taʾthīr*) with respect to the particularity under scrutiny should be explicitly indicated in the base text, or else indicated by *ijmāʿ* or an exhaustive inductive examination.[256] Failing transitiveness, a text can be seen to assimilate a particularity by appearing to be appropriate to a general interest which seems indicated by the nomothetic discourse, without this general interest being such in fact, for the intent of God is ineffable. This is so to such an extent that the sure knowledge, based on textual pronouncement, that for instance water is a cleansing agent appropriate for ritual purity, is by no means a knowledge based upon certainty arrived at by evidence or one based on knowledge of the reason for the appropriateness of water for cleanliness. The reason why water is said legally to cleanse and purify, and therefore the true coefficient of correlation in analogical judgements based upon the premiss that water has that particular property, is known only to God. Similarity and other, palpable connections between terms of an analogy are of a decidedly inferior grade and do not carry the compulsion of obscurer yet rather more divine connections.[257]

The *ʿilla* thus also imputes a general value to a particular statement about a particular, such as the statement that wine is forbidden, a statement generally (with the exception of some Ḥanafite jurists) extended by analogy to cover and ban all inebriating drinks, inebriation being the index of correlation.[258] As in metaphor, the particular comes to carry a general attribute after having been stripped of its particularity and assimilated to the illusory generality of the principal term. It acts as a member of a classificatory system in which the base term, represented by the *ʿilla* located in it, acts as a classifier, that is, as a criterion of inclusion in a class of things and exclusion from it (such as the class of forbidden beverages).[259] Devoid of intrinsic necessity, such analogies as are built on the basis of the authority of a text do not rest on the establishment of a relation, but on the suggestion of such a relation, as one modern scholar of Islamic thought remarked, and correlation appears based on a sign, as was argued in the foregoing paragraphs.[260] Analogy is the equivalence of two terms brought about by the index of correlation;[261] it is judgement passed upon a particular on the basis of the principles of another.[262] This is why analogy involves a more thoroughgoing process than metaphorisation, for whereas metaphor is ultimately a semantic phenomenon, metonymy is purely semiotic, and acts by mere indication, suggestion and decree, as analogy in Islamic law.[263] A base text acquires its generality only relatively: particular in themselves, as Fārābī noted,[264] these *uṣūl* are such in the sense that others, *furū'*, are built upon them, and that, correlatively, such judgements as had been made without recourse to the sanction of others.[265]

The content of the *aṣl* is therefore irrelevant, it being delimited by formal, not substantial criteria, involving considerations of certainty (authority) and economy.[266] What is important is that it has the major property of an *aṣl*, that it is transitive and that its judgements are transferable to other particular locations.[267] Analogy is, indeed, the transition of a judgement from one location to another.[268] An *aṣl* therefore possesses the oracular quality attributed by Berque to prophetic traditions in a more restrictive context,[269] and which could be generalised to encompass all *uṣūl*, all the enunciations of nomothetic discourse. As in all oracular pronouncements, that which matters is not the substance of the enunciation, but its authority; this applies equally to the Delphic priestess and to the Qur'ān. In both cases, enunciations are made which are sometimes clear in their import, sometimes truly oracular as are, for instance, the sequences of letters which open some Qur'ānic chapters and for which there are esoteric interpretations on the part of the esoterically minded, but which were normally the occasion for prudential silence on the assumption that they contain mysteries inaccessible to humanity.[270] In both cases, the enunciation is delivered with the express expectation that it should be correlated to a particularity according to principles of interpretation whose import is ineffable. But this ineffability does not vitiate their correlation with actualities on the part of specialised agencies, sagely seers and unofficial priests in Greece and *'ulamā* who have reached the station of *ijtihād*, individually or collectively as in *ijmā'*. Neither does ineffability vitiate the coercive power exercised by the planets over mundanities, or of numbers and the alphabet over elementals. Ineffability is the correlative of an absolute disparity in potency, and both are a register of the *status quo* as interpreted by those with the authority to do so. The harmony between the command of God and human conduct is guaranteed by the servility of the latter to the former, much like the assonances that relate elemental and occult qualities, mundane and stellar occurrences and the coherence of an elemental or humoural composite. Harmony in the universe as a whole, as indeed between its different constituents, is predicated on a disparity in power, and consequently on a disparity in value. The universe, and here we may adapt a saying of Marcus Aurelius which was quoted above, is eminently and decidedly political.

* * *

This unequal harmonious justice is premised not only on an exclusive potency, but on a correlative assumption of absolute knowledge by the creator and only very partial knowledge by the created, manifestations of which we have seen. In the fundamentally anthropomorphic universe that we have been reviewing, creative and other acts have an immediate epistemic correlate; God is no machine and knowledge is quite literally power. Furthermore, in this anthropomorphic universe, the metaphysics of animate/inanimate, will/nature, form/matter and their cognates is fully at work. This is why God not only tends the universe continuously,[271] but does so on the assumption of an absolute knowledge which cannot be obtained by mankind; it is the impossibility of such an absolute knowledge that constitutes the crux of refutations of astrology and alchemy, two forms of proto-technology.[272] It is the possession of such imponderables that assures God's absolute domination of the universe and ensures the fulfillment of fate.[273] It is clear that this runs parallel to the purpose discerned by many in the fact that the Qur'ān, for instance, is occasionally an opaque text, for had it not been so commoners and divines would have become the same, and their differentiation irrelevant.[274] Indeed, some esotericist mystics maintained that everything that God said to mankind was deliberately delusive, for had He unmasked the truth to them His dominion and omnipotence could not have been realised.[276] The secrets of creation, and the art of maintaining omnipotence, are thus correlative, and both the exclusive preserve of God, who encapsulated these secrets in what the European Hermetic and cognate traditions termed the Ineffable Name.

This Greatest Name, *al-ism al-a'ẓam* is occasionally said to have been known to some divines,[276] but is properly speaking accessible only to a select few whom some saw to be a particular line from the Prophet's progeny, although some were of the opinion that it is accessible only to the Messiah in the future.[277] Such a restriction was only natural, as this Name holds the key to creation, and its revelation would inevitably lead to a state of comprehensive confoundedness.[278] Thus it comes about that the exclusive possession of the secrets of things maintains the order of the universe and guards it against the presumptions of mankind, very much in the same way that the tip of the social order, the king, is meant to be in absolute and exclusive possession of the secrets of his kingdom and his own palace, to be shared with no one[279], for therein lie not only the secrets of the king's strength, but also of his potency.

Notes

1. On these and allied notions, see Tahānawī, *Kashshāf*, p. 106.
2. Pseudo-Sijistānī, 'Kamāl', p. 383.
3. Qazwīnī, *'Ajā'ib*, pp. 339–40.
4. Ibn Rushd, *Mā ba'd aṭ-ṭabī'a*, p. 166.
5. Ibn Khaldūn, *Prolégomènes*, vol. 1, pp. 95, 149–50; Miskawaih, *Tahdhīb*, pp. 46–7 and Maqdisī, *Bad'*, vol. 4, pp. 53–4.
6. Heat and humidity effect the tempers of people, and thus account for their mental disposition, according to principles common in medical works. See Ibn Khaldūn, *Prolégomènes*, vol. 1, pp. 84 ff., Qifṭī, *Tārīkh*, pp. 306–7 and Ibn Sīnā, *Qānūn*, vol. 1, pp. 79 ff. Some thought the alleged stupidity of negroes was attributable to a congenital weakness, as did Mas'ūdī on Galen's and Kindī's authority (*Murūj*, vol. 1, pp. 163–5), an opinion vigorously contested and refuted (Ibn Khaldūn, *Prolégomènes*, vol. 1, p. 157).
7. Ghazālī, *Mīzān*, p. 332.
8. Miskawaih, *Tahdhīb*, p. 46.
9. Ibn Khaldūn, *Prolégomènes*, vol. 2, p. 367.
10. *Ibid.*, vol. 1, pp. 149, 153–4 and see the sketch in Mas'ūdī, *Tanbīh*, pp. 22–5.
11. Avicenna, *De Anima*, p. 50.
12. *Ibid.*, pp. 248–50.
13. Ibn Sīnā, *Ḥudūd*, p. 61.
14. Ibn 'Arabī, *Inshā'*, pp. 4–5.
15. Tawḥīdī, *Muqābasāt*, pp. 209, 211–12. This capacity of commoners probably accounts for folk prognostications based on manipulating sand, stones, offals, etc. See Ibn Khaldūn, *Prolégomènes*, vol. 1, pp. 191–2.
16. Ibn Khaldūn, *Prolégomènes*, vol. 1, pp. 181–3.
17. *Ibid.*, p. 174.
18. Ghazālī, *Munqidh*, p. 111.
19. Ghazālī, *Mīzān*, p. 207 and Ibn Khaldūn, *Prolégomènes*, vol. 1, pp. 165–6. See the general account in Rāzī, *Mabāḥith*, vol. 2, p. 523.
20. Rāzī, *Mabāḥith*, vol. 2, p. 524 and Abū Rayyān, *Suhrawardī*, p. 306.
21. Avicenna, *De Anima*, pp. 199–201. Suhrawardī (*Lamaḥat*, pp. 147–8) says the same in an almost identical text.
22. Rāzī, *Mabāḥith*, vol. 1, p. 509.
23. See the general treatment of F. Rahman, *Prophecy in Islam: Philosophy and Orthodoxy* (London, 1958).
24. Ibn al-Khaṭīb, *Rawḍa*, pp. 519–20.
25. See the description of mystical gnosis in Ghazālī, *Munqidh*, pp. 101 ff.
26. Ibn al-Khaṭīb, *Rawḍa*, p. 580.
27. Affifi, *Mystical Philosophy*, p. 97.
28. For instance, Sarrāj, *Luma'*, pp. 396 ff.

29. Qushairī, *Risāla*, vol. 2, pp. 660–61.

30. *Ibid.*, pp. 521–2 and Sha'rānī, *Ṭabaqāt*, vol. 1, p. 7.

31. Rāzī, *Mabāḥith*, vol. 2, p. 424.

32. Bāqillānī, *Bayān*, para. 110.

33. *Ibid.*, paras. 7, 14, 17.

34. *Ibid.*, para. 111 and see para. 114.

35. *Ibid.*, para. 43. It is noteworthy that Bāqillānī (*ibid.*, para. 56) admitted saintly miracles.

36. Juwainī, *Irshād*, pp. 321–3 and Ibn Khaldūn, *Prolégomènes*, vol. 3, pp. 134–7.

37. Ibn Ḥazm, *Fiṣal*, vol. 5, pp. 2–3. This author (*ibid.*, pp. 109–10) assimilated the saintly miracles of Ḥallāj, the magic of Pharaoh's sorcerers and the forthcoming acts of the Antichrist (*dajjāl*) to the same category of wile.

38. See the general statement in Kalābādhī, *Ta'arruf*, pp. 87 ff.

39. Ya'qūbī, *Tārīkh*, vol. 2, pp. 34–5.

40. N. Abū Zaid, *Al-Ittijāh al-'aqlī fī al-tafsīr. Dirāsa fī qaḍiyyat al-majāz fī al-Qur'ān 'ind al-Mu'tazila* (Beirut, 1982), pp. 81–2.

41. See the comprehensive preliminary sketch in Bāqillānī, *I'jāz*, 33 ff. and the detailed developments throughout.

42. The question of eloquence, and the related question of whether the Qur'ān employed the techniques and tropes of soothsaying, was the subject of much discussion (the most recent and rigorous study of this matter affirms the soothsaying quality, and I think demonstrates definitely the distance between Qur'ānic Arabic and any vernacular languages of its age: M. Zwettler, *The Oral Tradition of Classical Arabic Poetry* (Columbus, 1978), pp. 101 ff., 128 ff., 156 ff.). It was a vulnerable point, virtually undemonstrable except by dogged affirmation and by ridiculing other texts (see the comments of Mandūr, *Naqd*, pp. 377 f. and I. 'Abbās, *Tārīkh al-naqd al-adabī 'ind al-'Arab* (Beirut, 1971), pp. 345 ff.) and there were attempts to take up the challenge and compose texts to compare with the Qur'ān, as did Al-Ma'arrī (one such text from whom is related in Yāqūt, *Irshād*, vol. 1, p. 177 and see *Tajdīd dhikrā Abī al-'Alā'* in T. Ḥusain, *Al-Majmū'a al kāmila li Mu'allafāt Ṭ. Ḥusain* (Beirut, 1974), vol. 10, p. 298) and the famous Ibn al-Rīwandī (Māturīdī, *Tawḥīd*, pp. 193 ff.) — Ibn al-Rīwandī does not appear to have been the only Mu'tazilite to hold this view. See Shahrastānī, *Milal*, p. 30 and for certain dimensions and contexts of this view, see an Isma'īlī text in A'sam, *Tārīkh*, p. 128). That seems to have been the starting point of Jurjānī's transformation of the canons of textual criticism into a comprehensive science of discourse (see Jurjānī, *Dalā'il*, pp. 6–7) and the reason why some were reported not to have included stylistic elements in the concept of inimitability — Naẓẓām is also said to have adopted this view (Ash'arī, *Maqālāt*, vol. 1, p. 271 — but this is denied by Khayyāṭ, *Intiṣār*, p. 28).

43. Avicenna, *De Anima*, p. 174.

44. Qushairī, *Risāla*, vol. 2, p. 715.

45. F. Meyer, 'Die Welt der Urbilder bei Ali Hamadani', in *Eranos-Jahrbuch*, 18 (1950), p. 123. To my knowledge, the most useful general account of Arabic dream theory is still that of N. Bland, 'On the Muhammedan Science of Tābir, or Interpretation of Dreams', in *JRAS*, 16 (1856), pp. 118–71. H. Gätje, 'Philosophische Traumlehren im Islam', in *ZDMG*, 109 (N.F. 34, 1959), pp. 258–85 treats specifically philosophical theories, while P. Schwarz, 'Traum und Traumdeutung nach 'Abdalganī an-Nābulusī', in *ZDMG*, 67 (1913), pp. 473–93, studies the treatise of the early eighteenth-century divine, Nābulsī, the most detailed in Arabic. Abul-Barakāt Baghdādī, *Mu'tabar*, vol. 2, pp. 418 ff., provides a neat and compact account. There is a striking similarity between Arabic dream theory and that of the Greeks, on which see E.R. Dodds, *The Greeks and the Irrational* (Berkeley and Los Angeles, 1951), pp. 104 ff. Ḥajjī Khalīfa, *Kashf*, cols. 416–17 provides a list of Arabic translations of dream treatises attributed to Plato, Aristotle, Euclid and Ptolemy. A number of interesting studies, rich in Arabic material, are assembled in *The Dream and Human Societies*, ed. R. Caillois and G.E. von Grunebaum (Berkeley

and Los Angeles, 1966).

46. Nābulsi, *Ta'ṭīr*, vol. 1, pp. 3–4; Ibn Ḥazm, *Fiṣal*, vol. 5, pp. 19–20; Avicenna, *De Anima*, pp. 179–80; Ibn Sīnā, 'Unique Treatise', p. 285; Rāzī, *Mabāḥith*, vol. 2, p. 420 and Fārābī, *Madīna*, pp. 48–50. Some scholars denied any role for humours and tempers in engendering dreams, natures and qualities being passive receptors of effect — for instance, Abū Ya'lā, *Mu'tamad*, para. 313.

47. On the principles of interpretation, see the account of J. de Somogyi, 'The Interpretation of Dreams in ad-Damīrī's Ḥayāt al-Ḥayawān', in *JRAS*, 1940, pp. 43 ff.

48. Avicenna, *De Anima*, p. 180.

49. See Bland, 'Muhammedan Science of Tâbir', p. 134.

50. Ibn Sīnā, 'Unique Treatise', p. 293.

51. Ibn Khaldūn, *Prolégomènes*, vol. 1, p. 185.

52. *Ibid.*, pp. 187–91.

53. Meyer, 'Welt der Urbilder', p. 132.

54. See 'Aẓma, *Al-Kitāba al-tārīkhiyya*, p. 111 and the references there.

55. Ibn Sīnā, 'Unique Treatise', p. 288.

56. *Ibid.*, pp. 286–7. It will do well to compare oneiromantic knowledge with the acquisition of rationality under the impact of the Active Intellect: see Avicenna, *De Anima*, pp. 234–5.

57. *Ibid.*, p. 292.

58. *Ibid.*, p. 294.

59. *Ibid.*, pp. 176–7.

60. Rāzī, *Mabāḥith*, vol. 2, p. 421.

61. Avicenna, *De Anima*, p. 177.

62. A general idea of these matters can be sampled from E. Galindo, 'Anthropologie et cosmogonie chez Avicenne', in *IBLA*, 22 (1959), pp. 287–323.

63. Tawḥīdī, *Imtā'*, vol. 1, p. 147 and see Pseudo-Sijistānī, *Ṣiwān*, p. 314.

64. Ibn 'Arabī, *Inshā'*, p. 22 and see Ibn Khaldūn, *Shifā'* (ed. Khalifé), pp. 51–2.

65. Ibn al-Khaṭīb, *Rawḍa*, p. 136. On the cosmic significance of Muḥammad, see A. Jeffery, 'Ibn al-'Arabī's Shajarat al-Kawn', in *SI*, 10 (1959), pp. 56 ff.

66. Details of this are well presented in Affifi, *Mystical Philosophy*, pp. 78 ff.

67. Jābir b. Ḥayyān, *Ikhrāj*, p. 50.

68. Ibn 'Arabī, *Tadbīrāt*, pp. 108–9.

69. See the account of Bin'abd al-'Ālī, *Fārābī*, pp. 86, 122–3.

70. Miskawaih, *Tadhīb*, p. 41.

71. Baghdādī, *Mu'tabar*, vol. 2, p. 390.

72. Rāzī, *Asās*, pp. 18–19.

73. Ash'arī, *Maqālāt*, vol. 1, p. 102.

74. *Ibid.*, and see pp. 102–4.

75. Ibn al-Jawzī, *Talbīs*, p. 87.

76. Isfara'īnī, *Tabṣīr*, p. 138 and see Juwainī, *Irshād*, pp. 174 ff. For a Hanbalite statement, see Abū Ya'lā, *Mu'tamad*, paras. 147–8.

77. Sukūnī, *'Uyūn*, para. 89.

78. Ash'arī, *Ibāna*, p. 31.

79. *Ibid.*, p. 35. The Ash'arite doctrine of divine attributes has been studied in detail by M. Allard, *Le problème des attributs divins dans la doctrine d'al Aš'arī et ses premiers grands disciples* (Beirut, 1965). it may be legitimate to inquire whether a crypto-anthropomorphic conception lay at the origin of the vehement and initially bloody dispute over the eternity of the *Qur'ān* and over whether it was ingenerate or not. For views on this, see Ash'arī, *Maqālāt*, vol. 2, pp. 231–44, and the characteristically judicious review of Ibn Ḥazm, *Fiṣal*, vol. 3, pp. 7–10. For the Ash'arite position, see Ash'arī, *Luma'*, pp. 33–4. On further semantic and ontological issues and refinements concerning elements in this topical nexus, which include the meaning of God's 'speech' and 'voice', the status of meaning, elocution and written text from the perspective of this problem, and whether

or not 'speech' inhered in God or not, see Juwainī, *Irshād*, pp. 109 ff., 131–2; Ghazālī, *Iljām*, pp. 50–51 and the convenient review of Kalābādhī, *Ta'arruf*, pp. 54–5 and the short critical comments of 'Abd al-Jabbār, *Faḍl*, pp. 156 f.

80. The first comprehensive statement seems to be that of Ash'arī's contemporary in Baghdad, and leader of the Ḥanbalites of his time, Barbahārī. The complete text of his *profession de foi* is given in the Ibn Abī Ya'lā, *Ṭabaqāt*, vol. 1, pp. 18 ff. For the doctrine of divine attributes of relevance here, see *ibid.*, pp. 19–20.

81. Ibn Qudāma, *Taḥrīm*, para. 73.

82. Ibn Taimiyya, *Muwāfaqa*, vol. 1, pp. 144–6.

83. Ibn Qudāma, *Taḥrīm*, para. 77 ff.

84. Ash'arī, *Luma'*, p. 25.

85. Frank, *Beings and their Attributes*, pp. 12–14, 16–19.

86. Shahrastānī, *Milal*, p. 22. It is noteworthy here that *mutakallimūn* often tried to assemble attributes into a small number of categories (*ibid.*, pp. 21–3; Ash'arī, *Maqālāt*, vol. 2, pp. 157 ff.), and this seems to have been an understandably common procedure. The Jacobite philosopher Yaḥyā b. 'Adī ('Un traité de Yahyâ Ben 'Adī. Défense du dogme de la Trinité contre les objections d'Al-Kindī', pp. 5–6) reduced them to generosity, wisdom and omnipotence, which he identified with, respectively, the Father, the Son and the Holy Spirit. See G. Graf, *Geschichte der christlichen arabischen Literatur* (Vatican City, 1944 ff.), vol. 2, pp. 235–6. Shahrastānī (*Milal*, p. 102) claims a connection between Nestorian doctrines of the Trinity and a Mu'tazilite conception of 'modes' which might be well worth an investigation.

87. Juwainī, *Irshād*, pp. 41–2, 115 ff.

88. *Ibid.*, pp. 80–81.

89. Isfarā'īnī, *Tabṣīr*, pp. 147–8.

90. Bāqillānī, *Tamhīd*, paras. 262–3.

91. For instance, Baghdādī, *Uṣūl*, pp. 114 ff.

92. Ash'arī, *Luma'*, pp. 23–4; Māturdī, *Tawḥīd*, p. 38 and Juwainī, *Irshād*, p. 143.

93. Bāqillānī, *Tamhīd*, para. 383 ff.

94. *Ibid.*, para. 267 ff.

95. Māturdī, *Tawḥīd*, pp. 93 ff.

96. Juwainī, *Irshād*, pp. 141, 143–4.

97. Ghazālī, *Faḍā'iḥ*, p. 39.

98. N. Frye, *The Great Code. The Bible as Literature* (London, 1982), p. 55.

99. Ibn Ḥazm, *Fiṣal*, vol. 2, pp. 117 ff.

100. For instance, Ibn Kathīr, *Bidāya*, vol. 2, p. 151. On the Arian position concerning God alone being ingenerate, in whom nothing participates, see J.N.D. Kelly, *Early Christian Doctrines*, 5th edn (London, 1977), pp. 227 ff.

101. Ibn Rushd, *Manāhij*, p. 168.

102. L. Massignon ('Inventaire de la littérature hermétique arabe', in *La Révélation d'Hermès Trismégiste*, ed. A.J. Festugière and A.D. Nock, 2nd edn (Paris, 1950), vol. 1, pp. 384–400, 438–9) presented some valuable historical and other general considerations on Arabic Hermeticism, and provided (pp. 388 ff.) important indications about the location and incidence of this Hermeticism. Important historical considerations are also given by A. Affifi, 'The Influence of Hermetic Literature in Moslem Thought', in *BSOAS*, 13 (1951), pp. 841 ff. The study of M. Plessner ('Hermes Trismegistus and Arabic Science', in *SI*, 2 (1954), pp. 45–59) unfortunately chases the red herrings of literalist and direct textual influence, thus ignoring the spread of the incidence of ideas with an Hermetic label, and it is difficult to speak of Hermetic or Hermetic-Sabean influence without due regard to the width of the intellectual area where it is at play, or to the coherence of Hermetic texts quoted. On the personality of Hermes in Islamic thought, see S.H. Nasr, 'Hermes and Hermetic Writings in the Islamic World', in Nasr, *Islamic Studies* (Beirut, 1967), pp. 67–8; on Hermetic lore in Arabic writing in general in relation to Sabean and Dualist Persian ideas, see E. Blochet, 'Etudes sur la gnosticisme musulmane', in *Revista degli*

studi orientali, 2 (1908–9), pp. 717–56, 3 (1910), pp. 177–203, 4 (1911–12), pp. 47–79, 267–300. It should be appreciated that the last Sabean temple in Ḥarran was only destroyed in 424/1032 (Chwolsohn, *Ssabier*, vol. 1, 541), that there were several treatises on Sabeanism (for instance, Qifṭī, *Tārīkh*, pp. 78, 120, 195) in circulation. With respect to Sabean doctrine in Arabic sources, some caution (but not hyper-scepticism) is called for — cf. Kraus in Rāzī, *Rasā'il*, pp. 192–3.

103. Dodds, *The Greeks and the Irrational*, pp. 246–7. Correspondences between various parts of the cosmos are common to all cultures. On the various dimensions and constellations of thought of Stoic, Hermetic, Platonic and Pythagorean provenance, enmeshed with Christian and Jewish ideas, and woven together in an 'orientalising' mode, see Lewy, *Chaldean Oracles, passim*.

104. On his teachings and his movement, see W.F. Tucker, 'Rebels and Gnostics: Al-Muğira Ibn Sa'īd and the Muğīriyya', in *Arabica*, 22 (1975), pp. 33–47.

105. Ash'arī, *Maqālāt*, vol. 1, p. 72.

106. Pseudo-Sijistānī, *Ṣiwān*, pp. 301–2.

107. See the table in Ullmann, *Natur und Geheimwissenschaften*, p. 350. For texts and a study of astro-medical matters, see F. Klein-Franke, *Iatromathematics in Islam. A Study of Yuhanna Ibn as-Salt's Book on Astrological Medicine, Edited for the First Time*, Hildesheim, Zurich and New York, 1984 (Texte und Studien zur Orientalistik, Bd. 3).

108. R. Guénon, 'Note sur l'angélogie et l'alphabet arabe', in *Etudes traditionelles*, 43 (1938), pp. 324–7.

109. Kraus, *Jābir Ibn Ḥayyān*, vol. 2, pp. 239–41, 252 ff.

110. H.G. Farmer, 'Al-Kindī on the "Ethos" of Rhythm, Colour, and Perfume', in *Glasgow University Oriental Society. Transactions*, 16 (1955–6), pp. 32 ff. The correlation of the four strings of the lute, and hence the four basic tonalities, with bodily tempers (the *zīr*, for instance, corresponding to fire and hence to bile) underlay musical therapeutics: the *zīr* corresponds to bile, and therefore, counteracts phlegm and associated diseases (Ikhwān al-Ṣafā', *Rasā'il*, vol. 1, p. 213). This underlay the use of music in hospitals (H.G. Farmer, *A History of Arabian Music to the XIIIth Century* (London, 1929), p. 197). Thus when the famous Andalusian musician Ziryāb introduced a fifth, intermediate string into the lute, this was seen to correspond to the intermediate and perfectly isonomic position that the soul occupies in the body (Maqqarī, *Nafḥ*, vol. 3, p. 126) — or justice in ethics.

111. Ikhwān al-Ṣafā', *Rasā'il*, vol. 1, pp. 229–32.

112. *Ibid*., vol. 1, pp. 52–3.

113. Muqaddasī, *Taqasīm*, pp. 37 ff. On the importance of, and for copious examples of, septenary divisions, see M. Steinschneider, 'Die kanonische Zahl der Muhammedanischen Sekten und die Symbolic der Zahl 70–73', in *ZDMG*, 4 (1850), pp. 145–70, Steinschneider, 'Die kanonische Zahlen 70–73', in *ZDMG*, 57 (1903), pp. 474–507, and J. de Somogyi, 'An Arabic Monograph on the Number Seven', in *Islamic Culture*, 32 (1958), pp. 245–9. For Greek use of the numbers seven and seventeen, see Kraus, *Jābir Ibn Ḥayyān*, vol. 2, pp. 207 ff.

114. Muqaddasī, *Taqāsīm*, pp. 41–2.

115. Other numbers are at play. Five had a special place for Ibn Arabī, who saw the five daily prayers to correspond to a variety of cosmic principles, each of which corresponds to an elemental nature (with the addition of light, to which the mid-day prayer corresponds — *Tanazzul*, pp. 54–5). But some thinkers, notably Asha'arites, refused such divisions of things in their zeal to deny any immanent regularities not subject to the direct creative will of God. Thus the division of colours and tastes into four is refuted on the assumption that colours and tastes are infinite in variety and number: Baghdādī, *Uṣūl*, p. 42.

116. Bāqillānī, *I'jāz*, p. 44. Bāqillānī's arithmetology, not to speak of his arithmetic, is manifestly dubious — or is the fault to be found with Bāqillānī's editor?

117. Ibn Khaldūn, *Prolégomènes*, vol. 2, p. 182.

118. Ḥajjī Khalīfa, *Kashf*, cols. 83, 86, 215, 650–51, though Ghazālī (*Faḍā'iḥ*, p. 69) stated that numerical and other associations are purely arbitrary, based neither on reason

nor tradition nor even the infallible Imam — for Ghazālī in this text was engaged in a refutation of Ismā'īlism, and relates in detail the correspondences they employed, some of which are very curious indeed (*ibid.*, 66 ff.).

119. Būnī, *Uṣūl*, p. 8.

120. See the account in Ibn al-Khaṭīb, *Rawḍa*, pp. 328–31.

121. Būnī, *Uṣūl*, pp. 8–16. See the Chaldean configurations of the lords 'of the hour', 'of the day', etc: Lewy, *Chaldean Oracles*, p. 230.

122. Ibn Khaldūn, *Prolégomènes*, vol. 3, pp. 146 ff., and see the diagram in F. Rosenthal, *Ibn Khaldūn: The Muqaddimah* (Princeton, 1967), vol. 3, following p. 204 and in the jacket inside the binding at the end of the volume.

123. The most comprehensive account of the properties of the stars and of zodiacal signs is probably that in Ikhwān al-Ṣafā', *Rasā'il*, vol. 1, pp. 114 ff.

124. On stars and humours, see Ibn Sīnā, *Ḥayy*, p. 48. On Greek and Avicennan views of the medical properties of planets, see P. Duhem, *Le système du monde* (Paris, 1914), vol. 2, pp. 363 ff.

125. A comprehensive account can be found in Ḥajjī Khalīfa, *Kashf*, cols. 725–6, 1114–15. See the practical details in Būnī, *Uṣūl*, p. 111.

126. See Ibn Khaldūn, *Shifā'*, pp. 66–7 and Ibn Khaldūn, *Prolégomènes*, vol. 3, pp. 125 ff.

127. Ibn Ḥazm, *Fiṣal*, vol. 5, pp. 4–5. Muqaddasī (*Taqāsīm*, p. 211) saw crocodile-repellent obelisks that functioned as planned.

128. Jābir b. Ḥayyān, *Ikhrāj*, p. 80.

129. *Ibid.*, p. 83 and see the further details in *ibid.*, pp. 84–8.

130. Ibn Sīnā, *Aqsām*, p. 75.

131. Ṭāshköprüzade, *Miftāḥ*, vol. 2, pp. 591–2.

132. Maqqarī, *Nafḥ*, vol. 2, p. 521.

133. *Ibid.*, p. 180.

134. Ibn Khaldūn, *Shifā'*, p. 67 and Ḥajjī Khalīfa, *Kashf*, col. 651.

135. Ibn Sīnā, *Aqsām*, p. 75.

136. Qazwīnī, *'Ajā'ib*, pp. 346 ff.

137. Ḥajjī Khalīfa, *Kashf*, col. 1131.

138. Miskawaih, *Hawāmil*, pp. 167 ff. and Ibn Sīnā, *Shifā' (Manṭiq, 4)*, p. 579. There is still extant a detailed treatise on this science: Rāzī, *Firāsa*, which starts with medical considerations on temperate dispositions of the body.

139. Ibn 'Arabī, *Tadbīrāt*, pp. 162 ff., 170 ff., 176.

140. Ibn Khaldūn, *Prolégomènes*, vol. 3, p. 85.

141. Ḥajjī Khalīfa, *Kashf*, col. 416.

142. Baghdādī, *Mu'tabar*, vol. 2, p. 417.

143. Ibn Sīnā, 'Unique Treatise', p. 299.

144. *Ibid.*, pp. 299–305.

145. Pseudo-Ibn Sīrīn, *Muntakhab*, p. 4.

146. Qifṭī, *Tārīkh*, p. 154.

147. Nābulsī, *Ta'ṭīr*, vol. 1, pp. 5–6 and Pseudo-Ibn Sīrīn, *Muntakhab*, p. 4.

148. Nābulsī, *Ta'ṭīr*, vol. 1, p. 8.

149. The main procedures are detailed in *ibid.*, pp. 7–8 and de Somogyi, 'Interpretation of Dreams', pp. 3 ff.

150. On the various types of magic, see Ḥajjī Khalīfa, *Kashf*, col. 981, and see also Rāzī, *Mabāḥith*, vol. 2, p. 424. On false magic, such as legerdemain and illusionism, see Ḥajjī Khālifa, *Kashf*, col. 1020 and Ibn Khaldūn, *Prolégomènes*, vol. 3, pp. 124 ff.

151. Ibn Khaldūn, *Prolégomènes*, vol. 2, p. 187.

152. Y. Marquet, 'Les cycles de la souveraineté selon les épitres des Iẖwān al-Ṣafā, in *SI*, 36 (1972), pp. 47–69.

153. Ibn Abī Uṣaibi'a, *'Uyūn*, pp. 326–7.

154. Ibn Khaldūn, *Prolégomènes*, vol. 1, p. 306. The connection between regular astral

conjunctions and the vicissitudes and 'stages' of Khaldūn's famous reflections on the state are manifest. See Al-Azmeh, *Ibn Khaldūn: An Essay*, pp. 36–7.

155. Ibn Khaldūn, *Prolégomènes*, vol. 2, pp. 245–6.

156. Text in M. Redjala, 'Un texte inédit de *la Maqaddima*', in *Arabica*, 22 (1975), pp. 321–2.

157. Ikhwān al-Ṣafā', *Rasā'il*, vol. 2, p. 92.

158. Qazwīnī, *'Ajā'ib*, p. 57.

159. Ibn al-Khaṭīb, *Rawḍa*, pp. 384 ff.

160. Tawḥīdī, *Muqābasāt*, pp. 67–8, 78.

161. Ibn Rushd, *Kawn*, pp. 27–8.

162. Ibn Khaldūn, *Prolégomènes*, vol. 2, p. 246 and text in Redjala, 'Un texte inédit', p. 322.

163. See on this matter Diogenes Laertius, *Lives*, vii.140, who adds that such relations are not only based on sympathy, but also upon tension.

164. Ibn al-Khaṭīb, *Rawḍa*, p. 578.

165. Ibn Sīnā, *Shifā', (Ṭabī'iyyāt, 2)*, p. 196.

166. *Ibid.*, p. 192.

167. Ikhwān al-Ṣafā, *Rasā'il*, vol. 2, p. 92.

168. Avicenna, *De Anima*, p. 199 and see Rāzī, *Mabāḥith*, vol. 1, p. 509.

169. See M.A.F. Mehren, 'Vues d'Avicenne sur l'astrologie et sur le rapport de la responsabilité humaine avec le destin', in *Le Muséon*, 3 (1884), pp. 387–8, 397.

170. Ibn Ḥazm, *Fiṣal*, vol. 5, p. 14.

171. Ibn Sīnā, *Shifā' (Tabī'iyyāt, 2)*, pp. 258–9.

172. See Ibn Rushd, *Ma' ba'd aṭ-ṭabī'a*, p. 51.

173. See, for instance, Ikhwān al-Ṣafā', *Rasā'il*, vol. 1, pp. 145–7, 277–8; vol. 2, p. 133; vol. 3, pp. 182–3 and see Ibn al-Khaṭīb, *Rawḍa*, pp. 573 ff. and Shahrastānī, *Muṣāra'a*, pp. 97–8.

174. Ibn Ḥazm, *Manṭiq*, pp. 66–7.

175. Ibn Sīnā, *Shifā' (Ṭabī'iyyāt*, 2), p. 125.

176. Tawḥīdī, *Imtā'*, vol. 2, p. 109.

177. Qazwīnī, *'Ajā'ib*, p. 275.

178. Ikhwān al-Ṣafā', *Rasā'il*, vol. 2, pp. 110–11.

179. Ibn Rushd, *Samā'*, pp. 100–1.

180. Ibn Sīnā, *Najāt*, 2nd edn, p. 214.

181. See, for instance, the remarks of Ṭabarī, *Firdaws*, p. 18.

182. For the senses of the term 'actor' (*fā'il*), see Baghdādī, *Mu'tabar*, vol. 2, p. 8. See Pines, 'Quelques tendances antipéripateticiennes', p. 212, for a discussion of force in a mechanical context.

183. Jābir b. Ḥayyān, *Ikhrāj*, p. 4.

184. Ibn Rushd, *Manāhij* (ed. Qāsim), p. 200.

185. Ibn Rushd, *Samā'*, p. 12.

186. *Ibid.*, pp. 19–20 and Rāzī, *Mabāḥith*, vol. 1, pp. 526, 530–1, 538.

187. Shāṭibī, *Muwāfaqāt*, vol. 3, pp. 81–2.

188. See the classic statement in Ash'arī, *Luma'* (ed. McCarthy), p. 39. See the general account by D. Gimaret, *Theories de l'acte humain en théologie musulmane* (Paris and Louvain), 1980.

189. See the classic statement of 'Abd al-Jabbār, *Faḍl*, pp. 169 ff.

190. Ash'arī, *Luma'* (ed. McCarthy), p. 44.

191. For a basic argument, see Ash'arī, *Luma'*, pp. 81, 93–4 and see the position of Māturīdī, *Tawḥīd*, pp. 308 ff.

192. Māturīdī, *Tawhīd*, p. 312 and see Ash'arī, *Luma'*, p. 84.

193. Ash'arī, *Luma'* (ed. McCarthy), pp. 45f. and Bāqillānī, *Tamhīd*, paras. 554–5, and see Ibn Rushd, *Manāhij* (ed. Qāsim), pp. 234–5, 238. See the intermediate position of Māturīdī, *Tawḥīd*, p. 266.

194. Ash'arī, *Lumā'*, pp. 115–16 and see the account of different nuances of this position in Juwainī, *Irshād*, pp. 238 ff.

195. For instance, Ibn Ḥazm, *Fiṣal*, vol. 3, p. 36 and see especially the classic Mu'tazilite critical statement of 'Abd al-Jabbār, text in A'sam, *Tārīkh*, p. 94. See the comments of Abū Ya'lā, *Mu'tamad*, para. 138, close to the Mu'tazilites.

196. Māturīdī, *Tawḥīd*. pp. 263–4. Perhaps the limit of this view of God's absolute latitude is that attributed to Suhrawardī and taken to have been one reason for the heresy on the basis of which he was executed: he is said to have maintained (in relation to himself?) that, although tradition has Muḥammad as the last of prophets, yet the infinite power of God makes the creation of yet another prophet possible (editor's introduction to Suhrawardī, *Lamaḥāt*, p. 11). Similarly, the Mirdāriyya Mu'tazilite sect conceded that it was indeed within God's power to do evil, but that if He did He would be evil Himself (Shahrastānī, *Milal*, p. 30). At the other extreme is the view of the Ka'biyya Mu'tazilites, that God had no will as such (Shahrastanī, *Milal*, p. 32). Whether this should be taken to mean (as in Ibn Khallikān, *Wafayāt*, vol. 3, p. 45) that His acts are involuntary is another matter.

197. Ibn Rushd, *Mā ba'd aṭ-ṭabī'a*, p. 87.

198. Ash'arī, *Maqālāt*, vol. 2, p. 196.

199. Bāqillānī, *Tamhīd*, para. 488.

200. Juwainī, *Irshād*, p. 219.

201. Ash'arī, *Luma'* (ed. McCarthy), p. 40.

202. Maturīdī, *Tawḥīd*, pp. 256–7.

203. Ibn Rushd, *Manāhij* (ed. Qāsim), pp. 225–6.

204. Al-Azmeh, *Ibn Khaldūn in Modern Scholarship*, ch. 5 and Al-Azmeh, *Ibn Khaldūn: An Essay, passim*.

205. 'Aẓma, *Al-Kitāba al-Tārīkhiyya*, pp. 77–8, and 'Aẓma, 'Al-Siyāsa', *passim*.

206. On the relation of Islam to previous religions, which is one of an almost Hegelian *Aufhebung*, see 'Aẓma, *Al-Kitāba al-tārīkhiyya*, pp. 113 ff.

207. Such is the meaning of the term *jāhiliyya*: see Al-Azmeh, *Ibn Khaldūn in Modern Scholarship*, pp. 134 ff.

208. Bāqillānī, *Tamhīd*, para. 477 ff.

209. Juwainī, *Irshād*, p. 226.

210. Ibn al-Ḥājib, *Mukhtaṣar*, p. 43.

211. *Ibid.*, p. 46.

212. On some such views, including very bizarre ones, along with a Mu'tazilite refutation, see 'Abd al-Jabbār, *Sharḥ*, pp. 477 ff. See Baghdādī, *Uṣul*, pp. 259 ff., for an Ash'arite account and *ibid.*, pp. 240 ff., for a refutation of the Mu'tazilite position that divine justice required for God should compensate, in the afterlife, beasts of burden for the wretchedness of their earthly lot. For Ḥanbalite positions, see Abū Ya'lā, *Mu'tamad*, paras. 207, 212.

213. For instance, Juwainī, *Irshād*, p. 3; Isfarā'īnī, *Tabṣīr*, pp. 162–4 and Ibn Ḥazm, *Fiṣal*, vol. 4, pp. 35, 41. See Shawkānī, *Irshād*, pp. 253–4, and the Ḥanbalite position of Ibn Qudāma, *Taḥrīm*, paras. 45–7.

214. See the retort of Rāzī, *Muḥaṣṣal*, p. 148.

215. Ash'arī, *Maqālāt*, vol. 2, pp. 218 ff.; Ibn Ḥazm, *Fiṣal*, vol. 4, p. 192 and Ibn al-Rīwandī, *Faḍīḥa*, fragments 4, 9, 14, 16, 143.

216. Baghdādī, *Uṣūl*, pp. 149 ff.

217. Ghazālī, *Mustasfā*, vol. 1, p. 69.

218. The Mu'tazilite 'Allāf rejected all intermediate categories of command and decreed them not to be go beyond obedience and disobedience (Ibn 'Aqīl, *Funūn*, p. 55).

219. Shawkānī, *Irshād*, p. 200.

220. Ibn Ḥazm, *Mulakhkhaṣ*, p. 6.

221. Ibn Ḥazm, *Iḥkām*, p. 953. For a review of this issue, see Rāzī, *Asās*, pp. 211 ff.

222. Ibn Hazm, *Iḥkām*, pp. 1050 and *passim*.

223. *Ibid.*, p. 931.

224. For instance: Ṭabarī, *Tafsīr*, vol. 1, p. 12. See the salvaging of the common position

on analogy by another textualist, albeit one with greater realism in this case: Ibn Taimiyya, *Radd*, p. 53.

225. Shawkānī, *Irshād*, p. 204. See I. Goldziher, *The Ẓāhirīs. Their Doctrine and Their History*, tr. W. Behn (Leiden, 1971), pp. 35–6. The reader should be alerted to the fact that Goldziher's book, although the only treatment of this school, is a collection of notes and not a properly constituted history or exposition of Ẓahirite doctrine.

226. For a statement of the Mu'tazilite position, see Baṣrī, *Mu'tamad*, pp. 177–9, and for a Ḥanafite statement of an analogous (though not homonymous) position, see Pazdawī, *Kanz*, pp. 611 ff. and see pp. 10 ff. For reviews of this controversial matter, see Ibn 'Aqīl, *Funūn*, paras. 363, 436, 480; Rāzī, *Muḥaṣṣal*, p. 147; Shāṭibī, *Muwāfaqāt*, vol. 2, pp. 31–2 and Shawkānī, *Irshād*, pp. 8–9. The Mu'tazilite 'Allāf maintained that a legal major should know God, good and evil even before the receipt of nomothetic discourse (Shahrastānī, *Milal*, p. 24).

227. Shāṭibī, *Muwāfaqāt*, vol. 1, pp. 63–4, 209–10, 245 ff.; vol. 2, pp. 3–4, 28–9, 76 ff., 212–13, 220–21; vol. 4, pp. 134 ff. and see also Shawkānī, *Irshād*, pp. 214–16.

228. See, for instance, Baṣrī, *Mu'tamad*, pp. 838–40; Shāṭibī, *Muwāfaqāt*, vol. 1, p. 16 and Shawkānī, *Irshād*, pp. 242–3.

229. For instance, Baiḍāwī, *Minhāj*, p. 12; Ibn Ḥazm, *Iḥkām*, pp. 758 ff.; for a Mu'tazilite reservation see Baṣrī, *Mu'tamad*, p. 301 and for an Isma'īlī statement see Qāḍī al-Nu'mān, *Majālis*, para. 220.

230. Shāṭibī, *Muwāfaqāt*, vol. 1, p. 185.

231. Ghazālī, *Mustasfā*, vol. 1, p. 93.

232. Āmidī, *Iḥkām*, vol. 1, p. 82.

233. Ibn 'Aqīl, *Jadal*, para. 42 and see the criticism of Ibn Sīnā, *Shifā' (Qiyās)*, p. 575 and the comments on the terms of this criticism by J. Van Ess, *Die Erkenntnislehre des 'Aḍudaddīn al-Īcī* (Wiesbaden, 1966), p. 392.

234. Ibn Jinnī, *Khaṣā'iṣ*, vol. 1, p. 48.

235. *Ibid.*, p. 51.

236. *Ibid.*, pp. 50–51.

237. See for instance, Āmidī, *Iḥkām*, vol. 1, pp. 113–24 and Ghazālī, *Mustasfā*, vol. 1, p. 63.

238. Shawkānī, *Irshād*, p. 222.

239. Baiḍāwī, *Minhāj*, p. 93.

240. On this scale, see Ghazālī, *Mustasfā*, vol. 2, p. 318.

241. Ghazālī, *Miḥakk*, p. 33.

242. Pazdawī, *Kanz*, p. 1014.

243. Āmidī, *Iḥkām*, vol. 1, p. 7.

244. Baiḍāwī, *Minhāj*, p. 78.

245. Qarāfī, *Tanqīḥ*, p. 165.

246. Rāzī, *Munāẓarāt*, paras. 71–2.

247. Shāṭibī, *Muwāfaqāt*, vol. 1, pp. 14–16, 10–11. These five necessities are agreed upon by legal scholars, though their status is in the context of 'interest', peripheral to theory, and relevant only marginally.

248. *Ibid.*, p. 44. See the Mu'tazilite distinction between necessary and indexical connectors in analogy: Baṣrī, *Mu'tamad*, p. 772.

249. Ibn Ḥazm, *Mulakhkhaṣ*, p. 41 and see the same point made in a non-polemical context by Ghazālī, *Mi'yār*, p. 161.

250. Pseudo-Qudāma, *Naqd*, p. 15.

251. Ghazālī, *Mi'yār*, p. 202.

252. It is perhaps not surprising that Bājī, *Minhāj*, paras. 47–8 contains one of the most succinct statements of this distinction, given that the author was engaged in disputation and polemic with no less a person than Ibn Ḥazm. For a rigorous discussion, see Ghazālī, *Mustasfā*, vol. 2, pp. 310–12 and the comments of Baṣrī, *Mu'tamad*, p. 700; Ibn Rushd, *Biyāda*, vol. 1, p. 8 and Khwārizmī, *Mafātīḥ*, p. 9.

253. Bājī, *Minhāj*, paras. 19, 300 ff.
254. Āmidī, *Iḥkām*, vol. 1, p. 227.
255. Baiḍāwī, *Minhāj*, pp. 83 ff.
256. Ghazālī, *Mustasfā*, vol. 2, p. 318.
257. *Ibid.*, pp. 310–11.
258. See Ghazālī, *Mi'yār*, pp. 170 ff. On this complex question, a good example of legislative rationality in Islamic law, see the excellent account of A.J. Wensinck, 'Khamr', in *EI*, vol. 4, pp. 995–7.
259. See the discussion of H. Konrad, *Etude sur la métaphore* (Paris, 1939), pp. 88, 91.
260. L. Gardet, 'La dialectique en morphologie et logique arabes', in *Ambivalence*, ed. Berque and Charnay, pp. 130–1.
261. Āmidī, *Iḥkām*, vol. 3, p. 273.
262. Baṣrī, *Mu'tamad*, p. 699.
263. On this distinction see P. Ricoeur, *The Rule of Metaphor*, tr. P. Czerny *et al.* (London, 1978), p. 198.
264. Fārābī, *Ḥurūf*, para. 112.
265. Āmidī, *Iḥkām*, vol. 3, pp. 273–4. For a logical account of relations of generalisation and particularisation in legal analogies, see Ibn Sīnā, *Shifā' (Manṭiq)*, pp. 555–6.
266. For a most comprehensive statement, see Shawkānī, *Irshād*, pp. 205–6.
267. Ibn 'Aqīl, *Jadal*, paras. 48–9.
268. Ghazālī, *Mustasfā*, vol. 2, p. 31.
269. Berque, *Essai sur le méthode juridique maghrébine* (Rabat, 1944), p. 21.
270. See, for instance, Ṭabarī, *Tafsīr*, vol. 6, p. 180 and *passim*.
271. Ibn Rushd, *Manāhij* (ed. Qāsim), p. 170.
272. The most comprehensive statement is that of Ibn Khaldūn, *Prolégomènes*, vol. 3, pp. 221 ff. 223 ff.; see also Ibn Sīnā, *Shifā' (Ṭabī'iyyat, 2)*, p. 198 and Ibn Qayyim al-Jawziyya, *Miftāḥ*, p. 189. Regardless of epistemological considerations, astrology and its analogues follow from the Stoic notion of determinism that these authors shared, see Sambursky, *Physics of the Stoics*, pp. 65 ff. and see the remarks of Duhem, *Système du monde*, vol. 2, pp. 287–8 and vol. 4, p. 494.
273. For instance, Tawḥīdī, *Muqābasāt*, p. 67.
274. For instance, Ibn Qutaiba, *Ta'wīl*, p. 62.
275. Ibn al-Khaṭīb, *Rawḍa*, p. 604.
276. For instance, Ibn Abī Ya'lā, *Ṭabaqāt*, vol. 2, p. 252 and Sakhāwī, *Ḍaw'*, vol. 1, p. 197. Not much is said about what people did with such knowledge, and no pattern of initiates is discernible except amongst the greater mystics. For the Name itself, which conservative divines did not want to admit as containing the secrets of creation or at least skirted this aspect, see the account of Suyūṭī, *Ḥāwī*, vol. 1, pp. 394–7 and Nawawī, *Fatāwī*, p. 305. The political connotations of eschatological and antinomian dimensions of the Greatest Name are brought out in very great detail in a study of seventeenth-century Jewish messianism by G. Scholem, *Sabbatai Sevi. The Mystical Messiah, 1626–1676* (London, 1973), pp. 402 and *passim*, a movement informed by the cabalistic lore which is very similar to esotericist conceptions of Arabic mysticism.
277. Ḥajjī Khalīfa, *Kashf*, col. 591.
278. *Ibid.*, col. 411 and Sha'rānī, *Ṭabaqāt*, vol. 2, p. 68.
279. Abū Ḥammū, *Wasīṭa*, p. 21, echoing many a *Fürstenspiegel*.

Chapter Three

A Special Relation: Signification

In an improved version of the accepted view on the epistemological properties of medieval Arabic thought, one modern researcher maintained that the learned culture of Arab-Islamic civilisation rested upon three epistemic systems — a linguistic, a gnostic and a rationalist.[1] Yet the incomplete descriptive justice of this classification of procedures does not in any way insure its validity when it aims, as it does, to be the criterion of interpretation for medieval Arabic thought. The procedures so classified do not constitute three modes of knowledge which severally institute types of discourse, which in their turn rule supreme in the context of a particular science of a particular school of thought. The three types indicated, in addition to others omitted, are in fact three types of epistemological material rather than three theories of knowledge, each of which is generally applied to a particular but not exclusive type of subject-matter, and which almost invariably coexist in the same text. The question thus devolves into the study, not of their analytical separability which is not open to doubt, but of their modes of active combination, and this requires a perspective other than that which takes textbook theories of knowledge as its point of departure.

Knowledge and its Object

In order more accurately to appreciate the three types of argumentation under review in the context of medieval Arabic thought, it is necessary to eschew the assumption, common to modern thought and the product of the modern philosophical tradition as epitomised by Kant, that formal knowledge is an autonomous field for the exercise of a 'faculty', and therefore the object of a particular scientific discipline commonly termed the 'theory of knowledge'. What today falls within the purview of epistemology would normally, in the context of medieval Arabic and other cultures, have fallen within the domains of psychology and linguistics. It is in the context of the theory of the mind (and this is itself part of the context of the study of the transition from mundane to supra-mundane existence) that topics belonging to the theory of knowledge in its modern acceptation were adumbrated, as any cursory look at the works of medieval Arabic philosophy would demonstrate. Rationality, in works of philosophy, is a simple substance and a divine quality as we have seen, while in the works of jurisprudence it is an instrumental manifestation of providence which allows for the perception of divisions between the licit and the illicit, the providential and the improvident.[2] In neither domain is it a self-sufficient and *sui generis* quality or ideal. In dogmatic theology, the mind was conceived in an instrumental mould. Just as it was sometimes considered a faculty of discernment whose particular instrument was logic,[3] dogmatic theologians took it for an aggregate of necessary knowledge,[4] what Ḥanbalites and others liked to term innate knowledge (*fiṭra*),[5] comprising such matters as the impossibility of the identity of opposites.

The criteria for the discrimination between veracity and falsehood, the task of the mental faculty, can be various. In addition to tradition of unimpeachable veracity, aspects of which are studied in various passages of this book, the two foremost criteria, additionally or autonomously, are logic and grammar. Some thinkers established a parallelism between the two, with logic guarding intellectual truth and grammar insuring the correct construction of linguistic utterances whose contents are not necessarily those of the intellect.[6] Correlatively, there are utterances which are linguistically correct but logically invalid, being based on sophistical, dialectical or poetical figures; in any case, grammar is confined to a particular language while logic is not so bound and is universal.[7] By way of counter-argument, the grammarian Sīrāfī, in a justly famous debate with the logician Abū Bishr Mattā (d. 329/940),[8] rejected the claims of logic on the assumption that they were based on the rules of the Greek language and were, as such, irrelevant to thinking in the medium of Arabic.[9] The distinction between the provinces of language and of thought upon which logicians insisted was rejected, not only by representatives of the doctrinally anti-logical and anti-philosophical tendency, but also by the likes of Ibn Ḥazm who sought to restate Aristotelian logic within the wider context of a theory of signification contained in his *Taqrīb*, whose cornerstone was the conviction that the criteria of logic are linguistic because language is factually and logically anterior to logic.[10] A similar position was maintained by later grammarians such as Sakkākī (d. 626/1228–9), who sought to reinstate the theory of the syllogism in grammatical terms.[11]

The position stated by Yaḥyā b. 'Adī (d. 363–4/973–4) that both language and logic were equally formal operations[12] must have displeased both logicians, who loved form but distrusted words, and grammarians, who loved language and distrusted formalism, although, as we shall see, formalism was not absent from grammatical theory.

Both language and logic are instruments conducive to the truth — except for the truth of the mystics which, based on a faculty of inwardness (*qalb*) and of transcendental sensibility (*dhauq*), is the result of immediate and unmediated apperception which is inexpressible,[13] and which is consequently always defective in expression and thus liable to charges of blasphemy.[14] Language, logic, gnosis, induction, authority and other means of attaining the truth, separately or in any discursive combination, may indeed be theories of knowledge. But this status which can, without unacceptable injustice, be imputed to them, does not justify the imputation of centrality to this status, for its status is never separate from a perfectly adulterated discursive practice. Their status as ideal theories never corresponds to practice and is never realised; what instances there are of realisation are very marginal and can only be considered as attempts fully and bookishly to realise certain theoretical prescriptions which do not correspond to the realities of discursive practice which underlie all utterances. The reality of discursive practice in the context of medieval Arabic culture is otherwise intended, and deploys these 'faculties' as forms of knowledge and forms of correspondence between truth and its object — forms of expression which represent forms of signification.

Truth, *ḥaqīqa*, is not the result of the passive epistemic forms referred to, but is of totally different provenance. Truth is not an absolute and unitary entity, but is relative to its provenance. Indeed, *ḥaqīqa* is a term of linguistic provenance, and it is classified as linguistic (in the lexical sense of a word designating an object), terminological and nomothetic (in the sense of the correspondence of word and object being prescribed by nomothetic discourse)[15] — an example of the last could be the term *ṣalāt* which, of all its meanings, came to stand exclusively for ritual prayer. *Ḥaqīqa* is a term inevitably inscribed in the study of the division of all utterance into literal and figurative designation. Similarly, syllogistic theory works on the basis of criteria of validity external to it, ones concerned with the metaphysic of categories and definitions which, alone, are the guardians of the ultimate validity of the syllogism and the causes of its falsity, being responsible for its premisses. Similarly, gnosis is the result of a long period of ascetic and other training which alone safeguards the integrity of gnostic union with God as opposed to communion with Satan. Knowledge is an activity, not the content of such activity as discourse exercises; it has no special and privileged ontologial status as knowledge, but is an utterance which runs parallel to ontological reality. Knowledge as such has no particular quiddity, except within the context of a rare Platonism where it was an assembly of archetypes and part of an ontology, not an epistemology. The absence of an epistemology in medieval Arabic thought as distinct from psychology or linguistics is the correlative of this state of affairs which, contrary to the duality of mind and matter with which Cartesianism inseminated modern thought and culture, did not conceive of reality and knowledge as states of differential quiddity.

Arabic thought in the Middle Ages did not admit of the ontological distinction between tangible entities that can be sensuously apprehended and entities of a spiritual or a subliminal nature. This is certainly a more catholic, and certainly a more realistic, view of things than is allowed for in terms of modern positivistic doctrines. Being is exercised at various levels and in several forms, none of which is less real than the other. Arabic thought deployed the notions systematised in Stoic theory, dividing being into three locations: verbal utterance (*lekton*), psychic representation (*fantasia logiki*) and reality (*tyxanon*)[16] — without this last in any sense having exclusive title to Being. Fārābī took up this view explicitly, attributing it to 'the Ancients', and assimilating representation to the entities of reason, the concepts.[17] Others rehearsed this division with the addition of a fourth location, that of script, existence having a four-fold division depending on whether the thing existed immediately in itself, or whether its like was graven in the mind (*dhihn, psyche*), composed of sounds which together indicate the psychic representation, or was manifested as characters standing for sounds by means of which speech indicates the psychic representation.[18] All four have a basic characteristic in common, which is existence.[19] And while some thinkers confined their typology of existents to the two genera of the mental and the immediate,[20] this did not render the verbal and the scriptural existentially suspect. They were part of a theory of signification. This had immediate and literal being as the signified, as the original existence, while its existence in the psyche forms part of the field of figurative discourse analysis.[21]

True knowledge of a thing, and the true articulation of the psychic representation which is knowledge, is measured by the adequacy of representation to the thing and the correspondence of the region of immediate being with that of being mediated into articulation and representation. Knowledge is an act of signification, and falsehood is not so much privation as anomalous signification; it is the dislocation of the correspondence between the sign in its psychic and locutionary forms and the signified. Ignorance and falsity are nothing but believing things to be as they are not,[22] such that falsity is very much like the spatial separation of two exactly isomorphous and equally immediate shapes made of different substances, the one tangible and sensuous, the other verbal or plastic. Knowledge as adequation is therefore the possibility of a full correspondence and conformity between the sign and the signified in such a way that every point in the region of representation and articulation is topologically correlated to a corresponding point in the region of immediacy. It is a commensuration, the recreation in another medium of sensuous reality in all its amplitude. There is therefore no epistemological basis for falsehood, for it is a misapprehension based upon the misapplication of the linguistic, logical or other means of attaining knowledge of the truth; it is a misappropriation of immediately tangible reality, a dislocated solipsism.

The analysis of falsehood bears out this contention, for falsehood was never attributed to mechanisms of knowledge or to epistemological processes, but was taken for the result of either deliberate design or some other species of dissimulation, or attributed to plain incompetence. Falsehood has its origin outside the sphere of knowledge, which is as closed as it is perfect in its self-sufficiency. The identification of truth and verisimilitude animated Ibn Khaldūn's celebrated criticism of historical transmission in terms of the psychology of the historian and his proneness to gullibility and mendacity.[23] The same recourse to the notion of correspondence and elicitation of failure of technique for the lack of correspondence animated the rather more profound analysis of falsehood by the great student of schism, Ghazālī. The human spirit is 'obedient to illusions', especially those born of association of a Pavlovian description, such as the drawing away from a rope on the part of him who had been bitten by a snake, or from a beautiful maiden should she happen to be called by a Jewish name. In all cases, preference for some things, including falsity, and the shunning of others, is the product of egotism.[24] It is an equally attractive illusion which induces the soul to accept poetical premisses to syllogisms,[25] and the philosophers do, indeed, go counter to their better judgement simply because a certain notion is associated with the names of Aristotle, Plato or Hippocrates.[26] False beliefs, and Ismā'ilism was always foremost in Ghazālī's mind in this context, persisted by virtue of the gullibility of men and their readiness to be misled by power-thirsty groups and individuals who, in order to conjure up a following, invented a schism[27] which was attractive to a host of disaffected commoners, ambitious individuals, scions of bygone dynasties, libertines who wished not to believe in damnation and other malcontents.[28] All schismatics based their work on dissimulation and the arousal of disaffection, and logic, according to an enemy, was a Byzantine attempt to subvert the Islamic faith.[29] The ample discourse on *taḥrīf*, the adulteration of the Christian and Jewish scriptures by Christians and Jews so as to reveal a content which is un-Islamic or which does not lend itself to a typological interpretation from an Islamic point of view, is also inscribed in the same terms.[30] *Taḥrīf* is fundamentally a phonetic term which designates the alteration of a word, by the rearrangement of its letters,[31] and, in the scriptural context, takes on the technical sense of a deliberate alteration of the text, or, less commonly and more charitably, an accidental one brought about by careless copying or by the vagaries of interpretation.[32] Indeed, differences amongst Islamic legal scholars are attributed by Ibn Ḥazm to matters akin to the charitable conception of *taḥrīf*, being due to the accretion of judgements intended to interpret the scripture.[33] And finally, Ibn al-Jawzī's *Talbis Iblīs*, the Deceptions of Satan, is a study of the various strands of thought with which the author disagreed — philosophy, some mystical beliefs and others — as imputations and insinuations of the Devil which otherwise have no basis. Satan's inroad into the human spirit is made of passions, and humanity's rampart is the mind, 'one of God's soldiers',[34] and the custodian of truth, correspondence with reality.

The fact that a particular community is prone to adopt particular beliefs because of predilections born of custom, ecology (which effects the somatic humours) and the configurations of the stars,[35] cannot therefore go counter to the technicist approach to truth under discussion. Falsehood has inroads into the truth not because of any intrinsic property of epistemological operations, but because of externally inspired defects, including passions born of livid and other tempers. Indeed, logic in the widest sense of a discriminating faculty, as the Measure of Science, *mi'yār al-'ilm*, is the ultimate touchstone according to which discrimination is possible between reason and passion.[36] The closest study of the intrinsic mechanics of falsehood in the context of differences within the scientific community ascribed falsehood to technical matters such as the difficulty and unwieldiness of some finer points.[37] Truth is one and unchangeable; difference must be either the result of misunderstanding (and reconciliation therefore becomes possible, as between the doctrines of Plato and Aristotle which Fārābī tried to unify on the assumption that the absence of difference in philosophy and religion is the index of truth),[38] or else, as we saw, they must be based on the error of one in a zero-sum game where the winner is the more accomplished technician. The reason why Ibn Sīnā's theology, according to Ghazālī, was based on error, unlike his truthful logical and arithmetical doctrines, is that his theological demonstrations were not of the same degree of technical accomplishment as that manifest in his logic and arithmetic.[39]

In all cases the truth, whether articulated in speech or represented in the psyche, is a fact of correspondence of an almost topographical nature between a tangible immediate existent, a verbal existent and a graphic existent. The ideal state of knowledge therefore seems to be one which seizes the very immediacy of the object of knowledge, one within the context of a nominalist paradigm in which the correspondence between word, concept and thing is complete. It is a state in which the object is so assimilated by its concept, or the concept so assimilated by the object, that they are interchangeable, as if knowledge were an act of beholding. In fact, it is in this sense that all psychological treatises refer to memory as a depository of sensuous experience, unadulterated by its temporal or substantial difference, and to intellectual acts as a combination of components so deposited.[40] It does therefore seem not implausible to argue that gnostic apprehension is the limiting case of types of knowledge as direct and immediate apperception, and the most extreme and consistent form of sensualist positivism which will have nothing less for knowledge than the absolute and immediate consumption of its object, or the mutual consumption of subject and object, of man and God. After all, the immediate apprehension of God, *ma'rifat al mushāhada*, absorbs and transcends scientific knowledge of God, as it does comprehension and utterance relating to God.[41] And although not all mystics explicitly stated so, this direct apprehension, in all its levels which ascend with ascetic and pious effort, involves a physical vision of subliminal beings such as angels.[42] Knowledge relates to its object in that the object is apprehended visually or quasi-visually[43] — a reference to gnosis, but also a reference to idealised knowledge in general, as is indicated by the use of the term *'ilm* here, and not *ma'rifa*, which is ordinarily used to indicate mystical gnosis as opposed to articulated knowledge which is science, along with such terms as *mukāshafa*, *ḥaqq*, *'ilm ladunī* and others.[44] The mind, reason, is an instrument of enslavement to the limits of humanity and not one for a vision of divinity.[45] Mystical gnosis is so direct that it is an entirely private experience for which the resources of language are inadequate, even for figurative expression which depends on some form of connection.[46] This is why apologists for mysticism defend expressions of *shaṭḥ*, blasphemous or heretical expressions and utterances which cost many mystics their heads (and occasionally more), as the result, not of heretical content, but of the lack of adequacy of language to that which is being expressed[47] — a sensation, a direct apprehension, an all-encompassing and absolutely adequate knowledge acquired in state of theolepsy (*jadhba*). This is why Ibn 'Arabī very sensibly urged his acolytes to reply to critics who taunt them with demands for proof of their statements by retorting that one never asked for a meaningful statement on the essence of things, nor for proof of the sweetness of honey or of the pleasure of intercourse.[48] Such matters are not amenable to articulate statement.

Gnostic solipsism lies at the extremity of both expression and comprehension — the former because the expression of its realities is necessarily defective and inappropriate to its content and the latter because it is located at the outer limit of knowledge, where comprehension is absolute and where the object of knowledge is seized by the subject in all its immediate fullness and plenitude. Full knowledge is the assimilation by the subject of the whole object, and the full representation of the object in the subject, a representation which is either absolute, such as that which comes about in the ontological union of subject and object in full gnosis, or relative and semiological, in which knowledge of the object represents this object, and can thus be said to correspond with it, although it is made of a different material — signs and signifiers, i.e. words and concepts. Short of the gnostic cannibalisation of the object of knowledge by its subject, the ideal of knowledge is one in which this full assimilation is semiotic, in which subject and object are related by full verisimilitude in which the subject fully recovers and calques the object, as in the Stoic *fantasia kataleptikē*. Ideally, therefore, the relation of knowledge to its object is iconic, or at the very least constructed according to an iconic metaphor, regardless of whether we are dealing with the connection of word and object, or of generality and particularity.

The subject and object of knowledge thus occasionally coalesce, but are always formally homologous and stand for one another. The ideal and most accomplished epistemic act is that which transcribes the form of the object in the psyche with a full correspondence, without accretions or omissions,[49] knowledge being the inscription of the form of the object in the soul and casting of the pscyhe after lineaments of the object.[50] The existence in the pscyhe of the object as knowledge is that of an exemplar and isomorph, just as a mirror reflects an object and acts as the location for the reality of the image.[51] And although a famous philosopher of Baghdad thought it necessary to underline his conviction, which he shared with everyone else, that the formal similarity of signifier (*dāll*) and signified (*madlūl*) is not also the similarity of the essence of an utterance about an object (*qawl*) and the essence of this object, yet this did not imply for him the falsity of the view that the verbal articulation of something fully represents the essential sense of the object in its immediate givenness.[52] This is why defects of knowledge are imperfections of a quantitive sort in which the primary criterion is fullness of correspondence, and it is this which warrants the classification of knowledge of an object into the complete and the incomplete, and correlatively, the general and the particular for, according to the epistemological nominalism which reigned supreme in Arabic thought, the ascent of knowledge to fullness is a descent from generality to particularity,[53] the subsumptions of particulars into species and genera is an Aristotelian classification on the basis of an induction.[54] The world is composed of particulars only, and the correspondence of a concept to its referent is not the presence of the concept in the world, as in some Platonic conceptions, but its correspondence to every particular it subsumes.[55] Arabic philosophical and sagely writing is replete with discussions on exactly how the mind, which naturally veers to the general, grasps the particular, and how sense, which thrives on particularity, contributes to the workings of the mind.[56] But this awareness of complexity was largely the response to polemical occasion[57] or to gratuitous sageliness,[58] and was discursively inoperative in so far as the general prevalent Aristotelian conception was concerned. It was this pervasive nominalism which constituted the *leitmotiv* of the refutations of logic, at the apex of which lay Ibn Taimiyya's work, and which belaboured the point that logic and reality can never be truly correspondent, an attitude which, when pushed, devolved into a sensualism.[59]

Knowledge and the Arabic Language

The relationship between knowledge and its object is therefore a sliding process of telescoping and focusing. But knowledge does not exist as such. It is never disembodied and separated from the medium of signification, for 'we name in as much as we know, and we indicate sense in as much as we name'.[60] Signification is the evidence as well as the mechanism of knowledge, and in the nominalistic sense under discussion, signification is the unamibiguous indication of the object by its conceptual subsumption in Porphyry's Tree for those who subscribed to an Aristotelian epistemology, or alternatively for those who did not so subscribe, by the word which designates it. Concept and word are as fully transitive and interchangeable as knowledge; they both repeat in the psyche the sensuous event by means of which the immediate object is apprehended. This is why the notion of correspondence (*muṭābaqa*) is central to and paramount in the very highly elaborate theory of signification within which the epistemology of Arabic thought is embedded. It is correspondence, and the various linguistic means by which correspondence is dislocated, that constitutes the subject matter of the theory of signification in Arabic thought.[61]

Correspondence as the touchstone of signification and the transitiveness of all locations of signification, chief among which are the conceptual and the verbal, are correlative with each other as they are with the nominalist assumptions upon which they are based. Alongside the Aristotelian convention according to which concept, embodied in a word, generically corresponds to the object by subsuming it as an exemplar, is the linguistic convention according to which a word designates its object by indicating all of the totality named by the word,[62] an indication as full and comprehensive as it is bereft of accretion or omission[63] — just like the concept encountered above. The concept which is intermediate between spoken utterance and object is based on the subsistence within the psyche of the image of the object[64] — without additions or any other alterations. Indeed, that which differentiates a word from a particle is that the former is meant for the singular and exclusive indication of one intention — being a noun if this intended meaning were not conjoined with time, otherwise being a verb.[65] It can be said that the grammatical definition runs parallel to the logical doctrine of definition, for both take due consideration of exhaustiveness of description (generic subsumption, *jam'*) as well as of the limits of applicability (specific difference, *man'*). Some grammarians explicitly underlined this point,[66] although others considered the employment of logical analogies and terminology inadmissible in grammar.[67] The ever clear-headed Ibn Taimiyya drew up a list of equivalences between linguistic and philosophical terms of use in the theory of signification.[68]

The main point animating the theory of signification is the univocality and unambiguity of signification as the normative state of knowledge and expression, and as the practical paradigm in relation to which all other, figurative and other, modes of knowledge and expression are to be scrutinised and assessed. It is perhaps this which led to the dubious status accorded to translation by such Arabic thinkers as gave it consideration and regarded it as, at best, a figurative approximation: language operates by the correspondence of words and particulars, and the particulars of one people, such as varieties of foodstuffs, do not necessarily correspond to what is available to another.[69] After all, language is based on *waḍ'*, the specific positing of a particular phonemic configuration, a word, to designate a particular sense.[70] This holds true regardless of the theory that a particular author held about the origin of language. Three such theories were available — that language was the result of a convention arrived at by sagely epigones, that it was directly instructed to mankind by God, and that it involved onomatopoiec and cognate operations.[71] In all cases, even the last and least widespread,[72] Ibn Sīnā correctly observed that the ultimate conception amounts to the same: that language is posited and dictated, for 'it is not in the nature of a noun to be a noun', but rather becomes one in the process of designating an object by means of it.[73] Once this positing, *waḍ'*, of a word and a particular object is accomplished and once it enters into general use and facilitates the communication that is necessary for humanity for whose sake language is posited, derivatives become possible, according to definite rules based on association and similar naturalistic criteria. A temporal process is thus postulated, one in which a graduation is in evidence, between the correspondence of particular words to particular objects, and more complex types of relation and association, until language is completed.[74] Alongside this conceptual gradation is one of a phonological nature in which words are derived according to equally naturalistic criteria, especially based upon sonority and the lightness of pronunciation, i.e. facility in accordance with the anatomy of the oral cavity.[75]

This denotative, almost naturalistic conception of language was the target of attack in the polemical pronouncements of some logicians, defending their art against the strictures and superior postures for some grammarians. Some saw words as incidental to logic, a formal art whose exclusive concern is with concepts (*ma'ānī*);[76] their opponents saw this very formalism of logic, such as that involved in the conversion of propositions, to be patently nonsensical.[77] But it does not seem that these mutual misgivings were active beyond the scope of polemic. The object of logic, according to Fārābī, the logicians' logician, is 'concepts in so far as they are denoted by words, and words in so far as they refer to concepts'.[78] For Sijistānī, grammar was an Arabic logic and logic a conceptual grammar which cannot, nevertheless, regard words in too cavalier a manner; perfection is to be had when conceptual logic and the logic of the senses, grammar, are combined.[79] Similarly, Sīrāfī asserted that grammar is a logic derived from the Arabic tongue, for it refers to concepts despite the ephemeral quality of all words to which concepts are conjoined.[80] In all cases, we find words and concepts conjoined, regardless of the origin and sanction of the former in ephemeral sensuous reality and of the latter in the more durable, divine, substance which is the mind.[81] Accomplished knowledge is the parallelism and correspondence between the entities and reality and those of language and the mind, and of the relations between these entities, for ultimately and ideally, just as logic is a mental form, so is grammar, according to Sijistānī, a traditional form, the form of sensuous experience.[82]

Ma'nā is both concept and 'sense' in a more diffuse manner. It denotes both a single representation of a single object or event, or a complex of related representations of related objects and events. In all cases, it is a representation denoting a reality, and is itself denoted by a word, unambiguously in its paradigm, so much so that Bīrūnī (d. 440/1048) criticised Sanskrit for the ambiguity of its vocabulary in which Sanskritists took so much pride.[83] A word corresponds to a sense, or to a concept, when it corresponds to a representation, a 'mental image', and is primarily posited with reference to this representation, not to the reality that this representation indicates.[84] The representation, *ma'nā*, mediates word and object without altering either or damaging the paradigmatic correspondence between them which, by the nature of things, has to go through it as through an intermediary layer. And if linguistic mistakes, such as 'I came to you tomorrow', lead to absurdity, it is mistaken representations, such as 'I carried the mountain', that lead to falsehood.[85] Indeed, some went so far as to advocate the fixing of representations in the mind prior to choosing words to convey them[86] although this position could be said to represent a certain *excès de zèle*, a careless expression which can have no practical consequence. Language translates representations[87] which, infirmed in the individual mind, must otherwise revolve around solipsism; words are intermediaries between minds, but are at the same time barriers between them,[88] for the original sensuous quality of knowledge in its immediacy is stunted.

It can be said that object, representation and expression relate to each other according to the tripartite division of the semiotic event in modern linguistics into sign, signifier and signified. Unlike the modern conception, an implicit iconic quality relates the three terms in Arabic thought, as the foregoing pages have been attempting to show. This iconicity is implied primarily by the paradigm of unambiguity, of pure and complete denotation, of the essential identity of the three terms, which are representatives of each other, although they each subsist in a particular domain of existence, as in the Stoic conception called forth at an earlier stage of this discussion. And while adequation and correspondence are the paradigmatic form of relation between object, representation and expression, the latter terms of the relationship are not always directly correspondent. Indeed, language was said to differ from logic in, among other matters, the use of figurative expression.[89] Indeed, it is the use of figures which is the decisive characteristic of language, and it is signification by means of figures — which, strictly, is a pathological mode of signification — which lies at the heart of the theory of signification, whose main concern thus devolves to the study of the manner in which figurative signification achieves correspondence.

This is not altogether surprising nor remarkable. Paradigms of denotation and iconic representation notwithstanding, the sciences of language are sciences of *'Arabiyya*, Classical Arabic, which is a particular natural language, and not *langue* as conceived by structural linguistics. The sciences of language have as their object the indication of *waḍ'*,[90] the association amongst Arabs of certain sequences of phonemes with particular objects and meanings, and this accords well with the definition of language as the collection of correspondences between sounds and meanings.[91] Divided into lexicography and grammar, the sciences of language deal with singular such correspondences, as well as with the relations between words as are treated in grammar, rhetoric and poetics.[92] And just as singular correspondences are the products of *waḍ'*, so are the grammatical schemata that form the rules of language, which are in their turn based upon spoken experience.[93] Indeed, grammar is, ideally, exhaustively descriptive, as grammatical treatises attest; a verb may well be, as we have seen, a word always associated with time and a noun that which is not so associated. But this characterisation is made over and above the essential description of nouns and verbs, which is an inductive enumeration of the properties characterising verbs and nouns in such usage as is acceptable to the grammarians, such as the noun, for instance, admitting of the genetive.[94]

Language is therefore usage, and the description of language, which is the task of linguistic sciences, is the description of such usage. The sciences of language therefore have as a fundamental task, not the description of the paradigmatic ideal, but of the actual means in which such an ideal of pure denotation is approximated. The major part of language is figurative,[95] which situation is therefore the main task of the actual, if not necessarily the official, description of language; for although language ought to be denotative in a simple world and in a direct sense, its workings are not so. Rather than executing an ideal and instantiating its paradigmatic structure, language as it is actually observed proceeds according to the rules of figurative denotation, quite apart from its obeying the rules of grammar. While unambiguous direct denotation is displaced, this does not effect the primary characteristic of language, which is denotation, for, after all, language is a purely utilitarian phenomenon,[96] and this purpose would certainly have been defeated if its denotative function were derogated from exclusive primacy. It is this concern with denotation and unambiguity (albeit in the context of Qur'ānic exegesis) that led Abū Isḥāq al-Isfarā'īnī (d. 418/1027) to adopt the position, which appears to have been unique in Arabic thought, of maintaining that there is no use of figurative expression in Arabic, and that even metaphorical use is based on the same sort of *waḍ'* as literal meaning, so that the designation of a brave man by the word 'lion' was originally posited in the same sort of way as 'lion' came to designate a particular feline.[97] Figurative expression is, indeed, not original to language, but is somewhat supererogatory, connected with the increasing complexity of life when literal denotation and singular expression have been surpassed.[98] Yet the fact that the figurative mode of denotation is not original to language does not make it any less actual. Rarely is expression literal,[99] and the Qur'ān itself is the greatest depository of figures, the lack of attention to which, according to a Mu'tazilite grammarian, is the prime condition for anthropomorphism.[100]

Figurative expression is an indirect form of denotation which does not alter the essential paradigm of expression, that of direct and unambiguous denotation, in which the levels at which a thing exists — utterance, representation and immediate phenomenal existence — stand for each other and correspond to each other in an iconic directness. Sense is divided into that representation originally posited for a word, *ḥaqīqa*, and that which is not part of the originally posited meaning of the word, *majāz*, figurative sense. This carries over the word into a semantic domain related by some feature to that of the original representation for which the word is posited by its *waḍ'*.[101] And just as the primacy of the signified, of the *denotatum*, is clear in the relation of correspondence linking object with concept and word, so is the signified equally primary when the object is removed from consideration and scrutiny is directed to the relation of representation (concept) and expression. The latter should correspond to the former in order for expression to have been truly fulfilled, because the representation itself has become the object of a secondary representation which is linguistic expression.

Despite the emphasis placed by some on the primacy of expression in the process of signification, the 'balance' and appropriateness of representation and expression, of word and concept[102] was central to Arabic poetics. After all, eloquence (*balāgha*) amounts to no more or less than the correspondence of word and concept,[103] of representation and expression, and the most accomplished expression is that which achieves this correspondence most fully and perfectly. And although poetic evaluation was based on the principle that representations are both common and limited,[104] being in fact *topoi* (much like those dominant in medieval Latin literature),[105] so that expression emerges largely as an art and skill of an ornamental type according to certain normative principles,[106] these principles of classicism were ultimately beholden to the principle of representation, for eloquence was a concept denoting excellence of expression, and this in turn was seen to have depended on the clarity with which the various aspects of the concept were rendered.[107] Representation is therefore in effect and in practice, primary, and expression derivative. Indeed, sophistical argumentation was seen to have been successful precisely because in it words are given primacy over meanings and substituted for them.[108] If a concept is chosen a word which is most specific to it, most revealing of it, and most concordant with it, in addition to ennobling it, among other things, it is considered the most accomplished of expressions.[109] And what, after all, is it that makes recourse to metaphorical expression desirable except for the superior elucidation metaphor affords, a superiority in representation which alone warrants discarding the literal sense of the word?[110] Figures ennoble meanings, but figures are no more than so many ways of ennobling the self same meaning, a mode of rendition at the base of which is a fundamental verisimilitude.[111]

The centrality of representation in signification, and its primacy with respect to expression, underlay the classicist emphasis on the form of the composition of discourse. It was this centrality which was deployed and developed by 'Abd al-Qāhir al-Jurjānī (d. 471/1078–9) in his theory of poetic and Qur'ānic composition, one of the most sustained, refined, rigorous and durable attempts to construct a theory of the production of meaning in discourse and of discourse analysis in any language and at any time.[112] To concepts is due the obedience of words, for they are their masters;[113] words are but the receptacles of concepts,[114] and whoever believes the contrary is simply one who believes that, because he notices that concepts are engendered in his mind only after words have reached his ears, these words must necessarily be primary.[115] Composition is order; it is order which obtains from the connection between the concepts to which words in composition relate,[116] and order endowed by the grammatical and rhetorical rules according to which the composition of words into discourse take place.[117] But the arrangement of words in discourse, inextricably connected to grammatical rules as it is, runs parallel to the composition and sequence of concepts in the psyche, which are themselves ordered according to the requirements of the mind.[118] But at this point Jurjānī went to the limit of the theory of representation and brushed against the paradigmatic confines of Arabic thought in this region, for he saw rhetorical figures to have constituted an autonomous sphere of signification which brought into play concepts such as the 'image of meaning', and the 'meaning of meaning'.[119] But this second order of signification, and its operational autonomy in the analysis of discourse, was theoretically conceived to have been ultimately reducible, albeit at a remove, to correspondent signification; it was conceived but instrumentally.

Figurative sense is elicited by the intersection of the posited and original *denotatum* of one word with those of other words. Words can be said to denote concepts in three senses — by correspondence, by implication and by association,[120] to which some, of a more catholic disposition and less beholden to terminological concensus and more accountable to linguistic reality, might add matters such as opposition.[121] Figurative expression is the transitive use (*isti'māl muta'addī*) of the concept posited for a word with the aid of an associative sign (*qarīna*).[122] Association and implication indicate the relation between the originally posited concept, *ḥaqīqa*, and ones imputable by the transitive use of the word conjoined to this original concept,[123] semantic relations which were well catered for by grammatical structures.[124] Figurative use could thus have been said to be primarily a manipulation of the semantic fields of words in which concept indicates concept.[125] And it is on the basis of these conceptions that was constructed the vast and exceedingly rich body of writing on metaphor, metonymy, analogy, synecdoche and other figures,[126] a body of conception so pervasive and conceptually so central to Arabic discourse and the theory of such discourse that even a purist such as Ibn Rushd employed its main conceptions and typologies of meaning structure and discursive composition as descriptions of semantic pathology leading to sophism, in the unlikely location of an epitome of Aristotle.[127]

Figurative usage is, as we saw, a manipulation of the original order of language. This manipulation does not in any way alter the original design, that of unambiguous denotation, but is deliberate ambiguity designed the better and more fully to accomplish the intended tenor of a denotation in a discursive content. The grounds and criteria of figurative use are entirely rhetorical; they are embellishments not grounded in the structure of language or its original design. Indeed, that metonymy is more eloquent than a straightforward statement, and that allusion is preferable to indication, is not something that involved conceptual alteration, but was simply a more emphatic form of statement.[128] The techniques of embellishment which involved the use of the vast body of figures deriving from the transference of meanings and the displacement of indication from the realm of *ḥaqīqa* to that of *majāz* depended entirely on the intent of the speaker, which lay at the heart of language which is, after all, a means by which people express concepts they intend.[129] Poetical rhetoric deals with the incidental embellishment of discourse, and is but a set of rules for acquiring the requisite skills.[130] Much like the quasi-proposition of the Stoics,[131] statements involving figures, and these comprise as we saw the bulk of language, involve a heightened tonality of expression, rather than a displacement of meaning. A metaphorical statement is not a false one necessarily, nor is falsity concomitant with it. It is a pleasurable one, based on the truth of the metaphor,[132] i.e. its emphasis of the original sense, the heightened tone of its impression.

Signification, whose substance and medium is language, is therefore curiously not a linguistic phenomenon, but a manipulation of language by extra-linguistic agencies, primarily the speaker. The bulk of signification, with the exception of that desired but rarely achieved by the intellectual austerity of some logicians and some Ẓāhrites, consists of affectation consonant with the desire of the speaker and his communicative intent. It was quite a common assumption that the *force majeure* preventing the austere and rigorous statement of religious and other realities was the commoners, who required the use of various rhetorical techniques in order to be swayed and kept in the state appropriate for them. Theological differences were attributed by Abū Sulaimān al-Sijistānī to just this,[133] and Bīrūnī and others explained various forms of idolatry as stemming from the desire of commoners for figural representation,[134] they being naturally inclined towards the sensuous component in representation rather than the more purely rational, to which the elite have a predilection.[135] Similarly, 'Abd al-Jabbār the Mu'tazilite attributed anthropomorphism to the commoners' sensuous imagination[136] — a charge which a late Ash'arite in his turn but less convincingly directs at the Mu'tazilites, viewing the common predilection for appearances and illusions at the root of their dogma.[137]

Commoners only understand by sensuous example and analogy with observable things. This is why, according to Ibn Rushd, God made the Qur'ānic statement that the cosmos was created in time, when in fact it was simply created *ex nihilo*, though not in time.[138] Similarly, Ghazālī would explain the various faculties of the psyche to the commoners by representing the senses as the spies of the king, who represents the rational faculty,[139] a topical representation particularly appropriate for commoners, whose *raison d'être* it is to be ruled. But not everyone subscribed to this theory of the duality of expression. And though both Ibn Taimiyya, who was furiously hostile to any binary truth conception,[140] and Ibn Rushd, who was one of its main exponents, both invoked the saying attributed to 'Alī b. Abī Ṭālib to the effect that commoners ought to be told only that which they can readily grasp, for they would otherwise deny what they are told by God and His Prophet,[141] proponents of this conception had a common-sensical conception of censorship unconnected with an underlying metaphysics and bereft of a double faith theory, except as was imputed to them by the adversaries: for every station of person a form of speech is appropriate and efficient communication depends on the appropriateness of what is uttered in the context of the hearers. 'Double faith' only existed in the context of thorough esotericism.[142]

Interpretation and Symbolism

It was with criteria other than those of the duality of expression that the mainstream of scholarship approached sacred texts, using the linguistic tools whose principles where sketched above for the elicitation of meaning, both theoretical of use in dogmatics and practical of use in jurisprudence. One relatively early compendium of interpretation detailed the various figures common in rhetoric and poetics as the means of matching words with concepts.[143] There was an invariable insistence that sacred scripture not only employed the linguistic techniques of the Arabs, these being the various rhetorical figures, but that, correlatively, interpretation should proceed according to the rules of the Arabic tongue as spoken by the Arabs.[144] So much at least was admitted by even the most exacting of exegetes, who insisted that books are written in order to be readily understood, and that the Qur'ān is God's direct discourse, but that it requires elucidation and exegesis on account of its rhetoric and the occasional density of its message, which itself reflects the grandeur of its author.[145] The task of exegesis, of textual analysis, is the assignation of true, or at least probable, meanings to terms, so that the construction of dogma and the business of legislation could proceed.

The truth of a text, much like that of other objects of knowledge, is singular, regardless of it being fully accessible or not, and not all scriptural truths are accessible, as the final section of the previous chapter hopes to have demonstrated. Representations seek out their original objects, which are then expressed as the truth, and words seek out the original meanings posited for them. Expression heightens the tonality of the concept in figurative usage the more to bring out the original reality of conceptual representation sought out by expression and denoted by it. Similarly, the exegesis of sacred texts seeks out the equivalent of the originally posited sense of a word, the primitive *waḍ'* which is its pristine truth. And just as the *waḍ'* of a word is originally conceived in the conceptual faculty as intention, and just as this sense is one which has a positive beginning in historical circumstance expressed in its etymology (whether this beginning be convention, a divine instruction as when God conferred language upon Adam, or a circumstance such as onomatoepeia), so is the sense of the Qur'ān inextricably intertwined with the circumstances of revelation, *asbāb al-nuzūl*, being an historical account of the circumstances in which each verse was revealed, and thus giving positive indication of divine intention, and hence, meaning. The circumstances of revelation form the topic of a particular branch of scholarly endeavour, and are an integral part of all exegetical effort, designed to elucidate matters such as whether or not verses were intended in a particular sense applicable to singular circumstances or in a general sense. The text of the Qur'ān is, moreover, divided into two groups of statements, those which involve ambiguity (*mutashābih*), and those whose sense is unambiguous (*muḥkam*) — although the precise delimitation of the two categories was the topic of some controversy the context of which appears to have been the attempt to distinguish and delimit areas within which divine intent was sufficiently imprecise in its expression as to allow for the expending of exegetical efforts of particular kinds. Among the verses that have been considered to have been unambiguous were explicit statements of prohibition, punishment and command to such matters as prayer; and among the types of statements considered ambiguous were matters such as the mysterious letters of the alphabet with which some chapters open and which, to the vast majority of Muslims, are secrets exclusively in the custody of God's ineffable wisdom. But regardless of varieties of differences over these matters, it does seem that, in practice, the whole of the Qur'ān, with the exception of exceptions such as the ineffable letters, was considered open to fruitful exegesis, regardless of what portions were considered *muḥkam* and which were not.[146]

Truth, as we have seen throughout this chapter, is singular and whole, and therefore accessible, except for that which is ineffable for reasons known to God only. Deviations from the truth are pathological displacements of a pre-existent correspondence, an original and 'natural' correspondence whose dislocation is the effect of external factors, such as sycophancy or passion, and ultimately, of Satan himself. The Qur'ān and traditional narratives attributed to the Prophet are subject to the same perspective. The truth originally intended for them is accessible by the ordinary means by which original correspondence of word and concept is restituted, in the methods of rhetoric. Mu'tazilite exegesis used this motif with remarkable rigour, and saw in *majāz* and the consideration of verses as figurative constrictions a means of transforming ambiguous verses into unambiguous ones.[147] But the full accomplishment of this rigour was pre-empted by the rigorous demands of Mu'tazilite dogmatics, which prescribed what verses should be subjected to figurative consideration and which should not, with the result that the Ash'arites, dogmatically averse to such procedures, figuratively interpreted verses that the Mu'tazilites interpreted literally and vice versa.[148] But whereas the interpretability of particular verses is dictated by extra-exegetical criteria, exegesis itself relied on the distinction between the manifest, *al-ẓāhir*, and that which is not so. The task of exegesis was application of linguistic and historical techniques in an attempt to obtain the same clarity and unamibiguity of designation, in so far as this is at all possible, in respect to passages which do not have the manifest, vitruous clarity of the *ẓāhir*. Yet the attitude most consistent with the theory of language that has been discussed was, not unnaturally, that of Ibn Ḥazm. He maintained that the pristine purity of correspondence between word and meaning should be rigorously maintained. As such, a meaning or a judgement should never go beyond the word, nor should it fall short of it: that is why the particularisation of statements is inadmissible, for it subtracts from religion what cannot legitimately be subtracted.[149]

Ẓāhir is that which may be said to be the equivalent in distinctness and iconic directness of the real immediate thing. Immediate existence, presentness, is not in need of representation, is not open to interpretation, and can only be considered as *ẓāhir*.[150] *Ẓāhir* is, in a manner of speaking, a substitute for immediate presence, and its direct representative, almost its physical translation. But *ẓāhir* is not a concept that exists independently of a wider semantic universe incorporating its alternative and textual correlative, the *mu'awwal*, that open to interpretation for the lack of definitive clarity and distinctness. *Ẓāhir*, manifest sense, is that which is clear of itself, a word whose utterance encompasses its meaning without there being a factor contravening this immediate signification.[151] It is that which signifies by virtue of its original posited sense which can be recovered by philological investigation, by virtue of its conventional sense such as the technical juristic term for excrement, *ghā'iṭ*, which originally signified a lonely location, and finally, for some jurists who are sensitive to the use of any term in exegesis except for *ẓāhir*, from the result of a justified interpretation.[152] *Ẓāhir* is, more straightforwardly, that which signifies by itself, unaided.[153] In these senses, the term corresponded to what some jurists, after the example of Shāfi'ī (d. 204/820) himself, termed *naṣṣ*, text, the quarry of legislation; both are truly equivalent, as Ibn Ḥazm in his austere intellectuality indicated, and the avoidance of the term *mu'awwal* was an added bonus.[154] Manifest content as *ẓāhir* is therefore also that which is liable to interpretation, being open to more than one visibly possible sense, such as an original and a nomothetic sense, or senses equally possible to the mind or senses possible because of synonymy.[155] But in all such instances, the competence of exegesis is fully comprehended by philological methods which ascend from simple lexicography and history to complex rhetorical investigation and the resolution of ambiguities — such was seen to be the primary task of exegesis,[156] though exegetical labour normally commenced with *asbāb al-nuzūl*.[159] But then this last was an historical discipline whose stock-in-trade was philological. In all cases, and whatever the philological discipline involved, exegetical work in the sense under discussion had as its central task the recovery of an original meaning, an original intention, the treatment of words as signifying without evoking anything:[158] the full recovery of sense, without residue, without accretion.

Correlation with the distinction between manifest and ambiguous denotation is one between *tafsīr* and *ta'wīl*, both of which designate exegesis, but which stand for distinct bodies of exegetical procedure and assumption, and distinct positions with regard to the limitations of *majāz*. This exponents of esotericist *ta'wīl* took as extending to the limits of expression, in which textual statements exemplify and typify a discourse unconnected with the manifest statement except by allegory. Some preferred the position that *tafsīr* referred to philological procedures: lexicographical and historical considerations (*asbāb al-nuzūl*, the sequence of Qur'ānic chapters and the abrogation, *naskh*, by later ones of earlier but contradictory statements and related matters) of the text. Others, such as Māturīdī, saw in *tafsīr* any interpretation which could be said to have been conclusively established to the degree that its author is prepared to take an oath on its veracity.[159] Thus *tafsīr* would be applied to *naṣṣ* or *ẓāhir*, depending on terminological commitment, and would refer to textual exegesis having as its exclusive aim the determination of sense intended by the literal utterance, but without going beyond the bounds of what we have seen to be ordinary and acceptable displacements of sense made for rhetorical effect.

In all cases, probable and certain, exegesis involves the recovery of original intended sense, and establishes a correspondence between utterance and meaning, between word and concept, between expression and representation. Rare were the occasions which saw practical consequence, or even forthright assent, to Ibn Ḥazm's exigent demand that the lexical-historical sense of the manifest content should alone suffice to determine the original intent of God (or of Muḥammad in the case of narrative traditions), and that any interpretation on the basis of figures should in itself have been manifestly signalled by the authority of either another text, or a legitimate consensus or of sensuous necessity in cases of the patent absurdity of a literal interpretation.[160] *Ta'wīl*, which is generally made to stand for departures from the lexical and historical, was generally considered to have been admissible, and was dealt with by the setting of conditions for its legitimate operation. Generally speaking, these involved the adherence by these operations to rhetorical figures attested in Arabic, and, in more elaborate interpretations, their being based on clear and explicit premisses.[161] Indeed, even the Ḥanbalites attributed to Ibn Ḥanbal the *ta'wīl* of three prophetic narrative traditions, and though this is based on the testimony of Ghazālī,[162] who related it on the authority of Ḥanbalites contemporary with him and who breathed the highly sophisticated Ḥanbalism, close in certain respects to Mu'tazilism, of Abū Ya'lā (d. 485/1066) and Ibn 'Aqīl (d. 513/1119), it is attested in different contexts.[163] *Ta'wil* is the generic term that covers all hermeneutical procedures. Like all such procedures, its task is the recovery of the original *waḍ'*; like the origin of language, it seeks out the original circumstance, and hence the original intention, and posits it as sense. The meaning of a statement is the revival of its beginning, a recovery of the origin.

The original intent recovered by exegesis was only rarely said to indicate a reality totally distinct from that explicitly denoted or connoted by the letter of the text. The underlying reality, *bāṭin*, the esoteric, for those to whom it was admissible, is an order of truth distinct from, and truer than, the truth as conveyed by the linguistic medium of the text, whose stock-in-trade is the procedures one employs in history, lexicography and the rhetorical figures prevalent amongst Arabs and employed in the Qur'ān. Truth is one and indivisible, and the reason why an exoteric order of utterance is called for is not, as we have seen, an epistemological matter, but was a sociological, indeed a political concern with the distribution and custody of knowledge which will be considered later on in this book.[164] At the interface between esoterism and exoterism are texts whose interpretation is called for by the patent absurdity to the mind of their content,[165] but whose contents cannot as such be denied because of their sanctity, such as the existence of a chthonian order of good and evil spirits known as the *jinn*,[166] or the paternity of God to Jesus.[167] Indeed, Ghazālī's rigorous analysis of the text of the Gospels with view to establishing the humanity of Jesus and denying his divinity, without recourse to Qur'ānic authority in his argumentation, is a prime example of the use to which such conceptions were put.[168]

Beyond this interface, and beyond linguistic techniques, lies a different sort of correspondence, one which accords primacy to an esoteric sense, and which derogates linguistic expression to the status of a representation, for commoners, of an ulterior intention. The exoteric statement represents the esoteric as in a rhetorical figure not normally admissible, that of allegory and, indeed, for some, as an enigma as an obscure allegory.[169] This held in the famous, and often misconstrued, position of Ibn Rushd,[170] notwithstanding his admission of numerous passages in holy texts whose meaning he held to have been readily and immediately present in the letter, and whose interpretation is readily accessible to *ta'wīl* on the basis of Arabic rhetorical principles, or already accomplished by the infallible concensus.[171] Ibn Rushd's argument that 'truth does not contradict truth', that the truth as unravelled by the trained mind and as stated in sacred texts is concordant,[172] may resemble a 'double faith' position. But it is one definitively attuned to the conception that such faith was not really a matter of 'faith', but concerned carriers of forms of the same faith, or rather of interpretations of the same statement whose truth is conceded, on faith, by all. That truth is multivocal, for Ibn Rushd does not imply that it is not one and indivisible. Ibn Rushd's five-fold classification of texts on the basis of their accessibility to truth and of the techniques of achieving correspondence with the original intent (which is the truth) is geared towards the recovery, or the impossibility thereof, of this original intent, and contains one of the most comprehensive statements of the question of figures, ulterior truths and interpretation in Arabic thought.[173] Philosophy does not only supplement textual truth, but amplifies it by recovering another original intention of the text.[174] This recovery is one which uses a particular mode of expression; it does not propose a truth anterior to, and incompatible with, the sensuous display suitable for the intellect and disposition of the commoners, but merely unravels a mode of expression more apposite to the truth as conceived by the intellectuals versed in philosophy. Truth is stratified, but it is yet one, manifested in three forms: demonstrative, dialectical (that of theology) and rhetorical (of the commoners). These three are but forms of expression, each deriving from a particular manner in which it was ascertained.[175] That Ibn Rushd employed the term *bāṭin* does not make him an esotericist in the mould of the pro-Shī'ite melodrama for the construal of Islamic philosophy,[176] and the stratification of the carriers of knowledge is at once a social one and one which manifestly proceeds in accordance with the principles of textual interpretation, not of esotericist decoding.

In comparison with thorough-going esotericism, Ibn Rushd was relatively modest. For whereas he wanted to ascertain the truths of philosophy in the domain of scripture with the aid of the pure intelligence, adherents to allegorical esotericism wanted to substitute for the entirety of the literal text another, anterior and superior one, established not with the aid of the unaided intelligence, but of a scriptural authority distinct from that which is exoterically manifest, and this was not a point that was lost on the more orthodox, hence the polemics, persecutions and cognate actions. Without professing esotericism, the whole of Sunnite Islam long employed what is, technically, a thorough allegorical method, and that was the typological interpretation of pre-Islamic sacred history, the history of pre-Islamic religions.[177] With the exception of the history of pre-Islamic evil such as that of Cain's progeny, the history of Adam, Moses, Abraham, Jesus and other recognised prophets was a pre-history of Islam, a sort of repeated proto-Islamism which culminated and ended with the revelation of Muḥammad. Adam was called, by God Himself, Abū Muḥammad. The Ka'ba was founded by Adam and refounded by Abraham. Friday was the day of the completion of creation and will be the last day of the world. Apocalypse and the prior advent of the Messiah, al-Mahdī, are acts which recapitulate and repeat previous events of divine history. Indeed, it could be said that the whole of history is a mere recapitulation of fate as it pre-existed in the knowledge of God and in the register of fate, *al-lawḥ al-maḥfūẓ*, the tablet upon which God's commands were registered before creation.[178] Typology could not but have been admissible: not only is it premised on the existence of an essentially invariant *waḍ'* (scriptures), but is, like Ibn Rushd's assumptions, based on the belief that the letter of all legitimate holy scripture does not involve untruth. The Torah cannot err; hence the possibility, and, indeed, the necessity of its typological interpretation. Similarly, the Qur'ānic statements on God's omniscience cannot know particulars, but yet is not its contrary: hence interpretation is necessary with a view to demonstrating an inner unity.[179] If the conclusion of the exegetical and irenical effort was that an allegory is involved, this is purely incidental to the impulse of the argument, for the split between sense and reference is not here, as in allegory, irreparable and absolute. The counterpart in exegesis is the conception of *naskh*: two contradictory statements, neither of which can be false, lead to the solution that the one abrogated the other, without invalidating its truth.

This was the case despite specific interdictions on the interpretation of *khabar*, narrative accounts such as those accounts of revelation history in the Qur'ān and prophetic tradition.[180] And though typological interpretation of prophetic history is not, technically speaking, allegory, *ta'wīl*, it does share a feature of allegory, for it is the substitution of one term for another one without there being a relationship of necessary designation between them. But whereas typological interpretation does not contravene existing dogma, attempts at the application of allegorical interpretation to all aspects of the sacred text do. Moreover, unlike the allegories of Ibn Rushd, it claims a higher authority which displaces that of the sacred text, and claims this authority in the aid of dogmas extrinsic to the content of the scripture. Words in the text, very much as in the Philonic beginning of allegorical exegesis,[181] are symbols of underlying truths. But whereas Philo, like Ibn Rushd, chose philosophical concepts to underlie the symbols inscribed in the text, true esotericists chose other concepts but employed the same method, that of matching individual symbols with individual underlying esoteric truths. It may come as a surprise to learn that the esotericist Ismā'īlīs denied that rhetorical figures were admissible in the text of the Qur'ān,[182] so that its *ẓāhir*, accessible to those not initiated into the sect, is to be literally taken. Similarly, one of the foremost representatives of the other major esotericist stance, Ibn 'Arabī the esotericist mystic, adhered to the Ẓāhirite doctrine in which anything but literal interpretation of the Qur'ān is inadmissible. But this is perhaps not as surprising as it may seem, and any surprise will probably have been occasioned by an implicit orientalist assumption of the adherence of esotericists to 'reason' or 'inwardness' and the orthodox to 'belief' or 'authority'. It appears that denying the commoners the right to speculate is correlative with the strict authority of esotericist interpretation. The master of an esotericist sect is endowed with an oracular vision which is not merely a private vision, but is of such cosmic significance as could credibly be claimed and enforced by such a master, and such credibility can only be had in a definite institutional setting, arrogating to the master a credibility whose fullness is only matched by the acceptance it receives from lower creatures.[183]

Ghazālī stressed the fact that Ismā'īlī esotericist interpretation rested on the authority of the Imām, and emphasised the denial by the Ismā'īlīs of the authority of reason in matters of religion.[184] Ibn 'Arabī did not take the trouble of trying to deny that the inner truths he claimed for the manifest utterances of the sacred text were based on his own revelation, and that the gnosis of the mystic is the highest and most divinely-inspired of all knowledge;[185] he even claimed that a saint had the right to disqualify any prophetic tradition which is not properly established by mystical revelation.[186] The *ẓāhir* not only constitutes a method of delivery appropriate for the commoners, i.e. those who have not been initiated into the secrets of the esotericist sect or of the mystical way. It is, most pronouncedly in the case of esotericist Shī'ite sects like the Ismā'īlīs (albeit only rarely the subject of explicit mention),[187] the custodian of the secrets of the faith by *taqiyya*, prudential dissimulation, which both protects the unorthodox from persecution in periods of turmoil, and restricts the circle of the privileged initiates in periods of ascendancy, as during the time of the Fatimid caliphate. But behind the *ẓāhir*, and on the authority of an alternative source of dogma, the Ismā'īlīs and the esotericist mystics discovered an original sense composed of philosophical, cosmological and theosophical concepts akin to the Eastern Neo-Platonism associated with Sabean beliefs and certain Manichean concepts. These were combined with magical and other concepts associated with the name of Hermes and pervasive in the Near East and elsewhere in Late Antiquity, and associated with Eastern Neo-Platonism. In addition, esotericist mystics had in common with the Ismā'īlīs a cyclical theory of history in which the fortunes of divinity, coincident with those of the Imāmate (or of sainthood in the case of the mystics), rise and fall in seven repetitive circles, the last of which is the advent of the Messiah at the end of time, a theory of history in which, especially for the Shī'ites, 'Ali played a very privileged role.[188]

Esoteric doctrines are expressed by means of allegory in exoteric pronouncements, and the task of interpretation, as is the task of all signification, is the establishment of correspondence between word and object which, in allegory, is totally displaced. And just as *ẓāhir* and *bāṭin* are allegorically related, so are, for the Ismā'īlīs, the *bāṭin* and its own *bāṭin*, which they termed *ḥaqīqa*, truth, knowledge of which is angelical and is reserved for persons with privileged positions in the cosmological order according to principles of the microcosm/macrocosm connection that have already been the topic of a previous discussion.[189] Indeed, interpretation is not only seen to have been dependent on the interpreter's position within the sectarian hierarchy and the concomitant access to cosmic and other secrets, but this position itself was the microcosmic counterpart of the cosmic order with which it is correlated.[190] The resulting situation is therefore one where secrets in their full amplitude are available to the infallible Imām only, who is consequently the sole arbiter of inferior truths. But this does not mean that other truths as are available to other members of the Ismā'īlī hierarchy are equally true. Indeed,

Ismā'īlīs were at pains to point out that the considerable differences in the interpretation of single Qur'ānic verses were the result of the differential status of interpreters.[191] This matter was both consonant with Ismā'īlī cosmology and organisation, as with their desire to affirm the ultimate unity of truth. It had the added bonus that the lack of firm interpretive bases which Ghazālī remarked upon could be explained away: why the stave of Moses should stand for his argument, for instance, is neither attested by the mind, nor even by a firm Ismā'īlī imāmic tradition.[192] Such thoroughly esotericist and allegorical interpretation was therefore not, strictly speaking, a textual exegesis, but a symbolic mode for the recovery of truth deliberately occluded, the recovery of sense by substituting for textual elements other, unrelated significations, according to a code; it is the substitution of one authority for another. Ultimately, the original *waḍ'* transmitted through the line of legitimate *imāms* goes back to the direct inspiration of God, but the *imām* of the day is the sole proof of his own veracity.

But if some allegories were patently facile and gratuitous, such as, for the great Ismā'īlī Al-Qāḍī al-Nu'mān (d. 363/973), circumcision standing for the revelation of the *bāṭin*,[193] and as those others parodied as a warning in a special treatise,[194] the most systematic variety rested on the correspondence of the corporeal and spiritual realms, as Ghazālī insisted in a famous mystical treatise which, starting from this premiss, established in the world of sense symbols of superior beings, such as the sun standing for the sovereign, and the angels, in their emanationist capacity, being represented by the heavenly bodies, and then went on to interpret the famous Qur'ānic verse of Light (24:17) along the same principles of similarity and appositeness.[195] In the same way, in a rather less systematic assimilation to metaphysical principles, the Qur'ānic term *'arsh*, God's Throne (69:17) was assimilated to the ninth firmament at the limit of corporeal existence, the eight other firmaments being the angels who carry the Throne.[196] Similarly, Ikhwān al-Ṣafā' interpreted God's promise that the skin of those in Hell will burn and be constantly replaced, to stand for body-loving souls that will forever alternate between generation and corruption under the lunar sphere in an unending cycle of reincarnations.[197]

The principle of the singularity of truth is fully at work here, as elsewhere. A symbol stands for a single truth, whatever else it may mean to neophytes, not to speak of the commoner — a term which, in this context, is of a sectarian and not only a social significance. There was no attempt to weave the interpretation of the Qur'ān into a single narrative, but interpretation by allegory, like that undertaken by means of linguistic and historical investigation, took as its unit of interpretation the single utterance, be that a word or, at most, a verse. This was much in keeping with the conception of the singularity of truth, as it was in conformity with the fact that comprehensive exegesis in its final form, in Islam as elsewhere, could only have been the sum total of partial exegeses, each of which was dictated by a particular situation calling for textual support for a doctrine or an act. It was also in keeping with the fact that the Qur'ān or any other text is interpretatively inexhaustible.[198] It is, moreover, itself not a text that can be so interpreted as to form a continuous narrative which might make possible its allegorical correspondence with, say, a long and continuous line of metaphysical argumentation, a myth of creation, or a moral tale possible, although the correspondence of its verses with a combination of these and other correspondents is possible. This was precisely the possibility utilised by esoteric exegesis. For each truth stood a symbol, and this made possible the encodement of the Qur'ān in such a way that it was seen to represent a prior truth — according to Al-Qāḍī al-Nu'mān, the Qur'ān is the utterance of Muḥammad in its manifest appearance, but its *baṭin* was the utterance of God.[199] It is manifestly impossible to encode a doctrine in a narrative as long and various as the Qur'ān, and instances of narrative allegories longer than a single verse are not concerned with the Qur'ān. Indeed, the exceedingly obscure philosophical tales that do exist in Arabic, such as Suhrawardī's Epistle on the Flutter of Gabriel's Wing,[200] his Ḥayy Ibn Yaqẓān,[201] or his Tale of the Western Wandering,[202] and indeed less obscure ones like Ibn Sīnā's own and original Ḥayy Ibn Yaqẓān,[203] were stories whose component elements, especially persons, places and objects, referred to metaphysical and mystical concepts. There is no connected narrative to speak of in these tales except for the bare essentials that connect one tableau to another, each of which is defined by a concatenation of metaphysical relations. What unfolds is not a drama, but a sequence of dramaturgical arrangements with no compelling narrative sequence, and whose connection is a function of an ulterior sequence knowledge of which cannot be obtained by the decypherment of the tale. Indeed, the code is unconnected with the narrative sequence, but is a collection of symbols each of which stands singularly and separately for a prior truth. For just as in a morality tale where action is a mere device for framing exemplary situations, so is narrative action, sequence, a frame for the display of metaphysical and mystical concepts.

The ostensible decoding of the Qur'ān which is the task of allegory is therefore and in fact just the reverse, an encodement of the Qur'ān in terms of a prior truth. It is a piecemeal encodement of disparate texts on the basis of a *waḍ'* on the part of the allegorical authorities themselves. It is therefore not allegory strictly speaking that was at play; enigma, an obscure allegory, hovered ever at the edges. Decoding by allegory is therefore more appropriately termed a decypherment here, and this is doubly appropriate in view of the dissociation of symbols and the unilateral singularity with which each denoted the truth it represented. The dissociation of symbols is the correlative of their contingent connection to their *denotata*, the results of *waḍ'*, for they were indeed based on a convention not far removed from that informing cryptography, or from the correspondences of use in astrology and other sciences that were studied in the foregoing chapter. Esotericism is the custody of a secret lore or learning which is the key to the understanding of exoteric texts and other objects, such as the alphabet which, for Ibn Sīnā, produced strange combinations which correspond to the cosmic order and the ultimate secrets of which are, as he explicitly noted, not suited for being committed to writing but have to be orally transmitted.[204] Ibn Sab'īn (d. 776/1268) attributed the encodement of universal secrets to the early Hermetics (*Harāmisat al-duhūr al-awwaliyya*), and proceeded to divulge them in terms of an accessible symbolism, reserving more profound matters for oral instruction.[205] And Ibn 'Arabī wrote of one of his treatises that it combined symbolism with clarity, and could therefore be grasped by the two categories of readers, those initiates seeking a sign, and commoners after a common understanding.[206] Symbols are riddles, 'rhetorical enigmae' (*alghāz khaṭābiyya*) concealing truth;[207] a symbol is an inner sense occluded by an explicit pronouncement, and the symbols of mystics are not to be found in their treatises, but in their private correspondence.[208] It is presumably the sort of oath to secrecy that Ibn 'Arabī spoke of[206] which kept secrets intact, making direct instruction by a master imperative, except to those exceptionally gifted with intuition[210] who would presumably then enjoy direct divine guidance. Gnosticism here is not, as it was in an earlier part of this chapter, a type of knowledge, but a method of attaining the truth — alongside the three methods proposed by Ibn Rushd.

It is arbitrary or quasi-arbitrary convention which establishes allegorical correspondences, therefore, just like the arbitrary correspondences that bind the alphabet with the sounds, stars and humours. It is arbitrary in the sense that Ibn Khaldūn suggested in relation to numbers and letters, in that they are not based on a correspondence which can be established by natural or rational criteria,[211] but which is necessarily based on Hermetic and vernacular principles, or on some gratuitous analogies drawn up for the purpose of scripturalist justification — but in all cases on an original invariant *waḍʻ*. They rest on the authority of the imām or on the intuitive and gnostic grasp of the order of things,[212] but are in essence the positing of a correspondence between individual symbols and their individual *denotata*, just as in the exegetical instances adduced above.[213] They are therefore an instance of cryptography, which occludes things in symbols (*alghāz*), or covers them with an alphabetical or numerical notation (*muʻammā*), or vice versa.[214] Such encodement was used in esoteric learning,[215] and, not unnaturally, in royal correspondence, some of which had a formal codified symbolism, but much of which was left to the mental dexterity of the corresponding cryptographers.[216] It was not surprising that divines of the stature of Subkī wrote on cryptography,[217] doubtless in the service of the state, but probably also in the far less momentous cause of veiled criticism,[218] not to speak of the training of the mind.[219]

Some codes were particularly far-fetched, and could well have represented instances of charlatanry,[220] as the author of a Jābirian text thought were those who saw the origins of alchemical lore in Pharaonic inscriptions;[221] some believed that the *Maqāmāt* of Ḥarīrī (d. 516/1122) and the fables of *Kalīla wa Dimna* were encoded alchemical dissertations.[222] But the distinction between authentic and spurious coding is irrelevant to the central fact of the matter in so far as the present discussion is concerned, that the encodement is arbitrary, based on the convention of a closed group of initiates, and that it is a symbolic mode of representation in which the restoration of correspondence between word and concept rests upon the assumption that truth is singular. But truth is also whole, and it is this conception which underlay the alternative type of esotericism, based on the dispersal of bits of the truth in different texts, and not as well-known as the symbolic.[223] This procedure, employed in alchemy,[224] was the principal means of occluding alchemical secrets in the Jabīrian corpus, and seems to have Greek and Hellenistic antecedents in the esotericism based on the arrangement of material.[225] It consisted of dispersing material in such a way that the exercise of the intelligence was concentrated on fitting it together again in order to recover the original sequence — the original order, therefore the original intent, which is hidden by deliberate hoaxes, delusions and snares — making recourse to instruction imperative.[226]

* * *

Knowledge is therefore but a particular type of signification. It is a signification which has representation and the expressive utterance of this representation as its main elements, an expression whose correspondence to representation constitutes knowledge, the correspondence of concept (or representation) to object constituting truth. The establishment and acquisition of knowledge is the certification of signification. The unit of signification being the single lateral chain linking word, concept and object, knowledge is therefore the restoration of the original array of correspondence between a particular *tyxanon*, its appropriate *fantasia logiki*, and the *lekton* originally posited to represent the signifier it denotes. Knowledge is then the restoration in the case of displacement, and the establishment in case of privation, of an ontologically prior, natural, order of things, and is the correlative in the sphere of knowledge of the sort of harmonious and immutable order that exists elsewhere. Regardless of whether the signification is iconic and infused with the immediacy of direct apprehension, or non-iconic, the consequence is the same, the restoration of the lateral correspondence of one particular sign and a particular signified in such a way that the former fully encompasses the latter in its entirety.

The unit of knowledge is thus the single expression, the word or the concept, signifying a single thing in its entirety. This is why Ibn Khaldūn, for instance, found epitomes of texts positively harmful in education, their words being 'over-crowded' with meanings,[227] the assumption being that for each word there naturally and originally stood one concept, and that an epitome abbreviates a text in such a way as to allocate to the care of one word meanings which should be represented by others. The same assumption of fostering was indicated by another author, who added to the technique of abbreviation the indexation of concepts and things, the indication of a signified by implication, such as 'town' standing for 'the inhabitants of the town'.[228] Correlatively, it was advocated that the textual adaptation, when required in preference to direct quotation, should not only convey the meaning of the text adapted fully, but should do so with a verbal correspondence,[229] a sort of extended synonymy. And conversely, a textual commentary is called for in order to manifest concepts crowded together by brevity, in addition to determine the precise sense of words which might have ambiguous meanings and to supply premisses missing in the text to be commented upon.[230]

In all cases, the elucidation of meaning is the recovery of the original comprehensiveness, integrity and lateral correspondence that should normally be found in a process of signification. Rare were the discussions of the integrity of a text as distinct from that of a lateral sequence of signification, such as 'Abd al-Qāhir Jurjānī's concern with the transcendence of singular denotations;[231] and without effect was the theoretical position of Ash'arī that the unit of Qur'ānic inimitability, i.e. the unit amenable to rhetorical and semantic study, was the whole chapter[232] rather than what was actually the unit, which was the verse or the singular utterance. Indeed, it was this procedural tendency of almost canonical status (in practical terms) that was the target of Shāṭibī's criticism and of his affirmation of the integrity of the Qur'ānic text and the strong advocacy of regarding all but purely lexical study to have as its object the concatenation of statements in the text.[233] Rarely was exegesis based on a conception of the text as a whole comprising interrelated units and Fakhr al-Din Rāzī's exegesis is almost unique in this respect and in its regarding the entire Qur'ān as a sequential unit or concatenation of sequential matter.[234] The unit of knowledge is the singular and integral signification. Over and above the unit of knowledge is not the whole text, but the sequence of bits of knowledge, the unit of statements on a particular class of objects held together by an extra-textual authority, which is a science, *'ilm*. This will be the object of the next chapter.

Notes

1. M. 'A. Jābirī, 'Khuṣūṣiyyat al-'ilāqa bain al-lugha wal-fikr fil-thaqāfa al-'arabiyya', in *DA*, 18/6 (1982), p. 62. The author then goes on to make the unfounded claim that the first is of Arabic origin, the second of Persian and the third of Greek.
2. See, for instance, Ibn Ḥazm, *Iḥkām*, p. 6 and see Ghazālī, *Mīzān*, p. 233.
3. For instance, Ibn Khaldūn, *Prolégomènes*, vol. 3, pp. 87, 108 and Tawḥīdī, *'Ulūm*, paras. 18–19.
4. For instance, Abū Ya'lā, *Mu'tamad*, para. 183 and Juwainī, *Irshād*, pp. 15–16 and see Ghazālī, *Mi'yār*, p. 287.
5. For instance, Ibn Taimiyya, *Naqd*, pp. 157–8.
6. Ibn Sīnā, *Najāt*, pp. 5–6 and Fārābī, *Iḥṣā'*, p. 16.
7. Fārābī, *Iḥṣā'*, p. 20.
8. An account of this debate is given by M. Mahdi, 'Language and Logic in Classical Islam' in *Logic in Classical Islamic Culture*, ed. von Grunebaum, pp. 51–83.
9. Tawḥīdī, *Imtā'*, vol. 1, p. 110.
10. See the analysis of S. Yafūt, 'Ibn Ḥazm wa manṭiq Arisṭū', in *DA*, 19/4 (1983), pp. 55–82 and the more general study of R. Arnaldez, *Grammaire et théologie chez Ibn Hazm de Cordoue* (Paris, 1956).
11. Shakkākī, *Miftāḥ*, pp. 207 ff.
12. Yaḥyā b. 'Adī, 'Maqāla', paras. 12–13.
13. For instance, Kalābādhī, *Ta'arruf*, pp. 104–5.
14. For instance, Tawḥīdī, *'Ulūm*, paras. 30–1.
15. On the species of truth, see Sakkākī, *Miftāḥ*, p. 170; Āmidī, *Iḥkām*, vol. 1, p. 38; Ibn al-Ḥājib, *Mukhtaṣar*, p. 19; Qarāfī, *Tanqīḥ*, p. 20 and the summing up of Shawkānī, *Irshād*, pp. 21–2.

16. Diogenes Laertius, *Lives*, vii.43–6 and Zeller, *Stoics*, p. 74.
17. Fārābī, *Iḥṣā'* (ed. Amīn), p. 75.
18. Ghazālī, *Miḥakk*, p. 108; Ghazālī, *Mi'yār*, p. 76; Ibn Khaldūn, *Prolégomènes*, vol. 2, p. 348 and Pseudo-Qudāma, *Naqd*, pp. 7 ff.
19. See the account of Affifi, *Mystical Philosophy*, pp. 6–7.
20. For instance, Baghdādī, *Mu'tabar*, vol. 1, p. 225.
21. See the useful general statement in Ṭashköprüzāde, *Miftāḥ*, vol. 1, p. 74.
22. For instance, Juwainī, *Irshād*, pp. 7, 14.
23. See Al-Azmeh, *Ibn Khaldūn: An Essay*, pp. 122 ff. and *passim*.
24. Ghazālī, *Mustasfā*, vol. 1, pp. 58–9.
25. Ghazālī, *Maqāṣid*, p. 101.
26. Ghazālī, *Tahāfut*, 4th edn, pp. 73–4.
27. Ghazālī, *Mīzān*, pp. 406–7.
28. Ghazālī, *Faḍā'iḥ*, pp. 34–6, 18–19.
29. Suyūṭī, *Manṭiq*, pp. 8 ff.
30. On this matter, see 'Azma, *Al-Kitāba at-tārīkhiyya*, pp. 32 ff. The Church Fathers charged the Jews with the same, and interpreted their refusal to sustain an allegorical interpretation of some Old Testament texts to their desire to avoid such conclusions: Wolfson, *Philosophy of the Church Fathers*, 2nd rev. edn (Cambridge, Mass., 1964), p. 74. For an account of the Muslim position on *taḥrīf*, see Ibn Kathīr, *Bidāya*, vol. 2, pp. 147 ff. For interpretations of the Old Testament with a view to indicating prophecies of the advent of Muḥammad, see Ibn Qayyim al-Jawziyya, *Hidāya*, pp. 51 ff. One author wrote a dissertation on such prophecies based on both the Old Testament and the writings of the philosophers: Ibn Abī Uṣaibi'a, *'Uyūn*, p. 567.
31. Ibn Jinnī, *Khaṣā'iṣ*, vol. 2, pp. 436 ff.
32. Ibn Khaldūn, *'Ibar*, vol. 2, p. 11.
33. Ibn Ḥazm, *Iḥkām*, pp. 237 ff.
34. Ghazālī, *Miḥakk*, p. 73 and Ibn al-Jawzī, *Talbīs*, pp. 2–3, 23.
35. Rāzī, *Muḥaṣṣal*, p. 22 and Ikhwān al-Ṣafā', *Rasā'il*, vol. 1, pp. 299 ff.
36. Ghazālī, *Mīzān*, p. 242.
37. Ghazālī, *Mi'yār*, pp. 65–6.
38. See the comments of R. Arnaldez, 'Comment s'est ankylosé la pensée philosophique dans l'Islam?', in *Classicisme et declin culturel dans l'histoire de l'Islam*, ed. R. Brunschvig and G.E. von Grunebaum (Paris, 1957), p. 251.
39. Ghazālī, *Tahāfut*, 4th edn, pp. 76–7 and see a similar argument with different emphases in Ibn al-Jawzī, *Talbīs*, p. 49.
40. A good general account of the psychology of knowledge is given by Ibn Khaldūn, *Prolégomènes*, vol. 2, pp. 364 ff.
41. Sarrāj, *Luma'*, p. 64.
42. Ghazālī, *Munqidh*, p. 107.
43. Ibn 'Arabī, *Inshā'*, p. 13.
44. See, for instance, Qushairī, *Risāla*, vol. 1, p. 301 and Ibn Khaldūn, *Shifā'*, p. 22.
45. Kalābādhī, *Ta'arruf*, p. 79 and see Ibn 'Arabī, *Tadbīrāt*, p. 117.
46. Ibn Khaldūn, *Prolégomènes*, vol. 3, pp. 78–9, and Ibn Khaldūn, *Shifā'*, p. 55.
47. For instance, Sarrāj, *Luma'*, pp. 453 ff.; Ghazālī, *Munqidh*, pp. 107–8 and Ibn Ṭufail, *Ḥayy*, pp. 60–1 and see Ibn Khaldūn, *Prolégomènes*, vol. 3, pp. 77–9, where Ḥallāj is taken up.
48. Ibn 'Arabī, *Tadbīrāt*, p. 115.
49. Miskawaih, *Hawāmil*, p. 52.
50. 'taṣawwur an-nafs bi ṣūrat al-ma'lūm': *ibid.*, p. 54.
51. Ghazālī, *Mi'yār*, p. 101.
52. Yaḥyā b. 'Adī, 'Maqāla', para. 20.
53. Baghdādī, *Mu'tabar*, vol. 1, p. 37.
54. For instance: Avicenna, *De Anima*, p. 222 and Ibn Khaldūn, *Prolégomènes*, vol.

3, pp. 108–9.

55. For instance, Shahrastānī, *Muṣāra'a*, p. 53.

56. For instance, the reflections of the Baghdadi philosopher Abul-Ḥasan al-'Āmirī as told by Tawḥīdī, *Imtā'*, vol. 2, pp. 84–5.

57. For instance, in the anti-philosophical position started by Ibn Khaldūn, *Prolégomènes*, vol. 3, p. 214, who subscribed to the general position, implicitly and explicitly, in other passages.

58. For instance, by Ibn Khaldūn's master al-Ābilī, quoted in Aḥmad Bāba, *Nayl*, p. 246.

59. Ibn Taimiyya, *Radd, passim*, and see, for instance, Rāzī's critical remarks on Ibn Sīnā's logic on similar assumptions, in *Lubāb*, pp. 15–16, 23, 48 and *passim*. For a reverse position, involving what we might call a spiritualist mentalism, see Miskawaih, *Nafs*, p. 11 of text (and see p. 27).

60. Baghdādī, *Mu'tabar*, vol. 2, p. 122.

61. That pre-Kantian philosophy did not distinguish logical from real causes and principles, *archai*, therefore reflects this state of affairs, and should not be regarded as a 'confusion' — most notably by A. Schopenhauer, *The Fourfold Root of the Principle of Sufficient Reason*, tr. E.F.J. Payne (La Salle, Illinois), 1974, pp. 9 ff.

62. Baiḍāwī, *Minhāj*, p. 18.

63. Sakkākī, *Miftāḥ*, p. 156.

64. Ghazālī, *Mi'yār*, p. 183.

65. Sakkākī, *Miftāḥ*, p. 4. This tripartite division of linguistic elements formed the customary commencement of Arabic grammatical theory. For a philosophical calque, which appears clumsy in its effort for terminological distinction, see Ibn Sīnā, *Najāt*, 2nd edn, p. 11.

66. Sakkākī, *Miftāḥ*, p. 205.

67. Zajjājī, *Miftāḥ*, p. 48.

68. Ibn Taimiyya, *Radd*, p. 25.

69. For instance, Ibn Taimiyya, *Radd*, pp. 49, 55–6 and see the polemical statements of Sīrāfī in Tawḥīdī, *Imtā'*, vol. 1, p. 112.

70. See the definitions in Suyūṭī, *Muzhir*, vol. 1, p. 38 and Ṭāshköprüzade, *Miftāḥ*, vol. 1, p. 130 and see Ibn Khaldūn, *Prolégomènes*, vol. 3, p. 289.

71. For a judicious account, see Ibn Jinnī, *Khaṣā'is*, vol. 1, pp. 40 ff.; vol. 2, pp. 28 ff. For a detailed review, see Suyūṭī, *Muzhir*, vol. 1, pp. 8–45. In an European language, see H. Loucel, 'L'origine du langage d'après les grammarians arabes', in *Arabica*, 10 (1963), pp. 88–208, 253–81; 11 (1964), pp. 57–72, 151–87. This matter had important theological and exegetical consequences which emerge clearly in the Arabic sources, and which are conveniently reviewed by Abū Zaid, *Al-Ittijāh al-'aqlī fit-tafsīr*, pp. 70–82.

72. Pseudo-onomatopoeic considerations were however paramount in Arabic etymology. Arabic historical literature is especially replete with fictitious etymologies. Eve (Ḥawwā') was so called because she was fashioned of a live creature (*ḥayy*), as in Ṭabarī, *Tarīkh*, vol. 1, p. 102, and there appear to be various possible etymologies of humankind (*insān*), reviewed by Nuwairī, *Nihāya*, vol. 2, pp. 5, 7. See the amusing parodies of such etymologies by Ibn Ḥazm, *Iḥkām*, pp. 1123–4. It does seem that the principles of etymology in Arabic literature were similar to those prevalent in medieval European literature — *ex causa, ex origine* and *ex contrariis*. See E.R. Curtius, *European Literature and the Latin Middle Ages*, tr. W.R. Trask (London, 1953), p. 44. It is particularly curious to note the parallelism between the origin of the word *homo* in the fact that man is made of *humus* (*ibid.*), and the derivation of the name of Adam from *adīm al-arḍ*, the soil of the earth's surface, related by Ṭabarī, *Tarīkh*, vol. 1, p. 88 and inserted in popular legend deployed in the *Arabian Nights* (*Alf Laila wa Laila*, vol. 2, p. 624).

73. Ibn Sīnā, *Shifā' (Manṭiq)*, pp. 2–3, 12.

74. See particularly the interesting pseudo-historical construction of Fārābī, *Ḥurūf*, paras., 116 ff., 123 ff.

75. One major example of phonological facility is *imāla*, the conjunction of a consonant and a vowel in the context of particular phonemes on which see Ibn Jinnī, *Luma'*, pp. 239 ff, who also refutes, by phonological argumentation, objections to the conception of *imāla* citing the conjunction of unvowelled consonants in some languages (*Khaṣā'iṣ*, vol. 1, pp. 90–1). See the succinct review of this matter by G. Bohas, 'Quelques aspects de l'argumentation et de l'explication chez les grammariens arabes', in *Arabica*, xxviii/2–3 (1981), pp. 205–7. Although Jurjānī (*Dalā'il*, p. 35) subscribed to a view of the arbitrariness of language, such that the word *ḍaraba* might very well have been *rabaḍa* without this effecting its sense (the verb to strike), it is unclear precisely what limits, if any, are admitted to this arbitrariness.

76. Baghdādī, *Mu'tabar*, vol. 1, p. 6.

77. Baṭlayūsī, 'Mas'ala', p. 83.

78. Fārābī, *Iḥṣa'* (ed. Amīn), p. 74.

79. Tawḥīdī, *Muqābasāt*, pp. 121, 123.

80. Tawḥīdī, *Imtā'*, vol. 1, p. 115.

81. *Ibid.* and Tawḥīdī, *Muqābasāt*, p. 123.

82. Tawḥīdī, *Muqābasāt*, p. 124.

83. Birūnī, *Hind*, p. 13.

84. Shawkānī, *Irshād*, p. 14; Baghdādī, *Mu'tabar*, vol. 1, p. 62. The position that words stood in an immediate relation to the reality they designate was not totally without representatives. See Suyūṭī, *Muzhir*, vol. 1, p. 42.

85. 'Askarī, *Ṣinā'atain*, p. 76.

86. Ghazālī, *Miḥakk*, p. 108.

87. Ibn Khaldūn, *Prolégomènes*, vol. 3, p. 274.

88. *Ibid.*, p. 275.

89. Baṭlayūsī, 'Mas'ala', p. 80.

90. Ibn Khaldūn, *Prolégomènes*, vol. 3, p. 283.

91. See the assembly of definitions in Suyūṭī, *Muzhir*, vol. 1, pp. 7–8. Thus it does not appear at all surprising that the assumption that synonymy is caused by an object having been the occasion of two distinct acts of positing was almost automatic, but not the only explanation: see Suyūtī, *Muzhir*, vol. 1, pp. 405–6. Other aspects of the relation between word and object (for instance, Ghazālī, *Maqāṣid*, p. 42, among many others) are fully comprehended by the considerations of plastic correspondence we have been speaking of — thus synonymy, overlapping, etc.

92. For instance, Fārābī, *Iḥṣā'* (ed. Amī), pp. 59–60.

93. For instance, the exhaustive definitions of Ṭāshköprüzade, *Miftāḥ*, vol. 1, p. 144.

94. For instance, Ibn Jinnī, *Luma'*, pp. 7–8 and Anṣārī, *Masālik*, pp. 3–5. It is on the basis of an initial classification of grammatical 'behaviour' into nominative, accusative and genitive, that the grammatical description of Arabic was constructed — see Ibn al-Ḥājib, *Kāfiya*, pp. 2–3 and 3 ff.

95. For instance, Suyūṭī, *Muzhir*, vol. 1, pp. 357–9.

96. For instance, Ibn Jinnī, *Khaṣā'is*, vol. 1, p. 33.

97. Suyūṭī, *Muzhir*, vol. 1, pp. 364–5 and Shawkānī, *Irshād*, p. 23.

98. Fārābī, *Ḥurūf*, para. 127.

99. Ibn Jinnī, *Khaṣā'iṣ*, vol. 3, p. 247.

100. *Ibid.*, pp. 247 ff., 245. The Ẓāhirites admitted figurative expression in Arabic but denied it in the Qur'ān, where an argument similar to that of Isfarā'īnī is deployed, making its text additionally privileged with a singular literal vocabulary over and above that of Arabic generally (see Ibn Ḥazm, *Iḥkām*, p. 413), a position described as a 'rigidity repudiated by fairness, denied by good sense, and eschewed by the mind' (Shawkānī, *Irshād*, p. 23). Some Ḥanbalites also maintainted this view for theological motives contrary to those of the Mu'tazilites (Ibn Rajab, *Dhail*, vol. 1, pp. 174–5).

101. For instance, Ibn Jinnī, *Khaṣā'iṣ*, vol. 2, p. 442 and Sakkākī, *Miftāh*, pp. 169–70.

102. A comprehensive exposition of the view emphasising word over content is given

by Ibn Khaldūn, *Prolégomènes*, vol. 3, pp. 344–5. See 'Abbās, *Tārīkh al-naqd*, pp. 155 ff.

103. Ibn Khaldūn, *Prolégomènes*, vol. 3, p. 291.

104. 'Askarī, *Ṣinā'atain*, pp. 201–3.

105. On these, see Curtius, *European Literature*, pp. 79 ff. and *passim*.

106. See the comprehensive expression of Ṭāshköprüzāde, *Miftāḥ*, vol. 1, p. 200 and the material sketched by G.E. von Grunebaum, 'The Concept of Plagiarism in Arabic Poetry', in *Journal of Near Eastern Studies*, 3 (1944), pp. 234–53. Not unnaturally in a topological literature, plagiarism was a conception often invoked in poetics. See the judicious account in Mandūr, *Al-Naqd al-manhajī*, pp. 354 ff., which, unlike Grunebaum's account, does not accord the conception of 'originality' a privileged analytical role, it being irrelevant in this context. For a proper interpretation, see Zwettler, *Oral Tradition*, pp. 82–3 and *passim*.

107. See the methodical sketch by Ḥajjī Khalīfa, *Kashf*, col. 260.

108. Ibn Rushd, *Safsaṭa*, pp. 5–6.

109. Jurjānī, *Dalā'il*, p. 31.

110. 'Askarī, *Ṣinā'atain*, p. 274 and Sakkākī, *Miftāḥ*, pp. 195–6.

111. This may have been the reason why the Aristotelian *mimesis* in Arabic philosophical poetics was indifferently translated by terms designating a variety of figures, metonymy, metaphor and others — see the editor's note no. 2 to Ibn Rushd, *Shi'r*, p. 57 and see the Averroeistic specification in *ibid.*, pp. 58–9.

112. Jurjānī's criticism of the purely verbal poetics espoused by others is detailed throughout his work, but a compact statement is given in *Dalā'il*, pp. 236 ff. On Jurjānī's theory, see the sound exposition of K. Abu Deeb, *Al-Jurjani's Theory of Poetic Imagination* (Warminster, Wilts), 1979.

113. Jurjānī, *Asrār*, pp. 5–6 and Jurjānī, *Dalā'il*, p. 271.

114. Jurjānī, *Dalā'il*, p. 37.

115. *Ibid.*, p. 242.

116. *Ibid.*, pp. 304 ff.

117. *Ibid.*, pp. 55 ff.

118. *Ibid.*, pp. 35 ff.

119. *Ibid.*, pp. 173 ff., 312 ff.; in the latter passage of which Jurjānī dismisses the theory of plagiarism as based on the erroneous assumption that one could measure discourse by the words employed in it. But such a measure was a fundamental working principle: how else could one explain that an author of the calibre of Ma'arrī was said to have written epitomes and commentaries on the poetical oeuvres of Abū Tammām, Buḥturī and Mutanabbī (Ibn Khallikān, *Wafayāt*, vol. 1, p. 114).

120. For instance, Ghazālī, *Maqāṣid*, p. 39 and Sakkākī, *Miftāḥ*, p. 156.

121. For instance, Pseudo-Qudāma, *Naqd*, pp. 19–20.

122. Sakkākī, *Miftāḥ*, p. 172.

123. *Ibid.*, p. 157.

124. Jurjānī, *Dalā'il*, pp. 59 ff. and *passim*.

125. *Ibid.*, pp. 301–2.

126. Some of the most accomplished and concise statements can be found in Jurjānī, *Dalā'il*, pp. 45–7; Shawkānī, *Irshād*, pp. 23–4 and the review of Rāzī's analysis in Suyūṭī, *Muzhir*, vol. 1, pp. 359–60. A long comprehensive exposition can be found in Sakkākī, *Miftāḥ*, pp. 156 ff. For an exposition in a deliberately jurisprudential mode, see Ibn Ḥazm, *Iḥkām*, pp. 368 ff.

127. *Safsaṭa*, pp. 27 ff. and *passim*.

128. For instance, Jurjānī, *Dalā'il*, pp. 48–9.

129. See the detailed analysis of linguistic affects by Sakkākī, *Miftāḥ*, pp. 84 ff., 98 ff.

130. For instance, Ṭāshköprüzāde, *Miftāḥ*, vol. 1, pp. 201–2.

131. Diogenes Laertius, *Lives*, vii.67.

132. Miskawaih, *Hawāmil*, p. 214.

133. Tawḥīdī, *Muqābasāt*, pp. 265–6.

134. Bīrūnī, *Hind*, p. 84 and Ibn al-Jawzī, *Talbīs*, p. 52.
135. Ibn al-Jawzī, *Talbīs*, pp. 18, 20.
136. 'Abd al-Jabbār, *Faḍl*, p. 149.
137. Ṭāshköprüzade, *Miftāḥ*, vol. 2, p. 163.
138. Ibn Rushd, *Manāhij* (ed. Qāsim), p. 205.
139. Ghazālī, *Mīzān*, p. 213. A similar analogy was employed by Ibn 'Arabī, *Tadbīrāt*, pp. 132–3 and Ibn Sīnā, *Ḥayy*, p. 50.
140. Ibn Taimiyya, *Muwāfaqa*, vol. 1, pp. 4–6.
141. *Ibid.*, vol. 1, p. 27; Ibn Rushd, *Faṣl* (ed. 'Amāra), p. 35.
142. 'Askarī, *Ṣinā'atain*, p. 141. This is a conception they shared with their opponents: Ibn Taimiyya, *Muwāfaqa*, vol. 1, p. 28. There was a corresponding distinction in early Greek thought, which presumably continued, between censorship as a mode of delivery with Socrates and the Sophists, and the esotericism of the Pythagoreans. See F.D.E. Schleiermacher, *Introduction to the Dialogues of Plato*, tr. W. Dobson (London, 1836), p. 10.
143. Ibn Qutaiba, *Ta'wīl*, pp. 213 ff. A fair exposition of stances towards exegesis in connection with the various theological tendencies, see L. Gardet and G. Anawati, *Introduction à la théologie musulmane* (Paris, 1949), pp. 394 ff.
144. See, for instance, the statements of Shāṭibī, *Muwāfaqāt*, vol. 2, pp. 56 ff.; vol. 3, pp. 255 ff.
145. Zarkashī, *Burhān*, vol. 1, p. 14.
146. Good accounts of the different interpretations and limits of the *muḥkam* and the *mutashābih* are given by Ṭabarī, *Tafsīr*, vol. 6, pp. 170–81 and Shawkānī, *Irshād*, pp. 31–2. On the mysterious letters, see especially Zarkashī, *Burhān*, vol. 1, pp. 173 ff.
147. See the discussion of Abū Zaid, *Al-Ittijāh al-'aqlī fit-tafsīr* (Beirut, 1982), pp. 183 and *passim*.
148. *Ibid.*, pp. 229 ff.
149. Ibn Ḥazm, *Iḥkām*, p. 1064. Conversely, going beyond the word, and imputing to religion what is not of it, includes all reasoning by analogy.
150. Ghazālī, *Faiṣal*, p. 179.
151. Bājī, *Minhāj*, para. 22.
152. Of those, see *ibid.*, paras. 22–5. See also Āmidī, *Iḥkām*, vol. 3, pp. 73–4 and the review of Shawkānī, *Irshād*, pp. 175–6.
153. Baṣrī, *Mu'tamad*, p. 320 and see Pseudo-Qudāma, *Naqd*, p. 14.
154. Shawkānī, *Irshād*, p. 176; Ibn Ḥazm, *Iḥkām*, p. 39 and Ibn 'Aqīl, *Jadal*, paras. 11–13.
155. Ghazālī, *Mustasfā*, vol. 1, p. 384; Ibn 'Aqīl, *Jadal*, para. 12 and Ibn al-Ḥājib, *Mukhtaṣar*, p. 149.
156. Zarkashī, *Burhān*, vol. 1, p. 15.
157. Suyūṭī, *Itqān*, vol. 2, pp. 185–6.
158. See the analysis of T. Todorov, *Symbolisme et interpretation* (Paris, 1978), p. 50–2.
159. See the review of various positions in Ṭāshköprüzāde, *Miftāḥ*, vol. 2, pp. 573–6 and Suyūṭī, *Itqān*, vol. 2, p. 173. Māturīdī adopted the sensible position that *tafsīr*, being a straightforward procedure based upon positive knowledge of the original intention of the Qur'ān, was the task of the *ṣaḥāba*, associates and contemporaries of the Prophet, while *ta'wīl* was the business of religious scholars. See M. Götz, 'Māturīdī und sein Kitāb Ta'wīlāt al-Qur'ān', in *Der Islam*, 4 (1965), pp. 31–2.
160. Ibn Ḥazm, *Fiṣal*, vol. 2, p. 122; vol. 3, p. 3 and *passim*.
161. Shawkānī, *Irshād*, p. 177 sketched the standard position.
162. Ibn Ḥazm, *Faiṣal*, pp. 184–5.
163. Rāzī, *Asās*, p. 101.
164. Thus it cannot be said that for Ibn Rushd, *ẓāhir* and *bāṭin* were related by opposition, as their relationship does not deploy the principles of opposition in Arabic thought taken up above. See comments on this and other matters in a very stimulating article by J. Berque on 'Averroès et les contraires', in *L'Ambivalence*, ed. Berque and Charnay,

pp. 139–40 and *passim*.

165. For instance, Ghazālī, *Iqtiṣād*, p. 212.

166. Baghdādī, *Mu'tabar*, vol. 2, p. 290. Fārābī was the author of a treatise on this subject: Qifṭī, *Tārīkh*, p. 280.

167. Bīrūnī, *Hind*, pp. 28–9.

168. Ghazālī, *Radd*, pp. 8 and *passim*.

169. The whole question of allegory in antiquity has been superbly studied by J. Pepin, *Mythe et allégorie: les origines grecques et les contestations judéo-chrétiennes*, 2nd edn (Paris, 1978) which treats enigma on p. 90.

170. See the comments of Al-Azmeh, *Ibn Khaldūn in Modern Scholarship*, pp. 89 ff.

171. Ibn Rushd, *Faṣl*, pp. 13–14.

172. *Ibid.*, p. 13.

173. Ibn Rushd, *Manāhij* (ed. Qāsim), pp. 248–51 and see Ghazālī, *Iljām*, pp. 15 ff.

174. See the comments of W. Sharārā, *Isti'nāf al-bad'. Muḥāwalāt fil-'ilāqa bain al-falsafa wat-tārīkh* (Beirut, 1981), p. 66 and *passim*.

175. Ibn Rushd, *Faṣl* (ed. 'Amāra), pp. 45–6.

176. Al-Azmeh, *Ibn Khaldūn in Modern Scholarship*, pp. 89 ff.

177. For the distinction between allegory and typology, see Kelly, *Early Christian Doctrines*, pp. 69 ff. For a conceptual analysis, see Todorov, *Symbolisme et interpretation*, pp. 110 ff.

178. On divine history, see the analysis of 'Aẓma, *Al-Kitāba at-tārīkhiyya*, pp. 109 ff.

179. Ibn Rushd, *Faṣl* (ed. 'Amāra), pp. 38 ff., and Ibn Rushd, *Mā ba'd aṭ-ṭabī'a*, pp. 149–53.

180. Ghazālī, *Iljām*, pp. 13 ff.

181. For instance, Philo, 'Allegorical Interpretation of Genesis II., III' (*Loeb Classical Library*, 226), I,I. 1–18 and I,XVII 56 ff. and see Wolfson, *The Philosophy of the Church Fathers*, vol. 1, pp. 30 ff. See Todorov, *Symbolisme et interpretation*, pp. 51–2.

182. Ḥ. al-Faqī, *Al-Ta'wīl, ususuh wa ma'ānīh fil-madhhab al-Ismā'īlī, 1: Al-Qāḍī al-Nu'mān (Dirāsa wa nuṣūṣ)* (Tunis, n.d.) (Al-Jāmi'a al-Tūnisiyya, *Silsilat al-dirāsat al-Islāmiyya*, 7), p. 42.

183. Al-Qāḍī al-Nu'mān (*Majālis*, paras. 83, 195, 220 and *passim*) has left us valuable transcripts of conversations with the voice of the ultimate authority, the Caliph Mu'izz, which indicate the workings of epistemic authority so absolute that the sole response to it was prostration.

184. Ghazālī, *Faḍā'iḥ*, p. 59.

185. For instance, *Tadbīrāt*, pp. 115–16.

186. Affifi, *Mystical Philosophy*, pp. 97–8 and Ibn 'Arabī, *'Uqla*, p. 50.

187. By a free spirit such as Pseudo-Qudāma, *Naqd*, p. 41 and constantly by Ibn 'Arabī and similar mystics in works which were presumably of very restricted circulation, for instance, Ibn 'Arabī, *Tadbīrāt*, p. 112 and Ibn Ṭufail, *Ḥayy*, pp. 130–1.

188. On the relations between mysticism and Shī'ism, see the detailed study of M.K. al-Shaibī, *Al-Ṣila bain al-taṣawwuf wat-tashayyu'*, 2nd edn (Cairo, 1969). A detailed account of Ismā'īlī and other Shī'ite exegesis, as well as of mystical exegesis, is given from a Sunnite viewpoint and without prejudice, by the late M.H. al-Dhahabī, *Al-Tafsīr wal-mufassirūn* (Cairo, 1961–2), vols. 2 and 3. On imāmic cycles, see Ibn Khaldūn, *Prolégomènes*, vol. 1, pp. 165–6 and P. Walker, 'Eternal Cosmos and the Womb of History', in *IJMES*, 9 (1978) pp. 355–6. Nowhere is the privileged role of 'Alī so explicitly brought out as in the secret *Kitāb al-Majmū'* of the Nuṣairites of Syria, where he is decreed to be a God in the *bāṭin* and imām in the *ẓāhir*, whose relationship to Muḥammad, as with the Ismā'īlīs, is one of *iḥtijāb*, occultation. See the text in R. Dussaud, *Histoire et religion des Nosairis* (Paris, 1900), p. 183, and see pp. 41 ff.

189. Faqī, *Al-Ta'wīl*, pp. 53 ff.

190. *Ibid.*, p. 62 and see Maqrīzī, *Khiṭaṭ*, vol. 1, pp. 391–5, for a concise and comprehensive sketch of the Ismā'īlī gradation of initiation and knowledge, in which microcosmic

questions are sketched on p. 394.

191. Faqī, *Ta'wīl*, pp. 18, 45.

192. Ghazālī, *Faḍā'iḥ*, pp. 57–9.

193. Faqī, *Ta'wīl*, p. 69.

194. Suyūṭī, *Itqān*, vol. 2, p. 187.

195. Ghazālī, *Mishkāt*, pp. 65 ff., 76 ff. Compare the spiritualist terminology of the interpretation with Ibn Sīnā's philosophical terminology in a similar interpretation of the same text in *Nubuwwāt* (ed. Marmūra), para. 18 ff.

196. Ibn Sīnā, *Nubuwwāt* (ed. Marmūra), paras. 31–3 and see Gardet, *La pensée religieuse d'Avicenne*, pp. 140–1.

197. Ikhwān al-Ṣafā', *Rasā'il*, vol. 1, p. 137. This interpretation of the text was disputed by Ian Netton who denies the Ikhwān held a belief in the transmigration of the soul (see his *Muslim Neoplatonists*, p. 113). The ascription of this doctrine to the Ikhwān is supported by G. Widengren, 'The Gnostic Technical Language in the Rasā'il Ikhwan al-Ṣafā' ', in *Actas do IV congresso de estudios árabes e islâmicos (Coimbra-Lisboa, 1968)* (Leiden, 1971), p. 183 (I owe these references to Ian Netton).

198. See the stimulating demonstration of the inexhaustibility of some New Testament texts in F. Kermode, *The Genesis of Secrecy* (Cambridge, Mass., 1979).

199. Faqī, *Ta'wīl*, p. 26.

200. Text and annotation to the symbols in the editor's introduction to Suhrawardī, *Lamaḥāt*, pp. 40 ff.

201. Suhrawardī, *Ḥayy, passim* and editor's introduction.

202. Annotations in Suhrawardī, *Opera*, vol. 2, pp. 274 ff.

203. Ibn Sīnā, *Ḥayy, passim*, and editor's introduction.

204. Ibn Sīnā, 'Al-Risāla al-Nairūziyya', pp. 95 f., 97.

205. Ibn Sab'īn, *Budd*, pp. 29–31, 131.

206. Ibn 'Arabī, *Tadbīrāt*, p. 106.

207. Ibn 'Arabī, *Tanazzul*, p. 35.

208. Sarrāj, *Luma'*, p. 414 and see Qushairī, *Risāla*, vol. 1, p. 229.

209. Ibn 'Arabī, *'Uqla*, p. 50.

210. Ibn Ṭufail, *Ḥayy*, p. 64.

211. Ibn Khaldūn, *Prolégomènes*, vol. 2, p. 182.

212. Ḥajjī Khalīfa, *Kashf*, col. 149.

213. See also the list of Ibn 'Arabī's equivalences in Dhahabī, *Tafsīr*, vol. 3, pp. 78 ff.

214. Qalqashandī, *Ṣubḥ*, vol. 9, pp. 250–1, 232 ff. and Ḥajjī Khalīfa, *Kashf*, col. 149.

215. See, for instance, Būnī, *Sharḥ*, p. 100.

216. Ibn Khaldūn, *Prolégomènes*, vol. 2, p. 349.

217. Ḥajjī Khalīfa, *Kashf*, col. 150.

218. Subkī, *Mu'īd*, p. 149.

219. Pseudo-Qudāma, *Naqd*, p. 58.

220. A flavour of this can be sampled from a text quoted by Sha'rānī, *Ṭabaqāt*, vol. 1, p. 168.

221. Kraus, *Jabīr Ibn Ḥayyān*, vol. 2, p. 32.

222. Ṭāshköprüzāde, *Miftāḥ*, vol. 1, p. 343.

223. This is clear from the imprecision of the discussion of an otherwise extremely well-informed authority, Ibn Khaldūn, in his *Prolégomènes*, vol. 3, pp. 192–3.

224. Būnī, *Uṣūl*, pp. 5, 7.

225. Kraus, *Jābir Ibn Ḥayyān*, vol. 1, pp. xxxi–xxxii.

226. See the texts in *ibid.*, notes to pp. xviii–xxx.

227. Ibn Khaldūn, *Prolégomènes*, vol. 3, p. 250.

228. Nuwairī, *Nihāya*, vol. 7, pp. 4–5 and 'Askarī, *Ṣinā'atain*, pp. 179, 181, 187 ff.

229. Nuwairī, *Nihāya*, vol. 7, pp. 183–4.

230. Ḥajjī Khalīfa, *Kashf*, Introduction, col. 37 and 'Askarī, *Ṣinā'atain*, p. 196.

231. Jurjānī, *Dalā'il*, p. 252.

232. Bāqillānī, *I'jāz*, pp. 254 ff.
233. Shāṭibī, *Muwāfaqāt*, vol. 3, pp. 278–9.
234. Zarkashī, *Burhān*, vol. 1, pp. 35 ff.

Chapter Four

The Constitution of Islamic and Foreign Sciences

The foregoing accounts will have indicated that the notion of certainty is very peculiarly placed in Arabic thought. With the exception of mystical solipsism and of philosophy and its ancillaries as a closed scientific system, a case could be made for the assertion that a profound scepticism marks Arabic thought in general. The fact that *fiqh*, as we saw in Chapter 2 above, was a science which produced judgements which, with few exceptions, are only probable, and that not even the Qur'ān yielded its meaning very willingly but had to be approached with the ruses of the tongue in mind, are facts in point. Though evidence has a paramount and incontrovertible veracity, recourse had in most cases to be made to an act of interpretation which restituted the original intention, an act whose result is by no means a foregone and secure conclusion, for the intention of God is ultimately ineffable, as the *'ilal* of *fiqh*, attest. The 'theory of knowledge' to be found in Arabic thought therefore, as distinct from the theory of signification, can find its bearings only within the bounds of this ultimate restriction. Certainty does not appear to be germane to the parameters within which Arabic thought charts its contours; what is more apposite is the practical compulsion which stands in for certainty, and makes statements appear as if certainty were their attribute. This does not occur in the abstract space of the single statement, but has a precise location, that of the register of connected statements attributable to a paradigmatic reference of a practical kind, a reference of what we might call an operational certainty. This register is a science, *'ilm*.

The Structure of Scientific Formations

A science is constructed on the basis of a number of premisses, *muqaddimāt* (s. *muqaddima*),[1] each of which is an utterance pertaining to the topics of the science, and which are considered to be apodictic within the bounds of that particular science. But prior to the constitution of these fundamentals are two primitive classes of knowledge into which all comprehension is divided, apprehension (*taṣawwur*) and judgement (*taṣdīq*). The former refers to knowledge of that which is designated by a single term,[2] or of a singular thing,[3] and in all events designates the imprint of a thing in the mind and its direct representation.[4] *Taṣdīq* entails the addition of a judgement and the relation of one thing to another or of one assertion to another, or indeed relating an assertion and a thing, such as asserting the veracity of something.[5] Authors averse to, or not practically familiar with, this terminology of philosophical inspiration employed a classification which is sometimes parallel and sometimes correlative, dividing knowledge into that which is necessary to the mind, and that which is in need of an artful acquisition; as with the division between apprehension and judgement, acquired knowledge is a judgement involving the necessary.[6]

The class of apprehensions not being in itself demonstrable, it is based upon sensuous or mental intuition — and indeed, the spiritual intuition of the mystic[7] — or upon the compulsion of a testimony without necessary relation to subject of this apprehension, and this testimony is tradition. That a particular object exists palpably, that a whole is greater than any of its component parts, or that fire burns, are incontrovertible statements.[8] The list of matters admissible as innate to the mind can be varied according to the affiliations of the author, as could the components of 'sense'.[9] Equally incontrovertible are matters of general knowledge such as the existence of a distant country, for this is based upon consensus which is not, in what it asserts, subject to demonstration — which incidentally makes the only possible retort, for those lacking in conviction, that of refutation.[10] Both the consensus based upon common agreement, and that stemming from the compulsion of dogma or some other particular distinction, are not open to question.[11] Inductive apprehension, based upon the repetition of associations according to the usual analysis of Arabic thought which is also premised on nominalist assumptions,[12] is analogous to consensus in its conceptual profile,[13] and is therefore similarly undemonstrable with any certainty, even though it carries an irrestistible compulsion.

Beyond self-evidence and the sensation of certainty there is no sanction of empirical truth except mutual testimony which cannot be elevated to the level of philosophical truth, for unless empirical truth were based upon the absolute and exhaustive register of all its particulars, it could not be demonstrative in the philosophical sense of the term.[14] Yet nevertheless, empirical truth, like the truth based on authority, is certain for all intents and purposes, and it is in this capacity that it formed the basis of judgements upon which specific types of action was contingent. In the sphere of law, it formed, as we have seen, the basis of interpretation, for grammar and rhetoric are based upon inductive inference from usage that is held to be valid. This was also the case in the context of such practical arts as astrology, whose validity was seen by some as resulting from cumulative experience,[15] and whose invalidity was inversely seen to reside in the impossibility of acquiring a sufficient fund of individual cases of events that occur as infrequently as they do in the heavens.[16]

The nature of apprehension was the topic of some controversy. Philosophers and theologians saw it in terms of either an Aristotelian definition involving genus and differentia, a description, *rasm*, involving the enumeration of visible characteristics, or an analogical inference, *tamthīl*.[17] This view was incorporated in later theology and was respectful of the philosophical procedures as well as of the theological sensibilities, which would not admit generic hierarchy among things but merely differentiated things.[18] It was this latter procedure which was welcomed by Ibn Taimiyya in what is probably the most incisive exposition of the matter in Arabic thought.[19] As against definition, Ibn Taimiyya declared himself for a severe sensualist and nominalist intuitionism[20] which would guard knowledge against infiltration by logical categories which might compromise revelation as the sole fount of knowledge — an attitude, it must be stressed, which made its author acutely attentive to the conceptual realities underlying terminological conventions, both his own and those of others, and consequently radically iconoclastic. For his part, that other iconoclast of genius, Ibn Ḥazm, preferred to defuse the issue by relegating definition to the vernacular sense of indicating the nature of a thing.[21] Indeed, such was the play of particular concerns, here as elsewhere, that a linguistic scientist explicitly declared description superior to definition, which he did not deny, because it took better account of particulars.[22]

Apprehension and judgement shade into each other; some authors used the former in the most restrictive sense of what is immediately apprehended without judgement.[23] This matter seems related to the debate just outlined and the correlative differences over whether, as Ibn Sīnā insisted, a thought sequence in the mind and the inference of conclusions from premisses is a deliberate operation, or whether it was automatic, as a critic of his maintained,[24] being realised by a providential intervention.[25] Judgement was normally subdivided into the three operations of syllogism, induction and analogy, which correspond to the three species of apprehension as definition, description and analogical inference[26] (to which were added the array of specifically theological and juristic procedures which may be subsumed under analogy very widely understood and designated by *naẓar*, a term of very wide reference).[27] Yet the description given to the modalities and operations of judgement were more often than not employed in the description of apprehension. That the two shade into one another, and that what is an apprehension in one context can practically be considered a judgement in another (without theoretical and explicit allowance having been made for this shift), are due to the fact that the two concepts are relative to the position of their *denotata* in a wider argumentative concatenation, that of the constitution of science from the premisses that are its own, and of the conclusions of one science serving as premisses of another.

Indeed, the principles underlying a science can belong to either of these categories and can consist of apprehensions just as much as of judgements.[28] These principles, *muqaddimāt*, have the quality of apodicticity, regardless of whether this be acquired on grounds of rationality, positivity or convention.[29] They are, in any case, postulates,[30] which are not demonstrable in the context of the science which postulates them; it is they, on the contrary, that demonstrate the theses of this science.[31] And though philosophers did attempt in their mode of exposition to arrange their topical material in parallel with the order of things, such as starting from the elements in the philosophy of nature and from the One in theology in accordance with the two senses of the chain of being, this attempt at a rigorously demonstrative procedure was rare. The extent to which the idealistic aspiration to inexorable serial demonstration was realised in practice still awaits a close study of the demonstrative structure of Arabic philosophical texts;[32] a recent analysis of the serial structures of Ibn Khaldūn's *Muqaddima* concluded that this ideal demonstrative seriality was heavily adulterated, but this is a text which deals with a particularly complex subject-matter and is subject to torsions to which a text on pure natural philosophy is not.[33] Whatever demonstrativeness there may or may not have been, this would not, and neither would other argumentative methods, have belonged to the structure of science, but would have been a procedural matter, an operational mode of logical form premised on the assumption, studied in the previous chapter, that logic runs parallel to the nature of the mind, and that this in turn corresponds to the order of nature. Demonstration, like analogy and other procedural modes, connects the premisses of a science, undemonstrable in the science itself, with its proportions and theses.

A science is not a demonstrative sequence, but a concatenation, which may be animated by demonstrative intent, of premisses, objects (*mauḍūʿāt*) and topics (*masā'il*). In the context of sciences specifically designated as demonstrative, an object is that which articulates the topics which are the subject for demonstrative action by the premisses, an action of affirmation or negation.[31] The object of a science is the region of sensuous and of spiritual reality to which its topics appertain; indeed, every reality accessible to the mind should have a science particular to it.[35] Such, for instance, are number, the object of arithmetic, and nomothetic judgements, the object of jurisprudence. One palpable object could also be the object of more than one science when approached from different premisses. Two or more sciences could share the same object if they were pitched at different levels of abstraction consonant with the flexibility and relativity of judgements and apprehensions, or if they intersected topically in that object, in the same manner as physics and medicine are hierarchically correspondent in their approaches to the human body (judgements of the latter being premisses of the former), or as the heavenly bodies are a location where physics and astronomy, the geometrical study of movement, intersect.[36] The premisses of one science, and some of its topics, could therefore well be taken from another of topical or objective proximity. When a physician asserts that a round wound heals slower than an oblong one, he is having recourse to the geometrical principle that the circle is the largest of all shapes.[37]

The hierarchical correspondence of sciences is one of generic connection between the objects of these sciences.[38] The object as such is not the immediate totality of the visible object, but respecting its scientific aspect only, as we have just seen. Thus the human body under the medical aspect, for instance, is the study of this entity in so far as it is normal or pathological,[39] not in any other capacity. The object is therefore that which is intermediary between the premisses of a science and its topical statements, its *masā'il*, a term which could profitably have been rendered as 'topic', but which could also be rendered by the technical Aristotelian term *aporia* (pl. *aporiai, quaestiones*).[40] Both topic and *aporia* imply a subject-matter, a topic, upon which a pronouncement can be made. In metaphysical terms, *aporiai* are related to the object of a science as its essential accidents; such was the convention not only in philosophical works, but in later theology and jurisprudential theory as well.[41] And whereas philosophical discourse insisted on proper and technically accomplished definition of the object[42] other discourses considered description to be perfectly adequate for the delimitation of the object whose attributes, the *aporiai*, form the main substance of scientific pronouncement.[43] Indeed, it is explicitly stated that, as was the case in fact, the object in all but self-consciously demonstrative sciences is not the subject of deliberate construction; but it is nevertheless identifiable, although its identification in matters such as literature requires much contrivance,[44] literature being to some totally without object, it being the skill of composition according to standard schemata.[45]

Sciences are thus concatenations of *aporiai*, a matter which prompted the not uncommon observation that Arabic sciences were fundamentally compilatory.[46] They are indeed so, not in the inchoate sense normally implied, but in that they are aporetic, although they have fairly strict boundaries to the admissibility of topics to the bounds of a particular science, as we shall see. A science seeks to establish its theses according to four categories of question that pertain to any matter under scrutiny — of existence, of identification or definition, or causality and of differentiation,[47] categories which another author stretched to nine and identified with the Categories.[48] It does so with reference to every topic. But it is not these categories of investigation that structure the science, for they appertain to each and every *aporia*, and each of these in turn appertains to the object. That which constitutes a science is not its method, for the methods of all sciences were mixed, but the concatenation of *aporiai*. It has been noted by a modern scholar that Islamic theology proceeds topologically,[49] and this observation can be generalised to all Arabic sciences, for they each consist of a concatenation of topics which *together* constitute the paradigm of the science: premisses, and a specific combination of *aporiai* — specific combination because some such topics could be common to two or more sciences. Thus the topic 'essence', for instance, is shared by both dogmatic theology and by philosophy. But this does not mean that the discussion of essence in theology is a philosophical activity, although theological discussions of this topic are certainly informed by the results of such activity. 'Essence' is only part of philosophy when it forms a part of the very specific combination of metaphysics, physics, psychology and ethics which, as a combination, constitutes the scientific paradigm *falsafa*.[50]

A science is thus a closed system, bounded by the parameters of its object. This is why it was possible to speak of the completion or consummation of sciences. Ibn Sīnā declared that, at the age of 18, he had sealed his knowledge of philosophy, the only development having subsequently intervened being maturity.[51] He also declared that his mnemotechnic poem on medicine, his famous *Urjūza*, contained the whole of medicine.[52] Similarly, Ibn Khaldūn declared, with respect to his new science of civilisation, that he had completed the foundation of the science by delineating its object and specifying its topics, and all that was left for subsequent generations was to complete its erection, not with the addition of further topics, but with the more detailed investigation of these.[53] Thus dissertation of any topic falls into seven types: the completion of the incomplete, the correction of the mistaken, the exegesis of the obscure, the epitome of a long text, the assembly of disparate but connected writings (and this seems understood in terms of a spatial metaphor, without the implication of synthesis), the organisation of disorganised writing and the extraction of what had not previously been extracted,, presumably from a given body of premisses.[54]

The paradigmatic closure of sciences does not seem to stem from the theoretical requirement of demonstrativeness, it not being in fact born of an ostensible demonstrative structure of science. Demonstration, we have suggested, is an operational mode, not a structural principle in the construction of science. Paradigmatic closure is the result of an historical evolution which is yet to be studied, one which looks into the circumstances that have made a particular topic invite inclusion into the paradigmatic body of a particular science. An example would be to try to account for the presence in theology of the *aporia* of whether God, being a good creator, could be responsible for evil, a matter that generated several responses, some of which have already been encountered. It can be suggested that theologians were engaged in a continuous argument with Persian dualistic theory on this matter, and that a point came when this topic joined the body of *aporiai* proper to theology as they came to constitute a repertoire which was registered, codified and schematised. Indeed, this debate with dualism was not an historical hangover from long-forgotten debates; one recent study has indicated that the most thorough and systematic expressions of the Persian dualistic argument on this particular matter took place as late as the tenth century A.D.[55] It could be shown with further research that a wider latitude for thought existed throughout the early Middle Ages than is normally presumed, and that non-Islamic thinking in the areas of the Islamic states and empires was not only preserved rather than simply wiped out by the Islamic conquests, but it continued to persist and flourish. Even a hasty glance at the *Tamhīd* of Bāqillānī, who died in A.D. 1013, would reveal a consummate debater engaged in a debate and refutation with ideas which were very much alive, ideas attributed to various Christian sects, to dualists, Manichaeans and many more. The aporetic character of Arabic sciences is the product both of historical circumstance and of topical contiguities and associations. The choice of which contiguities matter, and which do not, is again a result of historical circumstance. It would perhaps be useful to approach the history of closures by way of a study of terminology[56] and of the growing systematisation of treatises.[57]

The paradigmatic closure under discussion was only rarely attested directly by its adherents as the structural feature that it is, a feature displayed and made explicit in polemic as well as an organisation of the sciences. Polemic is the exercise of normalcy; it is the judgement made upon something from a normative perspective that takes exception to the lack of normalcy characterising its victim. The principles of a science safeguard the integrity of this science and guard it against the intrusion of theses not belonging to it.[58] This is why any attempt, for instance, to assimilate the science of *ḥadīth* to exegesis or to jurisprudence will only obtain very inadequate results,[59] regardless of the intersection of *ḥadīth* with them — indeed, as we shall see, *ḥadīth* stood to most traditional sciences as mathematics stands to modern natural sciences. The grammatical work of the Mu'tazilite Rummānī (d. 384/994) was logically so formalised that a contemporary declared it to be beyond the bounds of grammar,[60] and it was with such paradigmatic policing in mind that Suyūṭī in his treatise on grammatical theory was careful to declare his unwillingness to admit points that had not been vouched for by grammatical tradition.[61] The hostility to Ibn al-Ḥājib (d. 646/1248), the author of a standard textbook on jurisprudential theory and another on law,[62] on the part of Ibn Khaldūn, of his contemporary al-Qabbāb (d. 778/1376/7), and of the great Ibrāhīm b. Mūsā al-Shāṭibī[63] can be attributed to his paradigmatic indiscriminateness: he admitted into his treatise on law a number of *aporiai* from the Shāfi'ite Ghazālī, which were considered impermissible by his co-Mālikites,[64] a matter which Ibn Khaldūn attributed to his having been an autodidact, and one he considered confusing to students who might wish to use Ibn al-Ḥājib treatises.[65] A strong constituency of opinion in the Maghreb of the fourteenth century, when juristic theory was particularly cultivated,[66] was inimical to the later developments in the field which, starting with the work of Rāzī, imported elements of logic into the science.[67] Similarly, Shāṭibī himself objected to the inclusion of purely grammatical *aporiai* into the paradigmatic body of juristic theory because they do not fulfill the basic requirement for every *aporia* belonging to this science of serving as a premiss for the deduction of positive law.[68]

It was also in this sense that several thinkers rejected the importation of logic into theology, characterising the result as a tangle, an embroilment.[69] This and the inclusion within theology of philosophical topics (including physics and metaphysics) to such an extent that theology sometimes was something seen to have become indistinguishable from philosophy except for its utilisation of arguments and *aporiai* based upon textual topics and authority,[70] was attributed to the dialectical task of the science, which led it to admit some premisses held by its adversaries.[71] But over and above this historical explanation is another, that although philosophy and theology have independent objects and topics, yet they do give occasion to ambiguity due to the communality of certain *aporiai* (*maṭālib*) they pose in the course of demonstration.[72] It was indeed the case that it was theology that guaranteed the survival of philosophical topics after the decease of *falsafa*.[73] At a more arcane level, the Qāḍī ,Abū Rashīd al-Nīsābūrī (d. 450/1058) who took over the leadership of the Mu'tazilites after the death of the Qāḍī 'Abd al-Jabbār, was criticised for his unusual arrangement of material in a theological treatise in which he started with the discussion of substances and accidents.[74] The admissibility of Mu'tazilism into the body of theology was not often disputed in scientific terms, but when it was, it was only partly denied, for though it was said to belong to theology by virtue of its topics, its argumentative mode was special to itself, not resting exclusively on the arguments of authority which ostensibly distinguish true dogmatic theology.[75] Indeed, any science is distinguishable by the argumentative mode which preponderates in it, and it would be absurd to seek a dialectical argument in astronomy, or a logical demonstration in grammar.[76] Perhaps the most spectacular example of paradigmatic transgression, an act of eclectic genius whose result was historical oblivion, was Ibn Khaldūn's new science of civilisation. For careful as he was to assert that the topics of his science were only incidentally shared by other sciences, such as positive law, rhetoric, philosophical politics and statecraft,[77] yet he produced a new science whose object had been topically distributed in these sciences, and whose modes of argumentation were derived from both metaphysics and historiography, whose methods in turn were analogous to those of *ḥadīth*. The result was a satyr without historical viability.[78]

A paradigmatic dislocation therefore occurs when the argumentative modes proper to a particular topic are used in another, as Ibn Khaldūn had done, at the cost of contemporary incomprehension. But this type of occurrence was very rare. More relevant to historical reality was the transgression of the topical boundaries of a science. It could be said that when certain theologians took exception to the introduction of logic into the paradigmatic body of the science, their objection was not directed so much against the informal undeclared use of logic as against its formal incorporation as a topic to be studied in its own right. The topical structure of Arabic scientific knowledge has sometimes been remarked; theology has already been noted above, and positive law and jurisprudence have also been said to be only topically organised. But this awareness has not been systematic, and has not drawn the conclusions attendant upon itself. This structure was certainly correlative with the polemical context of legal theory,[79] and intimately connected with the organisation of the judiciary,[80] both of which matters will be treated later. To this we can also add other matters which are to be discussed later, such as orality of features of this structure which are connected with the technique of education, although the composite character of this technique will certainly cause much discomfort for recent discussions of literacy and orality,[81] although not despair.

Authority and the Classification of Sciences

The topical boundaries of the scientific paradigm are supposed to be set by its premisses, which structure its object. And indeed, this seems to be true to a large extent, at least in relation to systematic intent, provided one is attuned to irregularities and to inconsistencies. After all, history and an historical formation such as science cannot be expected to be logically consistent, but to be more attentive to consistency with historical circumstance and short and long term constraints born of ideology, culture, society and polity. The premisses of the science provide the guiding principles of integrity, and the object can be regarded as the receptable of topics born of scientific and extra-scientific associations which together constitute the paradigmatic, topical and methodological concatenation which is a particular science. That the object is defined, if ever, *post factum* is a supposition whose plausibility can only be confirmed by detailed historical studies which are yet to see the light of day. But the premisses still infuse much of the topical material which is brought into the science by historical compulsion and topical association. And we can well present premisses as falling into two major classes, traditional and non-traditional, which correspond to the great division made by Arabic thinkers themselves of sciences into the traditional, *'ulūm naqliyya*, and *'ulūm 'aqliyya*, those based on premisses other than tradition, exemplified but not exhausted by reason.

This division is adopted here for analytical convenience, and for its adaptability to the purposes of this chapter, and not as a statement of the deeper criteria of scientific and epistemic classification in Arabic thought, and certainly not with reference to the almost Manichean division by modern scholarship of Arabic thought into that part which is good for championing the mind, and that which is bad for opting for belief, and therefore irrationality. It should be stressed that this division is not the one exclusively used to classify sciences in Arabic thought, although it does correspond to the practical division of learning into letters, sciences of religion and philosophical sciences, according to which works were classified in Arabic libraries.[82] But in theory, sciences could be and were classified in terms of varying criteria, a fact which in itself makes nonsense of the standard position. A general work of the seventh century of the Hijra divided all knowledge worthy of acquisition into the seven arts of exegesis, *ḥadīth*, positive law, literature, medicine, mechanics and arithmetic.[83] More comprehensively, Ghazālī proffered five types of classification applicable to sciences. Sciences could be classified from the methodological standpoint depending on the type of authority employed in them and the resultant type of argumentation prevailing, and this accords with the standard division. Closely allied with this classification is another, based on the epistemic principle on which they are based. Sciences are also classifiable according to whether their objects were revealed or not, and whether these objects are necessary or probable. Sciences are moreover classifiable from the perspective of juristic obligation, depending on whether their acquisition is a duty for each and every Muslim or incumbent upon only a few members of the community. Finally, sciences could be classified on the basis of their aims.[84] A system of classifications of a similar sweep but obviously pertaining to a topically more restricted conception of science was proposed some centuries later: sciences are classifiable, in the conventional manner, according to whether they are properly Islamic or otherwise. Alternatively, they could be regarded as either theoretical or practical. And finally, they could be methodologically classified according to whether their topics were established by some form of deduction, were established by the senses or were apprehended by the soul.[85] It was also possible to adapt one of the Ghazālian classificatory principles, as was often done, and divide sciences according to religious criteria. Ibn Ḥazm first of all excluded those sciences he considered running counter to both religion and the mind, such as alchemy. The rest he divided according to whether they were Islamic, such as exegesis and jurisprudence, or not specifically Islamic, being either universal such as medicine and linguistic sciences or of a specific national origin, such as philosophy.[86] Classifications according to purely topical criteria, such as those of Fārābī, should also be mentioned.[87] Sciences are divisible into the theoretical and the practical,[88] or according to an hierarchy of honour[89] or any combination of the above.[90]

Sciences can therefore be classified according to a wide variety of criteria which depend on the purpose of the classification. Such classifications do not have as their exclusive purpose the division of all knowledge into the licit and the illicit, corresponding to that with revealed premisses and that according to reason, as the standard position of contemporary scholarship would have us believe. That a science falls within the category of the non-Islamic does not by implication make it illicit or illegitimate, neither does this imply methodological and epistemological distinction, and the struggle against philosophy is not exercised in the region of science but in the field of ideology, as we shall see. For Ibn Khaldūn, perhaps the most trenchant critic of philosophy and one of the most creative users of metaphysics in Arabic thought, it is not its employment of reason that disqualified it, nor was it its foreign origin that compromised it. Philosophy for Ibn Khaldūn was simply impossible, applying the faculties of the human spirit to subliminal matters for which they are inappropriate.[91] For Ibn Ḥazm, the classifier of sciences according to the criteria of religion, philosophy and logic were sublime instrumental sciences giving access to the realities of the world,[92] despite their non-Islamic appurtenance. And that greatest critic of logic, Ibn Taimiyya, eschewing all but clarity of the intellect and the requirements of reality, declared that tradition (*samā'*) and reason are both methods conducive to science, not in any way being antonyms, as the antonym of traditional rectitude is not rationality but doctrinal innovation.[93] Ibn Taimiyya further saw that there is nothing which renders a particular object knowable to reason or by revelation only, for the modality of apprehension is relative to the apprehension itself, not to the object apprehended. That is why it is absurd to give primacy to reason over revelation rather than respect the specialisation and autonomy of each, and that of revelation happens to be that which the mind has no access to.[94] That reason is viable in some domains does not entail its viability everywhere.[95] This is why Ibn Taimiyya so adamantly attacked the contentions of Rāzī and Ghazālī, and the entire theological tradition of Ash'arism, for what he took to be their abrogation of revealed truths in their call for the interpretation of those sectors of revelation which do not seem to accord with the mind.[96]

As was often the case, Ibn Taimiyya indicated and discussed the core of the problem, after a rigorously fundamentalist fashion. The core of the problem and the locus of contention and of option, is authority. Reasoning in the field of jurisprudence, Ghazālī contended, is not truly distinct from reasoning in the rational sciences; difference between these two classes of sciences is not fundamentally one of the criteria and principles or rules of reasoning, but consists of the distinction in premisses.[97] The term 'logic' ought not, according to Ghazālī, be regarded as emblematic of evil, nor as the sole preserve of philosophers, for it is really a technical name given to the laws of thought,[98] and was the subject of Ghazālī's treatise, *The Measure of Science*, which comprised all types of argumentation and was conceived as of instrumental value.[99] Logic is an instrumental science, like Arabic and arithmetic, and hostility to it was generally confined to the irreligious associations of its name and to its transformation to a *sui generis* undertaking unrelated to the master sciences it ought rather to have been serving.[100] Logic, the fetish of Reason, was not, in Arabic thought, the locus around which scientific distinctions and typologies were constructed. Logic, according to a major critic of philosophy and of the place of logic in Arabic thought, comes naturally to humanity in so far as it consists of thinking beings, and logic, along with natural science, mathematics and metaphysics, is natural to all peoples and is not appreciably different amongst different peoples.[101] The two major classes of science are constituted by the compulsion of two different and distinct authorities, revealed tradition and the tradition of rational sciences unrevealed by a divine agency. But in terms of the technique of reasoning, the two employ components of the same epistemological repertoire under the guise of different names and different sets of convertible terminologies. As early an author as Muḥammad b. Zakariyyā al-Rāzī wrote a dissertation on logic according to the terminology of the theologians.[102] Ibn Ḥazm's treatise performed the same function, avoiding the use of the term *qiyās*, and marrying logical concepts to legal concepts and topics.[103] Ghazālī followed suit and transformed Aristotelian terminology into one understandable and familiar to dogmatic theology.[104] Ibn Sīnā assimilated theological and juristic logical terms to the Aristotelian.[105]

Classified according to premisses, sciences are traditional or positive (*naqliyya, waḍʻiyya*), or else they are, for the lack of a better term, rational (*ʻaqliyya*) — rational not in the sense of constituting the opposite of the positive, but in a sense signalling their extra-revelatory provenance. And whereas the compulsion of tradition in the former is explicit, reflexive and the subject of extensive analysis and study, the compulsion of philosophical tradition, manifested in the almost sacerdotal status of authorities, is no less effective. We may wish to overlook the assertions of the philosophers' adversaries, that they rarely deviated from Aristotle[106] that they rarely deviated from his authority,[107] and that they were the slavish adherents of a monolithic body of teaching[108] culled from the redaction of Aristotelian doctrines by Themistius.[109] But that should not compel us to overlook a number of facts germane to our argument concerning authority, and which are articulated in the context of the teleology of knowledge according to which, as we saw, truth can only be one which was completed, once and for all, in the Aristotelian system.[110] Philosophy and other sciences of wisdom, *ḥikma*,[111] were indeed defined in such terms, irresistible to the nineteeth-century intellectual ambience which still marks much of orientalism, as a search for 'the realities of things',[112] as the knowledge of causes,[113] or as 'the scrutiny of things according to the requirements of demonstration'.[114] But this should not imply a free search for realities, but rather implies adopting the option of adherence to the doctrines of the Ancients (*al-aqdamūn*), Aristotle, Galen and others, who cannot err and who already arrived at realities and causes by demonstration. Without this fundamentalist assumption of a complete original knowledge and an essential unchanging truth, Fārābī's attempt to reduce to one the philosophies of Plato and Aristotle would have been unthinkable, nor the fundamentalist Aristotelianism bereft of centuries of commentary which lay behind the philosophical work of Ibn Rushd: what lay between the Commentator and the First Master in time was but the adulteration by commentators of the lone truth contained in the Aristotelian text. The preliminary task of epitome and exegesis for Ibn Rushd required not only the ejection of such accretions, but also the elimination of Aristotle's own dialectical arguments, doubtless made necessary by the First Master's preliminary searches for the truth and examination of *aporiai*, and before his discovery of truly scientific demonstration. They do not properly belong to the Aristotelian text, the very essence of original purity.[115]

The system of authority of use in Arabic philosophy not only rested on the assumption of one invariant truth that had been accomplished in the past, but also on a chain of authorities from Plato through Aristotle and Theofrastos, on to Alexandria, Ḥarrān, the Arabic translators, on to the Second Master, Fārābī and his pupil Yaḥyā b. 'Adī.[116] Despite the availability of accurate historical information, Arab philosophers constructed for themselves a fantastic mythological history which articulated a prophetic and quasi-prophetic genealogy and a philosophical one, thus linking, as a chain and in parallel, Greek philosophers with authorities going back to the legendary Luqmān the Sage and Idrīs-Hermes.[117] Prophecy and philosophy are of the same import, both containing two forms of a *philosophia perennis* in which discordance, as that between Plato and Aristotle (and in this matter Simplicius and others had preceded Fārābī), was illusory.[118] And indeed, just as language was seen to be the result of a *waḍ'*, so were the secrets of *ḥikma*, the philosophical, natural and occult sciences, the results of either a direct instruction by

God, or else of a convention amongst sages, which secrets were later transmitted along the genealogical lines indicated.[119] And as truth is one and invariant, the genealogy of philosophical knowledge is not a process of development or of improvement, but is the transmission of an invariant in which the past is simply a prior occurrence of the present,[120] and in which the origin is the most complete and consummate of instances: hence the fundamentalist philosophical puritanism of Ibn Rushd and, in another context, that of an Ibn Ḥazm. Genealogy was not a form of historical knowledge, but a mode of authority both external to philosophy and internal to it.

The premisses of philosophy are not Reason, whatever that may be, but compulsive theses and topics in the natural sciences and other fields, such as elements, the void, the faculties of the soul and others, matters which almost naturally demand their articulation in terms of comprehensive treatises and of commentaries, finalist forms of writing which are indeed predominant in Arabic philosophy and natural science. Ibn Rushd's vast philosophical output consisted of epitomes and commentaries which sought to restitute the primitive, original sense of the Aristotelian text, while Ibn Sīnā's output consisted of systematic treatises of varying length and geared towards varying audiences. Fārābī's output, though more varied, was composed in a period when philosophy was still paradigmatically unfinished, but no less finalist for that. Lesser philosophers composed short epistolary treatises, didactic works and polemical tracts, while some important ones such as Sijistānī perpetuated the science by word of mouth, having taught a great many pupils.[121]

If rational sciences are common in their particulars to all nations, positive sciences as are prevalent among religious communities are only generically connected, the prescriptions and dogmas of Islam having abolished antecedent revelations by means of *naskh*,[122] a technical term in Qur'ānic studies which designates the abolition of the import, but not the letter, of a verse by a subsequent and contradictory verse. This conforms perfectly well to the idea of history as not only a teleological process, but one in which the truth is pre-existent from the beginning, at the very least prefigured in terms of typology. The premisses of positive sciences and the compulsive grounds upon which they were built consisted of a body of statements and theses which have in common the quality of having originated from an infallible fount. Not unlike the case we encountered in philosophy, the apodictic compulsion of these fundamental statements, *uṣūl*, is not demonstrable, but is nevertheless fully authoritative, adherence to them being virtually a political choice, resting on the submission to a body of authorities, and exercising judgement, as Ibn Taimiyya showed, upon the basis of this assumption. Traditional sciences are based, according to the very accurate and exhaustive statement of Ibn Khaldūn, on 'narrative relating nomothetic positing'.[123] That which is posited, and which has authentic and legitimate value in terms of nomothetic requirement, is therefore to be adopted as a premiss to which facts of life or of thought are to be assimilated by either analogy or indication. The body of pronouncements considered to be legitimate for this purpose consists of the Qur'ān, *ḥadīth* and the concensus (*ijmā'*) of generations of scholars. The main task of the chief positive sciences is therefore to examine the grounds of authenticity of this corpus and the relations between its components. The sciences of language are also positive sciences, but they are ones based on the original positing of linguistic usage and on the traditions transmitting this original usage. Linguistic sciences, also traditional sciences like the nomothetic, consequently involve many of the same features of the sciences derived from sacred traditional sources.

The main substance and working material involved in the positive sciences were the narrative report, *khabar*, whose veracity is naturally the first and fundamental concern, and performative statements, *inshā'*, in the form of command, *amr* and its cognates; the proper manner of dealing with this matter has already been discussed in our sketch of *qiyās* above.[124] What distinguishes a narrative from a performative utterance is that it is equally possible for it to be true or to be false,[125] or, in philosophical terms, *khabar* is a propositional statement relating two entities and entailing a judgement upon the veracity of the relation maintained.[126] This standard definition, which seems to have been of Mu'tazilite origin,[127] was the occasion of severe criticism on various grounds, not least that it was tautological, the narrative itself being the ground of veracity which is in turn the ground of veracity of narrative, and veracity itself being external to both the narrative itself and the judgement pronounced upon its veracity.[128] But such criticism remained theoretical and had no practical consequence. The one systematic attempt to draw practical consequences from this original correlation between narrative and its referent, that of Ibn Khaldūn, and to construct a system of plausibility which could be utilised to test a narrative on bases other than the veracity of its transmitters, was an impossible undertaking. Not only was it impossible, as Bīrūnī realised,[129] to vouch for the veracity of any narrative relating a past occurrence, the most that one could do was to assert that they were not impossible. But Ibn Khaldūn was attempting to solve a question posed in the terms of the Rāzian criticism of *khabar* by means of conceptual tools proper to the sciences of *khabar*, an undertaking paradigmatically and theoretically, and therefore historically, impossible.[130]

It was only historically proper that this criticism should have remained without discursive effect. For questions of narrative were, strictly, just that, and not questions pertaining to the content of narrative, or to the reality of that which is purportedly related in narrative. Narratives were divided into two categories, the true and the false, and the latter comprised those narratives contradicting 'necessary knowledge' — i.e. common sense — or those running counter to stronger narratives, those with a more compelling pedigree, such as an infallible text or the concensus of scholars.[131] Falsehood is well provided for in the breasts of men, who are credulous, partisan and sycophantic.[132] But in all cases, narratives were taken or rejected on the basis of their pedigree, which vouchsafed or else sullied the veracity of the narrative. The primary criterion is therefore political, based upon submission to the epistemic compulsion of a pedigree without necessary regard to the substance related and transmitted by this pedigree. A true narrative of the past, received from an authentic line of truthful transmitters upon a truthful original testimony, such as that of Muḥammad, is equivalent in necessity for belief and certainty which it generates, to the compulsion of sensuous perception or that of innate truths, or to that of narratives so persistent as to be compelling.[133] A truthful narrative is also one which does not go counter to the concensus of the Islamic nation,[134] this unit being definable according to the doctrinal predilections of the person defining.

The veracity of narratives is a political fact in the sense that it depends on authoritarian criteria which entail the axial considerations of the authority of individual transmitters, the authority of consensus and the authority of narratives so persistent and constant (*mutawātir*) as to render impossible a compact (*tawāṭu'*) of untruth on the part of its individual transmitters.[135] Criteria for the probability of particular narratives which might be in question involving matters other than such as were related to transmission, were normally based on common sense regarding circumstance and simple grounds of plausibility, and were not very widely in use, probably due to not being considered as weighty or even as relevant as criteria pertaining to transmission.[136] Veridic narrative formed a corpus supplying history, *ḥadīth* and grammar (with linguistic instances), and through *ḥadīth*, providing the most important single source of legislation in positive law. After the middle of the third century of the Hijra *ḥadīth* had been brought together into a controlled corpus, almost a canon, of six major collections of such stature that a main one, the *Ṣaḥīḥ* of Bukhārī (d. 255/870), was almost routinely said to have been 'the truest of books after God's Book [the Qur'ān]'.[137] But in addition to these canonical texts, there was a vast corpus of *ḥadīth* which was never discarded. *Ḥadīth* criticism was built on the assumption that a controlled collection, a canonical tradition, was available, but that legislative and other purposes demanded that other traditions not be excluded from the bounds of authenticity, and that the received corpus in its various components, upon which so much rested — political and cultural traditions, law, exegesis, lexicography and very much else — should be treated with the regard that is due to the established canon according to which so much of everyday life is regulated. Thus it is not, for instance, due to the probability of slackness and unorthodoxy that someone like Ghazālī used uncanonical traditions, as was recently suggested in what is almost an automatic reflex in Islamic studies.[138] Uncanonical tradition on which so much stands, and even canonical tradition which might invite closer scrutiny, were matters to be handled with the greatest of care and gentleness, and their unassailability was premised upon their authority, not the guarantee of their veracity.

Thus although veracity was put forward as the cause and guardian of authority, it appears in fact that authority is the main ground for the assertion of veracity. And while this awaits the work of many scholars for its detailed historical demonstration, some indirect evidence can be proffered. For while the terminology and criteria of use in the criticism of authorities were very defined, developed and refined,[139] they appear to have been very charitably applied. When Ibn Khaldūn took the unusual step of subjecting canonical narratives on eschatological matters to a rigorous traditionalist criticism, he drew severe criticism based upon prudential grounds.[140] And while the criticism of narrative traditions continued ceaselessly, especially in the fundamentalist vein (as, for instance, any glance at the writing of the fourteenth-century historian and traditionist Ibn Kathīr (d. 774/1372–3) would reveal),[141] it steered well clear of narratives with a practical consequence, except in the fundamentalist criticism of Ibn Ḥazm. Divines and traditionists did not tire of exhorting prudence and charity; according to one, if criticism of authorities were allowed to become an open matter, 'not a single one of the Imāms will be saved'.[142] Another stressed that even those traditionists who are found to be mendacious ought not to be defamed.[143] Manuals of traditionists and dictionaries of authorities considered weak displayed contradictory opinions of the same traditionist, and assessments of their veracity based upon unconnected criteria, such as reputation and doctrinal affiliation, and which amounted more to a casting of aspertion rather than a positive judgement of prohibition on the use of narratives passed on by them.[144] Thus discretion was always in order, and charity eminently possible, and liable for scientific justification in terms of transmitted — and varying — opinions of the same authority in manuals of traditionists. Charitable and constructive scepticism was always in evidence, and prudent criticism always practised, while candour was only occasionally displayed. But rare was the forthrightness — but not the realism — of Rāzī when he declared that Bukhārī was no clairvoyant, but merely recorded what he honestly believed to have been the facts occurring at the time of the Prophet, and that one ought to have confidence in traditionists but should also be cognisant of the fact that they are not infallible, just like the Prophet's associates, and that, furthermore, it is not plausible that narratives relating sayings of Muḥammad and accepted as authentic could have recorded his very words, having been written down only two or three decades after they had been said — without detracting from their authority or their compulsion.[145] Bukhārī and Muslim (d. 261/875), another level headed commentator commented, assembled narratives with generally accepted veracity, and the rest of the six canonical collections were concerned with assembling those narratives of a practical utility.[146] Equally understandable was the conduct of Abū Ḥanīfa (d. 150/767), whose legal corpus emphasised expediency: his *ḥadīth* standards were particularly exacting;[147] he called a spade a spade.

Thus despite the fact that many traditionists considered their trade to be not a little suspect by standards of an ideal and perfect veracity,[148] the results were so compelling that they constituted the apodictic beginning of all sciences based upon narrative traditions. Once established as authentic, a narrative tradition acquired an unassailable stability and compulsion. Though some criticism of the content of such traditions was practised, it was generally disapproved of in Sunnite Islam, especially if it resorted to *ta'wīl*,[149] for Shī'īsm itself can be said to have been justified by one such *ta'wīl*, the famous reported saying of Muḥammad at Ghadīr Khumm construed as appointing 'Alī to be his successor. A narrative tradition relating an occurrence, moreover, is not liable to *naskh*, for it has to be either true or untrue,[150] matters irrelevant to reports of commands, although a minority of Mu'tazilite scholars permitted *naskh* in certain categories of *khabar*, such as those relating to historical events where accuracy in matters such as numbers describing life-spans is not vital for the integrity of the narrative.[151] But such criticism was not something that altered the content of narrative traditions. *Naskh* effectively displaces one statement in favour of another, abolishing it in effect; one scholar thought fit to indicate that the lexical sense of *naskh* is abolition and transference: when the sun displaces the shade, this is an act of *naskh*, from the verb *n-s-kh*.[152] Not all instances of *naskh* are agreed upon, neither was there full agreement as to what sort of text can abolish another: statements from the Qur'ān can do this for one another, statements containing certain, concordant and constant sayings and acts of Muḥammad (*sunna*), can likewise be connected by *naskh*, while varying degrees of disagreement are in evidence with view to *naskh* connections between other components of the narrative corpus, such as Qur'ān and *sunna*, or consensus, *qiyās* and *sunna*.[153]

Clearly, Arabic thought in its traditionalist mode was not as monolithic as might appear to be the case; indeed, modern legislators in the Arab world have tapped this vast corpus of disagreement in working out modern legislation which is no less orthodox for its deviation from the Ḥanafite, Shāfi'ite, and Mālikite consensus in the immediate pre-colonial period, and have indeed shown no hesitation in musing moribund Ẓāhirite legislation and general concepts derived from the radical juristic theory of Shāṭibī. While adherence to the corpus of tradition was compulsory, elements from this corpus formed the apodictic statements of traditional sciences. Choice within this corpus was fairly open, although there was a body of incontrovertible statement headed by the Qur'ān and the *sunna*, and closely followed by the consensus over particular issues. Indeed, to narrative traditions from the earliest Islamic times and contained in the Qur'ān and the *ḥadīth*, were added the opinions of legists and other divines which had acquired currency, and which, for the purpose of providing apodictic statements of science, were very effective. Ẓāhirite doctrine considered these to be admissible only if they were, in addition, positively confirmed by a text, and if they were confined to the concensus of the immediate associates of Muḥammad,[154] to the exclusion of later consensus which they took private opinion, and adherence to which would have been mere imitation, *taqlīd*. This, for Ẓāhirites and other fundamentalists, constituted foliage which grew over the pristine truths of the Qur'ān and the *sunna* and occluded them from the gaze of later generations. Yet it was generally accepted to take to the letter the famous saying attributed to the Prophet, that his nation will never concur upon an error, and that consensus is by implication infallible. Disagreements over concensus devolved upon the description of those whose common opinion constituted authentic concensus. But concensus cannot be groundless for, being the exercise of fallible human judgement, it must have some justification, although the definition of such justifications was very vague and could well be regarded as *post factum* desire for systematic order rather than to a will or wish to scrutinise concensus.[155]

And after all, there was almost total agreement on the slogan to the effect that every *mujtahid*, learned legist or theologian, is right. Law and its cognates, we saw, are not absolutely certain judgements, and all members of the professional class of legists who legislate legitimately. Truth is assimilated to legitimacy, whose definition is ultimately cultural and political, not intellectual or logical. That is why criticisms of this famous motto (*kullu mujtahidin muṣīb*) simply specified and nuanced its terms: every *mujtahid* will be rewarded for his effort by God, though not every *mujtahid*, is right, for truth is one.[156]

The willing submission to the corpus of traditional narratives and the treatment of these narratives as *ipso facto* apodictic was the fundamental criterion of positive or traditional sciences. Needless to say, this does not by any means imply a rejection of Reason, as modern commentators would like to believe. Reason was always praised as the specific attribute of humanity, that which distinguishes it from bestiality, and positive law was constructed on the assumption of legal majority, *taklīf*, which naturally presupposes reason. And even if, with very few exceptions, Arabic thinkers have almost always chided *taqlīd* without eschewing tradition,[157] this does not imply that Reason has to be asserted specifically in order for it to be made the very element of discourse. Reason is instrumental, acting upon apodictic statements, just as it does upon the apodictic statements of the philosophers. What marks off positive sciences was not unreason, but a specific provenance (not type) of premiss. From this common body of premisses were separated a number of thematic and topical repertoires, each of which constituted a science, and not all of which partook of the sacred. Positive sciences rested on the political choice of submission to apodictic beginnings, and on the equally political choice of charity towards these beginnings, not submitting them to too exacting an examination in order to perpetuate their validity, regardless of what latter-day historians might have wished.

The Content and Form of Islamic and Foreign Sciences

But the positive sciences rested equally upon a specific group of topics, for the world was divided into regions, and, knowledge being parallel to the world, was constrained into conforming to this division. Humanity occupies an intermediate position in the order of things, being at once sacred and profane, sublime and base, material and spiritual, natural and divine. It therefore straddles the sciences of nature and those of God, the knowledge of the elements and the knowledge of God. But being sacred and profane, humanity is equally neither sacred nor profane, neither sublime nor base, neither material nor spiritual, neither natural nor divine. Knowledge of humanity cannot therefore be had from the knowledge of nature, nor that of God. Knowledge of humanity is neither based upon the certainty of dogma, nor on the certainty of the senses. It is based upon a different element: it is based upon the uncertainty which is *khabar* — *khabar* about the past, this being history, *khabar* about the future, this being eschatology, *khabar* about the manner in which humanity should conduct itself in order to fulfill divine purpose, this being law, *khabar* about God's explicit description and wishes, this being dogmatics and devotions. All these matters are conjectural: God's wish is merely indicated; and God's nature is either the product of a probable interpretation, or the occasion for a fideistic attitude. But for the purposes of scientific and of pragmatic practice, these probabilities are apodictic.[158]

It is appropriate first to discuss the sciences of language. They are ancillary sciences, but like that other ancillary science, logic, they are essential for the proper exercise of the understanding in the field of positive sciences. Without proper knowledge of 'Arabiyya, there can be no proper understanding of the textual patrimony which constituted tradition, the apodictic statements of positive sciences.[159] Without it, there can be no access to the proximity of the original *waḍ'*. Like all other positive sciences, those of language stand upon a *khabar*, that of language, of linguistic use. Language — both as words and as rules, lexicography and grammar — was modelled upon a paradigmatic usage which, for reasons which are not entirely clear to us now, did not include the Qur'ān and *ḥadīth* except in a very peripheral manner. Instead, the paradigmatic usage consisted of the speech of a number of tribes whose usage was elaborately graded for its soundness and compulsion; and whereas lexicographers generally cited both poetry and prose, grammarians in effect regarded poetic usage as primary.[160] In all cases, concern was with fidelity of transmission: the famous dictionary of Fairūzabādī (d. 817/1415) was likened to be amongst lexical works the analogue of Bukhārī's canonical compendium of *ḥadīth* amongst collections of prophetic tradition.[161] For lexicography is the science of the posited conjunction of words and meanings,[162] and grammar (*naḥw*) is the adoption (*intiḥā'*) of the linguistic usage of the Arabs with regard to construction, plurals and such matters in order for those who are not native to this facility to be able to acquire the skill.[163]

Grammar is the adoption of rules of word combination in order for original meanings to be rendered.[164] Grammar therefore is built upon paradigmatic usage, and it is on the basis of this that rules are inferred and analogies constructed and judgements built upon these analogies varied in acceptability according to their viability in terms of closeness to the original usage.[165] Lexicography also considers meanings in terms of original references.[166] It was quite natural that linguistic sciences flourished and paradigms were sought: the Arabic culture area was vast, and no one seemed at all perturbed if a prominent Qāḍī in Baghdad spoke atrocious Arabic[167] — it was probably assumed that he wrote it perfectly. Similarly, the Andalus, particularly famous for grammar and lexicography, probably had this fame precisely because classical Arabic was not spoken and grammarians who actually spoke the classical were considered to be ludicrous.[168]

Not unnaturally, the use of analogy in linguistics was chastised by some, most notably Ẓāhirite jurists[169] and grammarians,[170] on the assumption that linguistics was a means for the preservation of language in all its integrity, not for its alteration, and that linguistic sciences are a register of linguistic usage, not inference from such usage. This criticism repeated the hostility of some to the use of analogies in other fields, and most specifically in those of law and theology, examples of which have been brought forward at various junctures of this book. This repetition is not surprising at all. There was a practical legislative solidarity between the two analogies, a linguistic analogy performing the analogy of a juristic judgement by means of the establishment of synonymy, such as decreeing homosexual sodomy to be adulterous fornication or wine to be an intoxicant.[171] There was also a more properly scientific connection, that the methods of linguistic study were parallel to those of use in other sciences, and especially in the principles of jurisprudence, and indeed used the conceptual and methodological terminology of the principles of jurisprudence. Grammatical theory is *uṣūl an-naḥw*, just as jurisprudential theory is *uṣūl al-fiqh*,[172] and it was also possible to draw up a dialectical method for grammatical debate based upon the principles of jurisprudential dialectics.[173] But, as a very prominent grammarian insisted, the indicative signs (*'ilal*) upon which grammatical analogies were built are far less certain than those of jurisprudence, and are in any case built upon a relatively small textual corpus, resulting in very incomplete induction[175] — hence the plethora of exceptions in Arabic grammar.[176]

Grammatical theory was a late development imposed upon an earlier, aggregative rather than systematic organisation of the science. This is not surprising, given that linguistics usage, of which there was a vast corpus, was apodictic. Some systematisations, like that of Ibn Jinnī, were based on direct acquaintance with what we might call the Arabic prototypes (Ibn Jinnī was well acquainted with Mutanabbī, among other things), and on the corpus of usage which went by the name of the Baṣra school,[176] whose system was the result of a trimming of cases and exceptions rather than the result of a true systematisation and the inference of rules from principles.[179] And indeed, the work of Ibn Jinnī is rather one of description of grammatical and semantic patterns. Similarly, the highly systematic work of Suyūṭī, though employing technical terminology, was really a register of examples and instances after they had been duly classified as falling under the various headings of types of analogy.[178] Highly systematic works such as that of Zajjājī (d. 337/948–9) object to the recourse of other grammarians, under the influence of logic, to present definitions of grammatical concepts in terms other than those derived from the description of these concepts: thus a noun was not taken by him to be a sound indicating a meaning independent of time, but rather one which behaves in a particular way in combination with other words.[179] Similarly, books on literary criticism before Jurjānī and the Aristotelian effort of Qartājinnī (d. 684/1285), and later, in spite of them, present a classified register of devices born of literary convention,[180] being virtually lexica of excellences of composition, just as grammatical works are registers of paradigmatic usage retrospectively classified.

Upon this knowledge of Arabic rested the understanding of *ḥadīth* which, like the statements of linguistic usage which form the apodictic beginnings of grammar and lexicography, consists of a corpus of paradigmatic singular statements later topically systematised in works of this science. Classified under headings such as ritual purity (*ṭahāra*), apocalypse (*fitan*) and rules of sectarian toleration pertaining to the treatment of non-Muslims (*aḥkām al-dhimma*) — when not organised according to authorities (*musnad* works) works of *ḥadīth* contain the entire repertory of precedents and exemplary statements, organised in a paradigmatically topical form, without the statements comprised in the corpus themselves not having been based on anything but the supposition of veracity. *Ḥadīth* is a corpus of verbatim and indirect statements, or at least the ready retrieval of these statements and of the chains of authority which constitute their traditions, and the linguistic and historical capacity to understand the content of these statements (*riwāya, dirāya*).[181] The quintessentially aggregative science of *ḥadīth*, whose topics can readily be dissociated into singular statements, is an auxiliary to all sciences, but is auxiliary in a very specific and important sense: it provides a corpus of statements and a body of *exempla* which have apodictic value in the construction of other sciences.

Like *ḥadīth*, but much more elaborately so, the sciences of the Qur'ān rested on a repertoire of linguistic and historical knowledge applied to a specific textual body, one that is definitive and apodictic in an absolute sense, but also one which *ḥadīth* served to interpret. A late compendium of Qur'ānic sciences, in detailing the sciences whose knowledge is required of the exegete, lists the various linguistic and rhetorical sciences in addition to pertinent *ḥadīth*, the history of the Qur'ānic text, as well as exogenous sciences of incidental relevances such as dogmatics and law.[182] Being a text the authenticity of whose received form was crucial, for it is the direct speech of God, the study of textual variants was essential. Of these there are seven (*qirā'āt*) which came to be considered canonical, although this matter took a very long time to settle.[183] On the basis of the certain text, though beset with several minor variations,[184] the student could proceed with scrutinising the text to study a vast range of topics, from the Divine Names to the grammar and grammatical peculiarities of the Book, the numbers of its letters, words and verses, on to matters such as non-Arabic words used in it, *naskh* relations it contains, its use of rhetorical figures and many more issues.[185] All in all, the structure of Qur'ānic sciences is heterogeneous and *ad hoc*, a not unnatural fact given that they consist of the application of many areas of knowledge and expertise whose only connection in this context is their relevance to a text.

Qur'ānic sciences are a prelude for the all-embracing and all-important science of exegesis. Exegesis could, as we saw in the previous chapter, be the occasion for the expression and justification of esoteric doctrines. But it was also the occasion for the expression and justification of exoteric dogmatics; the great exegesis of Ṭabarī, regarded as almost definitive from the linguistic and historical points of view at least, is replete with theological polemic directed at the Mu'tazilites and others. The exegesis of Zamakhsharī (d. 538/1144), almost the quintessence of rhetorical analysis, is very much in the service of Mu'tazilite doctrine. Rāzī's exegesis presents a repertoire of contrasting opinions on exegetical and theological matters and is the location where many philosophical matters were discussed.[186] Yet with the exception of Rāzī's effort, exegesis was a piecemeal procedure, a discourse that jerks quite easily from verse to verse, following the tempo of the Qur'ān which is not concerned with the integrity of sequence, but is rather a sequence of successive and not intrinsically connected verses that resulted from (or, for the exegete, that were conjoined with) particular circumstances. Exegesis follows the sequence of the Book, not the requirements of exogenous topics.

It was exogenous topics which converge in the two sciences of theology and jurisprudence that deployed the statements of the Qur'ān and *ḥadīth*, duly interpreted, and utilised them as apodictic statements which constitute the fundamentals, *uṣūl*, of these sciences. Apodictic statements do not force their own organisation on theology and jurisprudence, for they are formless, merely statements almost meant for quotation in multifarious contexts, and integrated simply by being considered to be components of an apodictic corpus. Their integration in the two sciences of principles — the principles of religion (*uṣūl ad-dīn*, dogmatic theology) and the principles of jurisprudence (*uṣūl al-fiqh*, juristic theory) proceeded according to the needs of these two sciences. These needs were topical, for each of these sciences was a paradigmatic formation consisting of a topical repertoire guarded by a name standing for an object and rehearsed, as the next chapter will attempt to show, by a specialist body of specialists. It is interesting to note that while legal theorists gave primacy to their art over that of mere lawyers and dogmatic theologians regarding their concern as having precedence over common dogmatics, mere lawyers and advocates of 'old women's religion' regarded themselves as undertaking the more authentic and legitimate of tasks. This displays a double realisation: that the *uṣūl* were theoretically anterior, but that law and dogma were practically anterior in that they were historically precedent as well as being the substance of which the *uṣūl* were the theorisation and systematisation. But ultimately, advocates of *furū'* were more realistic than those of *uṣūl*, for theirs were disciplines which were durable regardless of their theorisation, while theory justified by the ostensible task of generating and justifying the *furū'*. The apodictic statements of *ḥadīth* and Qur'ān were deployed by specific topics, and theory is the theoretically and historically retrospective conformation of these topics. *Uṣūl* have no justification without reference to *furū'*, while these latter are justified irrespective of *uṣūl*.

Some scholars, such as Ghazālī, asserted a theoretical primacy, an apodicticity, of theology with respect to legal theory, it being the only science based on true logical generality amongst positive science, and legal theory being, according to him, a science of the particular, dealing with particular nomothetic statements and legal judgements.[187] But this was very much a minority position, though the Qāḍī 'Abd al-Jabbār (d. 415/1024) adopted a close contention, that though both theology and legal theory are based on conclusive judgements (*qaṭ'*, not certainty, *yaqīn*), legal theory is also composed of probabilties.[188] But it was normally held in later, i.e. post-Rāzīan legal theory which was heavily influenced by the Mu'tazilite tradition exemplified by the treatise of Abul

Ḥusain al-Baṣrī (d. 436/1044),[189] that the priority of dogmatic statements in the theory of jurisprudence was on a par with the priority of its other apodictic elements, linguistic sciences and the statements of the Qur'ān and the canon of narrative tradition.[190] *Kalām* thus had none but an instrumental distinction over legal theory, and was not epistemologically privileged in the relationship, as in the position of Ghazālī. In this way, dogmatic theology was seen as covering statements of belief, legal theory being concerned with human action,[191] or alternatively, the former was seen to defend with rational arguments those premisses which are taken in the latter as merely given.[192] In all events, works of both *uṣūl* discuss the topics of one another.

Thus legal theory, *uṣūl al-fiqh*, is knowledge of the hermeneutical means, both apodictic and methodological, for arriving at legal judgements. These comprise sciences of the Qur'ān and of *sunna*, particularly concepts and methods used in generating sense out of statements, such as rhetorical methods, exegetical operations, linguistic, historical and logical principles of generalisation and logical principles of generalisation and particularisation of statements, abrogation of Qur'ānic and other statements (*naskh*). In addition to these interpretative procedures, legal theory had to deal with concensus, *qiyās* and provisions legally made for expediency, prudence, custom and other matters which cannot rigorously be subsumed under apodictic inference.[193] Thus the concern of legal theory was with all aspects and methods of study relevant to nomothetic discourse as constituted in a canon of sacred texts; the components of this science are the *aṣl*, the apodictic beginning, followed by that which is rational in the *aṣl* and its elaboration by reason, in addition to auxiliary roots such as expediency.[194] Equally ideally stated, theology is the science of dogmatics in the widest possible sense: it deals with God, with the afterlife, with the relation of human activity to divine will, with prophecy, faith and allied matters, all of which knowledge must be related to apodictic statements relating to these topics.[195]

This emphasis on the apodictic character not only of the nomothetic and dogmatic canon, but of the two sciences of *uṣūl qua* sciences as well, was the occasion of criticism by what were collectively known, and in the context of this particular dispute, *ahl al-ḥadīth*, which comprised fideists in the context of theology (earlier and later Ḥanbalites) and others, and opponents of the *via moderna* or *via theologica* in legal theory. Both in theology and in legal theory, the *via moderna*[196] was characterised by the ascription of a pseudo-Aristotelian demonstrativeness, a pseudo-axiomatisation, to the newly-systematised sciences. This is well studied in the context of theology,[197] and was identified and criticised by Ibn Taimiyya as having been signalled by Ghazālī's admission into the paradigm of legal theory the topics of definition and demonstration.[198] Later legal theorists working within this tradition customarily commenced their treatises with a discussion of the concepts of science and of knowledge,[199] and one later author epitomised a redaction of a text by Rāzī on *uṣūl* and called it 'The Euclid of *Uṣūl*',[200] although in North Africa, where Rāzī's influence has already been signalled, there was strong resistance to axiomatised legal theory which split legal theorists into two camps.[201]

This professed axiomaticism, however, appears to be spurious. There appears to be no overall systematic compulsion which ties together *uṣūl* treatises, and there is no serial concatenation of their component parts. Works on legal theory appear like a listing of topics, philological, logical and rhetorical, which come together only because they constitute, singly, hermeneutical procedures of applicability to nomothetic discourse. That such treatises were inaugurated by logical prolegomena seems almost artificial, and at best a programmatic statement which remained unrealised, for it was indeed unrealisable given the fact that the corpus of nomothetic discourse was composed of particular statements which jurists would not allow, as we saw, to yield a *ratio legis*. The one occasion on which serial rigour and the compulsion of programmatic pronouncement was realised was the great *Muwāfaqāt* of Shāṭibī, a work of supreme rigour, subtlety and originality, with an immensely rich conceptual structure, and perhaps the only treatise on legal theory which makes for compulsive reading. In it, the author decided, against the consensus already discussed, that legal theory was not only compelling, but certain, and then went on to deny the admissibility of any legal judgement which was not accompanied by inferences from the authority of nomothetic discourse, and to build upon the certainty yielded by authority a firm base of *ratio legis* (*maqāṣid shar'iyya*) in terms of the famous notion of *maṣāliḥ mursala*, the public weal, widely used in Mālikite jurisprudence. In this way, nomothetic discourse was no longer a mere aggregate of particular statements, but a body collectively employed to form the truly apodictic touchstone of legislation, *ratio legis*, that for the sake of which all legislation is made, and which is composed of three components, ranging from the necessary to the supererogatory but desirable, such as the ban on the killing of young boys in war. The latter, of course, are supererogatory with respect to the necessary five that we have already met: the preservation of religion, sanity, life, posterity and wealth.[202] Necessities had been generally thought, as we have seen, to be outside the bounds of law in the strict sense of that resulting from nomothetic *waḍ'* and legal discourse, being in the same conceptual category as other mundane and demonstrable needs, such as expediency. In making them the centre of legal theory, Shāṭibī could be said to have developed a legal theory based on natural law.

But the work of Shāṭibī was to remain within theoretical effect until this century, and was doubtless understood by his contemporaries not in terms of the theoretical mutation it truly constituted, but in terms of its topical peculiarities which would have been likely to have rendered it paradigmatically suspect as positive law, *fiqh*. It put forward the paradigmatically unusual combination of two traditions of positive law, that of Abū Ḥanīfa, and that of the Ibn al-Qasīm (d. 191/806) tradition within Mālikism,[203] the latter being the Cordoban tradition, based on Mālik as well as on the *corpus juris* grown of local conditions through Saḥnūn (d. 240/847) down to Ibn Rushd (d. 520/1198), the philosopher's grandfather, and which was a tradition of very great authority throughout North Africa.[204] And it was perhaps only proper that the work of Shāṭibī should have been regarded in these terms. For not only was it a theoretical transgression on established scientific paradigms; but this transgression, which would have made it theoretically irrelevant to conservative contemporaries, would have allowed the *Muwāfaqāt* — as Ibn Khaldūn's *Muqaddima* was by its contemporaries[205] — to be dissociated into its topical elements, and it is these topical elements which constitute positive law, *fiqh*, which ought not to be confused with *uṣūl al-fiqh*.[207] Given the structural properties of *uṣūl* works as described in the foregoing paragraphs, such a dissociation would appear understandable. Correlatively, it could be said that this points to the phylogenetic aspect of *uṣūl*, that it preserved its origins in the topical aggregates which constitute its paradigmatic boundaries.

These topical aggregates are the *furū'*, 'branches', inferred from the *uṣūl*, 'sources'. In jurisprudence, they correspond to positive law, the detailed judgements construed from the *uṣūl* (the nomothetic corpus, including consensus, and the analogical method), being what might be called 'religion in the modality of obedience', the *uṣūl* being 'religion in the modality of knowledge.'[207] And these topical aggregates constituted the organising principle of positive law as displayed in systematic treatises: purity, devotions (prayer, pilgrimage and allied topics), commercial transactions, marriage and inheritance, manumission, *jihād* and others, each painstakingly divided into topics of growing particularity. The four schools of Islamic law that have survived in the Sunnite fold (Ḥanafite, Ḥanbalite, Mālikite, Shāfi'ite), and one could say the same for

Ja'farite and other Shī'ite *fiqh*,[208] each consisted of a more or less consistent body of regulations regarding these legal topics. Disagreements between schools, though, as we shall see in the next chapter, social, political and often theological and allied to social and political issue, are legally expressed in terms of disputes over matters of detailed legislation within the context of these topics and with reference to varying interpretations of identical statements from nomothetic discourse and differing results from analogical operations. There was an abundant literature on these differences and some instituted it as the topic of a particular science subsidiary to *fiqh*. A flourishing literature on dialectics abounded alongside *khilāf*,[209] but this was not so much a formalised science as a guide for argumentation on the basis of a study of *uṣūl al-fiqh* with intent to argue points of detail.[210] Indeed, two dialectical works that have been used in this book, the *Kitāb al-Jadal* (Book of Dialectic), of the Ḥanbalite Ibn 'Aqīl and the *Minhāj* (Method for the Ordering of Arguments) of the Mālikite Bājī (d. 474/1081), are very much like treatises in legal theory.

Whereas works on legal theory were normally catholic with respect to the *uṣūl* literature of persons adhering to all legal schools, disagreement in positive law was perennial. For indeed, *fiqh* is the knowledge of judgements pertaining to the practical actions of men,[211] and indications are that knowledge of law was not necessarily expected to be accompanied with knowledge of legal theory, but the two fields were assumed to be quite separate and autonomous.[212] It is in the domain of positive law that the schools were constituted and the discordances of opinion between them were expressed.[213] These schools were each constituted, firstly, by a main body of judgements which derived from or were attributed to their eponymous founders, along with some early adherents, the subjects of emulation and of following, *taqlīd*, and judgements so definitive that with them the door of *ijtihād* was supposed to have been closed. The matter was in fact far more complicated, and such a closure was not only considered, with few exceptions, inadmissible in Islamic law, but also goes counter to the logic of history and can only be taken seriously on the assumption of a fictious and ahistorical specificity which distinguishes Islam.[214] Beside this original *corpus juris* were several others within each school, incorporating the results of historical change and other variations of circumstance; thus Mālikism, for instance, had several forms, which included the Cordoban, the Egyptian, the Baghdadian and that of Qairawān,[215] and the Egyptian was, through the teaching of Ṭurṭūshī (d. 520/1126), subject to a Cordoban admixture.[216] In the early sixth century of the Hijra, one scholar mixed the Iraqi and the Khurāsānian forms of Shāfi'ite law.[217] Within the North African traditions, the judgements of the Fez jurists themselves formed a particular *corpus juris* which was used in the judicial process, in addition to *'amal muṭlaq*, the practice of jurists and traditions from all Islamic lands, a kind of licence for expediency.[218] And as the conception of *'amal*, practice, indicates, it is without necessary reference to formal legislation. Practice based on custom, local conditions and expediency was incorporated within the *corpus juris* specific to a particular tradition, if not often formally as *exceptio necessitatis* which probably constitutes the real significance of particular *ijtihād*,[219] yet usually received formal doctrinal elaboration in terms of *qiyās*.[220] Mālikite law in the Maghreb and Spain was particularly acutely local and dissociated from definite links with *uṣūl* until the jolt received from Ibn Ḥazm and, later, from Ibn Tūmart (d. 524/1130) was felt,[221] to such an extent that Ibn Ḥazm declared that the adherence to Mālik's judgements as received by them were even more highly regarded than the principal nomothetic texts.[222]

Positive law was hardly influenced by legal theory, then. Positive law was not modified by the historically posterior science of *uṣūl*, which was really not a methodology of law but a legal epistemology.[223] Correlatively, later developments in positive law, especially the great movement of refinement that followed the fifth/eleventh century, were only rarely incorporated into works of legal theory.[224] Law was inseparable from the legal process; it had, as Berque maintained, the flavour of a case law, where the centre of gravity in the process of legislation was displaced from the rule to the application of the rule,[225] or perhaps rather positive judgement in the name of the rule. Positive law was codified in thematic terms relevant to mundane application,[226] and it was the rules themselves that were apodictic, not their justifications, which were probably retrospective.

The body of theology is similarly structured, with not much of a demonstrative distance between premisses and results, as Ibn Rushd rightly remarked with reference to all positive sciences and their modes of argumentation.[227] Like each *corpus juris*, each topical paradigm, a theological tendency was held together by a number of theses it maintained and methods it considered admissible, although the overlap between the methods and topics of two particular schools could be very great. A Mu'tazilite was only he who concurred to the five principles of the school: the unicity of God, His justice, a station intermediate between belief and unbelief, God's advertence to mankind (*wa'd wa wa'īd*) and the Qur'ānic injunction to good and the censure of evil.[228] The difference between Ash'arism and Māturīdism in anti-Mu'tazilite theology was itself the result of differences over some 50 points of aporetic detail, such as the Maturīdites having considered creativity to have been eternally subsistent in the divine essence, while the Ash'arites saw it as an attribute without the divine essence, and there were small departures within each school from adherence to particular statements.[229] As can be seen, a theological tendency is defined by a particular collection of topics whose conformation is held to be paradigmatic and thus constitutive of the school. Not all these topics are homogeneous: the five principles of the Mu'tazilite creed are not all theological, some being social and political. This points out to a supremely important fact, that far from being derived from apodictic premisses, theological positions are the result of the coalescence of topics which were the results of specific polemical and political encounters.

For indeed, theology was the polemical art of defending the basic dogmas of Islam — belief in God, Angels, Revelation, prophecy, fate and the afterlife — against all detractors, heretics or unbelievers.[230] It was a totally different matter from the deliberate elaboration of the dogma, although this was a natural development, especially, as Ibn Khaldūn realised, that ambiguous verses in the Qur'ān pertaining to divine attributes had to be properly scrutinised.[231] Theology as later systematised presented the conjunction and elaboration of topics addressed, and this fact is underlined by the character of theological works. Bāqillānī's *Tamhīd* has already been the occasion of comment. Ash'arī's *Luma'* was arranged into chapters and sections, each of which opens with the objection of an opponent, as if it were a repertoire of *responsa*. Later works, though opening with epistemological considerations, were arranged along the same pattern of topics into which the work of Ash'arī and Bāqillānī are dissociable: God's attributable, human responsibility, the Beatific Vision and allied topics, in addition to the question of the *Imāma*.[232]

The coherence of these works is not due to the epistemological discussions or the hermeneutical concepts discussed, but, as in works of legal theory, is *hors du texte*, and is a function of the historical convergence of topics and their coalescence in a paradigmatic set of statements. Methodological rules were indeed deployed, but the structure of the science was unaffected by them, and their distribution was, in any case, very uneven. Correlatively, the tenor of theological discourse is polemical[233] directed against particular charges, and deploying particular arguments that had become part of a repertoire by means of a set of specific operations, such as the method of division.[234] Apodicticity in the real sense was the property of singular statements, as in positive law, not of general rules. Logicisation was more a matter of programmatic intent, and the methods and concepts of dialectic which underlay theological reasoning was unaffected except in matters of detail by the pseudo-axiomatisation of later *kalām*.[235] The topical organisation of the science unaffected by serial compulsion is displayed most starkly in such limiting cases as that of a theological treatise of a Ṣadr al-Sharī'a al-Bukhārī (d. 747/1346–7) which followed an inaugural chapter on logic by dividing its material into seven chapters, the number seven corresponding to the auspicious number of verses in the *fātiḥa*, the inaugural chapter of the Qur'ān.[236] The conclusive accomplishment of a theological paradigm in terms of its topics is displayed in another such limiting case, of a treatise by Suyūṭī addressing the aporetic sub-topic of whether women also will be able physically to behold God in paradise.[237]

Of a different mode is the relation between the apodictic beginnings of all sciences of sacred reference, and the science of mysticism, *taṣawwuf*. There is no disagreement amongst mystical thinkers over the contention that the Qur'ān and, to a lesser extent, *ḥadīth*, are the apodictic statements upon which is built the theoretical and devotional structure of the discipline. But the similarity stops here. Mysticism was originally an ascetic discipline, and continued to be a devotional mode above all else.[238] In the Andalus, for instance, it grew independently of the sciences, and seems to have remained so for a long time, well into the sixth century of the Hijra.[239] In Baghdad, it was connected with Ḥanbalite devotions. But connection with the theology and law were inevitable. Some mystics brazenly decreed their discipline superior to all other sacred callings, being the highest form of devotion, and thus the highest form of knowledge of the true object of knowledge, God. Science, *'ilm*, was superficial, touching upon mere exoterica, and mystical apprehension, *ma'rifa*, is a direct contact with the one true being.[240] *Shar'* is thus distinct from proper devotion and access to the true nature of things, hidden by the Veil of Sense, and access to which is the result of long devotional and ascetic training through a succession of stations, *maqāmāt*, acquired by hard devotions and application, and dispositions, *aḥwāl*, which are divinely inspired, leading up to gnosis.[241] All these situations were described and justified by scriptural interpretation, although many technical terms and articulations of devotional and gnostic conditions are often figuratively articulated in the very profane terms of love and intoxication.[242] Direct apprehension was always the aim; Ibn 'Arabī was quoted as having written to Rāzī saying that a mystic cannot be considered to have reached the condition of true knowledge until he had acquired all he knew directly from God.[243] All that is not God occludes Him.[244]

The devotional discipline of mysticism developed its own hermeneutical techniques and incorporated a variety of esoteric doctrines and numerological and other esoteric procedures, for exegesis and for gnosis, matters which were especially encoded for the initiates. This we have already encountered in various passages above. But partly as a result of esotericism, of suspicions of relations with Ismā'īlism and of statements purporting the superiority of gnosis, the charge of antinomianism was never far away. That is why some mystical writers asserted that mystical sciences were only accessible for those who have mastered the sciences of *shar'*.[245] Others were obviously dissimulating by stating that *shar'* is the *aṣl*, while mystical truth is a *far'* based upon it, although the former encompassed all that is visible and the latter all that is invisible,[246] in effect being superior in mystical terms. More systematically, one of the foremost theoreticians of mysticism incorporated his art formally into the body of positive sciences by declaring that *Sharī'a* was concerned with acts, both exoteric and esoteric, and whereas the former were the subject of devotions and legal judgements, the latter were the lot of inwardness[247] — the province of stations and dispositions, the most superior of positive sciences.[248] Mystics generally practised both types of devotion and scientific activity, and rare were the ones who never stopped to the lower reaches of the sensibility or who wrote only in an indecypherable code.[249] No sūfī disagreed with the assertion of superiority of direct knowledge whose seat is the soul, the divine part of man,[250] a superiority the assertion of which was often the occasion for a severe criticism of logic.[251] And the art was elaborately codified, endowed with a technical terminology which, as we saw in the last chapter, was slightly coded. As is the case with other instituted paradigms, the definitive sign of accomplishment was the irruption of differences attributable to local traditions and conventions within the wider body: Abū al-Qasīm al-Qushairī (d. 514/1120) recorded a difference between the Iraqis and the Khurāsānis concerning whether the state of *riḍa* was a disposition or a station, and offered an irenical solution.[252]

* * *

Thus in the positive sciences, apodicticity was not truly generative, but only symbolically so. The connection between premiss and conclusion, as that between theoretical science and positive instances, is mediated by an authority external to the relation, the authority of the apodictic statement regardless of its relevance in any true or logical sense of the term. Analogy, generically the context of all such connections as are to be found in the positive scienes, was built on probability, as its practitioners insisted, and on the presumption of an identity, as its critics, most notably Ibn Ḥazm, maintained. Both these positions are amply justified. For apodicticity in the positive sciences was not a mode of demonstration, but of assimilation to an archetype which is less the source of the particular than its imputed model. Assimilation to a supposed beginning as a means of explanation is a means of eliminating the difference between archetype and instance, and in the context of positive sciences as in that of myths of origin, it is a means of eliminating history and liquidating the reality that intervenes between archetype and event. The event, which in the positive sciences conforms to the schema that justifies it, is only figuratively born of the archetype, which itself is made to conform to the schema that connects it to the event. And indeed, it is the schema that is the invariant, according to an analyst of scientific myth, 'instead of the tale being the origin of the schema'.[253] Intellectual disciplines without scientific status in Arabic thought bear this out very well, for such disciplines as history,[254] politics[255] and, as we saw, literature were constructed on the elimination of history. Not only were the criteria of literary criticism ahistorical, but the form taken by historical and political writing is one in which present events and any other, including the future, are seen as repetitions of past occurrences, not by being prefigured in them, but being instances of paradigmatic occurrences inaugurated by them.[256] Such were events in prophetic, salvation history in a very real sense. Profane events, such as calamities, battles, betrayals and reigns, in the instances when they were not reduced to the bored absurdity of dumb succession, and when an attempt was made to apprehend them in terms other than themselves, were reduced to prototypes and archetypes. That is why historical works announced themselves as ones containined the distilled wisdom of past examples and of action exemplary both for the good and the peril it brings; the past, when known by history, is as if it were lived here and now. Similarly, political works outside the political import of *fiqh* such as *Fürstenspiegel* were registers of exemplary behaviour designed to guide the actions of the sovereign for whom the treatise was composed. That is why it is not at all unnatural to find that political events such as the foundations of states, rebellions and new religions are explained with recourse to legend, be it Persian, Arab or otherwise, much like a myth of origin. And therefore when advice was proffered to a sovereign, in works on politics and of history, by recourse to a past action, the sovereign was called upon to adopt that particular example as a legendary beginning of his own contemplated act, as its myth of origin and as its archetype, although the sovereign's act, being the product of today and inseparable from this its true context and bearing, was merely said to have been related to another, alien act.[257] This is how knowledge took the form of relation to a beginning, whether in a positive science and with reference to a textual origin, or in philosophy, with Ibn Rushd, for instance, wishing to relate himself directly to the original fount, the one and singular truth, which is the authentic Aristotle. That is also why Fārābī thought it unthinkable that Aristotle and Plato could have differed — for truth is not only one, but correlatively, it can only have one origin. History is an incidental blemish on the smooth face of the truth, and this smooth surface is restituted to its original condition once the particularity is levelled.

The explanation of an event, and the theory in which an event was inserted, in history as in other positive sciences, was therefore inseparable from the event itself. Generic elevation is only nominal; apodicticity imputed. It appears that Ibn Ḥazm displayed a very robust realism when he maintained, as we have occasion to see, that analogy imputed to God what he did not intend, and that it added to the original fund of things matters which do not belong to it, being merely historical, and not belonging to the singular fount of authority which is sacred speech. Traditionalism has a rationality which is proper to itself, and which is no less compelling than positivist or syllogistic rationality. Traditionalism can assimilate anything by means of its rationality, for in the aid of this rationality is a fact already mentioned, that any singular text is inexhaustible and infinitely interpretable. Traditionalist rationality is distinct from the syllogistic; we must eschew culturalist narcissism, and realise that traditionalist rationality is not necessarily a privation of triumphalist positivism or of the syllogistics. The rejection of such narcissism would seem to spring not only from the rigorous compulsion of historical rationality, but from the interconnection of rationalities. For after all, just as in the positive sciences there is no room for theory as such, as the event and the explanation are coterminous, logic itself is a repeatable transformation which is both rule and instance, and logical inference proceeds by the citation of a structural similarity on which inferences are supposed to be based[258] — a sort of solipsistic self-justification, an analogy in which logic is grounded and of which it is a form.

Figure 1: The Classification of Natural Sciences According to Ṭashköprüzāde

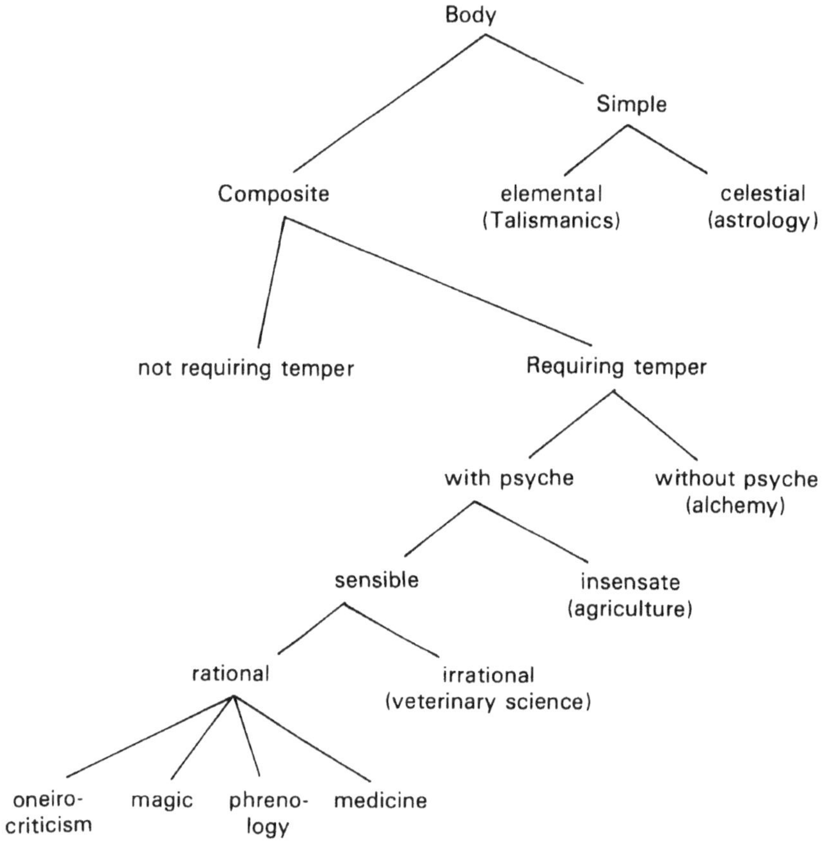

Apodicticity in the rational sciences is differently mediated; we have already discussed the salient points and will recapitulate some essential matters briefly. The degree to which these sciences came to fulfill their syllogistic intent is still an open question, as suggested above, and it is a question which bears detailed examination and ought not to be taken for granted, as it is in modern orientalist thinking. Rational sciences, which comprise natural sciences that study the world of the elements and, in some instances, the psyche, as well as logic, metaphysics and mathematics,[259] were often thought of as a distinct body of knowledge, one that is the patrimony of a particular class of people. Whereas natural science studied all bodies, simple and complex, elemental and celestial,[260] metaphysics took up the overall relations between things, while logic and mathematics studied determinate relations. Often designated as 'wisdom', *ḥikma*, these sciences existed both as paradigmatic formations, and as repertoires, elements from which were utilised in positive sciences and practical life. The infusion we encountered of theology with logical and metaphysical principles is a case in point. And references to works of philosophy, which were the locations for the elaboration and exposition of natural-scientific (and especially physical) knowledge, is a case in point for the general use of philosophical knowledge.[261] That metaphysical conceptions of a technical nature underlay, say, cosmology, did not imply the confinement of cosmology to philosophy. The matters investiged in the first two chapters of this book may, in some instances, have been technical matters in the context of particular sciences, occasionally suspected by pietistic individuals or taken for tokens of irreligion. But such matters supplied the main conceptions of medicine, cosmology and other fields of endeavour. Moreover, not only were they based on a uniform metaphysical base informed by conceptions such as hierarchy, conceptions which were most explicitly and theoretically studied in philosophy and remained untheorised and largely implicit elsewhere. They also often corresponded to religious and folk conceptions, albeit in a terminologically and technically distinct discourse. A case in point is the mutual translatability of angels, intellects, spheres and planets. It was, moreover and as already indicated, disciplines which were not strictly and formally philosophical that kept philosophical topics alive after philosophy had lost its intellectual and social density. The organisation of Rāzī's *Mabāḥith* and the strong element of the theological method of division within it has already been noted. The discussion of medical *aporiai* according to the paradigm of works on legal dialectics is another case in point.[262]

Philosophy was the umbrella of sciences, but only in the sense of a natural philosophy and a corpus of profane knowledge which has uses in other sciences and disciplines. And as we saw, even authors like Ibn Taimiyya admitted the physical-scientific component of philosophy, although such components as were acceptable to others were not generally known as philosophy, for philosophy, unlike the case in the European Middle Ages, did not come to be the name of intellectual endeavour in general.[263] Rather it stood for a paradigmatic discipline comprising various sub-sciences, a discipline so specific and self-contained that the heresiographer Shahrastānī (d. 584/1153) in his *Milal* mentioned the philosophers under a separate heading and as a self-sufficient sect amongst others. It was as the technical equipment which 'survived Christianity' that philosophy carved out for itself a position in Arabic thought;[264] and it was in this capacity that it incorporated the variety of Hermetic and other ideas within its purview and produced a paradigmatic conformation.

Arabic philosophy was not monolithic; it is possible to speak of a 'Platonism', associated with Muḥammad b. Zakariyyā al-Rāzī[265] and carried over in some respects by Abul-Barakāt al-Baghdādī,[266] a Jew converted towards the end of his life, although there seems to have been a more authentically Platonic current which is now obscure and whose existence is attested, among other things, by refutations of the conception of knowledge as *anamnesis*.[267] Pythagoreanism was, as we saw, clear in the numerological philosophy of Ikhwān al-Ṣafā' and elsewhere, and Yaḥyā b. 'Adī, Fārābī's pupil and the main avenue of his influence on Sijistānī and his school, was said to have studied Ibn Zakariyya al-Rāzī's works and to have been the only surviving authority on Pythagoreanism in Baghdad.[268] It is also possible to speak, with reference to Suhrawardī, of a 'philosophie néophythagoricienne et néoplatonicienne selon un ligne avicennisante fortement corrigé'.[269] But whatever overall influences one could thus indicate, they would merely be shorthand for particular conceptual profiles, and beyond a limited analytical facility they might provide, their value appears dubious.

Beyond this variety, and the primacy of Neo-Platonic ideas, philosophy, including the natural sciences, was one paradigmatic unit with many subdivisions based on local and other traditions. Philosophy was topically defined as the aggregate of its components, metaphysics naturally being important, but natural philosophy was equally prominent, as the science of natural bodies, simple and composite, at various removes from pure elementality, and including topics such as form, matter and *telos*.[270] Medicine was, in principle, comprehended under natural philosophy,[271] although some authors saw it as a mixture of science and practical skill (*technē*) based on experience and analogies from experience.[272] Under natural sciences were also subsumed matters such as oneirocriticism, although the divine inspiration it contains led some to remove it from the field of science or contamination with humours. Mathematical sciences were subsumed under philosophical studies, although they had many practical uses, not least in the science of inheritance division, a part of *fiqh*.[273] As for logic, it was well developed, had a succession of conventions,[274] and was systematised for extra-philosophical use by the terse textbook of Khūnajī (d. 646/1248),[275] a work of great diffusion and popularity.[276]

In all these cases, philosophical as well as only partly philosophical, apodicticity was in fact localised. Medicine commences with premisses involving elements and qualities, themselves derived from natural science in general, whose premisses are the same, although in natural science these premisses were part of a larger apodictic body involving the principles of bodies in general, in movement and at rest. Alchemy was based upon similar principles, while astronomy was based upon premisses derived from mathematical sciences, whose very principles were Euclidean in the case of geometry and derived from elsewhere in the case of arithmetic, which along with geometry formed the body of principles of use in the new science of Algebra. We have already had occasion to refer to the irrelevance of empirical evidence except in very particular contexts — it was theoretically inadequate on grounds of impossibility, as it was for those who denied astrology, and sub-theoretical in status for the mainstream opinion mentioned above in the case of medicine, which held to a firm differentiation between sciences and practical skills. And while the apodictic principles of, say, medicine, were concerned with the properties of humours, which figured in situations of increasing complexity, most notably in composite pharmacology (*al-adwiya al-murakkaba*), they were present with a remarkable rigour throughout the science.[277] Yet their permeation of their science down to the finest details, as the permeation of metaphysics by the basic principles of simplicity, complexity and hierarchy which have been studied in detail above, was not one which proceeded according to the principles of logic. The permeation of rational sciences by their premisses is one which proceeds naturalistically, according to a principle mentioned above: in the field of science concerned with corporeals, procedure followed the metaphysical order of nature detailed above, and proceeded from simplicity to complexity, from the elements to humours on to more complex combinations of humours and humoural processes. In metaphysics, this was again the case, but in reverse, descending order. Logic remained technically incidental, and was rather separate, as Arabic (*mutatis mutandis*) is separate in the field of traditional sciences, being instrumental in the procedure of particular arguments, and without impact on the overall operation of apodicticity. Indeed, the structure of logical knowledge itself was built upon metaphysical principles, on classificatory criteria premised on conceptions of individuality and generality, and related to the Categories, a metaphysical topic. Again logic followed the order of psychic nature, and moved from the simple to the complex, from propositions to categorical syllogisms on to conditional and hypothetical syllogisms, then to parasyllogisms, and other forms polluted with the matter of their propositions as dialectical and sophistical syllogisms. This movement not only ran parallel to that of the nature in the mind, but was also attested by its own historical and therefore authoritative myth of creation. For just as human collectivities are the result of a contractual legend, and language subject to a discernible (contractual or arbitrary) beginning, so also is logic the result of positive beginnings in the positing of words first of all, and in an order of ascending truthfulness, on to dialectical reason, and through sophistical argumentation to the ultimate consummation of demonstrativeness in the days of Aristotle.[278]

Philosophy as a form of heresy will be taken up in the next chapter. But we should briefly recapitulate the boundaries and components of its paradigmatic integrity. From unrevealed premisses, philosophy as the generic name for all non-traditional sciences comprised metaphysics and natural philosophy, some of which was implicitly or explicitly carried over into sacred knowledge, as in theology, and into everyday literate knowledge and practice, as medicine and meteorology, not to speak of inheritance division. That which constituted philosophy as a paradigm, and which removed a savant from the order of ordinary intellectuals and made him into a member of the order of philosophers, *falāsifa*, was not so much that intellectual's overlooking of traditional sciences, but his practice of the entirety of sciences associated with philosophy, including Platonic political and ethical theory. Especially pertinent in this context was the conception of philosophical happiness as contemplation, a conception we will see to be akin to many mystical notions, an association especially pronounced in the Andalus. Logic might have been the occasion of some reprobation, but natural sciences and medicine were not;[279] neither were mathematical sciences. What was at issue in determining philosophy as such was adherence to a number of metaphysical and prophetological doctrines pronounced heretical and definitely conducive to perdition, not adherence to the common fund of knowledge concerning nature and based on the elements and humours.

The definition of philosophy and philosophers is essentially historical, i.e. political and cultural, as we shall see in the next chapter. Fakhr al-Dīn al-Rāzī wrote on all philosophical topics save philosophical ethics and politics and was not considered a philosopher, although he is said to have been an alchemist[280] and to have written a book on astral magic, though some dispute his authorship.[281] But so did Ibn Sīnā, who though he did write on politics, wrote according to the 'contract theory' schema which was conventional in Arabic thought[282] although, unlike Rāzī, he propounded a philosophical prophetology. Philosophy was a paradigmatic formation whose name, 'philosophy', was used as a token of unbelief under determinate conditions, and not used under others, and there was nothing intrinsic in the paradigm itself which requires or justifies this distinction. What is true of philosophy is also true of occult sciences, which are both rational, resting on non-revealed premisses, and traditional, resting on the interpretation of sacred scripture,[283] as we already saw in our detailed discussions of alchemy, magic and similar sciences.

Notes

1. See the discussion of this term in Tahānawī, *Kashshāf*, pp. 1215–17.
2. Ghazālī, *Maqāṣid*, p. 33.
3. Ibn al-Ḥājib, *Mukhtaṣar*, p. 5.
4. Jurjānī, *Ta'rīfat*, p. 61.
5. *Ibid.*, p. 61. See, for instance, Ghazālī, *Mi'yār*, p. 182; Ibn Khaldūn, *Prolégomènes*, vol. 3, p. 109; Rāzī, *Muḥaṣṣal*, and see Ibn al-Ḥājib, *Mukhtaṣar*, p. 5 and the Peripatetic nuances on both terms in Ibn Sīnā, *Najāt*, pp. 3–4.
6. Bāqillānī, *Tamhīd*, paras. 8 ff.; Ibn Taimiyya, *Naqḍ*, p. 38 and Ibn 'Abd al-Barr, *Jāmi'*, vol. 2, p. 37.
7. For instance, Ghazālī, *Munqidh*, p. 63.
8. For instance, Ghazālī, *Mi'yār*, pp. 186 ff.: Bāqillānī, *Tamhīd*, paras. 12 ff.; Ibn Ḥazm, *Fiṣal*, vol. 5, pp. 108 ff. and see Rāzī, *Muḥaṣṣal*, p. 20 for an account of the arguments of those who deny the mind innate knowledge. Rāzī (*Mabāḥith, vol. 1, p. 322) spoke of clarity and distinctness.*
9. *See Tahānawī, Kashshāf*, pp. 304–5 and see Ibn Sīnā, *Najāt*, 2nd edn, pp. 62, 64–5.
10. For instance, Qarāfī, *Tanqīh*, pp. 4–5.
11. Ibn Sīnā, *Najāt*, 2nd edn, pp. 61–2, following the concensus of juristic and traditionalist thought.
12. See the account of Ghazālī, *Miḥakk*, pp. 50–1 and see Ibn Sīnā, *Najāt*, 2nd edn, p. 61. The most sophisticated analysis of induction in Arabic thought, which uses experiment as a cognitive tool and attributes more to sense perception than is normally allotted to it in the stricter and rather naive nominalism of Arabic thought, was that of Ibn al-Haitham. For a comprehensive account, see S.B. Omar, *Ibn al-Haytham's Optics. A Study in the Origins of Experimental Science* (Chicago and Minneapolis, 1977).
13. Ghazālī, *Mi'yār*, pp. 189–90.
14. Ibn Sīnā, *Shifā': Mantiq, 4*, pp. 558–60.
15. For instance, Ikhwān al-Ṣafā, *Rasā'il*, vol. 1, p. 144.
16. This is the standard charge in Arabic anti-astrological argument: Ibn Ḥazm, *Fiṣal*, vol. 5, pp. 38–9; Ibn Qayyim al-Jawziyya, *Miftāḥ*, pp. 148 ff. and Ibn Khaldūn, *Prolégomènes*, vol. 3, pp. 221–3, 237–8. For an overview, see C.A. Nallino, 'Sun, Moon and Stars (Muhammadan)', in *Encyclopedia of Religion and Ethics* (New York, 1951), vol. 12, pp. 91–3.
17. See particularly the accounts of Ghazālī, *Mi'yār*, pp. 68, 266–7 and Baghdādī, *Mu'tabar*, vol. 1, pp. 46 ff.
18. See the comments of J. Van Ess, 'The Logical Structure', pp. 37–8.
19. Ibn Taimiyya, *Radd*, pp. 10, 15–22, 32–4, 57–9 and *passim*.
20. For instance, in Ibn Taimiyya, *Naqḍ*, pp. 184–7.
21. Ibn Ḥazm, *Iḥkām*, p. 34.
22. Sakkākī, *Miftāḥ*, p. 206.
23. For instance, Suhrawardī, *Lamaḥāt*, p. 90.
24. Rāzī, *Lubāb*, p. 20 and see Ibn Khaldūn, *Prolégomènes*, vol. 3, p. 83.
25. Ghazālī, *Mi'yār*, pp. 183–4.
26. *Ibid.*, pp. 68–9, 131, 161.
27. For this term, see J. Van Ess, *Die Erkenntnislehre des 'Adudaddīn al-Īcī*, pp. 238 ff. For these procedures of argumentation, see the incisive account of Ibn Taimiyya, *Radd*,

pp. 163 ff. and see Tahānawī, *Kashshāf*, p. 1391 and the comments of Ghazālī, *Maqāṣid*, p. 66. For discussions on theological argumentations, see Van Ess, 'The Logical Structure' and 'A.S. Nashshār, *Manāhij al-baḥth 'inda mufakkirī al-Islām*, 2nd edn (Cairo, 1965).

28. Hajjī Khalīfa, *Kashf*, 'Introduction', p. 9.

29. Tahānawī, *Kashshāf*, p. 1215.

30. Ghazālī, *Maqāṣid*, p. 125: 'muqaddimāt musallama'. The normal term employed for 'postulate' was *muṣādara*.

31. Ibn Sīnā, *Najāt*, p. 158.

32. For a variant, see Baghdādī, *Mu'tabar*, vol. 2, p. 125 and Rāzī, *Mabāḥith*, vol. 1, p. 6.

33. Al-Azmeh, *Ibn Khaldūn: An Essay*, pp. 51 ff. and ch. 2, *passim*.

34. Ghazālī, *Mi'yār*, pp. 250–2; Ibn Sīnā, *Najāt*, pp. 106, 110; Baghdādī, *Mu'tabar*, vol. 1, p. 222 and Rāzī, *Lubāb*, p. 49.

35. Ibn Khaldūn, *Prolégomènes*, vol. 1, p. 63 and see Goichon, *Lexique*, para. 780.3 and Ibn Rushd, *Tahāfut*, p. 797.

36. Ḥajjī Khalīfa, *Kashf*, 'Introduction', pp. 6–8 and Ibn Sīnā, *Najāt*, 2nd edn, pp. 73–4.

37. Ibn Sīnā, *Najāt*, 2nd edn, p. 72.

38. *Ibid.*, 2nd edn, pp. 72–3, 208–9.

39. Baghdādī, *Mu'tabar*, vol. 1, pp. 221–2.

40. The later, Kantian use of this term, still with us today, which emphasises exclusively the dialectical sense of the term and brings it to the proximity of 'dilemma', is totally excluded here.

41. For instance: Ghazālī, *Maqāṣid*, p. 123; Tahānawī, *Kashshāf*, p. 688; Jurjānī, *Ta'rīfāt*, p. 256 and Āmidī, *Iḥkām*, vol. 1, p. 6.

42. For instance, Miskawaih, *Hawāmil*, p. 136.

43. For instance, Āmidī, *Iḥkām*, vol. 1, p. 6.

44. Hajjī Khalīfa, *Kashf*, 'Introduction', p. 57.

45. Ibn Khaldūn, *Prolégomènes*, vol. 3, pp. 294–5.

46. F.E. Peters, *Aristotle and the Arabs: The Aristotelian Tradition in Islam* (New York and London, 1968), p. 70.

47. Ghazālī, *Mi'yār*, pp. 248–9.

48. Baghdādī, *Mu'tabar*, vol. 1, p. 208.

49. Van Ess, *Erkenntinislehre*, pp. 20 ff., and *passim*.

50. See the remarks of R. Arnaldez, 'Falsafa', in *EI*, vol. 2, p. 775.

51. Qifṭī, *Tārīkh*, p. 416.

52. Ibn Sīnā, *Urjuza*, line 15. Writing from a strictly practical perspective, however, Ibn Maimūn (Maimonides) stated that medicine was the widest of all theoretical and practical arts, and a single lifetime is not adequate for its absolute mastery (text in M. Plessner, 'Al-Fārābī's Introduction to the Study of Medicine', in *Islamic Philosophy and the Classical Tradition*, p. 310).

53. Ibn Khaldūn, *Prolégomènes*, vol. 3, pp. 433–4.

54. For instance, Ibn Ḥazm, *Manṭiq*, pp. 10–11 and Ḥajjī Khalīfa, *Kashf*, 'Introduction', pp. 35–6. See Ghazālī, *Faḍā'iḥ*, p. 7.

55. M. Morony, *Iraq after the Muslim Conquest* (Princeton, 1984), p. 288.

56. It should be emphasised that terminology might exist without its being technical, which is the sense desired here. This question is still virgin territory, but we might fix the second half of the fourth century of the Muslim era as the period of crystallisation. We see that it was then that treatises on the terminology of law were composed (for instance, Ibn Khallikān, *Wafayāt*, vol. 4, p. 335). Khwārizmī's *Mafātīḥ* (pp. 3–4) was explicitly designed as a technical dictionary for all sciences and we still see Fārābī, at a slightly earlier date, in an agonising struggle to carve out a terminological preserve for philosophy uncontaminated with the common acceptance of words (*Ḥurūf*, paras. 111–13, 119, 155–8). One might undertake research on this matter in relation to linguistic study of certain transformations in Arabic vocabulary which were, according to L. Massignon ('Notes sommaires

sur la formation des noms abstraits en arabe et l'influence des modèles grecs', in Massignon's *Opera Minora* (Beirut, 1963), vol. 2, pp. 537 ff.), accomplished by the end of the third century. Study of earlier periods (for instance, Z.I. Ansari, 'Islamic Juristic Terminology before Shāfi'ī: A Semantic Analysis with Special Reference to Kufa', in *Arabica*, 19 (1972), pp. 255 ff.), seem obliged to remain inconclusive, or at least very highly specific to time and locality.

57. Gardet and Anawati, *Théologie musulmane*, pp. 157ff. have studied this matter well in relation to theology.

58. Fārābī, *Iḥṣā'* (ed. Amīn), p. 57.

59. Subkī, *Mu'īd*, pp. 115–17.

60. Yāqūt, *Irshād*, vol. 5, p. 281.

61. Suyūṭī, *Iqtirāḥ*, p. 208.

62. A casual count shows that there were no less than 20 commentaries on the theoretical treatise, and more on that on positive law, in the seventh century of the Hijra (Ibn al-'Imād, *Shadharāt*, vol. 6, *passim*). There were works specifically devoted to his terminology (Aḥmad Bābā, *Nayl*, pp. 32, 51), and his commentators included figures of such stature as Baiḍāwī, Subkī and Taftāzānī (Ḥajjī Khalīfa, *Kashf* (ed. Flügel), vol. 2, pp. 1853 ff.).

63. Aḥmad Bābā, *Nayl*, p. 73 and Ibn Ḥajar, *Durar*, vol. 2, p. 343.

64. Aḥmad Bābā, *Nayl*, p. 73; and Ibn Khaldūn, *Prolégomènes*, vol. 3, pp. 13–14 and Sakhāwī, *Ḍaw'*, vol. 4, p. 149. This did not mean that there was no Mālikite interest in his work. His compendium of positive law had the benefit of at least three commentaries (Ḥajjī Khalīfa, *Kashf*, col. 1256).

65. Ibn Khaldūn, *Prolégomènes*, vol. 3, pp. 12, 250.

66. Al-Azmeh, *Ibn Khaldūn in Modern Scholarship*, pp. 102 ff.

67. Ghubrīnī, *'Unwān*, pp. 73, 109–10 and *passim*. It should be stressed that this was a paradigmatic, not a dogmatic opposition to iniquitous logic, for many of those in opposition to the use of logic in jurisprudence utilised this discipline in theology and engaged in philosophical studies (*ibid.*). See Al-Azmeh, *Ibn Khaldūn in Modern Scholarship*, pp. 105–6.

68. Shaṭibī, *Muwāfaqāt*, vol. 1, p. 18.

69. For instance, Subkī, *Mu'īd*, p. 112. On the infusion of theology with philosophy, see G. Gardet, ' 'Ilm al-Kalām', in *EI*, vol. 3, pp. 1146–7.

70. Taftāzānī, *Sharḥ*, p. 14.

71. Ghazālī, *Munqidh*, p. 72.

72. Ibn Khaldūn, *Prolégomènes*, vol. 3, p. 123. Ibn Khaldūn makes the same argument for the connection between philosophy and mysticism.

73. Peters, *Aristotle and the Arabs*, p. 136.

74. Ibn al-Murtaḍā, *Ṭabaqāt*, p. 116.

75. Ṭāshköprüzāde, *Miftāḥ*, vol. 2, pp. 150–1.

76. *Ibid.*, vol. 1, p. 34.

77. Ibn Khaldūn, *Prolégomènes*, vol. 1, pp. 62–5.

78. Al-Azmeh, *Ibn Khaldūn: An Essay*, pp. 145 ff. and *passim*.

79. For instance, A.M. Turki, *Polémiques entre Ibn Ḥazm et Bāǧī sur les principes de la loi musulmane. Essai sur le littéralisme Zahirite et la finalité Malikite* (Algiers, n.d.), pp. 48–9, 449, and *passim*.

80. R. Brunschvig, 'Le système de la preuve en droit musulman', in *Recueils de la Société Jean Bodin*, 18 (1963), p. 174.

81. See the exposition of W. Ong, *Orality and Literacy* (London, 1982), pp. 37 ff. and the discussion of the form of Aquinas' work in *ibid.*, pp. 95–6.

82. Y. Eche, *Les bibliothèques arabes* (Damascus, 1967), pp. 325 ff.

83. Ḥajjī Khalīfa, *Kashf*, cols. 134, 2051.

84. F. Jabre, *Essai sur le lexique de Ghazali. Contribution a l'étude de la terminologie de Ghazali dans ses principaux ouvrages à l'excéption du Tahafut* (Beirut, 1970), s.v. ' 'Ilm'.

85. Ḥajjī Khalīfa, *Kashf*, 'Introduction', p. 11.

86. S. Yafūt, 'Taṣnīf al-'ulūm lidā Ibn Ḥazm', in *DA*, 19/5 (1983), pp. 58–91. For a close classification, see Ibn 'Abd al-Barr, *Jāmi'*, vol. 2, pp. 23 ff., 37 ff., 109 ff.
87. Fārābī, *Iḥṣā* (ed. Amīn), pp. 7, 108–9, and *passim*.
88. Ibn Taimiyya, *Muwāfaqa*, vol. 1, p. 48.
89. Ibn Sīnā, *Najāt*, 2nd edn, p. 73.
90. For instance, Ikhwān al-Ṣafā', *Rasā'il*, vol. 1, pp. 266–7.
91. See Al-Azmeh, *Ibn Khaldūn, An Essay*, pp. 115 ff.
92. Ibn Ḥazm, *Tawqīf*, p. 131.
93. Ibn Taimiyya, *Muwāfaqa*, vol. 1, pp. 116–17.
94. *Ibid.*, pp. 84–5 and see pp. 50–1, 79.
95. *Ibid.*, pp. 48, 50.
96. *Ibid.*, pp. 1–2. For Rāzī's statement on this topic, see *Asās*, pp. 210–11. For Ghazālī's position, quoted more than once above, see additionally his *Mustasfā*, vol. 2, pp. 137–8.
97. Ghazālī, *Mi'yār*, p. 60.
98. Ghazālī, *Tahāfut*, p. 71.
99. Ghazālī, *Mi'yār*, pp. 59–60.
100. For instance, Ibn Khaldūn, *Prolégomènes*, vol. 3, pp. 258–9.
101. *Ibid.*, pp. 86–7.
102. Ibn Abī Uṣaibi'a, *'Uyūn*, p. 424.
103. Ibn Ḥazm, *Manṭiq*, pp. 9–10 and *passim*.
104. See Van Ess, *Erkenntnislehre*, p. 287. The use by Ghazālī of Aristotelian concepts and the conscious use of Aristotelian definitions should not imply (as Van Ess, 'Logical Structure', p. 47) that Ghazālī reversed the topical structure of dogmatic theology and its consequences. Not even philosophy, as we will suggest later, can be said to have been successful in carrying out its programme for rigorous demonstrativeness.
105. Ibn Sīnā, *Shifā' (Mantiq, 4)*, pp. 568 ff.
106. Ibn Khaldūn, *Prolégomènes*, vol. 3, pp. 212–13.
107. *Ibid.*, p. 91.
108. Shahrastānī, *Milal* (ed. Cureton), p. 326.
109. *Ibid.*, p. 312.
110. For instance, Fārābī, *Ḥurūf*, para. 143.
111. For this term, see A.-M. Goichon, 'Ḥikma', in *EI*, vol. 3, pp. 377–8.
112. Jurjānī, *Ta'rīfāt*, p. 96.
113. Fārābī, *Fuṣūl*, p. 126.
114. Ibn Rushd, *Tahāfut*, p. 625.
115. Ibn Rushd, *Samā'*, pp. 2–3.
116. For instance, Mas'ūdī, *Tanbīh*, pp. 121–2.
117. For instance, Qifṭī, *Tārīkh*, pp. 5, 15; Ibn Khaldūn, *Prolégomènes*, vol. 3, p. 90 and see R. Arnaldez, 'L'histoire de la pensée grecque vue par les Arabes', in *Bull. de la Société francaise de Philosophie*, 72/3 (1978), pp. 125 ff., who also points to the Philonic filiation of Plato and Moses. See also Arkoun, *Al-Fikr al-'arabī*, pp. 90, 92.
118. Thus the Qur'ān was as pressing a matter for *aporiai* as the works of Aristotle. See Gardet, *Avicenne*, p. 203 and R. Arnaldez, 'La pensée religieuse d'Averroes', in *SI*, 7 (1957), pp. 99–114; 8 (1958), pp. 15–28 and 10 (1958), pp. 23–41. One author went so far as to see the birth of Muḥammad typologically prefigured not only in the Torah, but in the texts of philosophy as well (Ibn Abī Uṣaibi'a, *'Uyūn*, p. 567. The prophetic genealogy passing through Ḥarran was a means by which the Sabeans demonstrated their religious legitimacy (Chwolsohn, *Ssabier*, vol. 1, p. 643), but this matter was not their concern alone. Jibrā'īl b. Bakhtīshū' (d. 396/1005), scion of the famous Christian family of physicians, wrote a dissertation on the agreement of prophets and philosophers (Qifṭī, *Tārīkh*, p. 150) and Aristotle's refutation of the 'naturalists' (Pre-Socratics) was commended, but was seen to have been inadequate for the unavailability to its author of a divinely-inspired Book (*ibid.*, p. 51).

119. For instance, Qifṭī, *Tārīkh*, p. 3 and Ikhwān al-Ṣafā', *Rasā'il*, vol. 1, p. 186.

120. See the description of a theological historiography of theology by Van Ess, *Erkenntnislehre*, pp. 8–9.

121. Of general accounts of Arabic philosophy, a perceptive account is still to be found in T.J. de Boer, *History of Philosophy in Islam*, tr. E.R. Jones (London, 1903). Several times reprinted, this book is still conceptually not outdated in general studies of Arabic philosophy, a fact which indicates equally the care with which the book was written and the sorry state of studies on Arabic philosophy. M. Fakhry's, *A History of Islamic Philosophy* (New York and London, 1970), though fuller than de Boer, does not supercede it. The output of the Baghdadian school has never been properly considered in its wider context and has been the occasion of articles, except for the rather superficial sketch of 'A. A'sam, *Abū Ḥayyān at-Tawḥīdī fī Kitāb al-Muqābasāt* (Beirut, 1980) and the more careful account of N. Takrītī, *Al-Falsafa al-akhlāqiyya al-Aflāṭūniyya 'inda mufakkirī al-Islam* (Beirut, 1982). See also S.M. Stern 'Ibn al-Samḥ', in *JRAS*, 1956, pp. 31–44 and F. Jadaane, 'La philosophie de Sijistanī', in *SI*, 33 (1971), pp. 65–95, which is not, however, based on Sijistānī's own work. I have unfortunately not been able to see J.L. Kraemer's 'Abū Sulaymān as-Sijistānī, A Muslim Philosopher of the Tenth Century', unpublished Ph.D. dissertation, Yale University, 1967.

122. Ibn Khaldūn, *Prolégomènes*, vol. 2, p. 387.

123. *Ibid.*, p. 385.

124. On narrative and performative statements, see Tahānawī, *Kashshāf*, p. 1360; Ibn al-Ḥājib, *Mukhtaṣar*, p. 68; Suyūṭī, *Itqān*, vol. 2, p. 76 and Pseudo-Qudāma, *Naqd*, pp. 36 ff. See Van Ess, *Erkenntnislehre*, pp. 97–8. The topic of *khabar* was dealt with in detail in my *Al-Kitāba at-tārīkhiyya*, ch. 1.

125. For instance, Ibn al-Ḥājib, *Mukhtaṣar*, p. 68; Tahānawanī, *Kashshāf*, p. 410 and Baghdādī, *Kifāya*, p. 16.

126. Ibn Sīnā, *Najāt*, p. 17 and see Goichon, *Lexique*, para. 206.

127. Āmidī, *Iḥkām*, vol. 2, p. 7.

128. It appears that this criticism was most systematically levelled by Rāzī. See the account of Shawkānī, *Irshād*, pp. 42–3 and see Āmidī, *Iḥkām*, vol. 2, pp. 7 ff., Sakkākī, *Miftāḥ*, p. 206; Jurjānī, *Dalā'il*, pp. 344 ff. and Taftāzānī, *Sharḥ*, p. 28.

129. Bīrūnī, *Āthār*, p. 5.

130. See Al-Azmeh, *Ibn Khaldūn: An Essay*, pp. 121 ff.

131. Āmidī, *Iḥkām*, vol. 2, pp. 17 ff.; Bāqillānī, *Tamhīd*, paras. 635 ff. and Qarāfī, *Tanqīh*, p. 153.

132. The most comprehensive accounts of this matter are in Ījī, *Tuḥfa*, pp. 227–9 and Ibn Khaldūn, *Prolégomènes*, vol. 1, pp. 56–7 and *passim*.

133. For instance, Taftāzānī, *Sharḥ*, pp. 31–4.

134. For instance, Shawkānī, *Irshād*, p. 55.

135. On the notion of *tawātur* and the position of the minority averse to its use, see Baghdādī, *Kifāya*, p. 16; Suyūṭī, *Muzhir*, vol. 1, p. 114; Shawkānī, *Irshād*, pp. 46–8 and Anbārī, *Luma'*, p. 33. The point was also made that though *tawātur* might exclude the possibility of a compact, it does not exclude that of a common error (Shawkānī, *Irshād*, pp. 73 ff.).

136. For these criteria, see Ījī, *Tuḥfa*, pp. 236 ff. For discussions of particular instances of such matters, see A.D. 'Umarī, *Mawārid al-Khaṭīb al-Baghdādī fī tārīkh Baghdād* (Damascus, 1975), pp. 98–101 and B.'A. Ma'rūf, *Al-Dhahabī wa manhajuhu fī kitābihi tārīkh al-Islām* (Cairo, 1976), pp. 455–7. See also 'U. Muwāfī, *Manhaj al-naqd at-tārīkhī 'ind al-Muslimīn* (Alexandria, n.d.), pp. 146–7.

137. Ṭāshköprüzāde, *Miftāḥ*, vol. 2, p. 134.

138. By W. Montgomery Watt, *Muslim Intellectual. A Study of Al-Ghazali* (Edinburgh, 1963), p. 23.

139. See Ibn al-Ṣalāḥ, *'Ulūm*, pp. 10–114 and the modern discussion of Ṣ. Ṣāliḥ, *'Ulūm al-ḥadīth wa muṣṭalaḥuhu*, 11th edn (Beirut, 1979). Indications of terminological ambiguity

can be found in G.H.A. Juynboll, *Muslim Tradition. Studies in Chronology, Provenance, and Authorship of Early Ḥadīth* (Cambridge, 1983), pp. 176 ff.

140. Al-Azmeh, *Ibn Khaldūn: An Essay*, p. 90 and the accompanying footnotes, and Ibn al-Azraq, *Badā'i'*, vol. 1, p. 145.

141. 'Aẓma, *Al-Kitāba at-tārīkhiyya*, ch. 1, *passim*.

142. Subkī, *Ṭabaqāt*, vol. 2, p. 9 and see pp. 2–23.

143. Sakhāwī, *I'lān*, pp. 68–9.

144. For instance, Dhahabī, *Mughnī*, vol. 1, nos. 12, 102, 309, and *passim*.

145. Rāzī, *Asās*, pp. 205–9.

146. Ibn Khaldūn, *Prolégomènes*, vol. 2, p. 399.

147. *Ibid.*, pp. 405–6.

148. 'Abd al-Jabbār, *Faḍl*, p. 194.

149. For instance, Ghazālī, *Iljām*, pp. 13 ff.

150. For instance, Ibn Khaldūn, *Tārīkh*, vol. 2, p. 10 and Pseudo-Qudāma, *Naqd*, p. 41.

151. Baṣrī, *Mu'tamad*, pp. 419–20 and see Shawkānī, *Irshād*, pp. 186 ff.

152. Baṣrī, *Mu'tamad*, p. 394 and see p. 395.

153. A thorough review of this issue is given by Shawkānī, *Irshād*, pp. 190 ff.

154. Ibn Ḥazm, *Iḥkām*, pp. 495, 509, 590.

155. See particularly the discussion of Ibn al-Ḥājib, *Mukhtaṣar*, pp. 55–65.

156. Ibn Ḥazm, *Iḥkām*, pp. 647 ff. and see also Abū Ya'lā, *Mu'tamad*, paras. 484–5, and see para. 483 where this motto is denied in the field of dogmatics. On this slogan in general, see Shahrastānī, *Milal*, pp. 86 ff. and Subkī, *Mu'īd*, p. 106.

157. I will only cite here the Ḥanbalite Abū Ya'lā, *Mu'tamad*, para. 3.

158. See the curious statement of Ṭāshköprüzāde, *Miftāḥ*, vol. 1, p. 311, which might imply some awareness of this issue.

159. See the discussion of Ibn Khaldūn, *Prolégomènes*, vol. 2, pp. 385–6.

160. See Suyūṭī, *Iqtirāḥ*, pp. 52 ff. and the copious discussion of these issues by S. Afghānī, *Fī uṣūl an-naḥw* (Damascus, 1963), pp. 16 ff., who mentions doubts by grammarians and lexicographers about the literal exactitude of *ḥadīth*, and its liability to corruption due to non-Arab transmitters. The fundamental work on the history of Arabic is that of J. Fück, *'Arabīya: Recherches sur l'histoire de la langue et du style arabe*, tr. C. Denizeau (Paris, 1955), where the standardisation of the classical is studied on pp. 113 ff.

161. Suyūṭī, *Muzhir*, vol. 1, p. 101.

162. Ibn Khaldūn, *Prolégomènes*, vol. 3, p. 283.

163. Ibn Jinnī, *Khaṣā'iṣ*, vol. 1, pp. 34–6 and see other definitions in Suyūṭī, *Iqtirāḥ*, pp. 30–1.

164. Sakkākī, *Miftāḥ*, p. 37.

165. On grammatical analogies and their categories of viability, see Suyūṭī, *Iqtirāḥ*, pp. 39 ff., 115 ff.

166. Suyūṭī, *Muzhir*, vol. 1, pp. 1–4. Thus Arabic lexicography showed little concern with lexical development: W. Fischer, 'Die Altarabische in islamischer Überlieferung: Das Klassische Arabisch', in Fischer (ed.), *Grundriss der arabischen Philologie, Bd. 1: Sprachwissenschaft* (Wiesbaden, 1982), pp. 47–8.

167. Muqaddasī, *Taqāsīm*, p. 183 and se p. 128. A study of Muqaddasī's testimony on the state of Arabic in his world was made by Fück, *Arabīya*, pp. 163 ff.

168. Maqqarī, *Nafḥ aṭ-ṭīb*, vol. 1, pp. 221–2, quoting the famous linguist Ibn Sa'īd. It is interesting to compare this situation with that of Britain in the late antiquity, where Latin was particularly well and correctly cultivated and preserved in a linguistically alien environment: E. Auerbach, *Literary Language and its Public in Late Latin Antiquity and in the Early Middle Ages*, tr. R. Manheim (London, 1965), p. 85. Arabic technical terminology must have profited from the fact that Arabic was not the everyday language: cf. *ibid.*, p. 274.

169. Ibn Ḥazm, *Manṭiq*, p. 168.

170. Ibn Maḍā', *Radd*, p. 80.

171. Shawkānī, *Irshād*, pp. 16–17.

172. See the discussion of the man commonly regarded as the founder of this science in the formal sense, Anbārī (d. 577/1181), *Luma'*, p. 27, and see the pretentious but enlightening account of Suyūṭī, *Iqtirāḥ*, pp. 21 ff.

173. See the 'Introduction' to Anbārī, *Luma'*, p. 7 and Ibn Ḥajar, *Durar*, vol. 3, p. 332.

174. Ibn Jinnī, *Khaṣā'iṣ*, vol. 1, pp. 87 ff. and see Ibn Maḍā', *Radd*, pp. 80 ff. and *passim*. For particularly developed analyses of grammatical *'ilal*, see Zajjājī, *Īḍāḥ*, pp. 64–5 and see Bohas, 'Quelques aspects', pp. 208–9.

175. On the relation of exceptions to grammatical regularity, see Ibn Jinnī, *Khaṣā'iṣ*, vol. 1, pp. 97 ff. and see pp. 184–5. Ibn Jinnī insisted that if the paradigmatic Arab made an utterance which contradicted or otherwise departed from what one expected to be said according to the rules, one must eschew what one thus expected, a matter that Suyūṭī (*Iqtirāḥ*, p. 209) likened to the jettisoning of any legal judgement if it transpired that it disagreed with a textual statement. Similarly, the Fatimid Caliph al-Mu'izz likened the apodicticity of beduins in matters of language to the authority in religious matters of the Prophet's line — Al-Qāḍī al-Nu'mān, *Majālis*, para. 97.

176. For a judicious review of the Baṣran-Kūfan school issue, much exaggerated in scholarship, see Afghānī, *Uṣūl an-naḥw*, pp. 197 ff. For technical details on points of difference, see Sh. Ḍaif, *Al-Madāris an-naḥwiyya* (Cairo, 1968). Consensus in grammar is based on common opinion of these two schools: Suyūṭī, *Iqtirāḥ*, p. 88.

177. Afghānī, *Uṣūl an-naḥw*, p. 72.

178. For instance, Suyūṭī, *Iqtirāh*, pp. 176 ff.

179. Zajjājī, *Īḍāḥ*, p. 48.

180. See 'Askarī, *Ṣinā'atain*, pp. 11, 15, and 'Abbās, *Tārīkh*, *passim* and Mandūr, *Al-Naqd*, *passim*.

181. See for instance Ḥajjī Khalīfa, *Kashf*, col. 635. Ibn al-Jawzī (*Talbīs*, pp. 114 ff.) chided many of his contemporary *ḥadīth* specialists for confining their knowledge to memory and their ignorance of the wider, legal and other implications of their knowledge, and for their pride in obscurities and even their ignorance of Arabic.

182. Suyūṭī, *Itqān*, vol. 1, p. 181 and see also Ḥajjī Khalīfa, *Kashf*, cols. 427–8.

183. This matter is well reviewed by A.T. Welch, 'Al-Ḳur'ān', in *EI*, vol. 5, pp. 408–9.

184. A very convenient description of these variations is given by Ibn Qutaiba, *Ta'wīl*, pp. 28–9.

185. For instance, Zarkashī, *Burhān*, vol. 1, pp. 9 ff.

186. On the exegesis of Rāzī and its reputation and influence, see Dhahabī, *Al-Tafsīr*, vol. 1, pp. 295 ff. See also R. Arnaldez, 'Apories sur la predéstination et le libre arbitre dans le commentaire de Rāzī', in *MIDEO*, 6 (1959–61), pp. 123–6, and Arnaldez, 'Trouvailles philosophiques dans le commentaire coranique de Fakhr al-Dīn al-Rāzī', in *Etudes philosophiques et littéraires*, 3 (1968), pp. 11–24.

187. Ghazālī, *Mustasfā*, vol. 1, p. 4.

188. 'Abd al-Jabbār, *Faḍl*, p. 184.

189. Baṣrī (*Mu'tamad*, p. 10) was concerned that the Mu'tazilite conception of divine justice and providence should have legal consequences. The history of legal theory is yet to be written, but a good idea of it, as of the Baṣrī-Ghazālī-Rāzī tradition can be obtained from Ibn Khaldūn, *Prolégomènes*, vol. 3, pp. 21–3 and Ḥajjī Khalīfa, *Kashf*, col. 1878. This tradition also seems to have been particularly influenced by the Ḥanafite legal tradition, celebrated for its use of non-traditional argumentation — see Ibn Khaldūn, *Prolégomènes*, vol. 3, p. 21 and Ḥajjī Khalīfa, *Kashf*, col. 110.

190. For instance, Āmidī, *Iḥkām*, vol. 1, p. 9; Ibn al-Ḥājib, *Mukhtaṣar*, pp. 2–3 and Shawkānī, *Irshād*, pp. 5–6.

191. For instance, Tawḥīdī, *'Ulūm*, paras. 13–14, and Ṭāshköprüzāde, *Miftāḥ*, vol. 2, p. 5.

192. Fārābī, *Iḥṣā'* (ed. Amīn), p. 132.

193. A particularly clear and concise statement of these matters is given by Baṣrī,

Mu'tamad, pp. 11-12. See also Ibn Khaldūn, *Prolégomènes*, vol. 3, pp. 17-18 and the linguistic statement of all these matters in Pazdawī, *Kanz*, pp. 26-8.
194. Bājī, *Minhāj*, para. 19.
195. See particularly Jurjānī, *Ta'rīfāt*, p. 194.
196. Although modern scholarship on theology dates the *via moderna* with Juwainī and his pupil Ghazālī, Arabic authors often reserved this term for authors who succeeded Rāzī and who were epitomised by the formalist scholasticism of 'Adud al-Dīn al-Ījī: see Sakhāwī, *Ḍaw'*, vol. 4, pp. 148-9 and Ghubrīnī, *'Unwān*, p. 226. This applies more especially to legal theory, but see also Ghubrīnī, *'Unwān*, pp. 109-10.
197. Gardet and Anawati, *Théologie*, pp. 65-6, 71-2.
198. Ghazālī, *Radd*, pp. 194 ff. Ghazālī (*Mustasfā*, vol. 1, pp. 7 ff.) declared that his propedeutic chapter was a preface to all science, not only to legal theory.
199. For instance, Ibn al-Ḥājib's, *Mukhtaṣar*.
200. Aḥmad Bābā, *Nayl*, p. 32.
201. See Ghubrīnī, *'Unwān*, pp. 109-110, 230, 301 and *passim*, and Maqqarī, *Nafḥ*, vol. 2, p. 113 and *passim*.
202. Shāṭibī, *Muwāfaqāt*, vol. 2, pp. 4-6, 9 ff. and see Ibn Khaldūn, *Prolégomènes*, vol. 2, p. 97. The affinity between some of Ibn Khaldūn's conceptions (such as necessity/supererogatoriness, 'natural law' consonant with divine intent, etc.) and those of Shāṭibī are manifest. See 'A. Fākhūrī, *Al-Risāla ar-ramziyya fī uṣūl al-fiqh* (Beirut, 1978), p. 69n., and M.A. 'Ālim, 'Muqaddimat Ibn Khaldūn: Madkhal ibistimūlūjī', in *Al-Fikr al-'Arabī*, 1/6 (1978), pp. 35-50, *passim*. Perhaps both were strongly under the subtle influence of the crypto-Ẓāhirism that will be discussed in the next chapter. They were also under the influence of Ḥanafite legal theory, much praised by Ibn Khaldūn (Sakhāwī, *Ḍaw'*, vol. 4, pp. 148-9), which came to North Africa with Bājī (Ibn Khaldūn, *Prolégomènes*, vol. 3, p. 7) and which, was Pazdawī at least, emphasised the certainty of legal theory and the 'naturalistic' theory of law, to the extent that a later Ḥanafite had to edit Pazdawī's treatise in a manner which satisfied the enemies of Mu'tazilism (Ḥajjī Khalīfa, *Kashf*, cols. 496, 498).
203. Shāṭibī, *Muwāfaqāt*, vol. 1, p. 7 and see vol. 2, p. 288 for an impassive indication that the author might have expected resistance to his work.
204. Maqqarī, *Nafḥ*, vol. 1, p. 556; vol. 3, p. 216. See A. Turki, 'Veneration pour Malik et la physiognomie de malikisme andalou', in *SI*, 33 (1975), pp. 45 and *passim*.
205. Al-Azmeh, *Ibn Khaldūn: An Essay*, pp. 159-61.
206. See *Lisān al-'Arab*, vol. 17, p. 418.
207. Shahrastānī, *Milal*, pp. 19-20 and see Ibn 'Aqīl, *Funūn*, p. 7. The most satisfactory introduction to Islamic law is that of S. Mahmassani, *Falsafat al-Tashri fi al-Islam. The Philosophy of Jurisprudence in Islam*, tr. F.J. Ziadeh (Leiden, 1961).
208. The concerns of Shī'ite *uṣūl al-fiqh*, its structure and its topics, were very much the same as those of the Sunnites, complicated (but not very much) only by the infallibility of the imām, with whose judgement consensus must accord (R. Brunschvig, 'Les *uṣûl al-fiqh* imāmites a leur stade ancein (x[e] et xi[e] siecles)', in *Le Shi'îsme Imâmîte*, ed. T. Fahd (Paris, 1970), p. 209 and *passim*): substitute the prophet's companions for the imām and a position emerges not unlike that of Ibn Ḥazm. In positive law, the positions of the Twelvers accorded normally with one or other of the four main Sunnite positions, and a juristic particularism, though present, was not very significant (Y. Linant de Bellefonds, 'Le droit imâmîte', in *Le Shi'îsme Imâmîte*, pp. 185 and *passim*).
209. See the concise and comprehensive account of Ibn Khaldūn, *Prolégomènes*, vol. 3, pp. 26 ff.
210. See the indications of Ghazālī, , *Mustasfā*, vol. 1, p. 5.
211. For instance, Ibn Khaldūn, *Prolégomènes*, vol. 3, p. 1.
212. See, for instance, Ibn Rajab, *Dhail*, vol. 1, p. 360; Sakhāwī, *Ḍaw'*, vol. 1, p. 19 and Ibn al-'Imād, *Shadharāt*, vol. 6, pp. 266, 347.
213. I will refer the reader to one outstanding text, Ibn Rushd, *Bidāya*, which (vol.

1, p. 5) makes an important programmatic statement. See also the learned and perceptive study of C. Chehata, 'L'Ikhtilāf et la conception musulmane du droit', in Berque and Charnay (eds.), *Ambivalence*, pp. 258–66.

214. See the account of the various positions in Shawkānī, *Irshād*, pp. 253–4. This matter has recently been the subject of a thorough review: W.B. Hallaq, 'Was the Gate of Ijtihad Closed?', in *IJMES*, 16 (1984), pp. 3–41.

215. Ibn Khaldūn, *Prolégomènes*, vol. 3, p. 248.

216. *Ibid.*, pp. 12–13.

217. Ibn Khallikān, *Wafayāt*, vol. 2, p. 135.

218. M. Milliot, 'La conception de l'état et de l'ordre légal dans l'Islam', in *Academie de droit international. Recueil des cours*, 75 (1949), p. 645.

219. See Berque, *Méthode juridique*, p. 84 and ch. 6, *passim*.

220. See Chehata, 'L'Ikhtilāf', p. 262.

221. See Turki, *Polémiques*, pp. 48–9, 50–1.

222. Aḥmad Bābā, *Nayl*, p. 191.

223. C. Chehata, 'Logique juridique et droit musulman', in *SI*, 23 (1965), pp. 16–17.

224. Hallaq, 'The Gate of Ijtihad', p. 19.

225. Berque, *Méthode juridique*, p. 21.

226. See the characterisation of Andalusian Mālikism which is of wider applicability, by Turki, *Polémiques*, pp. 48–9.

227. Ibn Rushd, *Manāhij* (ed. Qāsim), p. 148.

228. Khayyāṭ, *Intiṣār*, p. 93.

229. See the Editor's Introduction to Māturīdī, *Tawḥīd*, pp. 19–25 (and p. 25 n. 4 for the literature on the discordances between these two schools), and Gardet and Anawati, *Théologie Musulmane*, p. 61.

230. Ibn Khaldūn, *Prólegomènes*, vol. 3, pp. 27, 35.

231. *Ibid.*, pp. 36 ff. On p. 43 the author concludes that this science is no longer justified due to the extinction of enemies of the faith. Ḥadīth narratives of the same import were the concern of Ibn Fūrak, *Mushkil*, pp. 3 and *passim*.

232. On the topical history of theology as gleaned from the strucutre and content of theological treatises, see Gardet and Anawati, *Théologie Musulmane*, pp. 136 ff.

233. *Ibid.*, p. 313 and *passim*, and L. Gardet, 'Quelques réflections sur la place du *'Ilm al-Kalām* dans les "sciences religieuses" musulmanes', in *Arabic and Islamic Studies in Honor of H.A.R. Gibb*, ed. G. Makdisi (Leiden, 1965), pp. 259, 263–7.

234. This method was also familiar from later Platonic dialogues and subsequent philosophy: Lloyd, *Polarity and Analogy*, pp. 148 ff.

235. See, for instance, Gardet and Anawati, *Théologie Musulmane*, pp. 71 ff. The correlation of abandonment of old methods of argumentation and 'logicisation', as seems to be implied by the discussion of Rāzī by Van Ess (*Erkenntnislehre*, pp. 30–2), is thus unjustified. Also unjustified is the assertion (pp. 31–2) that Rāzī abandoned the method of division: a glance at his philosophical compendium, the *Mabāḥith*, would reveal division as an important tool of argumentation.

236. Ḥajjī Khalīfa, *Kashf*, col. 419.

237. *Ibid.*, col. 77.

238. This historigraphical paradigm was current in Arabic thought, and is historiographic orthodoxy amongst scholars of today. See Ibn Khaldūn, *Shifā'*, pp. 110–11 and *passim* and Ibn al-Jawzī, *Talbīs*, pp. 164–6.

239. D. Urvoy, *Le monde de ulèmas andalous du V/XIe au VII/XIIIe siècle* (Geneva, 1978), p. 45.

240. Kalābādhī, *Ta'arruf*, p. 82; Qushairī, *Risāla*, vol. 1, p. 296 and Ibn Sab'īn, *Budd*, pp. 123 and *passim*.

241. See the general statements of Ibn Khaldūn, *Shifā'* (ed. Khalifé), chs. 2 and 3 and see pp. 41 ff. For *maqāmāt* and *aḥwāl*, see Qushairī, *Risāla*, vol. 1, pp. 234–6 and Sarrāj, *Luma'*, pp. 65–6. For a relatively concise description of the series of stations and

dispositions, see *ibid.*, pp. 68 ff., 82 ff. For a detailed sketch in a European language, see mistitled article of E. Blochet, 'Etudes sur l'esoterisme musulman', in *Le Muséon*, N.S., 7 (1906), pp. 189–212, 295–324; 8 (1907), 318–42; 9 (1908), pp. 85–102, 255–76 and 10 (1909), pp. 5–38, 175–205, 295–330.

242. See Ibn Khaldūn, *Shifā'* (ed. Khalifé), pp. 69, 74 and *passim*. See Sarrāj, *Luma'*, pp. 422–3 for description of ecstatic perception and ecstatic expression.

243. Sha'rānī, *Ṭabaqāt*, vol. 1, p. 5.

244. Ibn al-'Arīf, *Maḥāsin*, p. 81.

245. Sha'rānī, *Ṭabaqāt*, vol. 1, p. 4.

246. *Ibid.*, p. 166.

247. Sarrāj, *Luma'*, pp. 43–4.

248. *Ibid.*, pp. 456–7.

249. For instance, Sha'rānī, *Ṭabaqāt*, vol. 2, pp. 15, 21.

250. See Ibn Khaldūn, *Shifā'*, pp. 21 ff. and Ibn al-Khaṭīb, *Rawḍa*, pp. 110 ff.

251. Most thoroughly by Ibn Sab'īn, *Budd*, pp. 96 f. and *passim*.

252. Qushairī, *Risāla*, vol. 2, p. 422.

253. M. Serres, *Hermes: Literature, Science, Philosophy*, tr. J.V. Harari and D.F. Bell (Baltimore and London), 1982, p. 88.

254. 'Aẓma, *Al-Kitāba at-tārikhīyya*, pp. 131 ff.

255. 'Aẓma, 'Al-Siyāsa wa al-lā-Siyāsa', *passim*.

256. 'Aẓma, *Al-Kitāba at-tārikhiyya*, ch. 3, *passim*, for the present account.

257. See the analysis of Sharārā, 'Al-Malik, al-'āmma', pp. 42–3 and Sharārā, *Isti'nāf al-bad'*, pp. 132 ff. and *passim*.

258. W. Sacksteder, 'Analogy: Justification for Logic'', in *Philosophy and Rhetoric*, 12/1 (1979), pp. 27–9 and *passim*.

259. See, for instance, Qifṭī, *Tārīkh*, p. 1.

260. See the elaborate classification of Ṭāshköprüzāde (*Miftāḥ*, vol. 1, pp. 325–6) of sciences and their object from the body: see Figure 1, p. 182.

261. As for instance, the account of meteorology in Qalqashandī, *Ṣubḥ*, vol. 2, pp. 175 ff. or of cosmology in *ibid.*, pp. 154–5.

262. By one Ibn Labūdī in the seventh/thirteenth century: Ḥajjī Khalīfa, *Kashf*, col. 382.

263. See E.R. Curtius, 'Zur Geschichte des Wortes Philosophie im Mittelalter', in *Romanische Forschungen*, 57/2–3 (1943), pp. 294 ff.

264. Peters, *Aristotle and the Arabs*, p. xx.

265. Pines, *Madhhab adh-dharra*, pp. 78 ff.

266. Pines, 'Abul-Barakat', in *EI*, vol. 1, p. 112.

267. Rāzī, *Mabāḥith*, vol. 1, pp. 375–6. For other indications, see *ibid.*, pp. 111–12 and Ibn Rushd, *Mā ba'd aṭ-ṭabī'a*, pp. 47–9, 57–8.

268. Mas'ūdī, *Tanbīh*, p. 122.

269. Gardet and Anawati, *Mystique musulmane*, 2nd edn (Paris, 1968), p. 56.

270. See the judicious review of Ibn Khaldūn, *Prolégomènes*, vol. 3, pp. 116–17 and the detailed division of Fārābī, *Iḥṣā'* (ed. Amīn), pp. 117–19 and see Baghdādī, *Mu'tabar*, vol. 2, p. 27.

271. Ibn Khaldūn, *Prolégomènes*, vol. 2, p. 316.

272. Baghdādī, *Mu'tabar*, vol. 2, p. 232 and M. Plessner, 'Al-Fārābī's Introduction to the Study of Medicine', pp. 309, 312.

273. See Ibn Khaldūn, *Prolégomènes*, vol. 3, pp. 87–8 and Khwārizmī, *Mafātīḥ*, p. 200.

274. Ibn Khaldūn, *Prolégomènes*, vol. 3, pp. 112–13.

275. Khūnajī, *Jumal*.

276. See among others Ḥajjī Khalīfa, *Kashf* (ed. Flügel), vol. 2, pp. 623–4.

277. The magical remedies with which Arabic medicine was full (Ullman, *Islamic Medicine*, pp. 107 ff. and see the Prophetic examples in Ibn Qayyim al-Jawziyya, *Ṭibb*, pp. 124, 141 and *passim*) are assimilable to talismanic and other qualitative conceptions.

278. See Fārābī's construction of the pre-history of philosophy in *Ḥurūf*, paras. 118

ff., 141–3.

279. Apology for natural science was often made with recourse to its association with the thoroughly commendable science of medicine. See, for instance Ghazālī, *Iḥyā'*, vol. 1, p. 22.

280. Qifṭī, *Tārīkh*, p. 292.

281. On this dispute, see Hajjī Khalīfa, *Kashf*, cols. 989–90. Ibn Khaldūn, who was particularly well informed on these matters, does not doubt the attribution, though he had not read the book (*Prolégomènes*, vol. 3, p. 131).

282. See 'A. Zai'ūr, 'Madkhal ilā dirāsat al-fikr as-siyāsī li Ibn Sīnā', in *Al-Bāḥith*, 1/2 (1978), pp. 50–69.

283. One author (Ṭāshköprüzāde, *Miftāḥ*, vol. 2, pp. 593–4) assimilated divinatory sciences to Qur'ānic sciences on the assumption that their proper object concerns the Letters of the holy book.

Chapter Five

The Institution and Continuity of Scientific Formations

We have spoken of sciences as involving closure, authority, the apodicticity of premisses whose axiomaticism is arbitrary with respect to the sciences, not being derived or derivable from them. We have spoken of the inclusion and exclusion of topics which constitute the integrity and limits of science, but which were not necessarily generated by the often putative 'object' of science, but which were rather the results of an *ad hoc* incorporation in specific historical circumstances and in response to such circumstances. We have spoken of premisses bearing a compulsion not necessarily connected to inferential or other strictly rational relations, being more properly the function of extra-epistemic compulsion. These generated, so to speak, lines of force that compelled intellectual relations to run parallel to themselves. We have spoken, in short, of sciences as political systems, maintained as paradigms by relations of force built upon willing consent, and hence hegemonic rather than coercive. In other words, we have spoken of sciences and their paradigms as institutions rather than systems of ideas, as units embodied in history rather than as the ethereal creatures of the 'history of ideas'. If sciences are to have any integrity and effectivity, they would have to be units whose continuity in time (paradigmatic tradition) and in space (paradigmatic unity) is maintained. This maintenance is assured by closure and authority, and these in turn are only possible in view of the extra-scientific body of science: the scientific institutions of education and of schools, both of which are also composed of scientific personnel, who are in turn embodied in society and polity.

But that the integrity and continuity of scientific paradigms in Arabic thought was legitimised institutionally by recourse to myths of origin involving founding fathers, inaugural events or texts, does not grant us licence to indulge in myth-making of our own and to adopt the Manichean reason/belief antinomy upon which much modern scholarship is based. Reason and belief are not antithetical substances, but are strands of apodictic origin woven into the meshes of scientific paradigms and of individual intellects, as we have seen in many instances above and we shall have occasion to witness in many locations below. The line dividing incompatible statements does not lie along a fault dividing the two imaginary terrains of Reason and Belief, but relates to the specific and local relation of statements and positions to criteria of topical admissibility and apodictic relevance. Thus 'Ḥanbalism' is vastly more complex than what it is normally served up to be, as the paragon and very quintessence of unreason and spiritual aridity, which is thus incompatible with philosophy and mysticism, which lie on the other side of the great divide. The facts of the matter are, of course, otherwise.[1] Indeed, it might be said that the fundamentalist rigour of Ibn Taimiyya, for one, was geared towards clearing verbiage off the ground by the exercise of rigorous reason. Appeals to the unadulterated original texts amongst the Zāhirites were, similarly, occasions for the direct exercise of the mind upon the inexhaustible original text and without the dead weight of tradition. The spurious aridity and authoritarianism of Ẓāhirism was not, in fact, a factor that inhibited adherence to this legal school by a personality thoroughly saturated by that alternative and antithetical substance, doctrinal freedom and spirituality, as Ibn 'Arabī himself,[2] for whom the writ of the original meaning of the text was written on his eschatological imagery.[3] Indeed, Ibn 'Arabī was also the author of epitomes of canonical *ḥadīth* works, of a *ḥadīth* compendium, and of legal works, no less than of esoteric works some of which, he said, God had not commanded him to reveal.[4] Similarly, the great Andalusian esoteric mystic Ibn al-'Arīf (d. 536/1141) was an avid scholar of Qur'ānic variants and other traditional material,[5] which his spiritualist substance, according to much modern scholarship, should have rendered inadmissible, or at least irrelevant. And finally, it will not be irrelevant to note that Ibn Sīnā, who is said to inhabit intellectual territory unadulterated by Belief, wore the *ṭailasān*, the distinctive head-dress of juristic divines, for at least a period of his life.[6]

Sciences such as positive law, and schools such as the Mu'tazilite, are historical entities whose boundaries were established and changed by historical circumstances, and for whom the admissibility and inadmissibility of topics and other matters were matters pertaining to topical boundaries which are historically determinate. They were not beholden to binary incompatibilities (Reason/Belief) generated by the Enlightenment to denote the target of its polemic. A science is an historically specific paradigmatic space guarded by scientific authority and the sanction of unscientificity, and a school is a determinate historical combination of sciences and of extra-scientific connections and sanctions; historical determinants outside the paradigmatic space can dictate topics which a science incorporates or rejects, and generates the force that welds together disparate topics and apodictic systems into determinate paradigmatic formations. The same type of historical determination is at work in the determination of the legitimacy of particular scientific pursuits, such as astrology, alchemy and philosophy. Sciences were differentiated by honour in the usual hierarchical manner, and the honour and status of a science in the pecking order of hierarchical legitimacy was a function of the status of the result of the science, and of the certitude of its procedures.[7] Reprehensible sciences, which were scientific nevertheless, were those which are harmful either to the community, such as magic and talismanics, or to their practitioner, such as the belief in extra-divine agencies, conducive to the perdition of astrologers.[8] Such was the standard view in principle, and the high point of the polemic directed against philosophy, astrology and alchemy, that of Ibn Khaldūn, deployed the full rigour of all previous such argument, maintaining that they were not only sciences that will lead to damnation, but are also scientifically impossible, pretending to have access to knowledge which transcends the capacities of human experience and intellect,[9] without implying that such knowledge is in itself unthinkable.

Over and above the moral and legal aspects of scientific legitimacy are the central facts that the practical result of a science is incidental, that a science, once constituted, is in fact pursued for its own sake,[10] and that much of the hostility existing between sciences and the self-arrogation of superiority by the practitioners of a science, are functions of scientific narcissism[11] and, so to speak, defences of scientific territoriality. In short, once constituted, sciences are pursued whenever questions about their legitimacy do not lead to the destruction of their institutions and personnel, and so long as these institutions are capable of self-sustenance and scientific self-reproduction and have not become moribund.

It was only very rarely that sciences were completely delegitimated, and then for short periods only. By and large, all sciences were cultivated, even in conditions of acute stigma, and rarely was there an inquisitorial system set up for the determination of legitimacy and the imposition of a sole set of admissible propositions, or even *ad hoc* inquisitorial processes (*imtiḥānāt*, s. *imtiḥān*),[12] set in motion. It was only rarely that such sciences as *falsafa*, philosophy, or schools such as Mu'tazilism, became the object of explicit and effective interdiction, i.e. a negative judgement upon legitimacy backed by the executive authority and power of the state. It was in circumstances of adversity that schools were most sharply defined, for not unnaturally, objects of condemnation have to be made clear.

Criteria of Illicit Knowledge

Muslim scholars and jurists were exceedingly wary of condemning propositions as *kufr*, a term for which 'unbelief' rather than 'heresy' would be a closer rendition. It implies an act rejecting canonical testimony, and thus being beyond the pale of Islamdom, and consequently in direct antithesis to it.[13] A judgement of *kufr* is a legal judgement, and is one which carries the statutory punishment prescribed for apostasy, of which it is the analogue:[14] death and the confiscation of property. The charge of *kufr* is therefore a very grave one (theologico-political debates over it were a crucial element in the early development of dogmatics), and implies additionally a judgement on the eternal damnation of a *kāfir*. It is one which can only lead to a positive judgement after exhaustive deliberation employing the most thorough technical means available to jurisprudence for the examination of the proposition on the basis of which *kufr* is alleged. And one indeed has the impression that some texts detailing these matters deliberately went to considerable lengths in order to make the proof of such a charge almost impossible.[15] There is little doubt that such legal arguments were made, and such stringent checks developed, in order better to control the excesses that have occasionally been displayed in Islamic societies which, like other societies, sometimes pass through periods of acute tension which is articulated in religious and sectarian terms, and in which political and social struggles take place in the context of religion and of ideology. For indeed, as Ibn Taimiyya indicated, *kufr* cannot be pronounced against anyone belonging to *ahl al-qibla*, those who pray in the direction of Mecca, and *kufr* is no less than the contradiction of prophetic narrative.[16]

Kufr was thus sparingly employed with its full rigour, though it has been applied irresponsibly in many a polemic. Invention, *bid'a*, however, with its connotations of fatuity and transgression over established authority, was a different matter. Invention does not exclude its author from the community of those who pray towards Mecca. And indeed, in a system of thought built upon the premiss of a unity overriding societies, histories and schools, and incorporating *ijtihād*, local traditions and similar means of admitting diversity, mutual tolerance was not unnatural, but was indeed realistic, so that there was never agreement on what constituted *bid'a*, and there was even the notion of *bid'a mustaḥsana*, a discretionary invention that is commendable.[17] In fact, unlike *kufr*, invention was not a legal matter, and the literature pertaining to it was not legal,[18] for it is impossible to classify, given the equal validity and legitimacy of the various schools, despite occasional resort to intellectual and political violence. Innovation results in no practical legal consequence except in special circumstances characterised by acute social (and consequently sectarian) tensions, and in these circumstances legal judgements would tend to be contrived.

Thus under *kufr* (for Sunnites) would fall such matters, each within its context of historical relevance, as belief in the infallibility of the Imām and the correlative condemnation of non-'Alid caliphate.[19] Equally outside the pale of Islamdom were the proponents of such anomalous beliefs as metempsychosis, and of such practices as legitimising marriage with daughters-in-law, and similar matters that contradict divine or prophetic ordinance and pronouncement.[20] Also in contradiction with Islam were such philosophical doctrines as the eternity of the world or the multiplicity of divinity.[21] Annals supply us with many instances of execution of individuals for *kufr* or any of its synonyms. Two men were executed in 786/1384 in Damascus and in Tripoli, for adhering to Nuṣairite beliefs.[22] Many instances exist of execution for extreme Shī'ite positions involving the ritual cursing of the Prophet's associates.[23] Executions for mysticism-related beliefs and associated antinomianism also took place,[24] as did executions for aspertions cast upon the Prophet's veracity.[25] But equally, there were instances in which persons escaped a dire fate because of positions they occupied in society,[26] or persons who endured an *imtiḥān* with happy results.[27] More spectacularly, a true heretic such as Ibn al-Rāwandī (d. 245/859) not only escaped execution,[28] but also left posterity divided over his heresy,[29] despite his denial of Prophecy and his ridiculing of paradise as described in the Qur'ān, which he saw as a place that could provide joy only to rude rustics, 'wearing such rough material, and drinking milk and ginger, like a Kurdish bride'.[30] Similarly, Abul 'Alā' al-Ma'arrī (d. 449/1057) not only lived under tolerant circumstances, but his condemnation by posterity was by no means universal,[31] as can be seen from the number of epitomes of his works.[32] Even Ḥallāj, executed in 309/922, had an ambiguous reputation;[33] the Ḥanbalite Ibn 'Aqīl had to recant his earlier pronouncements on the sanctity of Ḥallāj,[34] which was no doubt a belief unofficially maintained in the mystical circles of Baghdad, in which the Ḥanbalites figured prominently.

There were clearly no hard and fast rules for the conditions under which *kufr* was invoked. These conditions were specific to time and locality and were, by the nature of things, aspects of cultural and more immediate forms of politics. Whereas there was, in principle, a general concept of *kufr*, no such conception like those of acceptable versus reprehensible innovations, and like the boundaries of sciences and schools of thought, are historical. We should in principle be able to indicate the political circumstances of each of the events mentioned in the previous paragraph. The sole instances where legal consequences might have become incorporated into the system of law were matters relating to the status of some communities with respect to *dhimma*, protected status under Muslim dominion, and whether these should be applied or whether a community, such as the Bāṭiniyya (proto-Ismā'īlīs), should be subject to the laws of apostasy.[35]

But even then, repentance is not foreclosed, and Ibn Taimiyya, after condemning Rāzī as a *kāfir* for the contents of writing on astral worship ascribed to him, did not exclude the possibility of his subsequent repentance and return to Islam.[36] But matters such as these were almost never definitely decided with reference to law; the lot of the Ahmadiyya in Pakistan today is very unusual. Inadmissibility in terms of religion and with reference to law was often declared by a scholar, or physically enforced by the state with the agreement of sections of scholars and divines. But it was virtually never elevated to the status of incontrovertible consensus, *ijmā'*.

Thus though no-one is likely to have contested Ibn 'Aqīl's point that inventors in matters of religion should be mercilessly treated, such invention being in religion the analogue of sedition in politics,[37] agreement about what constituted criminal invention was not available, save for the basic position that *kufr* is whatever denied the authority upon which canonical texts rest, i.e. their veracity, apodicticity and certainty. *Kufr* is the act of challenging or contravening the premisses upon which the Islamic validity of a statement is based. Just as individual sciences are premised upon apodictic statements, so is the class of all statements which belong to Islam and therefore fall in the context of the specifically Islamic positive sciences, those based upon positing by the ultimate nomothetic authority. Occult sciences were considered reprehensible by the majority, and sorcery especially was statutorily punishable with death, because they involved recourse to creative and active authorities other than God in fields not under the control of humanity.[38] Such was the lot of talismanics, although talismans were common, and a legal judgement by a famous conservative jurist specifically ruled against their interdiction, though it affirmed their reprehensible character.[39] Ghazālī himself was the author of a work on the occult science of Letters, a work on which there was to be at least one commentary,[40] and we have already mentioned occult works by Rāzī and others. The *zā'irja*, knowledge of which was closely guarded by Ibn Khaldūn,[41] was equally closely guarded by others who were familiar with it.[42] Alchemy was also widely practised, not necessarily according to the principle enunciated by Ibn Khaldūn that, generally speaking, the rich would not believe in its possibility whilst the poor would avidly pursue it:[43] there is much evidence of its practice by famous scholars and divines,[44] and sovereigns seem to have employed and honoured alchemists, but this latter was risky, and careless charlatans could come to a very bad end indeed.[45] Astrology, especially that connected to political and pseudo-historical prognostication, was very widespread both in court, where it was tolerated, and amongst messianic mystical groups, where it often led to insurrection and was thus very harshly treated,[46] not to speak of the populace at large.

The only evidence of large-scale persecution of mystics is in evidence with regard to certain North African and Andalusian esotericists attached to the Almeria school which so influenced Ibn 'Arabī, who call for special study, and who set up messianic communities one of which led to the formation of a short-lived hagiocratic state in Algarve under the fascinating and mysterious wonder-worker Ibn Qasī in 537/1142.[47] Generally speaking, none but spectacularly ecstatic and politically dangerous mystics were the object of persecution or of accusations of *kufr*. Not only had mystical scholars tried to explain in acceptable terms ecstatic pronouncements of the likes of Ḥallāj and Bisṭāmī (d. c. 260/874),[48] but they also asserted that they subscribed to the theological and dogmatic beliefs considered safest,[49] and adhered to whatever matters of positive law that were common amongst the four schools whenever this was possible.[50] One of the most esoteric of mystics explicitly insisted that any antinomian behaviour constituted *kufr* because it contradicted the prescriptive authority of God and the Prophet.[51] Though Suhrawardī was executed in Aleppo in 587/1191 upon the orders of Saladin, and although his teachings included a fair amount of astral and political lore which quite clearly constituted seditious *kufr*,[52] both his contemporaries and posterity differed over his heresy and sanctity.[53] The same applies to the famous Ḥallāj, whose execution was clearly a political decision,[54] but who, though not treated in the *Risāla* of Qushairī, was the object of much controversy,[55] venerated by mystics (but not too openly),[56] and condemned as a charlatan by others.[57] Ibn 'Arabī himself, though quite explicitly esotericist and professedly a believer in the supreme cosmological station of sainthood and in his direct inspiration by God, was highly venerated both in his lifetime and by posterity, though he was controversial,[58] to such an extent that some are said to have been given to urinating on his grave.[59] Though the monism associated with the name of Ibn 'Arabī was seen by some as a restatement of the standard Christian position on the Trinity,[60] and though his position on sainthood and its hidden politico-spiritual network of *qutb, abdāl, nuqabā*'[61] was sometimes considered a restatement of Ismā'īlī political theory,[62] it was so highly venerated a mystical system that one less imaginative mystic was subjected in the middle of the eighth century A.H. to an inquest for his criticism of the poetry of Ibn al-Fāriḍ (d. 632/1235), who wrote erotic love poems to God.[63]

Like mysticism, philosophy was tolerated, although philosophical activity was sometimes looked upon with disfavour. Occasionally, accusation of philosophy was the cause for persecution and even on occasion for execution.[64] Still, on other occasions, it was cultivated by kings such as the Almohad Abū Ya'qūb Yūsuf, whose physician was Ibn Ṭufail (d. 581/1186),[65] and was studied, secretly and unsuccessfully, by prominent opponents such as Ibn al-Ṣalāḥ (d. 643/1245) the *ḥadīth* scholar.[66] We have already seen how widespread was the use of philosophical knowledge, of knowledge generated by philosophical discourse. But philosophers tended to subscribe to three theses which, as of the time of Ibn Ḥazm, but more surely since the days of Ghazālī's refutation of Ibn Sīnā, were considered heretical: the eternity of the world, the denial that God knows particulars, and the figurative interpretation of salvation and damnation to relate to philosophical knowledge and the lack thereof.[67] Nevertheless, no legal consequences were necessarily attendant upon this. Other matters addressed by philosophers could not be the object of radical condemnation, for many of their theses were shared by various theological schools well within the bounds of Islam and were only condemned by those who equated inventions with *kufr*.[68] There are also philosophical concepts which run parallel to non-philosophical ones, as we saw, and differences here are purely nominal; other philosophical topics were unrelated to dogmatics, such as many topics in natural science.[69] And indeed, as a conservative saw, philosophers are not necessarily given to heresy, but are just a bunch of people with bizarre views.[70] Philosophy was seen moreover, especially in the Andalus, as a form of moral discipline,[71] which readily reveals Andalusian philosophy as very closely allied to certain mystical disciplines, as any reading of Ibn Ṭufail or Ibn Bāja (d. 534/1138) would reveal.

Thus relatively rare was the stridency with which someone like Suyūṭī condemned philosophy, and logic as a matter conducive to philosophy.[72] More usual was the simple declaration that philosophy, though heretical, should not imply the interdiction of logic for the learned.[73] Such were widespread attitudes, but without much practical consequence.

And not very rare were sober correctives by some who, like Ibn Taimiyya, relegated philosophical heresies to foggy thinking,[74] though this was only one aspect of Ibn Taimiyya's position on the matter. But it appears that, generally speaking, philosophers were particularly the targets of attack on the strength of their ethico-epistemological doctrine of salvation, with the suggestion that salvation is attainable by philosophical knowledge, not by prophetic guidance.[75] It was matters relating to the fate of the soul and in the context of philosophical salvation that Ibn Ṭufail criticised in Fārābī;[76] it is similar matters under the heading of '*siyāsa madaniyya*' (civics, as distinct from Islamic law) that marred the posthumous reputation of Ibn Bājā,[77] and which led Ibn Sīnā to accommodate prophetic nomothesis in the context of practical philosophy.[78] The doctrine of felicity towards which all this was geared, that salvation lay in the felicity (*sa'āda*) brought about by absolute philosophical knowledge, was one which was sharply called into question as to its very possibility by Ibn Khaldūn in his refutation of philosophy.[79] It was also well elaborated in mystical terms reminiscent of the solipsistic gnosis of mystics.[80] Indeed, the two modalities of absolute knowledge were sometimes decreed equivalent, though appropriate for different ages in the life of a person, discursive knowledge being more appropriate for youth on account of the application and diligence it requires.[81] And though philosophical arguments in defence of this doctrine, which were based on the assertion that it did not contradict canonical conceptions of salvation and damnation which only had to do with the body,[82] were not taken very seriously and, as we saw, condemned for inadmissible allegorism, some scholars like Ibn Taimiyya gave the philosophical intention all the benefit of the doubt: philosophical ethics were certainly superior to those of such people as savages without prophecy, and are indeed concerned with the public weal, which is, however, better served by prophecy.[83]

Scientific legitimacy is therefore a matter vastly more complex, and indeed far more interesting, than is allowed for by orientalist discourse, to whose antithetical categories they are by no means reducible. Philosophical topics were often coterminous with topics of other sciences, natural, theological and mystical. In all cases, the identification of that which is pure philosophy is either, as we suggested in the previous paragraph, indicated by the topical confluence of all matters philosophical in a self-conscious comprehensive and systematic form as in some compendium by Ibn Sīnā or specialist treatise by Fārābī, or else it is the accusation of heresy, an accusation which derived its force from the association of some philosophical ideas with concepts inimical to those vouched for by religion, and not from some anti-religious philosophical enterprise or impulse. Such accusations amount in effect to applying the philosophical label to ideas which may have been philosophical in origin, but which are more importantly, philosophical in association and in constituting a topical component of the philosophical paradigm. Such a label was not applied to the same ideas (such as that of essence) in other contexts such as *kalām* except in a polemical or (rarely) and neutrally historical description. We have witnessed instances of all these matters, and taken together they indicate that whenever the paradigmatic (topical) and the doxographical or heresiographical (political) descriptions of philosophy overlap, and this is not very often the case, they do so not because the political impulse of doxographical designation has grasped the truth of its subject, or because, conversely, the pure philosophical truth has found its phenomenal manifestation. When the paradigmatic and doxographical units of philosophy meet on the territory of a particular idea, or on that of the intellect of a particular personality, this constitutes the confluence of two separate entities. There is the paradigmatic unit which particular historical and cultural circumstances of the day impel towards meeting with a second entity: a body of thinkers or of doctrinal associations which the day considered suspect or inadmissible for reasons not necessarily connected with these ideas and thinkers themselves. Particular conjunctures make for the need to reclaim and evoke the connotations of godlessness and non-Islamic, and therefore in these conditions anti-Islamic, connotations of the term philosophy or the terms associated with it. It is only under determinate historical conditions that ideas were singled out and branded inadmissible and illegitimate; this has nothing to do with the ideas themselves, or with the ideas held by their opponents, for ideas do not clash, but what clashes are men in particular relations of antagonism, in determinate historical conjuctures. Ideas are admissible in certain contexts, and inadmissible in others; such for example was 'nature' which is practically admissible as such and in the context of medicine, but inadmissible formally in the context of the theory of human action propounded by certain schools of theology. The heresy of philosophy, when philosophy was taken as a token of heresy, lay beyond philosophy, since in a polemical context, philosophy and other tokens of irreligion are less determinate ideas than a semiotic value, a reference in a situation of antagonism, irrespective of the 'objectively' denotative rigour with which the content of this reference is defined.

Philosophy does not, therefore, float in an antiseptic space of Reason, unadulterated by Belief and in opposition to it. Philosophy consists of live ideas within a vigorous history, like other schools and sciences. Philosophers were constantly engaged with discussion of non-philosophical ideas, polemically and otherwise. Muḥammad b. Zakariyyā al-Rāzī wrote a treatise in defence of *kalām*, a polemic against the Mu'tazilite Jāḥiz (d. 225/869), and an epistle on habit. Fārābī wrote on the *jinn* and polemicised against the Mu'tazilites, while Yaḥyā b. 'Adī refuted atomism and the doctrine of *kasb*.[84] Ibn Sīnā is supposed to be the author of an epistle supporting the view that all human acts were created by God, and it is this that occasioned Yaḥyā b. 'Adī's retort that has just been mentioned.[85] Ibn Sīnā also refuted atomism and retorted constantly to theological arguments.[86] Christian philosophers wrote in defence of philosophy, on its agreement with Christianity, and disputed with Muslim theologians and philosophers on various topics.[87] More importantly, Ibn Rushd justifies philosophy in legal terms as a matter made obligatory on the basis of nomothetic discourse,[88] and defines it as theologians did, as the consideration of creatures in so far as they indicate their maker.[89] Likewise, Ibn Sīnā utilises the same procedure and, like theologians and unlike true philosophers according to his definition, proves the existence of God by the argument *a contingentia mundi* — a point which did not escape the attention of Ibn Rushd, who criticised Ibn Sīnā for it.[90]

Ibn Rushd was perhaps the most rigorously exacting of Arabic philosophers, though his syllogistic demands were often sacrificed for his legal arguments. There was no slight amount of sophistical argumentation in the cases that he made, and these were well catered for in terms of his theory of the levels of discourse. His criticism of others, especially of theology, is stupendously rigorous, especially with the demand that all arguments should show syllogistic rigour and eschew sophistics and dialectics. Indeed, his refutation of Ghazālī's refutation of philosophy was explicitly stated to be an examination of Ghazālī's arguments from the point of view of demonstrative certainty, and Ghazālī was deemed to have failed because he compromised too much with his age.[91] But such protestations of logical purity and exhortations to it were intended to preserve the integrity of the philosophical endeavour, for philosophy, unlike virtually all other disciplines, did not possess an institution that guarded over its paradigmatic continuity. It was rare for an individual to be merely a professional philosopher; in the Andalus, he would probably have been a professional physician or astrologer, as was the case elsewhere. A philosopher could also have been a copyist, merchant, a politician like Ibn Sīnā, or a courtier and intellectual showpiece, as was Fārābī for a while. Some, like Sijistānī, were paupers for much of their lives. Ibn Rushd was, like his grandfather, a prominent jurist, professor of jurisprudence, of Arabic and perhaps of *ḥadīth*,[92] in addition to being a renowned physician, philosopher and judge. A brief discussion of the circumstances of his *imtiḥān* will serve, it is hoped, as a cautionary example for discussions of *falsafa* and its position in Arabic thought, as well as to introduce disciplines whose paradigmatic boundaries were guarded by institutions.

When Ibn Ṭufail introduced Ibn Rushd to the Almohad Caliph Abū Yūsuf Ya'qūb al-Manṣūr in Marrakesh, the meeting started with a circumspect Ibn Rushd pretending he knew nothing of philosophy, and seems to have ended with an order to write epitomes of works by Aristotle the sovereign found obscure.[93] When later on the Caliph visited Cordoba, where Ibn Rushd had been Supreme Judge (*Qāḍī al-Jamā'a*), he publicly cursed the philosopher as a heretic in court, exiled him along with many others and ordered all philosophical works to be burnt except for those treating topics in medicine, arithmetic and aspects of astronomy.[94] But no sooner had Abū Yūsuf returned to Marrakesh than he reprieved Ibn Rushd and the others in exile, and called him back to his court in Marrakesh, which the philosopher did, only to die very soon after.[95] The charge which brought about this persecution was subscription to vague heresies dubbed *falsafa* and *zandaqa*.[96] But what seems to have been at issue was not a sudden decision by the soveriegn to satisfy some atavistic craving for philosophical blood amongst the populace and divine establishment of Cordoba. Neither was it simply a trumped-up charge by members of another, rival, prominent Cordoban scholarly and juristic family.[97] For philosophy to become unbelief, and for professional and social jealousy to become negotiable currency, and for the one to come to be related to the other, they have to intersect at a particular nexus.

Though it is probably impossible to discover exactly what this nexus was, suggestions regarding its context are eminently feasible. The context is not a sort of primordial anti-philosophical impulse, for philosophy was not a live issue but a token of other matters — in this instance, an issue connected with the religious and legal policies of the Almohads and their connection with Mālikism and the obscure fecundity of Ẓāhirite ideas in the Maghreb and the Andalus.[98] It has long been realised that Mālikism under the earlier Almohads was strongly admixed with Ẓāhirite ideas, although it does not seem that to speak of the latter supplanting the former is warranted.[99] But it was true that Ẓāhirism was a complementary component in judicial life;[100] it was complementary in that, though Mālikism was not officially abolished, its physiognomy was subjected to a very important change. Contrary to the customary picture of Mālikism as akin to a system of case-law in which the tradition of Ibn al-Qāsim in practice had precedence over all else, including nomothetic discourse itself, a picture which perhaps applies best to Mālikism under the Almoravids,[101] Mālikism under Abū Yūsuf Ya'qūb was distinct and was being recast according to an unstated Ẓāhirite model: he ordered jurists to eschew the standard local works, and it is reported that he had the *Mudawwana* of Saḥnūn burnt, a text that was the fount and origin of Maghribi Mālikism. He also commanded jurists to turn back to the original nomothetic discourse, to compile canonical *ḥadīth* and to continue the work of the founder of Almohadism Ibn Tūmart, with the compilation of a rival system of positive law.[102] The Almohads were obviously aiming at creating a new system of positive law, probably one more consonant with their time and circumstances, and, as we suggested, rigorous systems of fundamentalism are almost always innovatory in intent.

There was considerable resistance to the imposition of the new legal system, and considerable animosity to Ẓāhirisim as a result.[103] The responses of Almohad sovereigns to this resistance sometimes took the form of abolishing the *imām* status of Ibn Tūmart expressed in the proclamation of the Friday sermons in his name, but this was not always the case.[104] But the Ẓāhirite orientation of Almohad law, though it did not necessarily involve the name of the Ẓāhirite school, went counter to local legal traditions. In this, the position of Ẓāhirism was parallel to that of official Almohad theology, which was close in many respects to the Ash'arite tradition. A recent study had convincingly demonstrated, I think, the kinship between the positions of Ibn Rushd on a number of crucial theological issues and those of Ibn Tūmart.[105] Moreover, the position of Ibn Rushd on juristic theory was Ẓāhirite-inspired and counter to local Mālikism in one very central respect: he dismissed the validity of consensus independent of the original nomothetic discourse, and opted for an independent form of *ijtihād*, untrammeled by established solutions, and close to theological positions. He also asserted, as Ibn Ḥazm never tired of doing, that to admit consensus over and above the original divine and prophetic message was to adulterate the purity of the law by allowing the addition of accretions not allowed for originally, which amounts to presuming to speak for God and the Prophet.[106] Added to this pro-Almohad position in the Andalus, which was volatile at this time and whose cities were known for their turbulence and where the sacrifice of unbelievers by sovereigns to gain the support of the townspeople was not unusual,[107] was the fact that, on some apparently minute matters of positive law, Ibn Rushd was not as forthright in pro-Almohad legislation as might have been wished.[108]

The treatment of Ibn Rushd at the hands of his sovereign cannot therefore strike us as particularly surprising in an age of absolute despotism, no matter how enlightened, for the Cordobans had to have their circus after all, and the man on display, though not intended for the lions, still was to be served with a warning. Philosophers, whenever discovered or invented, were for the purposes of political spectacle, and it was specifically for the purposes of such a spectacle that they were invented and that philosophy as such and as a manifestation of unbelief was identified. Philosophy was a token, in times of need, for unbelief as a sacrificial object, and the significance of this is not that there was a visceral and congenital need for such sacrificial blood, but that certain historical conjunctures called for it in terms both of political calculus and of social and cultural economy. And while philosophy could easily be used as such a token, and could not use others as such tokens, these others found it very difficult antagonistically to relate to each other with such absolute professions of anathema. For other schools and sciences were instituted, and antagonisms between them, when acute, were tantamount to civil war. Often enough, these were waged in the name of purity of the faith, in which case resort to accusations of philosophy were used to bite at the defences of the antagonist. In all cases, antagonism was the result not of the clash of ideas, but of those who carried those ideas, as we saw in the case of Ibn Rushd, and the history of ideas and antagonism between systems of ideas and the persecution of some, can be understood only in terms of the everyday arcana attaching to these ideas and their associations — matters arcane only to us today because our criteria of importance and unimportance have occluded the body of relevant ideas and made visible only those which we can readily and lazily apprehend.

The Formation of Dogmatic and Legal Schools

Though each of the major theological and legal schools came to be instituted in a body of personnel — and historical study will show that institutionalisation in this sociological sense was paralleled with paradigmatic and terminological specification — their fortunes and the positions they occupied in Islamic societies and histories were various. Like philosophy, they are protean, and names after which schools were called were highly polyvalent, at times quite mystifying, but always definable in terms of local contemporary arcana. There were certainly always calls for eschewing verbal differences and of shedding animosities based on terminological and not substantial disputes. But it is not surprising that such calls were ignored. They were ahistorical in perspective, not having taken account of the fact that naming and labelling are not innocent or stupid acts, but that they are intended to set limits, establish boundaries and interdict communication and access. Naming is full of institutional, and hence political, significance for a name is also a token which is negotiable in the arena of cultural politics. Equally historical were the calls for unity: that of Shāṭibī was animated by his scholarly catholicity which was resisted by established local Mālikism,[109] while that of Subkī[110] was clearly apologetic and connected with the defence of a particular theological position in the face of opposition.[111] Ghazālī, for his part, was attempting to prove the superiority of gnosis over the merely relative truths of the theological schools, none of which is superior to another.[112]

We must therefore be wary of classifying schools — legal, theological and other — on the basis of the classifications available in medieval Arabic doxographies. These works are invaluable for the minute historical reconstruction of various opinions and the wider connections of such opinions. But their criteria of classification are not truly historical. Shahrastānī classified his charges according to the four great topical nodes of divine attributes, divine justice and predestination, divine advertence and reason and tradition,[113] while others such as Isfarā'īnī[114] and Ash'arī[115] fell into the pitfall he criticised, attributing school status and a name to virtually every person who propounded a special proposition on a particular topic. While Shahrastānī was forced in his account to specify and name the proponents of each detailed position within his topical nodes and thus appears at once ahistorical in his general conception and micro-historical in his detailed account, others attributed ahistorical status to every point of detail proposed by their protagonists. What confounds this already bewildering situation is what we observe throughout Arabic literature of the attribution of particular positions on, say, matters of grammar to theological schools. This might indicate that the schools, once we actually identify them historically, are more coherent at an earlier date than is so far conceded. It might also indicate that the attribution of a position to a school is not in itself indicative of that particular school and not an essential paradigmatic constituent, although grammatical positions, for instance, were of paramount importance for the theological and legal conceptions of a particular school, forming an essential component of their hermeneutic techniques. We must therefore study schools not only in terms of medieval doxographic classifications, but from an historical perspective which recognises the interdependence of speculation in the various fields of endeavour. We must look at the connection between these positions and the institutional situation of a school, at the fact that many positions are shared amongst members of different schools without this leading to the ejection of members of schools for their adoption of positions identified with another. We should also work with the consequences of the fact that schools were perfectly capable of modifying and rejecting previous positions, in addition to adopting new ones, without altering their nominal integrity, with the historical depth and the associated patrimony that this depth implies. It is also perfectly understandable that some schools take over others, such as the coalescence of Kullābiyya with the school named after Ash'arī and its disappearance within the more generic name, the transcendance of Qadariyya by the Mu'tazilites, and the absorption of Qarmaṭism ('genuine' or otherwise) at a particular point within Bāṭinism (which later became the Ismā'īliyya).[116] And finally, we must not forget the absorption within later Ash'arism of much of Mu'tazilism.[117]

Generally speaking, there was a great degree of mutual tolerance between the various legal schools, although this did not necessarily imply mutual affection or the lack of bigotry. Especially after the four schools of law were definitively established, it was not very unusual for an individual to teach or act according to more than one, or indeed to pass on from one to another without incurring censure, though the reasons for such a shift may have been personal advantage.[118] Jurists generally admitted that a *muftī*, regardless of his own legal school, should judge according to the requirements of the state.[119] But there were circumstances where communities were fractionalised along lines identified with adherence to particular theological or legal schools, and in such cases bloody confrontations were not unusual.[120] The most spectacular instance of such a situation was the Shāfi'ite-Ḥanafite dispute which persisted in Nīshāpūr for centuries, eventually leading to the destruction of the city. And while a general identification of Shāfi'ism with Ash'arism and mysticism is discernible, along with that of Ḥanafism with Mu'tazilism, these do not in any way explain the conflict or its persistence.[121] They explain the terms in which a social conflict of obscure bases was articulated and exercised, the political language of this conflict, but not the conflict itself or the binary division of the city, which is comparable to other historical instances.[122] In addition to the Nīshāpūr situation, which is also true of the whole of Khurāsān but without the same ferocity, the conflict between Ḥanbalites and Shī'ites in Baghdad is roughly comparable, although here the social and political bearings of the conflict are clearer. This involved discernible groups in Baghdad allied to the caliphate and to the dynasties — Būyid and Saljūq — to which power was delegated by the caliph in imperial terms and disputed in local terms, as well as to the related but independent conflict between the 'Alid patriciate and the caliphate, in alliance with merchants and the *petit peuple* respectively.[123] Otherwise, conflict was manifested in much milder forms in defence of vested interests, such as objections by the Shāfi'ite legal establishment against the attrition of its monopoly of judicial posts by Ḥanafites in the Mamlūk empire,[124] or the anti-Ḥanbalism with which the increasing influence of Ḥanbalite scholars and merchants in Damascus in the seventh century A.H. was met with mildly riotous Ḥanbalite reactions.[125] Similarly, it appears that the conflict between the two grammatical schools of Baṣra and Kūfa did not have conceptual issues as the overriding concern, although grammatical concepts was the field in terms of which were expressed regional interests in competition for caliphal patronage[126] — conflicts which, not unnaturally, provided technical matters with the opportunity to build their own momentum.

The terms of such conflicts were not always homogeneous. They are occasionally portrayed as antagonisms between pietistic and later theologico-legal movements, such as Ḥanbalism, and sectarian-legal movements, such as Baghdad Shī'ism. Again, they have been represented as conflicts between Ash'arism, a theological school, and Khurāsānī Ḥanafism, which was often associated with Mu'tazilism and later with Māturīdism (and the adversaries in the famous disputations of Rāzī in Transoxiania).[127] But in all cases, the topical boundaries sometimes intersected, as for instance in what Subkī, out of a wish to avoid using the accurate but risky description of Mu'tazilism, characterises as the Ḥanafite view on certain theological matters which prominent Ash'arites adopted,[128] without these Ash'arites ceasing to be so and despite the gravity in principle of the Mu'tazilite positions they adopted — not the least of which being the Mu'tazilite conception of divine justice adopted by Ghazālī, Ibn Daqīq al-'Īd (d. 716/1316), and Abū Isḥāq al-Isfarā'īnī.[129] But the lack of homogeneity does not imply ignorance on the part of Arabic authors, nor should it be regarded as a cause for confusion. After all, Arabic writers reporting such conflicts were writing of live issues, and not engaged in careful scholastic classifications, and accurately reflected the tokens in the names of which conflicts were exercised.

The *leitmotiv* of theological differences, as we have seen at various points above, concerns the interpretation of Qur'ānic verses relative to divine attributes, while legal disputes concerned matters of positive law and also points of legal theory allied to theological and methodological positions. And despite intersections and individual departures, a central core of propositions was always present as the paradigmatic body of dogma or of legislation which defined the school. In theology, such central bodies of opinions were formulated as short texts of *professions de foi*, *'aqā'id* (s. *'aqīda*), valid for a particular locality and tradition, such as that of Tahāwī (d. 321/933) or of Abū al-Qāsim al-Qushairī which Damascus Ash'arites took to be definitive,[130] or that attributed to a certain unnamed Nīshāpūrite, who may well have been Qushairī, and introduced by Saladin to Egypt as official dogma.[131] It was indeed in terms of such central propositions on divine attributes that Ibn Taimiyya was subjected to an *imtiḥān*, as a result of which he had to refute the charge of anthropomorphism by writing a statement of dogma asserting that the Qur'ān was an eternal divine attribute, neither physical speech nor linguistically conceived, and that God's position on his Throne (the Qur'ānic *istiwā'*) is not to be literally understood and must be conceived in a fideistic manner.[132] Ibn Taimiyya was not the only one persecuted in Damascus under charges of anthropomorphism. About a century earlier, another Ḥanbalite of Damascus was pronounced *kāfir* for insisting on the literal sense of Qur'ānic statements pertaining to divine attributes, an insistence which was not withdrawn — but the sole practical consequence of which was the forced emigration of Shaikh Taqī al-Dīn al-Jamā'īlī (d. 729/1329) to Cairo,[133] where apparently theology was of less consequence, and Ḥanbalites in any case only insignificantly present at a time when their influence on Damascus was increasing. But though anthropomorphic positions were normally associated with Ḥanbalites,[134] not all adherents to this position were of this school. There was for instance a Shāfi'ite who turned Ḥanafite and also adhered to Ibn Taimiyya's *mu'taqad*, belief, a term most probably referring to theological position.[135] Further, it should not be assumed that the charge of anthropomorphism indicated anthropomorphic positions: like philosophy, anthropomorphism was also a token negotiable in political and social struggles. The early history of Damascene Ḥanbalism, marked by a great increase in the wealth and authority of this, originally foreign community, is marked by much conflict and a great many accusations of anthropomorphism.

Baghdadian Ḥanbalism was thought to have been initially unruly in addition to being heretical — its supposed anthropomorphism was officially proscribed and the school decreed outside the community of

Islam in 323/935, both by proclamations of the Caliph himself.[136] But just over half a century later, under the resuscitated caliphate of al-Qādir, Ḥanbalism was very much on the ascendent and inspired a *credo* delivered by the Caliph as official dogma, a set of propositions opposed to the creeds of the Mu'tazilites, the Ash'arites and the Shī'ites.[137] Politically, this seems to have been directed against the Būyids, both in Baghdad and elsewhere, and to have been in favour of the rising Saljūqs.[138] But it was later, in the sixth/twelfth century, that Baghdadian Ḥanbalism had reached its 'grande époque':[139] it was then that Ḥanbalites were chosen for the Vizirate (such as the famous scholar from Zabīd in Yemen, the vizier of al-Muqtafī, Ibn Hubaira) and other high offices of state and the legal apparatus.[140] It was then that Ḥanbalism reigned supreme in Baghdad, its social constituents, such as popular militias (*'ayyārūn*) and sections of the Quraishite nobility, had had the better of Shī'ites, Mu'tazilites and Ash'arites, all of whom had discernible political complexions within Baghdad and in terms of wider international connections.[141] It was also in this period that Ibn al-Jawzī, the great preacher and close associate of the Caliph al-Mustaḍī' was given what have been described as virtually inquisitorial powers for dealing with a variety of departures from orthodoxy, particularly politically sensitive ones connected with the status of the Prophet's associates[142] — and hence the legitimacy of the 'Alid as opposed to the Hashimite lines. Indeed, Baghdadian Ḥanbalism, along with that of Isfahān, appears to have been popularly articulated in eschatological terms very akin to those of the Shī'ites; but whereas Shī'ite eschatology was 'Alid, that of the Ḥanbalites involved the veneration of Mu'āwiya, one of the main protagonists in Shī'ite demonology.[143] It was also roughly at the same time that Ḥanbalism acquired its important position in Baalbeck, Ḥarran (where Ibn Taimiyya's family originated), Isfahān, and to a lesser extent in Khurāsān, especially in Herat where there was a riotous Ḥanbalite community,[144] as well as in Mosul, where Ḥanbalites were few but vigorous.[145] The second great centre of Ḥanbalism, Damascus, came under the influence of this school during the reign of Saladin, when relations with Baghdad were very important, and when Ibn al-Jawzī himself was often sent on embassies to Damascus.[146]

Ḥanbalism was at once a theological school and a legal-moral creed.[147] And though its theological position was often fideist and occasionally anthropomorphic, it did have a number of theologians actively engaged in philosophical studies.[148] Ibn 'Aqīl, who was Ghazālī's student in the Niẓāmiyya, had to recant his allegorisation of divine attributes,[149] although another great Ḥanbalite theologian Abū

Ya'lā, equally under the influence of Mu'tazilism, was unscathed and indeed a pillar of his community, not having tampered with this particularly sensitive issue. It is noticeable that the theological tasks of the Ḥanbalites had later almost totally (with the two exceptions just noted) devolved to the Ash'arites and that, with time, the theological capability available to the Ḥanbalites became threadbare except for the affirmation of simple basic positions. A very wide gulf separates Abū Ya'lā's *Mu'tamad* and the *Taḥrīm* of Ibn Qudāma, the representative of Damascene Ḥanbalism who died in 620/1223; while the former was a sophisticated systematic treatment of dogmatic theology, the latter was concerned with refuting the theology of Ibn 'Aqīl and of interdicting theological activity altogether. Ibn Taimiyya was too austere in his consistency and clarity of purpose to have been part of the Ḥanbalite mainstream. It may well be that the waning of the theological facility of Ḥanbalism was partly due to the direct populist and devotional role it played and the membership in it of members of the minor orders of scholarship and devotion — a fact brought out very well by the Ḥanbalite biographical dictionaries which, unlike other such works, detail the lives of members of the lower orders of society. The human constituency of Ḥanbalism was decidedly wider than the elite membership of the Mu'tazilites and the Ash'arites which, for regional and other conditions, was recruited amongst members of other legal schools.

The theological facility at the disposal of Baghdadi Ḥanbalism was indeed that developed and refined by the Ash'arites. Ash'arī himself explicitly commended Aḥmad Ibn Ḥanbal for his positive assertion of divine attributes without allegorical intervention,[150] a matter which seems to account for inclusion of Ash'arites by the dispassionate Khwārizmī (d. after 366/976) in the category of anthropomorphic schools.[151] Indeed, Ḥanbalites of the middle period in Baghdad, in the age of Ibn 'Aqīl, considered Ash'arites as belonging like the Ḥanbalites to the category of *ahl al-ḥadīth*, albeit with the difference that they admitted some allegory in statements concerning divine attributes,[152] and a relatively early Ash'arite included in this category those who reasoned (i.e. Ash'arites) and traditionalists (i.e. Ḥanbalites).[153] This connection was not lost on subsequent generations. Later Ash'arites underlined this connection, explicitly bringing out Ash'arism as having initially been the theological arm of Ḥanbalism,[154] a matter also underlined by Ibn Taimiyya.[155] It was more than a century after the death of Ash'arī *circa* 320/932 and after the further elaboration of his school by Bāqillānī, Isfarā'īnī and Ibn Fūrak (d. 406/1015–16) that division set in seriously. It appears that Ash'arism was constituted as a separate theological school in Khurāsān, especially in Nīshāpūr, and was reintroduced into Baghdad, suitably transformed into its new guise, in 469/1076–7 by Abū al-Qāsim al-Qushairī, grandson of the great mystical scholar, and with a decidedly anti-Ḥanbalite tenor that led to much commotion and to the forced departure of Qushairī.[156] But in the period of gestation before the reintroduction of this school to Baghdad much commotion was involved.[157] Very soon before the affair of Qushairī, in 456/1064, the Saljūq vizier Kundurī convinced the Sultan Alp Arslan that the Ash'arites, along with the Shī'ites, should be publicly anathemised, which was duly undertaken, leading to the departure from Khurāsān of Qushairī and Juwainī.[158] This action, like previous ones during the reign of Ṭughril Beg (429/1038–455/1063), was attributed to the favour in which the Mu'tazilites stood and to the Ḥanafite bigotry associated with it and used as a vehicle for its legitimation.[159] But soon after Kandarī's execution and early in the vizirate of the illustrious Niẓām al-Mulk, these conditions were reversed, and the Ash'arites became the favourites of the Saljūq state, a matter which seems to stem from Niẓām al-Mulk's pro-Shāfi'ite policies in Nīshāpūr (but not necessarily elsewhere),[160] and what seem to have been consequent carrying out by theological means the struggle between the Sultanate and the Caliphate, which had hitherto, as modern research has shown,[161] been carried out in terms of the Ḥanbalite-Ḥanafite division. The association of Ash'arism with Shāfi'ites, which started in Khurāsān, was thus carried over into the mainstream of Arabic thought[162] but first in Baghdad, where the demise of the Mu'tazilites, who had been associated with the Shī'ites anyway, left no pillar with which the Caliphate could be challenged culturally by the Sultanate.

Ash'arism, it is true,[163] never became the dominant school of theology. But this is true only in the sense that it never unequivocally became certified as such. What the great apologist for Ash'arism, Subkī, declared as the character of his school is true: it is not a properly constituted school, but is a manner of stating and defending orthodoxy along traditionalist lines.[164] Defeated in Baghdad, never continuously maintaining its position as official dogma, it always lingered with a steady potency. But this was not an officially acknowledged position. The significance and importance of Ash'arism derive not from an officialisation, which may not always have been sought, but rather from constituting a body of statements and dogmatics which could always be construed as orthodox (and we exclude here certain positions starting with Juwainī). This derived less from positive dogmatics than from the fact that the Ash'arite orientation was based on the avoidance of error and on the attempt to eliminate the possibility of error. If Ash'arism in the tokenist, historical and political sense was not always important, the substantial aspects of this orientation were vital as a ground upon which uncontroversiality could have been established. That is why we find, for instance, that attempts to prove the orthodoxy of mysticism did not appeal to the name of this school, and did not take the form of adopting adherence to this school specifically, but were stated in terms of fideist positions on divine attributes, on eschatology and on the imāmate, which are customarily associated with Ash'arism but were not named as such.[165] In this sense, the polemic and apologetics of Subkī, based on protestations of centrality and uncontroversiality, are based on the observation of a fact which became the prevalent condition of Ash'arism in the later Middle Ages and after its Baghdadi period. This was followed by migration to Egypt and the Fertile Crescent when central Asia was experiencing the ravages of the Mongols during which the major seat of learning in central Asia, Nīshāpūr, was destroyed. In this period, the serious theological purpose of Juwainī and his followers, adulterated with Mu'tazilism and thus uncomfortably compromised, had waned. If Ash'arism before Juwainī and after Rāzī (with very few exceptions) had a positive theology over and above statements designed to avoid error in matters of religion, it is to be found in later developments which incorporated controversial philosophical concepts and in the extension of the probity with which divinity is attended to other regions of reality. If God is the creator, then creatures are absolutely created, and hence absolutely dependent, and hence 'nature' cannot exist. This projection of theology onto other territories of creation was the hallmark of Ash'arism and prompted Ibn Taimiyya to attack their denial of nature as going counter to common sense.[166] Ash'arism is a neutral common ground: born in association with Ḥanbalite attempts to avoid the errors involved in allegory, it carried on this attempt while Ḥanbalism hardened doctrinally and politically, including amongst its enemies erstwhile associates, now associated with the Sultanate and with Shāfi'ism. The basic position of Ḥanbalism as elaborated by Ash'arism remained alive, as a sort of doctrinal haven in times of adversity. As was often the case, Ibn Taimiyya in his austere rigour appears to have the final word: Sunnite Islām is Ḥanbalite irrespective of adherence to the legal school named after Aḥmad.[167]

The fact that Niẓām al-Mulk supported the Ash'arites in Baghdad should not automatically be understood to imply that he was doctrinally bound to them. He was a politician aware of the role of scholarship and culture generally in life, but mindful of political conditions and politic considerations. He also had Mu'tazilites in his entourage who belonged to the Zaidiyya of the Shī'ites.[168] The Mu'tazilites were various, some adhering to the Sunna, others to the proto-Shī'ite and the Zaidiyya.[169] After their early heyday in which their doctrine was pronounced official dogma under Ma'mūn and his immediate successors in the ninth/third century, they were persecuted and fell to a minority position in Baghdad during and after the restoration of Mutawakkil (232/847–247/861), and were very much associated with Shī'ite positions on the imāmate and therefore on the legitimacy of the Abbasids[170] — unlike Baṣran Mu'tazilites.[171] They were occasionally on the ascendent in semi-official terms, such as during periods of Būyid rule,[172] under some of the Khwārizm-Shāhs,[173] and under Maḥmūd of Ghaznī (d. 398/1030),[174] the conqueror of India and patron of Bīrūnī. But they were normally a maligned and small minority, who persisted in certain rural areas[175] (indicating their association with extra-theological groups), and otherwise transient, as in the Maghreb and the Andalus.[176] In all cases, and though they were intellectually very vigorous, their ideas were only explicitly adopted by members of the school, whose name many preferred to avoid after the policies of Mutawakkil. But that the name was avoided does not imply that their ideas were without effect. In fact, as we suggested in the previous chapter, the particular fecundity of this school seems to have been manifested less in its official prosperity than in providing raw material for theological and other speculation under a different rubric — that of Ash'arism, Māturīdism or legal theory. Additionally, Mu'tazilism had developed a very rich and elaborate body of *responsa* for use against various opponents; we are told that the famous Bishr b. al-Mu'tamir (d. between 210/825 and 226/840) had composed these in a 40,000-line mnemonic poem.[177] We must also bear in mind the persistence of ideas undesirable from the Islamic point of view until relatively late. We are told, for instance, that after the murder of Abū Muslim al-Khurāsānī, the military leader of the Abbasid revolution, his disciples used some of the doctrines he himself used (such as transmigration of souls) and founded a particular community in Transoxiania led by a self-proclaimed vicar of Zoroaster and which persisted until the twelfth century A.D.[178] Indeed, Zoroastrians were prominent in the court of the Būyid 'Aḍud al-Dawla,[179] who entrusted the Mu'tazilites with many tasks[180] — perhaps due to their connections with the Zaidiyya, who had anyway converted the Būyids to the rudimentary Shī'ism that the dynasty adopted.[181]

Just as Subkī, an apologist for Ash'arism amongst Shāfi'ites, identified the latter wholly with the former, so Mu'tazilites sought to identify their school with the immediate teachings of Abū Ḥanīfa and Abū Yūsuf[182] — an identification denied, as was any association between the two, by other Ḥanafite legists.[183] In the case of both the Mu'tazilites and the Ash'arites, such an identification was not only a means of legitimation by recourse to an appeal to the authority of the eponymous fathers of legal schools and to the religious associations of law. It was also, and in historical terms this is more important, an attempt to embed theological tendencies in the body of the social mass of law schools and of their correlative institutions, such as mosques, the legal system and educational institutions. This was, at best, indirect, as theology impinged upon the substance of law only through incorporation in legal theory, as we saw in the previous chapter. Legal schools might be said to have been the reality-principle of theological schools. They were the nearly exclusive formal vehicles of scientific activity; it was for them that educational institutions were constructed and funded, as was the funding and consecration of prayer-niches, prayer leaders and the pecking order of the legal institutions, headed by the Supreme Qāḍī, which oversaw all educational, legal and religious institutions.

The four legal schools of Ḥanafiyya, Ḥanbaliyya, Mālikiyya and Shāfi'iyya, monopolised legal and related institutions as of the early twelfth/fifth century.[184] In Spain, the initial Awzā'ite school gave way to Mālikism after its introduction by Yaḥyā b. Yaḥyā al-Laithī (d. 234/848–9).[185] The same development took place in Ifriqiyā and other parts of the Maghreb, although Ḥanafism lingered on under the Aghlabids.[186] The story of Ẓahirism in Spain and the Maghreb has already been outlined, and the school had some importance in Iran and, to a lesser extent in Oman and Sind, in the fourth/tenth century.[187] The last of Awzā'ite and Ẓāhirite judges in Damascus — and the school of Awzā'ī was the Syrian school par excellence, just as Ḥanafism was the Iraqi school and Mālikism the Medinan school — are in evidence in the fourth/tenth century.[188] The Jarīriyya, named after the great historian and exegete Ibn Jarīr Ṭabarī, was still in evidence in Baghdad more than half a century after Ṭabarī's death in 310/923, a Jarīrite judge being on record,[189] and the minor school named after Sufyān al-Thawrī (d. 161/777–8) was treated as a separate school in Ṭabarī's own book on *khilāf*.[190] Khurāsān was, as we saw, divided between Ḥanafites and Shāfi'ites and Baghdad and its dependencies appear to have been officially uncertain although strongly marked by Mālikism,[191] but this waned and from the middle of the fourth/tenth century Shāfi'ite judges are in evidence.[192] Indeed, a perusal of Subkī's biographies of Shāfi'ites shows very few Iraqis before about this time and a predominant proportion of

Khurāsānīs. As for Ḥanbalism, there was considerable controversy over its status as a legal school. Ṭabarī does not mention Aḥmad Ibn Ḥanbal in his *Ikhtilāf*, and explicitly denied him the status of legist, considering him purely a traditionist, as was still done by the great traditionist al-Khaṭīb al-Baghdādī (d. 463/1071) as late as a century and a half after Ṭabarī. While this has been attributed to factionalism,[193] it perhaps also points to the possibility that the constitution of Ḥanbalism as a legal system was a lengthy process, and that this school, like Shi'ism, was not initially constituted as such, but as a poltico-theological school, albeit opposed to the Mu'tazilites and the Shi'ites. It is on record that a certain Dārikī of Baghdad, who died in 375/985–6, was castigated for making legal decisions counter to the tradition of Abū Ḥanīfa and Shāfi'ī, to which he retorted that direct recourse to *ḥadīth* was superior to both[194] — a retort which might have easily come from a Ḥanbalite or indeed a Ẓāhirite. But Dārikī did not profess adherence to a particular legal school, and this lends some credence to maintaining an initial connection between Ḥanbalism and Ẓāhirism[195] in which the latter may have emerged as the specifically legal counterpart of the former, wider devotional and theologico-political school, a legal counterpart which may then have become enmeshed in its localities and unresponsive to the needs of Baghdad, where the Ḥanbalites were later to muster their own specifically legal institution and its body of cases.

With the exception of Baghdad at periods that have already been mentioned, there have been no Ḥanbalite states, if we except contemporary Saudi Arabia. Iraq, Syria and Egypt were to emerge as largely Shāfi'ite until well into Ottoman times with sprinklings of Mālikism and Ḥanbalism,[196] and the Maghreb and Spain were to remain Mālikite. Arabia was most often Mālikite, whereas Khurāsān and other eastern regions were to settle into predominantly Ḥanafite communities, perhaps after Shāfi'ite 'migration' to the east. It is perhaps clear from the foregoing that the monopolisation of legal and educational life by the four schools was relatively late. This is perhaps due to the fact that it was only then that the schools could be said to have been provided with institutions over and above the paradigmatic ones based on a body of legists. And indeed, the professionalisation of the schools occurred at the same time as their institutionalisation in academic contexts.[197]

The Institutionalisation of Learning

Whereas before what is sometimes known as the Sunnite consolidation under the Zangids, the Ayyubids and Saljūqs, scientific activity and scholarship seem to have been the concern of persons who were otherwise occupied in procuring a living, or who did not need to do so, the twelfth century A.D. saw the professionalisation of *'ilm*, manifested in specialised institutions of learning and scholarship, and in the recruitment of graduates of such institutions into state service.[198] And indeed, at this time Baghdad witnessed the separation of positive law from other fields of scholarly endeavour, the pursuit of which was in itself a gainful activity and the membership of whose community were distinguished by a distinctive dress.[199] It was perfectly legitimate for the Qāḍī 'Abd al-Jabbār to defend theology by protesting that it was pursued only for the love of God, not for gain in this world.[200] Before the inception of the Colleges, the *madāris* (s. *madrasa*) formal teaching took two forms. One was confined to a small minority and designed directly to cater for the needs of the state. Paradigmatic among these was of course the famous *Dār al-Ḥikma* of Ma'mūn, designed to support the very elitist preoccupation with translation from Greek and Syriac, to unify a corps of astrologers and to sustain Mu'tazilism.[201] The Fatimid *Dār al-'Ilm* in Cairo was meant as a teaching and propaganda institution to serve Ismā'īlism,[202] and was modelled on its Baghdadian precursor, a model which institutionally later served for the *madāris*.[203] But these institutions were not meant for instruction in *fiqh*, which remained the business of informal, but not necessarily unstructured or irregular, circles of teachers and pupils in various mosques and other public locations.

Prior to the era of the *madāris*, mosque circles catered for the teaching of law, of ḥadīth and of a variety of other subjects including grammar. These circles, centred around a particular person, were also the context for preaching, disputation and the solicitation of legal opinion.[204] And all these activities persisted through the era of the Colleges, but in a very peripheral manner. It was in the earlier part of the fifth/eleventh century that we are told the first College was built — before the birth of Niẓām al-Mulk who is normally credited with having initiated this institution. The Baihaqiyya was built in Nīshāpūr, followed by three others before Niẓām al-Mulk's famous Niẓāmiyya, where Juwainī taught and Ghazālī studied and later taught, and before Colleges spread under the impact of Niẓām al-Mulk to Balkh, Herat, Isfahān, Baṣra, Mosul and Merv, culminating in the great Niẓāmiyya of Baghdad, completed in 457/1065.[205] If Niẓām al-Mulk is to be credited with initiating anything it was the vital system of scholarship, the lynchpin of these institutions.[206] Syria and Egypt did not lag far behind; the first College was constructed in Damascus in 491/1097[207] and in Cairo not long after, and by the middle of the Mamlūk era Maqrīzī in his *Khiṭaṭ* listed 73 Colleges in Cairo and Nu'aimī (d. 927/1521) in his *Dāris* listed more than a hundred in Damascus alone. The Maghreb and Spain were, by contrast, poorly endowed, and the construction of Colleges lagged behind Syria and Egypt by nearly two centuries.[208]

Of course not all Colleges were alike. Some were magnificent, some mean. Not all had separate quarters; some Colleges consisted of circles in a particular mosque.[209] What qualified such institutions as Colleges was the type of endowment deed on which they were based,[210] and this deed not only stipulated the manner in which control over the College was to be exercised and the scholarships of students and emoluments of various members of staff for whom allowance was made in the endowment, but the topics taught. It was almost invariably the case that a College was devoted to teaching the *fiqh* of a particular one of the four schools. Grander establishments made provision for the teaching of up to the four schools.[211] In all cases, the person who endowed a College normally made quite detailed provisions for the upkeep of the building, the sort of food, clothing and allowance to be granted the students (the lot of students seems to have been very poor indeed), in addition to the subjects taught and whatever additional conditions he deemed fit.[212] Some of these special conditions could be quite peculiar, like the provision of one endowment that the College should never be entered by a woman,[213] or by an anthropomorphic Ḥanbalite.[214]

The Colleges were inseparably bound with the legal schools. But this does not imply that nothing but jurisprudence was taught in them, although it must be said that subjects taught were of the nature of topics auxiliary to *fiqh*, in the sense of being necessary for its proper study. At the Niẓāmiyya in Baghdad *khilāf*, theology and legal theory were taught,[215] and grammar, exegesis and other matters were taught at Damascus Colleges.[216] In exceptional circumstances reflecting both the wealth of the College and the diversity of intellectual life, subjects were taught that were not strictly linked to law. Such, for instance, was the teaching of medicine at the Manṣūriyya in Cairo[217] or of literature at the Niẓāmiyya of Baghdad[218] and at the Ruwāhiyya in Aleppo.[219] Auxiliary subjects such as the all-important propedeutics, *ḥadīth* and the Qur'ān, were naturally enough taught at Colleges, but they were, additionally, taught in specialised colleges which were established later on, especially in Damascus where 16 *ḥadīth* colleges were established as of the beginning of the sixth/twelfth century, in addition to seven Qur'ān colleges (beginning with the eighth/fourteenth century) and three combined Qur'ān and *ḥadīth* colleges (starting with the seventh/thirteenth century).[220] By contrast, Cairo possessed only one *ḥadīth* college,[221] a contrast which reflects that fact that Damascus was the centre of all later important *ḥadīth* scholarship — most of the important later traditionists were either natives or residents of Damascus, such as Ibn 'Asākir (d. 571/1175–6), Ibn al-Ṣalāḥ (d. 643/1245), Nawawī (d. 677/1277), Mizzī (d. 742/1341–2), Dhahabī (d. 748/1347) and Ibn Kathīr (d. 774/1372–3). And such was the distinction of some Colleges, that all the traditionists just mentioned held professorships at the Ashrafiyya *ḥadīth* college.[222] In addition, some of the larger mystical residential and devotional establishments, the *khwāniq* (s. *khānqāh*) had in their deeds of endowment provisions for the teaching of *ḥadīth* and either particular systems of positive law or all four schools.[223] One such establishment restricted scholarships to foreigners and, failing their availability, to local Cairene Shāfi'ites and Mālikites who subscribed to Ash'arite theology.[224] Finally, Colleges also had libraries with varying degrees of accessibility to outsiders and different regulations on borrowing, though the age of truly great libraries maintained by the Umayyads of Cordoba or the Fatimids in Cairo was overtaken by the era of the Colleges.[225]

The *madāris* remained, academically and otherwise, the core of the higher educational system, and this they did in direct connection with the schools of law. Indeed, it appears now inconceivable that the four schools would have monopolised educational and legal life in Islamic societies had it not been for the professionalisation and institutionalisation of their personnel in the context of the Colleges. The Colleges were the means of control over scholarly and intellectual life in general, the *modus operandi* of its homogenisation and of its paradigmatic continuity and refinement. The Colleges both fixed the schools of law and their ancillaries, and acted as the means of their separate continuity and of the constancy of their boundaries, as of the paradigmatic boundaries of other sciences which became much more than books, having been transformed into particular educational traditions whose continuity and cumulativeness was assured by the Colleges, where they became components in a curriculum after having been mere ideas, positions and methods — and therefore having become normatively established ideas, topics, positions and methods and, by extension, texts and authors. The maintenance of paradigmatic continuity and integrity, the preservation of boundaries within which sciences are constituted, is a matter assured by the structure of authority in the educational system and by educational techniques by means of which it operates.

Most superficially, this structure of authority is displayed in the gradation of stations within each educational establishment. Though modern scholarship uses the term *faqīh* generically to designate Islamic scholars and divines, this rests on the careless misuse of an epithet. *Faqīh* (pl. *fuqahā'*) technically came to mean an advanced student,[226] and it is therefore not surprising that the bright young Ghazālī took offence at being addressed as a *faqīh* by his teacher Juwainī.[227] Nevertheless, there were times when the term was used by extension of its literal sense of 'savant' to designate particularly accomplished scholars.[228] Similarly, in the context of *ḥadīth* colleges, advanced students were designated by the term *muḥaddithūn*, and like their analogues in the *madāris*, were presided over by more advanced students, *shuyūkh al-riwāya*, equivalent to the *mu'īdūn* (s. *mu'īd*), repetitors, of the *madāris*, who were themselves graded[229] and organised in a guild-like context, headed by a syndic, *naqīb al-fuqahā'*, and controlled and administered by, among others, a *kātib al-ghaiba*, an officer in charge of the roll-call.[230] These gradations were reflected, as often the case in many societies, in a formal, almost ritual manner, with the seating arrangement in class reflecting the differential stations of the students.[231] At the tip of this hierarchy was the *mudarris*, professor. The more famous and accomplished, the more professorships the *mudarris* simultaneously held, to such an extent that teaching could be delegated almost completely to a principal repetitor, and there were many *madāris* which, because of this as well as because of the lengthy lapses in filling professorial posts, were run entirely by repetitors.[232] Subkī's tract criticising the ills of his time specifically referred to perfunctory teaching by some professors as an act allowing unworthy persons the audacity and presumption to aspire to positions which ought to be reserved for the worthy few.[233]

Further below, we shall have the opportunity to refer to the differences within the ranks of the *mudarrisūn* and other scholars, generically termed *'ulamā'* (s. *'ālim*). In formal terms, it appears that whoever qualified for a professorship and was no longer a student was termed an *'ālim*, a savant: and it should be kept very much in mind that there were no formal qualifications, but that this derived from recognition, normally by peers, but also by the state and its legal hierarchy which was in charge of educational appointments. The highest grade in the scholarly and legal corps is that of *mujtahid*, a term opposed to *muqallid*,[234] one bound to receive legal decisions, and designates a scholar of such attainment that he could be entrusted with the solicitation of reliable legal and other judgements on the basis of the apodictic bases, judgements which could later be accepted by concensus or added as a separate judgement in the *corpus juris*, as we have seen. But again, the attainment of this station was dependent more on acceptance by peers, by posterity, or by the legal and political hierarchy, than any formal criteria,[235] although there was no lack of attempts formally to lay out criteria which qualify for *ijtihād*, criteria which were neither too exacting nor implying a rarity of their attainment.[236] Similar stations of excellence were described for *ḥadīth*[237] and Arabic,[238] and *ijtihād* in law seems also to have been topically divisible, a person attaining this station in a particular field, such as divorce legislation.[239] Once the station of *mujtahid* was attained, a person reached the top of the scholarly hierarchy, and might qualify for classification, by peers or by posterity, as Shaikh (master) of the Shāfi'iyya', '*Shaikh* of the *muḥaddithūn*', or some such title designating the principal scholar in a particular field. Such were the stations hoped for by Suyūṭī, for instance, when he prayed to God, as he was drinking the holy water of Zamzam on pilgrimage, that this might help him attain the station of Bulqīnī (it is unclear whether reference is being made to 'Alam al-Dīn (d. 868/1464), Suyūṭī's teacher or the teacher's more celebrated father, Sirāj al-Din (d. 805/1403).[240]

There was therefore an hierarchy of scholarly standing, normally correlated with an hierarchy of attainment, which might be subject to political disturbance at the top, stretching from the common run of ordinary students, *ṭalaba* (s. *ṭālib*) to the illustrious scholars of influence and authority. This was an institution, at once scientific and social, based upon seniority; it was a scientific and civil means for the transmission of science, and for the preservation and perpetuation of scientific authority. As scientific endeavour was based upon the assumption of all Arabic thought that knowledge pertaining to a particular topic is complete and indivisible, it does not come as a surprise to us that educational theory should not address the contents and substance of the educational process, but that it should be a formal statement of pious purpose and moral exhortation. Knowledge being pre-given, complete and indivisible, the knowledges of various topics are analogous *qua* knowledge, each consisting of a collection of particular and general statements which constitute the content of a science, and which are eminently exhaustible as well as of a clearly delimited scope dictated by the apodictic body of statements on which they rest and which constitutes the scientific boundary. Educational curricula such as that suggested by Ibn Khaldūn, purporting to programme learning according to the nature of the human mind and to follow the gradient of the mind from simplicity to complexity and from fundamentals to details,[241] fell out of the bounds of the purely institutional, almost entirely administrative, conception of education based on the assumption that it is the process whereby are imparted specific topical sets of propositions, and that all that occurs when topics are altered is the alteration of propositions, not requiring altered methods of instruction.

Pedagogic Authority and the Formation of Traditions

Thus a popular treatise on education, the *Ta'līm* of Zarnūjī, a Khurāsāni who died sometime between 591/1194 and 640/1242–3,[242] consists of sections detailing proper conduct, very much like a treatise on political wisdom. It exhorts the student, by example and *ḥadīth*, to be serious, pious and perseverent, and details a number of points of etiquette to be followed in dealing with peers, superiors and inferiors. Such were the matters deemed to constitute the conditions of learning which, the author said, his contemporaries fell short of or ignored.[243] Scientific knowledge is not retained or forgotten according to pedagogic criteria, for pedagogic methods do not figure within the conditions of knowledge. One forgets not so much because one has learnt badly: Zarnūjī ascribed the lack of retention to the consumption of fresh coriander, to the sight of a crucified man, to reading epitaphs and to casting live lice to the ground.[244] The same pre-givenness and completion with regard to the topic of education is clear in a *ḥadīth*-educational handbook by Sam'ānī (d. 562/1167): proper knowledge of *ḥadīth* is guaranteed by a number of rules of conduct to be followed by teacher and student alike, concerning dress, seating, demeanour, bearing, ink and quills.[245] Some centuries later, the same type of prescription was the basis for the description of education pertaining to all subjects, similarly supported by exemplary stories.[246] In all cases, what is at issue was that the conditions attaching to conduct ensure that teaching is undertaken by those for whom such activity is appropriate, not by ignorant upstarts;[247] in all cases, in other words, concern is with the integrity and purity of transmission, modelled on *ḥadīth*, of that which is definitively established. Conduct ensures exemplary and definitive behaviour, a ritual confirmation of relationship of power, for such as is exemplary in education amounts to a ritual choreography which constantly reaffirms the exemplariness of authority transmitted from teacher to student on behalf of the science with whose authority the teacher speaks and the authority of whose statements he merely carries over. After all, teaching and learning of intellectual matters are composed of an anterior knowledge and a prior science. Teaching passes on knowledge, conceived here as a mass, from a person who has it to one who lacks it.[248] Instruction passes on a mass from one location to another, and what is involved is a handing over, a transmission, almost by porterage, of a finished material, regardless of the material or of the means of carriage. Education ensures the safety of the goods transmitted.

Education is therefore, like everywhere else but with a pronounced directness and deliberateness, the transmission of an implicit apodictic system, one whose apodictic statements, as we have seen, are taken on trust, on the assumption of their validity, and with the sanction of authority. Indeed, not only are the prolegomena of sciences apodictic, but so also are, in effect and for the students, all its separate theses relating to its objects. For just as in other societies and settings, even where the contrary is professed, education is a process which instils in its charges what has been termed, in a more generalised sense of education, a 'cultural arbitrary'.[249] Pedagogic action upon pedagogic subjects imposes a set of propositions, or sets of propositions, which by the very nature of things cannot be liable to demonstration, as Arabic thinkers realised with reference to the apodictic beginnings of each science. In this sense, they are arbitrary from the pedagogic point of view, demonstrated only by the authoritativeness of their transmission, just as language is arbitrary.

The first and most direct manifestation of the mystification upon which pedagogic authority rests is the fact that the educational system under scrutiny venerated the source from which authority emanates in the most immediate sense and through which it speaks. The veneration of teachers is axiomatic and of paramount significance; education is a social operation, and isolation is tantamount to insubordination with respect to one's duties.[250] That education is social means that it is hierarchical, and that it operates with due regard to the relative positions of things, and in this regime of things the teacher is almost to be sanctified, certainly always obeyed, and revered to the extent that his children should also be venerated.[251] For indeed, in a hierarchical universe, companionship is naturally divided into three: with those above you, and this is, in essence, a form of service; with your equals, and this implies altruism born of sharing the same station; and with those beneath you, which calls for patronage, pity and protection.[252] We have already seen how suspicion of autodidacticism was sufficient cause to reject a scholar and sufficient explanation for his errors, as was the case with Ibn Ḥazm among others.[253] For though a teacher is not in himself the author of authority, but is the mouthpiece of this epistemic and legislative oracle, yet the oracle itself, or any base text in itself, cannot yield its secrets to a fallible mind without the guidance of a teacher. The teacher interposes tradition between basic text, scientific propositions and the learner.

This interposition is the factor which assures integrity and continuity in science, for we have seen that apodictic beginnings are, for all intents and purposes, arbitrary, and that they act within the discourse of science as a myth of origin and legend of beginning. The authority of science is mediated through the teacher, who represents the authority of the tradition within which he acts as a cultural and scientific being, and with a view of imposing, by pedagogic action, conformity to this tradition upon younger generations. This is why it was impossible for pedagogic techniques such as that suggested by Ibn Khaldūn to be enracinated in the scientific universe under review, for it would have required, after a fashion which we might call Ẓāhirite, direct unmediated access to *Urtext* of any science and every science, and the *Urtext* is occluded by tradition.

Teaching and certification based on the transmission of individually authoritative texts (epitomes, glosses, etc.), at the expense of a real or putative *Urtext*, scatters scientific authority and prevents the articulation of its parts, thus preventing the emergence of a comprehensive compulsive structure, and confirming each component in its own separate force and vested interest; such is precisely the import of education as conservative transmission of propositions; nothing overrides the separate authorities. In the Arabic scientific context, science was instituted and its integrity policed by a specific mode of teaching and a collateral mode of certification, which were also the means for the preservation of the integrity of scientific and other texts in the sphere of societies for which the techniques of printing were unavailable, and where therefore writings could easily have been subject to corruption, deliberate or undeliberate, by copyists and evil-doers.

The collation of copies and originals was normally very careful indeed,[254] the work of professional stationers (*warrāqūn*).[255] Some people prided themselves on possessing libraries which contained only books whose collation was certified up to the original reception, written or oral, from the author himself.[256] This was in tune with the scrupulous care with which Arabic scholars normally used their sources and indicated their quotations.[257] But this could not have been a process amenable to complete control. Some libraries lent books without restriction as to being copied or provisions for the control of copying,[258] and there is some evidence of unscrupulous persons expurgating parts of books they were charged with copying in order to finish the task all the more quickly.[259] The preservation of texts studied before the age of mechanical reproduction was very laborious indeed, and the only absolutely reliable copies of works were those whose accuracy could be guaranteed by an unbroken line of oral and written reception of the text going back to the author himself. This process ran parallel to the pedagogic process.

The pedagogic process is one of transmission involving textual material, in which knowledge is transferred to the learner so it might be borne by him (*taḥammul al-'ilm* is an expression very often used in Arabic pedagogy) for the purposes of preservation and further transmission. That which the pedagogic process transmits is a particular text, to preserve its integrity and accuracy both in the physical sense and in the intellectual sense of it being a fund of particular statements whose authority is binding and is reaffirmed by the tradition of its transmission represented by the teacher. To study the same text under more than one teacher was therefore a way of checking, as exhaustively as possible, the transmission of a particular text, as much as a manner of exposing oneself to different traditions, not necessarily of different interpretation, but of the concurrence and concordance of authorities on the prior authority of their common text. This was of course most pertinent in the study of *ḥadīth*, and what a person like Ibn 'Asākir would have accumulated from his studies of this subject in Damascus, Baghdad, Herat, Isfahān, Nīshāpūr and elsewhere,[260] amounted to what modern scholars might call a concordance of *ḥadīth*, all in the space of the memory and notebooks of one person. And for each sector of his studies, Ibn 'Asākir is likely to have received an *ijāza*, a licence further to transmit, i.e. to teach, the texts received from a particular master.[261] The *ijāza* was the pillar of the system of pedagogic certification and guardian of transmission. It was a licence to repeat particular texts, but in a very specific form and after a very specific convention: it allowed the repetition of text on the authority of a particular tradition, such traditions as would normally have been written in the *ijāza* document. And though there came into use a general-*ijāza* (*ijāza 'amma*) allowing a particular work, by its author or on their behalf, to be transmitted by all Muslims, or by all Andalusians, or some such collectivity,[262] this normally pertained to works of a deliberately general, perhaps devotional or moral, orientation and intention. Moreover, the solicitation and granting of an *ijāza* in absentia to an infant,[263] or the granting of a general *ijāza* to a person permitting them to repeat all the master knew, did occur.[264]

The history of these abuses is obscure, but they do not particularly effect pedagogic conceptions, though they might detract from their efficiency; the abuse of a standard is not its abolition as a standard. Properly used, this is a system of certification by authority for the transmission of authority, and the units transmitted, as befitted traditions rather than general conceptions, were very particular indeed. A *fahrasa* or its synonyms, a sort of an academic *curriculum vitae* indicating what works or portions of works one had studied under each of one's teachers, was the basis for further certifications emanating from that particular scholar, and the limits of his scope to certify.[265] When delivering his inaugural lecture as a professor of *ḥadīth* at the Ṣarghatmushiyya in Cairo, Ibn Khaldūn could not omit the traditions, *asānīd*, from which he received the text he was about to teach, the *Muwaṭṭa'* of Malīk.[266] Rāzī likewise took great pride in the tradition through which he received theology, which passed, among others, through Juwainī, Isfarā'īnī, down to Ash'arī himself and his Mu'tazilite master, Jubbā'ī (d. 303/916), and that through which he received *fiqh*, which went to Shāfi'ī through a particularly illustrious tradition.[267] The pedagogic process, channelled through the institution of the *ijāza*, is the bearing of a particular text through a particular line, and the technique of this transmission is the live reading of the text so that its accuracy might be ascertained, and its further transmission legitimised.

The academic licence to carry science is almost fully constituted and comprehended by the technique of which an *ijāza* is a result. An *ijāza* is a specific permit pertaining to a specific text, full or in part, and the manner in which the text in question was acquired reflects itself directly in the worth of the *ijāza*. The general licence mentioned above is obviously the most inferior and defeats the purpose of pedagogy, lending its texts out of the control of scientific authorities, and some jurists pronounced it totally inadmissible.[268] The crux of the certification system, in which *ijāza* is axial and its use almost generic, is the oral delivery, by the master or the student, of a text which the other follows in writing (*qirā'a* and *samā'*) or the dictation of a text by a master which the students copy (*imlā'* — sometimes, in large classes, with the master's dictation relayed to distant students by an official *mustamlī*),[269] and the precise manner in which the text was received is specified both in the licence certificate and by the master who is about to transmit a received text.[270] Reading and dictation could be accompanied by the collation of a manuscript, or by a commentary or discussion.[271] Moreover, the precise manner of reception is transcribed into a specialised terminology of use when a person is quoting an authority, and specifies the manner in which the quotation was received, in terms that seem to have been derived from a *ḥadīth*-transmission paradigm.[272]

Comprehension appears peripheral in comparison with the exactitude of transmission and the fastidious concern with the manner of transmission. Pedagogy is here the transmission of a facility, not of a capacity, during which process authority is reaffirmed by rehearsal and continued rehearsal. Pedagogic techniques affirm an authority, and reaffirm it by its recreation in the mind of the learner as a skill, a *habitus*, and Ibn Khaldūn clearly saw that education is a skill-creating process of training, much like apprenticeship in crafts.[273] And indeed, it is as institutionalised apprenticeship that the educational system functions through its pedagogic techniques outlined, and which at once preserve the physical and the intellectual integrity of authority.[274] Authority had to be explicitly present in order for learning to have any validity; there were instances of great scholars having read works by contemporary authors, which they then insisted on receiving formally by audition with the participation of the author.[275] Masters could teach from memory without censure after having gone blind, and at least one instance is reported of a master who relied totally on memory, as he was illiterate, again without censure.[276] He had presumably acquired the mnemonic skill to transmit particular texts, on the same assumption as that of the great mystic Shādhilī (d. 656/1258) who declared that his books were his companions.[277] In fact, a book, just like the portion of a book or even a single *ḥadīth*, is certifiable by an *ijāza*, and its certification is based on direct oral contact with the master, who could well be considered as a transhistorical agency which links the reader and the author by way of a tradition which certifies the work of the author, by excising history, as it were, but in fact reaffirming history by interposing a tradition between the reader and the author. And while the orality of transmission is seen as a guarantee of authority, oral transmission is also mystified into a pedagogic mode which is conducive to the best bearing of science for some divinely-inspired quality that intervenes in the direct relationship between master and pupil, one that is enhanced by the fact that physical proximity improves comprehension, be this proximity that of master and pupil, or of eyes and ears.[278] Indeed, such was the status of orality that the writing down of science is seen as no more than the means for allaying the effects of forgetfulness.[279]

The mystification of orality, like the explanations of forgetfulness that we saw were connected with the consumption of coriander and the treatment of lice, miss the point in order to affirm a received technique whose locus is the affirmation of authority which direct oral control ensures. It would not be correct to say that this emphasis on the superiority of oral delivery, besides its undoubted usefulness for the preservation of textual integrity, is a throwback to an oral culture. There are many features of Arabic thought that we have studied — a certain aggregativeness upon which is superimposed an apodictic relation, a closure, a positivism, a conservatism — which are associated with oral thought.[280] And indeed, we saw that pedagogic technique is premised on the primacy of orality. Moreover, much of intellectual debate and controversy was oral, with polemic being exchanged in educational institutions and in the presence of sovereigns, and such are matters which cannot be pursued with elaborate discursivity, but in dialectical fashion, by the methods of division into argumentative sections which could fairly comfortably be handled in a situation of debate.[281] Live debates in any case do not involve general points, but very specific theses.[282] And there is evidence that the topological and schematic redaction of *ḥadīth* had, as formal conditions, certain mnemotechnical constraints,[283] certain implicit stylistic and other canons which facilitate its commitment to memory and the recall of what is memorised.[284] But these matters ought not to lead to the supposition that we are here dealing with an oral culture which was merely transcribed onto paper for the pragmatic reason of preservation, as some Arabic traditionists supposed. Not only is this not in itself possible, but such a supposition ignores the role of orality in the Arabic language. This role is one for the direct control of learning by the agencies and institutions of learning, and of not allowing learning to be the unmediated access to sources, for such open access is contrary to the logic of any control. Orality ensures not only control, but control of a specific agency, that of the tradition through which a text is transmitted rather than through the text itself, although the text may have been transmitted absolutely intact. The *Urtext*, after all, is chosen and glossed ceaselessly. The matter is therefore one of the affirmation and reaffirmation of the transmitting authority. The master makes of the text taught an authority,[285] but it is equally true that it is in effect the master, through his institution, who makes an authority of the text, by presenting it as such, as a complete and integral mass, to be borne by his pupils as it was borne by him. And though there is some sense in the supposition that epitomes and such works which proliferated in Arabic thought, and that codified *quaestiones* and *responsa* which developed out of marginal glosses (*ḥāshīyya* into *ta'līqa*),[286] are manifestations of a declining vigour, of a sclerotic process, but this should rather be seen as an over-ripeness, a superabundance. It was born of the self-confidence of traditions which could set out their own texts as representing the truth which previously only the original texts of the great authorities could do — a matter criticised by, among others, Ibn Khaldūn as inimical to learning.[287]

But such were circumstances, and such was the actual primacy of the present over the past, that mnemotechnic aids sometimes were substituted for direct dealing with original texts. Normally in the sprightly poetical mode of *rajaz*, for study were available mnemonic poems which might have constituted, for some, the entirety of knowledge of a particular topic. One of the most famous is, of course, the *Shāṭibiyya*, in which Shāṭibī (d. 590/1194, no relation of the legist) composed the Qur'ānic variants, and the *Alfiyya* in which Ibn Mālik (d. 672/1274) composed the elements of grammar. There were also similar poems in which were codified, for ready retrieval, the principles of dialectics,[288] of particular works like the famous dogmatic treatise of Nasafī (d. 537/1142).[289] Such works were not only memory aids, but contained the entirety of their science — they were in effect science. A similar treatment meted out to the exegesis of the Qu'rān was considered to have been mildly *risqué*, having tampered with the rhyme of the Holy Book.[290] But a particular legal tradition did not run such risks,[291] and the accretion of exegeses of exegeses, and exegeses of mnemonic poems, simply underline the primacy of tradition as a present, over tradition as a frozen past, for history does not admit the lack of change, or the primacy of the past over the present, except as myth. That epitomes, mnemonic poems, certified portions of great works or of an *Urtext*, were the stuff of learning is only in conformity with history. For a textual tradition is substituted a live tradition, as is only natural, based on texts that are actually transmitted, texts which do not so much derogate the integrity of the *Urtext* as certify its importance and authority via the live authority of the teacher and the text he transmits — in effect, bringing out clearly the nature of the *Urtext* as a myth of origin. Scientific closure upon the apodictic beginnings expresses in actual fact closure upon the contemporary reception of these beginnings, the contemporary reception embodied in epitomes and in the disassociated parts of the *Urtext*. Closure is exercised with reference to particular texts, not to tradition as such, which does not exist; no tradition is worthy of the name if it were not alive. And these particular texts are the present and the life of tradition, and are indeed the custodians and guarantors of tradition. It is through them that tradition is expressed and kept alive, as mnemonic poems, as case law, as particular traditions embodied in an *ijāza*. Further, it is through the *ijāza*, the very life of tradition, that the differentiation of scientific paradigms is effected, for such differentiation is not only theoretical, but more importantly, is a differentiation embodied in educational and professional practices. It is through the *ijāza* that a person becomes a particular kind of scholar — grammarian, jurist, traditionist. And though many polymaths are in evidence, the protoplasm of live tradition, and of effective education, were the specialists, differentiated in practice by the texts they transmitted, and through which the closure of sciences, the correlate of differentiation, was practised. It may well be, therefore, that the sciences of *uṣūl* owed their particular wealth, diversity and development to their not having been as solidly instituted as the more basic branches of learning.

The *madrasa* and allied institutions were therefore the physical context in which the bearing of knowledge was regulated, organised and controlled. What little that is known about the teaching of non-traditional sciences does not reveal controlling agencies of the same scale, which transform books into authorities, except in medicine and allied sciences such as opthalmology. Nu'aimī listed three medical colleges in Damascus,[292] and wealthy physicians are also known to have endowed private medical colleges.[293] Additionally, medicine was normally studied as crafts were, by apprenticeship, and larger hospitals, which sometimes had substantial medical libraries, were the location for medical study, both practical and theoretical.[294] Heads of the great hospitals, *bīmāristāns*, such as the 'Aḍudī in Baghdad and the Nūrī in Damascus, were presumably in charge of both the administration of the hospital and the educational work within it. The formation of medical dynasties of extraordinary longevity — the Bukhtīshū' of Baghdad, hospital heads and physicians to Caliphs, lasted from 148/765 to 450/1058,[295] and others in other cities lasted much less[296] — whatever the causes, was certainly conducive to the formation of scientific traditions, and could probably be said to have been a substitute for the formal educational institutions of *fiqh* and allied topics. We are told of a Syro-Egyptian school in the seventh/thirteenth century,[297] and of a continuous line of teachers of medicine and philosophy in Baghdad between AD 850 and 1100.[298] And indeed, there was considerable uniformity in medical theory and practice, though control over the profession was exercised at the behest of the legal hierarchy through the office of the *muḥtasib*,[299] but this seems to have been directed to the prevention of quackery and abuse above all else.[300]

Whatever the means of control, the substance of what was learnt was not formally different from the situation prevailing in the *madāris*. What was learnt was medical authorities, on the assumption that medicine was a closed and finished science, the occasion for the composition by Ibn Sīnā of a mnemonic poem that we have already referred to. A physician received a licence to practise, and *ijāza* of very specific reference: the licence to repeat a particular medical treatise or to practise a specific task such as bleeding.[301] In cases where the examiner was a non-medical authority, and the *muḥtasib* as controller of trades had the right to examine physicians, incumbents were questioned about matters occurring in a small number of given texts.[302] The only case available of a wholesale examination of all medical practitioners at a certain location, the medical *imtiḥān* ordered by the Caliph al-Muqtadir in 319/931 and entrusted to the famous physician Sinān b. Thābit b. Qurra, involved also such an examination, and sought to ascertain under whom the 860 or so incumbents had been trained.[303]

Not unusually given the textual specificity towards which the pedagogic enterprise of medicine and other rational sciences such as philosophy was geared, the pedagogic technique was based upon reading and audition, the bearing of text. The terms *samā'*, *qirā'a*, and their associates are customarily used to designate the pedagogic process.[304] Not surprisingly, the close adherence to a textual corpus of binding and compelling validity is particularly pronounced in other 'rational' sciences which have an esoteric bent. Not only were there secrets which are so precious as never to be committed to writing or divulged except in private and orally,[305] but esoteric exclusivity is preserved by a limited circulation of texts. Some of the writings of Ibn Sīnā were such,[306] as were some by Ghazālī.[307] The key to these writings is either divine inspiration, or the teaching of a master, as we saw — in both cases, the authority of an interpretative agency, the former standing euphemistically for an undeclared tradition. The more exclusive a secret society, the inner circle of the initiates, happens to be, the more traditionalist and rigid in its received lore should one expect it to be. In the case of esoteric teaching, texts are interpreted by an allegorical transcription whose key is tradition as represented by its living authority. Similarly, in medicine or in philosophy, meaning is imposed and maintained by the integrity of the text borne and transmitted, much as with texts treated in the *madāris*.

In all these cases, we see that the manner of transmission, the pedagogic technique, is the institutional and civic manner in which an intellectual closure, that of a science, is maintained. In the educational system the closure of sciences and their folding in upon themselves is realised, not atemporally by the sheer preservation of a textual body (*fiqh*, medicine, or other) by its faithful transmission, but historically, with the affirmation of a tradition by means of its constant redaction and as present in the institution through which learning is borne and imparted — *madrasa, bīmāristān* or initiation into a secret society. It is through the local and timely presence of tradition that apodicticity is preserved, for its preservation is not that of a relic, but of an authority which is alive and constantly reiterated and reaffirmed through the civil ritual of education and initiation. Apodicticity and the closure each of its *modes dictate* are realised in every present, though they might be served up as preserves from a long time past which stand for the present and constitute its reality. It is always the present which constitutes the past, after its own image, or at worst after its own requirements and imperatives, for what is truly past and not present is only beholden and displayed, never used. It goes counter to the logic and reality of history to conceive of any present as passive. It is not the past, 'tradition', that lives in the present, but it is rather the present which reclaims that past, and this it has never done except very selectively, ever renewing it, but always attributing this reclamation and renewal to the past itself, and undertaking it in the name of the past. Like philosophy and anthropomorphism, the past, 'tradition', is a token, one negotiable in the present, for the purpose of the present, a present without which the past will at best be relegated to the museum, to be beholden at a very deliberate, and not always respectful, distance. The integrity of tradition is a myth of origin articulated in many forms, as logical or exemplary apodicticity, as positive origins; it is a myth which unifies a culture by the provision of a uniform sphere of reference in terms of which, by means of education, paradigms are differentiated. It is also a myth which, by magical fiat, makes present knowledge appear as if it were nothing but the recapitulation of the past, be that a syllogistic premiss or a textual compulsion.

Notes

1. For a thorough review and refutation of the standard position on Ḥanbalism, see G. Makdisi, 'Hanbalite Islam', in *Studies in Islam*, ed. M.L. Swartz (New York and Oxford), 1981. I will just add some instances: the theological work of Abū Ya'lā (*Al-Mu'tamad*); the great mystical tradition of Jīlī, a Ḥanbalite, with many fellow Ḥanbalites as followers, ecstatics and miracle-makers like all others (Ibn Rajab, *Dhail*, vol. 1, pp. 290 ff., 306 ff.; vol. 2, pp. 269 ff. and *passim*); and the currency of humoural theory amongst Ḥanbalite physicians as well as of standard cosmology (Ibn 'Aqīl, *Funūn*, para. 62).
2. Maqqarī, *Nafḥ*, vol. 2, p. 164.
3. Goldziher, *The Ẓahiris*, p. 170.
4. Ibn 'Arabī, *Fihrist*, pp. 356, 527 and 534.
5. Ibn Khallikān, *Wafayāt*, vol. 1, p. 169.
6. *Ibid.*, vol. 2, p. 159.
7. Ghazālī, *Mīzān*, p. 351 and the same in Ṭāshköprüzāde, *Miftāḥ*, vol. 1, pp. 33–4.
8. This standard position can be found in a vast array of texts and in various forms from Ghazālī, *Iḥyā'*, vol. 1, pp. 35–6 to Ṭāshköprüzāde, *Miftāḥ*, vol. 3, p. 11.

Figure 2

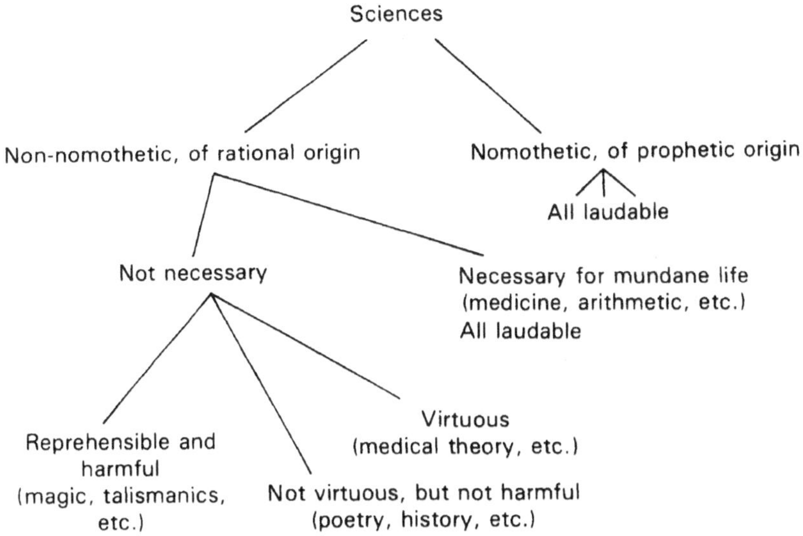

9. Al-Azmeh, *Ibn Khaldūn: An Essay*, pp. 115 ff.

10. Ḥajjī Khalīfa, *Kashf*, 'Introduction', p. 10.

11. Jurjānī, *Dalā'il*, 'Prologue (*Fātiḥa*)', p. 3.

12. For procedural aspects of an *imtiḥān*, see Nubāhī, *Tārīkh*, p. 201. It should be added here that comparisons with the Catholic inquisition and with Christian notions of heresy are not particularly relevant or illuminating. The purity of Catholic dogmatics was far more rigorously maintained; the central apparatus of the Church assured that heretical propositions were meticulously and uniformly identified, and, above all, condemned simultaneously by a multitude of authorities. See for instance the texts of condemnation relative to Marsiglio of Padua and of Errors at the University of Paris in E. Peters (ed.), *Heresy and Authority in Medieval Europe. Texts in Translation* (Philadelphia, 1980), no. 45 ff.

13. The reader can still read with profit an excellent article by B. Lewis, written before his scholarship was overtaken by the imperatives of Zionism: 'Some Observations on the Significance of Heresy in the History of Islam', in *SI*, 1 (1953), pp. 43–63.

14. For instance, Ghazālī, *Faḍā'iḥ*, p. 156.

15. For instance, the warning of Subkī in Sha'rānī, *Ṭabaqāt*, vol. 1, p. 13 and Ghazālī, *Faiṣal*, p. 201.

16. Ibn Taimiyya, *Muwāfaqa*, vol. 1, pp. 53, 146–7.

17. See M. Talbi, 'Les *Bida'* ' in *SI*, 12 (1960), pp. 61 ff. and *passim*. See the Andalusian opinion, which assimilates *kufr* to the larger class of innovation, in *Thalāth wathā'iq fī muḥārabat al-ahwā' wal-bida' fī al-Andalus*, ed. M.'A. Khallāf (Cairo, 1981), pp. 35–7.

18. See C. Cahen, 'Considerations sur l'utilization des ouvrages de droit musulman par l'historien', in *Atti del terzo congresso di studi arabi e islamici (Ravello, 1966)* (Naples, 1967), p. 241.

19. Ghazālī, *Faḍā'iḥ*, pp. 146–7.

20. Ibn Ḥazm, *Fiṣal*, vol. 2, p. 114.

21. *Ibid.*, vol. 1, p. 3.

22. Ibn al-'Imād, *Shadharāt*, vol. 6, p. 294.

23. For instance, *ibid.*, p. 140 and Ibn Ḥajar, *Durar*, vol. 3, p. 40. It is noteworthy

that Arabic literature is replete with denunciation of such ritual cursing and Ghazālī (Ibn Khallikān, *Wafayāt*, vol. 3, p. 288) specifically banned the cursing of Yazīd.

24. For instance, Maqrīzī, *Sulūk*, vol. 1, pp. 923–5; Ibn Ḥajar, *Durar*, vol. 1, pp. 308–16 and Dhahabī, *'Ibar*, vol. 4, p. 286.

25. Ibn al-'Imād, *Shadharāt*, vol. 6, p. 10.

26. For instance, Sakhāwī, *Ḍaw'*, vol. 2, p. 15.

27. Ibn Ḥajar, *Durar*, vol. 3, p. 325.

28. A'sam, *Tārīkh*, p. 155.

29. *Ibid.*, *passim*.

30. Text quoted in *ibid.*, p. 163.

31. Yāqūt, *Irshād*, vol. 1, p. 179.

32. Ḥajjī Khalīfa, *Kashf*, cols. 992–3.

33. Ibn Khallikān, *Wafayāt*, vol. 2, p. 140.

34. Ibn Rajab, *Dhail*, vol. 1, pp. 144–5.

35. See, for instance, the discussion of Baghdādī, *Uṣūl*, pp. 331 ff.

36. Ibn Taimiyya, *Naqḍ*, p. 47.

37. Ibn 'Aqīl, *Funūn*, para. 130.

38. Ibn Khaldūn, *Prolégomènes*, vol. 3, p. 127.

39. Nawawī, *Fatāwī*, p. 305.

40. Ḥajjī Khalīfa, *Kashf*, col. 698.

41. Ibn Ḥajar, *Durar*, vol. 3, p. 377. It is interesting to note that the early reputation of Ibn Khaldūn in the West, in the sixteenth and seventeenth centuries, was of him as an authority on the occult sciences, a reputation that may have initially been the responsibility of the renegade Leo Africanus. See Al-Azmeh, *Ibn Khaldūn in Modern Scholarship*, p. 58, n. 1.

42. Ṭāshköprüzāde, *Miftāḥ*, vol. 2, p. 593.

43. Ibn Khaldūn, *Prolégomènes*, vol. 3, p. 241.

44. For instance, Tawḥīdī, *Imtā'*, vol. 1, p. 35 (for Miskawaih), Ṭāshköprüzāde, *Miftāḥ*, vol. 1, p. 343 (for the famous Shāfi'ite jurist Ibn Daqīq al-'Īd).

45. For instance, Maqrīzī, *Sulūk*, vol. 2, pp. 322, 333–4.

46. For instance, Ibn Khaldūn, *Prolégomènes*, vol. 1, p. 290.

47. See M. Asín Palacios, *The Mystical Philosophy of Ibn Masarra and His Followers*, tr. E.H. Douglas and H.W. Yoder (Leiden, 1978), pp. 119 ff., 123 ff., along with the discussions of P. Nwiya, 'Note sur quelques fragment inédits de la correspondance d'Ibn al-'Arîf avec Ibn Barrajân', in *Hespéris*, 43 (1956), pp. 217 ff. and Affifi, *Mystical Philosophy*, pp. 174 ff. For the Algarve state and its leader, see Ibn Al-Khaṭīb, *A'māl*, pp. 285 ff. See also D.R. Goodrich, *A 'Sufi' Revolt in Portugal: Ibn Qasi and his 'Kitāb Khal' al-Na'layn'*, unpublished Ph.D. Thesis, Columbia University, 1978.

48. For instance, Ibn al-Khaṭīb, *Rawḍa*, p. 203.

49. For instance, Kalābādhī, *Ta'arruf*, pp. 57 ff., 72 ff.

50. *Ibid.*, pp. 101–2.

51. Ibn Sab'īn, *Budd*, p. 100.

52. See Abū Rayyān, *Suhrawardī*, pp. 48, 88 ff.

53. Ibn Khallikān, *Wafayāt*, vol. 6, p. 273.

54. See, for instance, the indications of the wider context of his execution in Miskawaih, *Tajārib*, vol. 1, pp. 76 ff. and of that of similar contemporary personalities, perhaps associates, in Yāqūt, *Irshād*, vol. 1, pp. 296, 298.

55. Isfarā'īnī, *Tabṣīr*, pp. 116–17.

56. For instance, the hostile account of Ibn al-Jawzī, *Talbīs*, p. 172.

57. Bāqillānī, *Bayān*, para. 87 ff. and *passim*.

58. Suyūṭī, *Naẓm*, p. 99 and Maqqarī, *Nafḥ*, vol. 2, p. 179.

59. Sha'rānī, *Ṭabaqāt*, vol. 1, p. 188.

60. Ibn Khaldūn, *Prolégomènes*, vol. 3, p. 67.

61. The clearest account of this is by Suyūṭī, *Ḥāwī*, vol. 2, pp. 241 ff., 252.

62. Ibn Khaldūn, *Prolégomènes*, vol. 3. pp. 72–3 and see Ibn al-Jawzī, *Talbīs*, pp. 164 ff.

63. Ibn Ḥajar, *Durar*, vol. 1, pp. 329–30.

64. For example: Yāqūt, *Irshād*, vol. 7, p. 126; Maqqarī, *Nafḥ*, vol. 2, p. 245 and Ibn Ḥajar, *Durar*, vol. 3, p. 233. An example of the kinds of official persecution and interdiction is given by Nu'aimī, *Dāris*, vol. 1, p. 393.

65. Marrakishī, *Mu'jib*, pp. 310–11. For the changing fortunes of philosophy in the Maghreb and the Andalus, see the editor's introduction to Ibn Bāja, *Rasā'il*, pp. 11–13 and D.M. Dunlop, 'Philosophical Predecessors and Contemporaries of Ibn Bājjah', in *Islamic Quarterly*, 2 (1955), pp. 100–16. On the changing fortunes of philosophy in Ayyubid Damascus, see J.A. Gilbert, *The Ulama of Medieval Damascus in the International World of Islamic Scholarship*, unpublished Ph. D. thesis, University of California, Berkeley, 1977, p. 151.

66. Ibn Khallikān, *Wafayāt*, vol. 5, p. 314.

67. See the compact review of this and related legal matters in Qifṭī, *Tārīkh*, pp. 51–3.

68. Ghazālī, *Tahāfut*, 4th edn, pp. 309–10.

69. *Ibid.*, pp. 79–81.

70. Ibn al-Jawzī, *Talbīs*, p. 49 and see Ibn Taimiyya, *Radd*, pp. 143–4.

71. Ibn Ḥazm, *Fiṣal*, vol. 1, p. 94; Qifṭī, *Tārīkh*, p. 234, with reference to Abū Muslim Ibn Khaldūn, the ancestor of the famous thinker and see Jurjānī, *Ta'rīfāt*, p. 176.

72. Suyūṭī, *Ḥāwī*, vol. 1, p. 259. Suyūṭī's, *Manṭiq* quotes a very large amount of anti-philosophical opinion.

73. For instance, Subkī, *Mu'īd*, pp. 110–11.

74. Ibn Taimiyya, *Muwafāqa*, vol. 1, p. 181.

75. For instance, Ibn Ḥazm, *Tawqīf*, p. 135.

76. Ibn Ṭufail, *Ḥayy*, pp. 62–3.

77. Qifṭī,. *Tārīkh*, p. 406 and Ibn Khallikān, *Wafayāt*, vol. 4, pp. 429–30, for quotation of a very hostile assessment of the unfortunate Ibn Bāja.

78. Ibn Sīnā, *Aqsām*, pp. 73–4.

79. Ibn Khaldūn, *Prolégomènes*, vol. 3, pp. 215–17.

80. Ibn Bāja, *Ittiṣāl*, p. 166 and *passim*.

81. Ghazālī, *Mīzān*, pp. 221–7 and see the comments of Ibn Khaldūn, *Prolégomènes*, vol. 3, p. 214. On meeting a certain mystic, Ibn Sīnā declared that he knew what the other saw, and the mystic declared that he saw what Ibn Sīnā knew: V.V. Bartold, *Turkistān min al-fatḥ al-'Arabī ilā al-ghazū al-Maghūlī*, tr. Ṣ.'U. Hāshim (Kuwait, 1981), p. 458.

82. Ibn Sīnā, *Najāt*, pp. 477–8.

83. Ibn Taimiyya, *Naqḍ*, p. 171.

84. Qifṭī, *Tārīkh*, pp. 274, 276, 279, 280 and 362.

85. Ibn Abī Uṣaibi'a, *'Uyūn*, p. 318.

86. Ibn Sīnā, *Najāt*, pp. 165–6 and *passim*.

87. Graf, *Geschichte*, vol. 2, pp. 157, 235, 238–40, 244 and *passim*.

88. Ibn Rushd, *Faṣl* (ed. 'Amāra), pp. 22–8.

89. *Ibid.*, p. 22.

90. See 'A. Ḥarb, 'Al-Huwiyya wa al-ghairiyya fī al-maqāl al-falsaī al-'Arabī' in *DA*, 18/4 (1982), p. 89.

91. Ghazālī, *Tahāfut*, pp. 55, 93–4, 196, 208 and *passim*. Such criticism of theology was quite commonplace amongst philosophers. See, for instance, Tawḥīdī, *Muqābasāt*, pp. 203–4, and the remark on the reputation of Kindī in R. Walzer, *Greek into Arabic. Essays on Islamic Philosophy* (Oxford, 1962), p. 194 n. 3.

92. Ibn al-Abbār, *Takmila*, vol. 2, pp. 542, 554 and 941.

93. Marrakishī, *Mu'jib*, p. 315.

94. *Ibid.*, p. 385. On some of those also exiled with Ibn Rushd and reprieved with him, see Ibn Abī Uṣaibi'a, *'Uyūn*, p. 532; Ghubrīnī, *'Unwān*, pp. 208–10 and Maqqarī, *Nafḥ*, vol. 2, p. 240.

95. Marrakishi, *Mu'jib*, p. 385.

96. See the terms in which Ibn Rushd was lampooned: texts in S. Munk, *Mélanges de philosophie juive et arabe* (Paris, 1859), p. 517.

97. Marrakishī, *Mu'jib*, p. 384 and Nubāhī, *Tārīkh*, pp. 111, 124.

98. Ẓāhirism seems only to have been officialised for a short period during Ibn Ḥazm's sojourn in Majorca (Turki, *Polémiques*, pp. 46, 52–3), and its local form seems to have taken the name of Ḥazmiyya (Goldziher, *Ẓahiris*, p. 112). By the eighth/fourteenth century, it became a school without masters, derided, and of use by the lowest class of lawyers (Ibn Khaldūn, *Prolégomènes*, vol. 3, p. 4 and 'Uqbānī, *Tuḥfa*, para. 62, 64). But we would be mistaken in believing that Ẓāhirism disappeared with the disappearance of its name. The effect was durable, and the impulse to reflection untrammelled by convention seems to have permeated much of Maghribi thought, partly accounting for its sensitive receptivity to later juristic theory, and also partly accounting for the remarkable untrammelledness of Ibn Khaldūn's thought, as well as of the free spirit that animated Shāṭibī's *Muwāfaqāt*, which is premised on a very Ẓāhirite axiom, that the intent of nomothesis can only be established with certainty if it is based upon the certainty of tradition.

99. Goldziher, *Ẓāhiris*, pp. 159–61 and A. Bel, *La religion musulmane en Bérbèrie* (Paris, 1938), pp. 254–6.

100. Urvoy, *Le monde des ulémas andalous du XIVe au VII/XIIIe siècle: étude sociologique* (Geneva, 1978), p. 187 and R. Brunschvig, *La Berbérie orientale sous les Ḥafṣides* (Paris, 1947), vol. 2, p. 288.

101. This led to Almoravid jurists being lampooned with the couplet: 'you acquired worldly wealth with the school of Mālik, and you divided wealth according to Ibn al-Qāsim' — Marrakishī, *Mu'jib*, pp. 235–6.

102. *Ibid.*, pp. 354–6. The Almoravids had reputedly burnt the books of Ghazālī (*ibid.*, p. 237), and it is reputed that Ibn Tūmart had met with Ghazālī in Baghdad, and that at this meeting mention was made of a *malḥama*, a futuristic poem, which indicated Almohad victory over the Almoravids (Ibn Qunfudh, *Fārisiyya*, p. 100). This meeting may have been legendary — see *ibid.*, p. 207 n. and R. Le Tourneau, *The Almohad Movement in Africa in the Twelfth and Thirteenth Centuries* (Princeton, 1969), pp. 6–10. It does not appear, moreover, that Ibn Tūmart was a Ẓāhirite: R. Brunschvig, 'Sue la doctrine du Mahdī Ibn Tūmart' in *Arabica*, 2 (1955), pp. 137–48.

103. See, for instance, Ibn al-Abbār, *Takmila*, vol. 2, p. 616 and Aḥmad Bābā, *Nayl*, pp. 138, 184.

104. Dhahabī, *'Ibar*, vol. 5, pp. 118, 166; and see R. Le Tourneau, *History of North Africa*, tr. J. Petrie (London, 1970), pp. 194–6.

105. D. Urvoy, 'La pensée Almohade dans l'oeuvre d'Averroès', in *Multiple Averroès. Actes du Colloque international organisé a l'occasion du 850e anniversaire de la naissance d'Averroès, Paris 20–23 September 1976*, ed. J. Jolivet (Paris, 1978), pp. 45–8. Urvoy also ('La pensée d'Ibn Tūmart', in *BEO*, 27 (1974), pp. 41–2) argued that Ibn Rushd and Ibn Ṭufail were official Almohad thinkers. See also W.M. Watt, 'Philosophy and Social Structure in Almohad Spain', in *Islamic Quarterly*, 8/1–2 (1964), pp. 46 ff.

106. Ibn Rushd, *Bidāya*, vol. 1, p. 9 and see Ibn Ḥazm, *Mulakhkhaṣ*, p. 6 and *Iḥkām*, *passim*. On Ibn Rushd's opening to Ẓāhirism, see A. Turki, 'La place d'Averroès juriste dans l'histoire du Malikisme et de l'Espagne musulmane', in *Multiple Averroès*, pp. 35–6, 39–40, and see R. Brunschvig, 'Averroës juriste', in *Etudes d'orientalisme dediées a la mémoire d'Evariste Lêvi-Provencal* (Paris, 1962), vol. 1, p. 44.

107. See for instance Maqqarī, *Nafḥ*, vol. 1, pp. 219, 221.

108. Brunschvig, 'Averroès juriste', pp. 38–9.

109. Shāṭibī, *Muwāfaqāt*, vol. 4, pp. 140 ff.

110. Subkī, *Ṭabaqāt*, vol. 3, p. 386 and *passim*.

111. On Subkī's propaganda, see G. Makdisi, 'Ash'arī and the Ash'arites in Islamic Religious History', in *SI*, 17 (1962), pp. 57 ff.

112. Ghazālī, *Faiṣal*, pp. 127–9, 131–3.

113. Shahrastānī, *Milal*, pp. 2–3. For an account of this and some other works, see H. Laoust, 'L'herésiographie musulmane sous les Abbasides', in *Cahiers de civilization mediévale*, 10 (1967), pp. 157–78.

114. Isfarā'īnī, *Tabṣīr*.

115. Ash'arī, *Maqūlāt*.

116. On the Kullābiyya, which survived until the fifth/eleventh century, and its supersession by Ash'arism, see J. Van Ess, 'Ibn Kullāb', in *EI*, Suppl., pp. 391–2. The question of the retrospective Ash'arism of Ash'arī was discussed by Allard, *Attributs divins*, pp. 287 ff. and Makdisi, 'Ash'arī and the Ash'arites', pp. 40 ff. On Qarmaṭism and Ismā'īlism, see S.M. Stern, 'Ismā'īlis and Qarmaṭians' in *L'Elaboration de l'Islam* (Paris, 1961), pp. 99–108. I should like to emphasise that the tenure of a Bāṭinī doctrine, and the commitment to a specific (or even general) 'Alīd genealogy, are historically distinct matters which, however, very often intersect. 'Alīd genealogy and other doctrinal matters also intersect in Shī'ism generally, although these are probably, again, historically distinct.

117. See, for instance, Subkī, *Ṭabaqāt*, vol. 2, p. 386 and W.M. Watt in *EI*, vol. 1, p. 697.

118. For instance, Ibn Khallikān, *Wafayāt*, vol. 4, pp. 152–4; Ibn al-'Imād, *Shadharāt*, vol. 6, pp. 326–7; Ibn Ḥajar, *Durar*, vol. 2, pp. 287–8; Shakhāwī, *Ḍaw'*, vol. 2, p. 174 and Ibn Farḥūn, *Dībāj*, p. 324.

119. See Maqqariī, *Nafḥ*, vol. 1, p. 556 and see Yāqūt, *Irshād*, vol. 6, p. 12 and Subkī, *Mu'īd*, pp. 145–6.

120. See, for instance, Muqaddasī, *Taqāsīm*, pp. 336, 371 and 395–6.

121. On the difficulty attendant upon understanding this conflict, see the excellent work of R. Bulliett, *The Patricians of Nishapur. A Study in Medieval Islamic Social History* (Cambridge, Mass., 1972), esp. pp. 33 ff.

122. For comparative material which also points to similar difficulties, see A. Cameron, *Circus Factions. Blues and Greens at Rome and Byzantium* (Oxford, 1976).

123. C. Cahen, *L'Islam dès origines au debut de l'empire ottoman* (Histoire Universelle, 14) (Paris, 1970), pp. 153, 158.

124. Maqrīzī, *Sulūk*, vol. 3, pp. 196, 359.

125. Ibn Rajab, *Dhail*, vol. 1, p. 199 and Nu'aimī, *Dāris*, vol. 1, p. 85.

126. See Afghānī, *Uṣūl al-naḥw*, pp. 197 ff.

127. Rāzī, *Munāẓarāt*. On the local enracination of Māturīdism in Samarqand, and its near fusion with, and attribution to, the Ḥanafite school, see W. Madelung, 'The Spread of Māturīdism and the Turks', in *IV Congresso de estudios àrabes e islamicos. Actas* (Leiden, 1971), p. 123.

128. Subkī, *Ṭabaqāt*, vol. 3, pp. 378 ff.

129. *Ibid.*, p. 387.

130. Subkī, *Mu'īd*, p. 107.

131. Maqrīzī, *Khiṭaṭ*, vol. 2, p. 358.

132. Ibn Taimiyya's text is given by Ibn Taghrī Birdī, *Manhal*, vol. 1, p. 339. On this particular inquest and its circumstances, see Maqrīzī, *Sulūk*, vol. 2, pp. 17–18 and Ibn Rajab, *Dhail*, vol. 2, pp. 396–7.

133. Ibn Rajab, *Dhail*, vol. 2, pp. 9–10, 22, 24. See *ibid.*, pp. 20–2 for anti-Ḥanbalite resistance in Damascus. On the failure of Ḥanbalism in Egypt, see H. Laoust, 'Le Hanbalisme sous le Califat de Bagdad (241/855–656/1258)', in *REI*, 27 (1959), p. 126.

134. For Baghdad, see Ibn Abī Ya'lā', *Ṭabaqāt*, vol. 2, p. 10; for Damascus, Nu'aimī, *Dāris*, vol. 2, pp. 123–4.

135. Maqrīzī, *Sulūk*, vol. 3, p. 70.

136. Laoust, 'Le Hanbalisme sour le Califat', p. 83. This was so despite the efforts of the Ḥanbalites to give ideological support exemplified by the position of Barbahārī on the Caliphate — see Ibn Abī Ya'lā, *Ṭabaqāt*, vol. 1, pp. 21–2.

137. G. Makdisi, *Ibn 'Aqīl et la résurgence de l'Islam traditionaliste au XIe siècle* (Damascus, 1963), pp. 299 ff.

138. *Ibid.*, pp. 311–12 and Laoust, 'Le Hanbalisme', p. 91.
139. Laoust, 'Le Hanbalisme', p. 107.
140. For instance, Ibn Rajab, *Dhail*, vol. 1, pp. 392 ff.; vol. 2, pp. 190 f. On Ibn Hubaira, see *ibid.*, vol. 1, pp. 251 ff. and Ibn Khallikān, *Wafayāt*, vol. 6, pp. 233–4.
141. See the valuable indications in Makdisi, *Ibn 'Aqīl*, pp. 320, 325 ff.
142. Laoust, 'Le Hanbalisme', p. 113.
143. See Muqaddasī, *Taqāsīm*, pp. 126, 399. The major Ḥanbalite divine Barbahārī wrote a dissertation exonerating Mu'āwiya (Ibn Abī Ya'lā, *Ṭabaqāt*, vol. 2, p. 205).
144. This is based on biographies in Ibn Rajab, *Dhail*, who is the source also for the information on Herat (vol. 1, pp. 54–6, and see Subkī, *Ṭabaqāt*, vol. 4, pp. 272–3). See also Laoust, 'Le Hanbalisme', pp. 105 ff.
145. H. Laoust, 'Le Hanbalisme sous les Mamlouks Bahrides (658/784–1260/1382)', in *REI*, 28 (1960), p. 3 — but no source is cited by the author.
146. On the introduction of Ḥanbalism to Damascus, see Ibn Rajab, *Dhail*, vol. 1, pp. 69–70. Damascus Ḥanbalites tended to form dynasties of scholars some of which were long-lived. On their beginnings, see Laoust, 'Le Hanbalisme sous le Califat', pp. 121 ff. The Hanbalites only succeeded in obtaining their particular prayer-niche (*miḥrab*) in the Great Mosque of Damascus in 617/1220 (Laoust, 'Le Hanbalisme sous les Mamlouks', p. 5). See *ibid., passim*, for the history of the school.
147. Laoust, 'Le Hanbalisme sous le Califat', p. 67.
148. For instance, Ibn Rajab, *Dhail*, vol. 2, pp. 40, 67, 71.
149. *Ibid.*, vol. 1, pp. 144–6. See Makdisi, *Ibn 'Aqīl*, pp. 430 ff. for political aspects of this affair.
150. Ash'arī, *Ibāna*, pp. 46–7 and see Gardet and Anawati, *Théologie Musulmane*, p. 59.
151. Khwārizmī, *Mafātīḥ*, p. 27.
152. Ibn Abī Ya'lā, *Ṭabaqāt*, vol. 2, p. 210. This may have been a minority view.
153. Ibn Fūrak, *Mushkil*, p. 3.
154. Ibn 'Asākir, *Tabyīn*, p. 163 and see Subkī, *Ṭabaqāt*, vol. 4, p. 32.
155. Ibn Taimiyya, *Naqḍ*, pp. 10–11, 18.
156. Ibn Abī Ya'lā, *Ṭabaqāt*, vol. 2, p. 239 and Ibn Rajab, *Dhail*, vol. 1, pp. 19–22.
157. Ibn Abī Ya'lā, *Ṭabaqāt*, vol. 2, pp. 247–8 and Subkī, *Ṭabaqāt*, vol. 4, pp. 129–31.
158. Ibn Khallikān, *Wafayāt*, vol. 5, p. 138 and Ibn 'Asākir, *Tabyīn*, p. 108.
159. Ibn 'Asākir, *Tabyīn*, pp. 108–9 and Subkī, *Ṭabaqāt*, vol. 3, pp. 390 ff. It should not be assumed, however, that Ash'arism was under constant persecution during that time. An account of these events is related by Madelung, 'The Spread of Māturīdism', pp. 126 ff.
160. Bulliet, *The Patricians of Nishapur*, p. 74.
161. Maqdisi, *Ibn 'Aqīl*, p. 291.
162. This association does not imply identity, but simply points to the fact that Ash'arites were normally Shāfi'ites and, in the Maghreb, Mālikites, while the Ḥanafites in Khurāsān later became Māturīdites after an uncertain Mu'tazilite association disturbed by the association of the Mu'tazilites with Zaidism and other Shī'ite sects, as we shall see. See Gardet, 'Quelques reflexions', pp. 266–7 and Makdisi, 'Ash'arī and the Ash'arites', pp. 44 ff. Not unnaturally, Ḥanafites could also be Ash'arites — for instance, Sumnānī of Mosul who died in 444/1052–3 (Ibn Quṭlūbughā, *Tāj*, p. 61). On Ḥanafism and Maturīdism, see Madelung, 'The Spread of Māturīdism', pp. 112 ff.
163. Makdisi, 'Ash'arī and the Ash'arites', *passim* and *ibid.*, pt. 2, in *SI*, 18 (1963), pp. 19 ff.
164. Subkī, *Ṭabaqāt*, vol. 3, p. 365.
165. For instance, Kalābādhī, *Ta'arruf*, pp. 66 f., 72 ff.
166. Ibn Taimiyya, *Radd*, pp. 94–5, 310–11.
167. Ibn Taimiyya, *Muwāfaqa*, vol. 2, p. 166.
168. Subkī, *Ṭabaqāt*, vol. 5, pp. 121–2.
169. On these affiliations, see A.N. Nader, *Le système philosophique des Mu'tazila* (Beirut, 1956), pp. 322 ff. Lineaments of this complex relationship are explored in W.

Madelung, 'Imamism and Mu'tazilite Theology', in *Le Shi'isme imâmite*, pp. 13 ff.

170. On this matter, see 'A. Rāwī, *Al-'Aql wal-ḥurriyya. Dirāsa fī fikr al-Qāḍī 'Abd al-Jabbār al-Mu'tazilī* (Beirut, 1980), pp. 61 ff., 448 ff. See *ibid.*, ch. 1, for a good account of the history of this school.

171. Shahrastānī, *Milal*, p. 34.

172. Maqrīzī, *Khiṭaṭ*, vol. 2, p. 358. This was particularly true during the 18-year vizirate of the urbane and tolerant vizier Ibn 'Abbād — see Sukūnī, *'Uyūn*, para. 346 ff.

173. 'Abd al-Jabbār, *Faḍl*, p. 138.

174. Ibn al-Murtaḍa, *Ṭabaqāt*, p. 118.

175. Balkhī, *Bāb*, pp. 108–9.

176. Ibn Ḥazm (*Ṭawq*, p. 45) speaks of a leader of Andalusian Mu'tazilites, implying the existence of a school. By the time of Ibn Rushd, it had obviously ceased to exist and Ibn Rushd (*Manāhij* (ed. Qāsim), p. 149) explicitly stated that Mu'tazilite works were unknown to him and unavailable in Spain. There also seem to have been Mu'tazilites in Ifriqiyā at the time of the Fatimids (Al Qāḍī al-Nu'mān, *Majālis*, para. 196 and *passim*, where they are refuted — but this may have been in response to their own anti-Ismā'īlī polemics in the East).

177. Ibn al-Murtaḍā, *Ṭabaqāt*, p. 52.

178. Bartold, *Turkistān*, pp. 314, 319–20.

179. E.G. Browne, *A Literary History of Persia* (Cambridge, 1928), vol. 2, p. 114.

180. Ibn al-Murtaḍā, *Ṭabaqāt*, p. 106.

181. See M.A. Shaban, *Islamic History, A New Interpretation* (Cambridge, 1976), vol. 2, p. 162. Muqaddasī (cited in Makdisi, *Ibn 'Aqīl*, p. 278) reported that 'Aḍud ad-Dawla was a Ẓāhirite.

182. For instance, see Ibn Quṭlūbughā, *Tāj*, p. 29.

183. Pazdawī, *Kashf*, pp. 10 ff. Pazdawī and others, of various schools, used Mu'tazilite ideas, but denied the connection, as we have seen.

184. G. Makdisi, *The Rise of the Colleges. Institutions of Learning in Islam and the West* (Edinburgh, 1981), p. 6, dates this a century later.

185. Maqqarī, *Nafḥ*, vol. 2, pp. 10, 45 and see vol. 3, p. 230.

186. There is evidence of a Ḥanafite grand judge of Tunis until the end of the third/ninth century — Ibn Quṭlubughā, *Tāj*, p. 63.

187. Goldziher, *Ẓahiris*, pp. 106–7 and Subkī, *Ṭabaqāt*, vol. 1, p. 328.

188. See Gilbert, *The Ulama of Damascus*, pp. 90–1 and the history of legal schools in Syria and Egypt in Subkī, *Ṭabaqāt*, vol. 1, pp. 326–7, vol. 3, p. 196.

189. Ibn Khallikān, *Wafayāt*, vol. 5, p. 224.

190. Ṭabarī, *Ikhtilāf*, *passim*.

191. Ibn Farḥūn, *Dībāj*, p. 257.

192. Ibn al-Jawzī, *Muntaẓam*, vol. 7, pp. 17–18 and Subkī, *Ṭabaqāt*, vol. 3, pp. 343–4.

193. See Yāqūt, *Irshād*, vol. 1, p. 251 and the comments of Laoust, 'Le Hanbalisme sous le Califat', p. 72. It is noteworthy that Ṭabarī's funeral was accompanied by a hostile riot.

194. Ibn Khallikān, *Wafayāt*, vol. 3, p. 189.

195. Laoust, 'Le Hanbalisme sous le Califat', p. 78.

196. When in 661/1263 for instance, it was decreed that Aleppo should have a judge for each of the schools, no Ḥanbalite could be found to fill the position (Maqrīzī, *Sulūk*, vol. 1, p. 501). The first appointment of a Ḥanafite to the position of judge in Alexandria was in 772/1370–1 (Ibn Ḥajar, *Durar*, vol. 1, p. 94).

197. The geographical distribution over time of Ḥanafites has been studied by Madelung, 'The Spread of Māturīdism', *passim*, and of Shāfi'ites by H. Halm, *Die Ausbreitung der Šāfi'itischen Rechtsschule von den Anfängen bis zum 8/14. Jahrhundert* (Wiesbaden, 1974) (Beihefte zum Tübinger Atlas des vorderen Orients, Reihe B, Nr. 4). There are no comparable studies of other schools, although the outlines are well known — see the more restrictive study of A. Bekir, *Histoire de l'école malékite en Orient* (Paris, 1962), more

properly a study of Mālikite tradition.

198. Gilbert, *The Ulama of Damascus*, pp. 59, 69, 78 and *passim*. Gilbert's findings on Damascus can safely be generalised.

199. A. Mez, *Al-Ḥadāra al-Islāmiyya fi al-qan al-rābi' al-hijrī*, 3rd edn, tr. M.'A. Abū Rida (Cairo, 1957), vol. 1, pp. 302–3.

200. Ibn al-Murtaḍḍā, *Ṭabaqāt*, p. 113.

201. Eche, *Les bibliothèques arabes*, pp. 41 ff., 53, 56.

202. *Ibid.*, pp. 88 ff., 143 ff.

203. *Ibid.*, pp. 150 ff.

204. For instance, Yāqūt, *Irshād*, vol. 5, p. 18 and Ibn Rajab, *Dhail*, vol. 1, pp. 33, 39, 78, 139.

205. See the account of Subkī, *Ṭabaqāt*, vol. 4, pp. 313–14; vol. 5, p. 171 and see the account of Maqrīzī, *Khiṭaṭ*, vol. 2, p. 363.

206. Subkī, *Ṭabaqāt*, vol. 4, p. 314.

207. Nu'aimī, *Dāris*, vol. 1, p. 537.

208. See Ibn Marzūq, *Musnad*, pp. 19–20, and the comments of 'Umarī, *Waṣf*, p. 9. For the political and cultural circumstances of the foundation of Colleges by the Merinids, see M. Shatzmiller, 'Les premiers Mérinides et le milieu religieux de Fès: l'introduction des Médersas', in *SI*, 43 (1976), pp. 115–16.

209. For instance, Nu'aimī, *Dāris*, vol. 1, pp. 313, 438.

210. For a detailed account, see Makdisi, *The Rise of the Colleges*, pp. 28, 31, 35 ff. and Maqrīzī, *Khiṭaṭ*, vol. 2, pp. 295–6.

211. For instance, Nu'aimī, *Dāris*, vol. 1, pp. 152, 545 and Maqrīzī, *Khiṭaṭ*, vol. 2, pp. 374–5.

212. For detailed accounts, see for instance Nu'aimī, *Dāris*, vol. 1, pp. 301–3; vol. 2, pp. 111–12. Eche, *Bibliothèques*, p. 177, found that the allowance of a student at the Mustanṣiriyya in Baghdad was equivalent to the income of its menial employees. See Makdisi, *Rise of the Colleges*, pp. 171 ff.

213. Nu'aimī, *Dāris*, vol. 1, p. 206.

214. *Ibid.*, p. 276.

215. Maqqarī, *Nafḥ*, vol. 2, p. 241.

216. Subkī, *Mu'īd*, pp. 153–4.

217. Maqrīzī, *Khiṭaṭ*, vol. 2, p. 380 and Suyūṭī, *Muḥāḍara*, vol. 2, p. 265.

218. Ibn Khallikān, *Wafayāt*, vol. 6, p. 192.

219. *Ibid.*, vol. 7, p. 48.

220. Nu'aimī, *Dāris*, *passim*.

221. Suyūṭī, *Muḥāḍara*, vol. 2, p. 262.

222. Nu'aimī, *Dāris*, s.v. 'Dār al-Ḥadīth al-Ashrafiyya'.

223. For instance, Maqrīzī, *Khiṭaṭ*, vol. 2, pp. 241, 249. Maqrīzī lists 23 such establishments in Cairo, in addition to 38 other mystical institutions; some were wealthy and treated their inmates with some largesse (for instance, *ibid.*, vol. 2, pp. 422–3), while others were almost proverbial for their sparse condition (for instance, Sakhāwī, *Ḍaw'*, vol. 1, p. 236. On the beginnings of these institutions in Khurāsān under the Saljūqs and in association with the rise of Shāfi'ism, see J. Chabbi, 'Khānḳāh', in *EI*, vol. 4, pp. 1025–6.

224. Maqrīzī, *Khiṭaṭ*, vol. 2, p. 416.

225. See Qalashandī, *Ṣubḥ*, vol. 1, pp. 466–7; Maqrīzī, *Khiṭaṭ*, col. 2, p. 395 and Subkī, *Mu'īd*, p. 159.

226. For examples from different times and places, see Subkī, *Mu'īd*, p. 155; Ibn Rajab, *Dhail*, vol. 2, p. 236; Nu'aimī, *Dāris*, vol. 1, p. 368; Ibn Khallikān, *Wafayāt*, vol. 6, p. 77 and Ibn Abī Uṣaibi'a, *'Uyūn*, p. 462.

227. Subkī, *Ṭabaqāt*, vol. 5, p. 185.

228. For example, *Nu'aimī*, vol. 1, p. 109.

229. On these positions, see Subkī, *Mu'īd*, pp. 159–60, 154–6 and the detailed account

of Makdisi, *Rise of the Colleges*, pp. 192 ff. Similarly, *shaikh al-'iqrā'*, organised elementary instruction and training in the context of Qur'ānic recitation.

230. Subkī, *Mu'īd*, p. 157; Nu'aimī, *Dāris*, vol. 1, p. 373 and Makdisi, *The Rise of the Colleges*, p. 220.

231. Makdisi, *The Rise of the Colleges*, pp. 91 ff.

232. *Ibid.*, pp. 167 ff., 195.

233. Subkī, *Mu'īd*, pp. 152–3.

234. For instance, Ibn al-Ḥājib, *Mukhtaṣar*, p. 232.

235. See the terms in which *ijtihād* is generally described by, for instance, Ibn Khallikān, *Wafayāt*, vol. 1, p. 28.

236. For instance, Ghazālī, *Mustasfā*, vol. 2, pp. 350–2; Shaṭibī, *Muqāfaqāt*, vol. 4, pp. 68–9 and Ibn al-Ukhuwwa, *Ḥisba*, pp. 205–6. This latter, practical manual, refers to practical reality, whereas conditions imposed by, for instance, Shawkānī, *Irshād*, pp. 250–2, refer to requirements impossible except for precious few, such as the author himself.

237. Subkī, *Mu'īd*, p. 116.

238. Suyūṭī, *Muzhir*, vol. 2, p. 312.

239. See Hallaq, 'The Gate of Ijtihad', pp. 6–7.

240. Suyūṭī, *Muḥāḍara*, vol. 1, p. 338.

241. Ibn Khaldūn, *Prolégomènes*, vol. 3, pp. 251–7, and see pp. 263–4 and vol. 2, pp. 315, 262–3. For examples of usual curricula, see Nu'aimī, *Dāris*, vol. 1, p. 61 and Brunschvig, *Bérbèrie*, vol. 2, pp. 364 ff. A particularly thorough education was obtained by Ibn Khaldūn — see his *Ta'rīf*, pp. 15–16, 19–20, 22, 37.

242. For these dates, see the editor's introduction to Zarnūjī, *Ta'līm*. For the work's popularity, see the 'Introduction' of T.M. Abel and G.E. von Grunebaum to Zarnūjī, *Instruction of the Student: The Method of Learning* (New York, 1947), p. 1, n. 1.

243. Zarnūjī, *Ta'līm*, p. 57.

244. *Ibid.*, p. 133.

245. Sam'āni, *Adab, passim*.

246. Ṭāshköprüzāde, *Miftāḥ*, vol. 1, pp. 6 ff.

247. See the explicit statement of Baghdādī, *Kifāya*, vol. 1, pp. 3–5.

248. Baghdādī, *Kifāya*, vol. 1, p. 203.

249. P. Bourdieu and J.-C. Passeron, *Reproduction in Education, Society, and Culture*, tr. R. Nice (London and Beverley Hills, 1977), para. 1 ff.

250. Ṭāshköprüzāde, *Miftāḥ*, vol. 3, p. 271.

251. Zarnūjī, *Ta'līm*, pp. 78 ff. Not unnaturally given esoteric teachings and the importance of devotional techniques, mystical writers stressed this point most eloquently. See, for instance, Ibn 'Arabī, *Tadbīrāt*, pp. 226 ff. and Sha'rānī, *Ṭabaqāt*, vol. 1, pp. 166, 176.

252. Qushairī, *Risāla*, vol. 2, p. 574.

253. See, additionally, Shāṭibī, *Muwāfaqāt*, vol. 1, pp. 58–9. Ibn al-Jawzī, a truly major figure, was also criticised for autodidacticism (Ibn Rajab, *Dhail*, vol. 1, pp. 403, 414) — though this might be a charitable interpretation by fellow Ḥanbalites for his criticism of excessive traditionalism and use of *ta'wīl*, which was ascribed to faulty learning rather than to more serious causes. See Ibn al-Jawzī, *Talbīs*, pp. 114 ff.

254. See Eche, *Bibliothèques arabes*, pp. 274 ff.

255. See Ibn Khaldūn, *Prolégomènes*, vol. 2, pp. 308, 349 and the general account of Ḥ. Zayyāt, 'Al-Wirāqa wa al-warrāqūn fil-Islām', in *Al-Mashriq*, 41 (1947), pp. 305–50.

256. See, for instance, Ibn Khaldūn, *Ta'rīf*, p. 20. Some manuscripts have very interesting histories. The edition of Ibn Ḥazm's *Mulakhkhaṣ* used in this book is based on a manuscript in the hand of Dhahabī, copied from the hand of Ibn 'Arabī, which copy is based on a direct line of transmission.

257. On this and related matters, see F. Rosenthal, *The Technique and Approach of Muslim Scholarship* (Rome, 1947).

258. See Eche, *Bibliothèques arabes*, p. 379, and the remarks of Ibn Khaldūn,

Prolégomènes, vol. 2, pp. 351–2.

259. For instance, Subkī, *Mu'īd*, p. 186 and see the warning of Mas'ūdī, *Murūj*, vol. 1, p. 17.

260. Ibn Khallikān, *Wafayāt*, vol. 3, p. 309.

261. See Baghdādī, *Kifāya*, vol. 1, pp. 311–55; Qalqashandī, *Ṣubḥ*, vol. 14, pp. 322–35 and see F. Sezgin, *Geschichte des arabishen Schrifttums* (Wiesbaden, 1967), vol. 1, pp. 53–84.

262. For instance, Ibn al-Abbār, *Takmila*, vol. 2, pp. 642, 678 and Nawawī, *Adhkār*, p. 369.

263. For instance, Ibn Khallikān, *Wafayāt*, vol. 2, p. 344; vol. 5, p. 345.

264. For instance, licences by Ibn Khaldūn to some of his students: M.B.A. Benchekroun, *La vie intellectuelle marocaine sous les Merinides et les Wattasides* (Rabat, 1974), pp. 352–3 and H. Ritter, 'Autographs in Turkish Libraries', in *Oriens*, 6 (1953), p. 83 and plate 17.

265. See C. Pellat, 'Fahrasa', in *EI*, vol. 2, pp. 743–4. For examples of the punctilious scrupulousness with which particulars were recorded, see, for instance, Suyūṭī, *Muḥāḍara*, vol. 1, p. 377 and Maqqarī, *Nafḥ*, vol. 2, p. 549. See the studies assembled in G. Vajda, *La transmission du saviour en Islam (VIIe–XVIIIe siècles)*, ed. N. Cottart (London, 1983) and the translation and commentary of original texts by J. Sublet, 'Les maîtres et les études de deux traditionnistes de l'époque Mamelouke', in *BEO*, 20 (1967), pp. 11–99.

266. Ibn Khaldūn, *Ta'rīf*, p. 297.

267. Ibn Khallikān, *Wafayāt*, vol. 4, p. 252.

268. Shawkānī, *Irshād*, pp. 63–4 and Ibn Ḥazm, *Iḥkām*, pp. 255–6.

269. Sam'ānī, *Adab*, pp. 84 ff.

270. Sam'ānī, *Adab*, p. 8 and Shawkānī, *Irshād*, pp. 61 ff.

271. Makdisi, *Rise of the Colleges*, p. 143 and Suyūṭī, *Naẓm*, p. 149.

272. See the detailed review in Suyūṭī, *Muzhir*, vol. 1, pp. 144–62 and Sezgin, *Geschichte*, vol. 1, pp. 77 ff. On the particularities of Qur'ān transmission, see Suyūṭī, *Itqān*, vol. 1, p. 101.

273. Ibn Khaldūn, *Prolégomènes*, vol. 2, p. 376 and *passim*.

274. See Bourdieu and Passeron, *Reproduction in Education*, para. 3 gloss 2; para. 4.1.1.2. gloss 1.

275. For instance, Ibn Khallikān, *Wafayāt*, vol. 3, p. 206 and Dhahabī as quoted in the editor's introduction to Sulamī, *Ṭabaqāt*, p. 45.

276. Makdisi, *Ibn 'Aqīl*, p. 101.

277. Sha'rānī, *Ṭabaqāt*, vol. 2, p. 13.

278. See for instance Shāṭibī, *Muwafaqāt*, vol. 1, pp. 60–1 and Ibn Abī Uṣaibi'a, *'Uyūn*, pp. 563–4.

279. For instance, Ibn 'Abd al-Barr, *Jāmi'*, vol. 1, pp. 63 ff., 70 ff.

280. See the description of Ong, *Orality and Literacy*, pp. 37 ff.

281. On orality and the form of *fiqh*, see Turki, *Polémiques*, pp. 449 and *passim*. For a convenient summary of debating practice and technique, see Ṭāshköprüzāde, *Adab*, pp. 30 ff.

282. See the examples transcribed in Sukūnī, *'Uyūn*, paras. 322 ff., 329 ff., and *passim*.

283. E. Stetter, *Topoi und Schemata im Ḥadīth* (Tübingen, 1965), conducts an examination of texts from Bukhārī to find schematised expressions and topoi for the organisation of events and succeeds, albeit formally and superficially, in locating them. An attempt to study such matters in Arabic historical writing can be found in 'Aẓma, *Al-Kitāba at-tārīkhiyya*, pp. 67 ff.

284. For a review of the literature on these matters, which started in Homeric scholarship, see Ong, *Orality and Literacy*, pp. 16 ff.

285. Eche, *Bibliothèques arabes*, pp. 159–60.

286. Ḥajjī Khalīfa, *Kashf*, col. 623 and Makdisi, *Rise of the Colleges*, pp. 116 ff.

287. Ibn Khaldūn, *Prolégomènes*, vol. 3, pp. 248 ff. and see Ibn Maryam, *Bustān*, pp. 216–17.
288. Ibn al-Khaṭīb, *Iḥāṭa*, vol. 1, p. 355.
289. Sakhāwī, *Ḍaw'*, vol. 2, p. 115.
290. Ḥajjī Khalīfa, *Kashf*, col. 454.
291. Milliot, 'Conception de l'état', p. 645 and see also Sakhāwī, *Ḍaw'*, vol. 2, p. 195.
292. Nu'aimī, *Dāris*, no. 155–7.
293. Ibn Abī Uṣaibi'a, *'Uyūn*, p. 733.
294. A. 'Īsā, *Tārīkh al-bīmāristānāt fil-Islām* (Damascus, 1939), pp. 34, 38, 102.
295. Ibn Abī Uṣaibi'a, *'Uyūn*, pp. 183 ff., 214. See the account of Graf, *Geschichte*, vol. 2, pp. 109 ff. and the family tree of C. Elgood, *A Medical History of Persia* (1951) (Amsterdam, 1979), p. 596. Members of this family are said to have guarded their knowledge and confined it to the family and close associates: Qifṭī, *Tārīkh*, p. 174.
296. For instance, Ibn Abī Uṣaibi'a, *'Uyūn*, p. 614.
297. Meyerhof and Schacht, 'Introduction' to Ibn al-Nafīs, *Risāla*, pp. 8–9.
298. Meyerhof, 'Von Alexandrien nach Baghdad', p. 428.
299. Elgood, *Medical History*, pp. 240 ff., 244.
300. For instance, 'Īsā, *Bīmāristānāt*, p. 52.
301. 'Īsā, *Bīmāristānāt*, pp. 43, 45.
302. *Ibid.*, pp. 53–5.
303. Qifṭī, *Tārīkh*, p. 191.
304. G. Endress, 'Handschriftenkunde', in *Grundriss der arabischen Philologie, Band I: Sprachwissenschaft*, ed. W. Fischer (Wiesbaden, 1982), p. 288 and 288 n. and see, for instance, Qifṭī, *Tārīkh*, p. 365.
305. For instance, Ibn Sīnā, *Nairūziyya*, p. 97 and Ibn Sab'īn, *Budd*, pp. 31, 131.
306. Ibn Abī Uṣaibi'a, *'Uyūn*, p. 457.
307. Ibn Ṭufail, *Ḥayy*, p. 64.

Chapter Six

Concluding Notes: Scientific Knowledge and the Social Order

Science in its capacity as a specific form of knowledge has been studied in some detail in the foregoing pages. Yet science does not only have to do with knowledge, and the occasion has already arisen for treating it in its capacity as a field where extra-epistemic conflicts are articulated and, indeed, fought out. In this respect, science provides the terms in which historically determinate social and political groups — schools of thought — muster the power of naming the authorities on behalf of whom an utterance is being made. In this way, science allows the social and political groups which carry it and consolidate its authority and which constitute its historicity to engage in a relationship of co-operation or of competition in the distribution of that fund of knowledge contained in the sciences, that fund which is institutionalised and therefore consolidated and continued by virtue of the scientitic institutions we have studied, the scientific paradigm, the school and the college or other educational means, such as initiation, each of which instils an apodicticity refashioned over generations. And in all these matters, the utterances of science have determinate relations to the utterances that form part of the general culture of the place and time in question.

The connection between science and the order of society and polity is therefore a complex one which cannot be reduced to the instrumental 'role' of science, nor to that of scientists, though these matters are not irrelevant for narrative history (*histoire événementielle*) of the moribund yet not quite despairing type, which regards the task of the historian complete once the narrative sequence and directly causal sequences of events are registered, and which instrumentally conceives of the location of ideas in the body of history in terms perhaps best articulated by means of what the sociology of knowledge terms the 'particular' conception of ideology.[1] Nor are the sociological and other substrata of science merely areas which empirically mediate the impact of science on the social and political orders, for strictly speaking, there are not such mediations, and the various instances of a historical formation — economy, society, polity, culture, science and others — relate to each other not by mediation, but by means of the relative values of each within the overall structure in terms of which they are determined; causality is structural, not unilineal. The relationship between the socio-political order and the scientific order is one of correlativeness, not of unilateral determination.

The Social and Utopian Being of the 'Ulamā'

But before some suggestions respecting these matters in the field of Arabic thought and Islamic societies are made, it is well to look into some aspects of the location of science and its agents in a concrete manner, and before we suggest some glances at the web of interconnections between science, culture and ideology, and the connection of all this with the good order of society and polity. The institutions that were the object of study in the foregoing chapter are the means of production of a competent and specialised body of scientists who could be counted upon to reproduce and disseminate the knowledge of which they were custodians. This body of specialists is generically known as the *'ulamā'*, the possessors of *'ilm*, science, a term variously translated as scholars, doctors, savants, divines. They were indeed the carriers of the literate memory of Arabic culture, but the fact that a generic name is applied to them has obscured the fact of their differentiation, which is far more important and historically relevant than their common nomenclature. There is no justification for the view, standard in modern scholarship, that the *'ulamā'* were a 'multicompetent, undifferentiated and unspecialised communal elite'.[2] This view is premised only incidentally on the fact that they belonged to various occupational groups[3] which they collectively overrode; more important, this quaint conception is premised on an untenable view of the fissiparous and gelatinous constitution of 'the Islamic City' and is meant to service this particular figment of the orientalist imagination.[4] The occupational affiliations of the scholarly class indicate diversity, differentiation and specialisation.

The *'ulamā'* were not, sociologically speaking, a corporate group. Moreover, they neither represented 'society' as such, nor the state, but different denominations had positions within both, and the notion of 'representation', often used in the sociological analysis of ideas, is irrelevant to sociological investigation, being a legal fiction and not a sociological concept of relevance to particular political systems. Prior to the establishment of the Colleges, scholarship was not always a profession, and was most often combined with a different occupation, in commerce or industry,[5] though devotional and legal offices were filled, and royal patronage of learning was rarely meagre. It was with the establishment of the Colleges that scholarship was thoroughly professionalised under state patronage,[6] at once for the training of specialised personnel and for the political purpose of containing and closing the schools of law and making them, as we saw, the main receptacles of knowledge, its production, its dissemination and its control. Within the compass of learning and scholarship, thus circumscribed, there were two great professional classes, the legal and the devotional, in which the former was superior in both status and remuneration, with the exception of the great devotional offices, such as that of Preacher (*imām*) at such places as the Umayyad mosque in Damascus.[7] It was also quite natural that the Colleges should also produce the state administrative personnel, the *kuttāb*, who everywhere seem to have been distinguished from the legists and divines in dress,[8] but who could and were classified in the same category as the legists, both being state functionaries.[9] In addition to these corporate professional distinctions, there were horizontal distinctions that cut across them. There were scholarly patriciates in the cities of Islamdom, many of them of astounding longevity and great influence. These retained control of the higher offices by what one scholar has termed 'natural' promotion and selective co-optation built into the collegiate and certification systems,[10] so that the upper reaches of the legal hierarchy were severely restricted. Indeed, the office of Supreme Judge was not the apex of a legal career, for there was no ladder that led to this particular office,[11] which was granted by the sovereign in accordance with the position the incumbents, through their families, occupied in the social structure and the politics of patrician family coalitions.[12]

Such were the great scholarly families of Damascus, like the Banū Ṣaṣrā who prospered between the middle of the fifth/eleventh and the end of the eighth/fourteenth century,[13] and the Ḥanbalite Banū Qudāma and Banū Munajjā.[14] Such was also the case of the Banū Jamā'a, originally from Ḥamā in central Syria who became the dominant Shāfi'īte family in the Mamlūk empire, monopolising the office of Preacher of the Aqṣā mosque in Jerusalem until the sixteenth century, and occupying the post of Supreme Judge for no less than 61 of the years between AD 1291 and 1383, in addition to other offices, such as custody of properties in trust and the office of *shaikh al-shuyūkh*, the supreme mystical office, in both Damascus and Cairo.[15] The Banū Marzūq were similarly situated in the Maghreb,[16] as were the Banū Shahrazūrī, judges of Mesopotamia,[17] and the descendants of Ibn al-Jawzī who were exterminated, along with the caliph, when Baghdad was sacked by the Mongols in 656/1258,[18] not to speak of the earlier Banū Ḥammād b. Zaid,

Mālikite judges in Iraq for some three centuries.[19] This naturally indicates extraordinary social stability in terms of urban social and political structures which are yet to be studied. It also indicates great wealth and immense status and prestige attaching to the higher offices. Ibn Daqīq al-'Īd (d. 716/1316) married his son to the Caliph's daughter.[20] Extensive land ownership is attested for this class in Damascus,[21] and its members were often granted *iqṭā'* fiscal land concessions in the Levant as well as in the Maghreb,[22] and one judge in Fez, when offered the choice of tax concessions, chose the tax on wine.[23]

Equally important as a source of great wealth was perhaps supervision of *awqāf* endowments, especially when many such endowments are supervised simultaneously, as was the case with Ibn Khallikān (d. 681/1282) who was in charge of all the important *awqāf* of Damascus, in addition to holding the office of judge of all Syria from Al-Arish to the Euphrates and seven professorships.[24] Indeed, the multiplicity of offices held must have been sufficient in itself to enrich a scholar: Badr al-Dīn Ibn Jamā'a for instance, held in 701/1301 the offices of *shaikh al-shuyūkh*, Supreme Judge of the empire, and Supreme Preacher, in charge of the Preachers' guild,[25] and Ibn Bint al-A'azz, at a slightly earlier date, simultaneously held the offices of Supreme Judge, Preacher of the Azhar mosque, state treasurer, superintendent of all *awqāf, shaikh al-shuyūkh*, trustee of the Sultan Baibars legacy, in addition to several professorships.[26] There was a very notable centralisation of offices during the course of the Māmluk state, and this has causes which are yet to be investigated, but this centralisation is not uniquely Mamlūk. Juwainī himself, much earlier, was superintendent of all Nīshāpūr *awqāf*, in addition to having been a professor, an *imām* and a preacher.[27]

It is therefore little wonder that high legal office was much sought after.[28] In comparison, emoluments from professorships, the stipends sometimes paid to judges,[29] and the income from lower legal and devotional offices were insignificant. The legal and religious establishments were indeed sharply cleft; at the top was a patriciate likened to European landed aristocracy, steeled with judicial power,[30] and it could be shown that this constituted part of the local patriciate, legal and otherwise.[31] There were several horizontal divisions below this, and these would have to be distinguished according to particular locality, the preachers of major mosques being distinct from suburban mosques or those in poorer areas, just as professors at the great schools constituted a class apart from those at smaller and poorer ones. In fact, teaching at the greater Colleges was often a family monopoly,[32] and some particularly great Colleges, such as the 'Ādiliyya in Damascus, often attracted as professors persons who had been, or were to become, supreme judges.[33] And whereas the lower rungs of the devotional and legal-educational establishment were stable and under the jurisdiction and control of the judges and persons in cognate professions, the highest offices were conferred directly by royal appointment, and could therefore be similarly revoked upon changes of regime or of favour.[34] Professorships in Cairo were granted by superintendents of the *awqāf* (s. *waqf*) of particular colleges,[35] who were normally senior Mamlūk officers[36] and who accounted for almost two-thirds of persons endowing *waqf* educational and other establishments,[37] except in the case of some major colleges that were the sovereign's preserve,[38] while in Damascus professorships were granted by the Viceroy.[39] In such circumstances, it is not surprising that some venality was observed in the conduct of some judges, who co-operated with Mamlūk grandees intent on usurping *waqf* properties,[40] including such prominent judges as the caliph's in-law Ibn Daqīq al-'Īd[41] and members of the usually punctilious and honourable Ḥanbalite hierarchy.[42] It is equally unsurprising that some judges stood firmly in opposition to this and similar actions,[43] and that the formidable Ibn Taimiyya refused the offices of judge and of *shaikh al-shuyūkh*,[44] like his teacher Ibn al-Mu'ammil, who refused to charge the usual fees for his teaching.[45] There were some who, having bent the *Sharī'a* to please some grandee, proceeded to write a legal defence of their actions,[46] and the corruption resulting from close relations with the state was often decried with the support of a repertory of *ḥadīth* deployed for this purpose.[47]

A great social cleavage therefore cut across the major division between devotional and legal offices. There was also a scholarly differentiation of intellectuals into classes of academic specialisation. Although these undoubtedly possessed a corporate sense of unity evinced in specialised biographical dictionaries of grammarians, *ḥadīth* specialists and others, yet they do not seem to have had a consequential corporate structure except in cases of parallelism with educational, legal and devotional organisms, such as the corporation of Qur'ān reciters (*dīwān al-qurrā'*),[48] whose members shared both the academic specialty of the Qur'ānic texts and their variations, and a professional bond in terms of both the academic and the devotional establishments. One could also mention here the corporate organisation of physicians under a master appointed by the state,[49] an organisation which had a physical location, the hospice, which was once a workshop and an educational establishment. Grammarians, for instance, had no such corporate structure. The celebrated Ibn Mālik was a relatively senior member of the devotional establishment, having been the prayer leader of the 'Ādiliyya college in Damascus.[50] Abū Sa'īd al-Sīrāfī was a deputy judge in Baghdad, and was at various times a professor of inheritance law, grammar and the Qur'ān, in addition to having been a professional copyist.[51] Indeed, one finds that, amongst grammarians, it was only exceptionally the case that a person was exclusively engaged in grammatical scholarship,[52] and one would surmise that in such cases grammar must have been the passion of a gentleman-scholar of independent means. The closest grammarians would have approached a corporate organisation was through their collegiate activities, which, however, involved the teaching of other subjects beside grammar.

What has been said about the differential wealth of members of the devotional and legal hierarchies is applicable in the same way to members of the various scholarly classes of people, whose livelihood, we saw, was determined by their professional engagement in the legal, educational and devotional establishments. Naturally enough, great differences of wealth are in evidence amongst physicians,[53] as they are among members of all other professional groups, and differences in the lot of the physicians are sometimes related to the extra-medical professional and scholarly activities of physicians, for some were also judges,[54] mystics,[55] engineers, *ḥadīth* scholars, logicians and astrologers, not to speak of merchants and legists.[56] At the apex of all professional and scholarly groups was an elite, generalised and socially probably homogenous, closely related to the state, and equally participating in a refined culture, *adab*, based on knowledge of some appropriate sectors of knowledge, literary and historical in the main, and suitable for leisurely cultivation — an amateurish culture (barring the individual specialties of each), in which members of the state could participate.[57] Indeed, as one Arabic author noted, the types of sciences patronised by kings reflected their predilection: Persians lent towards sententious sageliness and history, the Islamic kings to poetry, language and history, while the Mongols encouraged astrology and arithmetic, sciences of government.[58] But regardless of predilection, Arabic culture generally developed *adab*, a general knowledge not inappropriately termed 'scribal',[59] and involving history, political and moral maxims and poetry.

Adab was, of course, a form of refined entertainment,[60] both for refined persons and for kings; that is why poets were patronised, in addition to propagandistic functions that their panegyrics fulfilled. Rather more useful amongst the royally favoured scholarly endeavours were matters such as alchemy and astrology; it will suffice here to indicate that the famous alchemist Ṭughrā'ī (as his name indicates) was in the employ of the Saljūqs and almost acceded to the vizirate,[61] and that a certain Ibn Zuqā'a of Gaza, an astrologer and talismanic expert, was elevated from his profession of tailor to being an almost constant companion and advisor to the Sultan Barqūq.[62] Such persons would then have been the counterparts of what we today would consider as technical experts, whose sciences, not to speak of their social origins, were often suspect to the mainstream of the intellectual classes. The technical expertise of the mainstream was useful to the state in other ways, such as the issuing of rulings directed against a participant in a struggle for power, as for instance as illustrated by the episode in which Ibn Khaldūn was a signatory to such an opinion against Barqūq, who had been his patron and who came back to power soon afterwards and was more merciful towards Ibn Khaldūn than he might have been.[63] Similarly, and more significantly, one could cite the *fatwa* signed by the prominent legists of the Mashreq, including Ghazālī and Ṭurṭūshī (who was of Andalusian origin), advocating the removal of the Banū 'Abbād by the Almoravids,[64] more capable of fighting Western Crusaders. It was also through the good offices of Ibn Sab'īn that the Ḥafṣid Mustanṣir, engaged in a struggle for legitimacy with the parent Almohad state, obtained the support of Meccan legists.[65]

The *'ulamā'* therefore occupied many positions and performed multifarious functions, religious, legal, educational, political, examples of which could be cited almost indefinitely. This is not so much undifferentiated multicompetence as much as specialist distinction. And while the particulars of each function and of the variety of socio-economic locations occupied by *'ulamā'* help in explaining the course of historical events and the participation of members of this imaginary class in the whole range of social, economic, political and intellectual activities that constitute the substance of history, they do not really help towards comprehending the more stable structures through which science and the socio-political order are articulated. And though it is true that science was financially patronised by the state and other powers, it will be incorrect to assume that it was subject to serious influence, for though men of science often did the potentates' bidding, this was done in a private capacity, as science is an historical paradigmatic formation which cannot simply bend to the sovereign's will, neither does a corrupted rule cease being a rule. What the state could and did do was work with scientific material (schools, etc.) that was given. If Mu'tazilites, for instance, were suppressed, the term would have referred to the social and political institution, not to the components of its paradigm, which were alive under different names, and which was a particular permutation of elements drawn from the pools of possible thought that the first few chapters of this book tried to describe. And if the Almohads were attempting to develop a new system of law, their innovation consisted of the employment of elements whose legitimacy was unimpeachable but which were then unusual. And finally, if the Saljūqs encouraged the Shāfi'ites in Baghdad (they were themselves Ḥanafites), they were performing a political act with available material.

We have seen that educational establishments were under the control of those in the hands of whom their endowments were entrusted, and that these were in many cases members of the ruling class, 'men of the sword' and 'men of the pen'. Similarly, devotional and legal offices were under the control of the judiciary as represented by the supreme judge, and the judiciary itself was always subordinate to the political authority[66] as an office of state. The separate devotional establishment of mysticism was similarly regulated by the state through the office of *shaikh al-shuyūkh*.[67] But what this amounted to was not a thorough instrumental value of these establishments from the state's perspective, but rather a *modus vivendi* between the state on the one hand, and on the other, scientific and professional hierarchies subordinated to it in the last instance only, a last instance which, like all other last instances, never actually comes. Additionally, the state related to the various professional and class sections of the *'ulamā'* as it did to other members of society who were similarly or analogously placed.

The 'last instance' we spoke of is the domain where the political relations between the various sections of the *'ulamā'* and the state were played out in concrete historical senses and circumstances that cannot be taken up here. It constituted the domain where the possibilities of both savage political expediency and of Islamic utopia were explored, and where they interacted, clashed or reached concord. The Islamic ideology that everyone carried, *'ulamā'* and sovereigns alike, consisted of descriptions of a utopia in which life is regulated according to divine will — an impossiblity due to the imperfection of man. For man though God's *khalīfa* as we witnessed, remains under the influence of Satan, and also due to the inscrutability of divine will, reflected in the probability, not the certainty, of jurisprudence, a point we have encountered more than once above. And though a proper caliphate is the *sine qua non* for the meticulous application of God's writ within the limits of humanity's capacity, such an institution is a rare phenomenon, whether it existed in name or not. Caliphate almost inevitably reverts to natural kingship,[68] or at the very least becomes, like that of the Abbasids after less than a century in the 768-year life of this dynasty, a nominal caliphate, captive to the sultan. This captivity itself was legislated for by jurist *'ulamā'* under the title of *imārat al-istīlā'* as a matter made necessary for reasons of expediency, notably by Māwardī (d. 450/1058) whose treatise was almost canonical, having been the subject of a commentary by as late an author as Suyūṭī.[69] Yet it was the caliph himself who actually, though *post factum*, appointed the sultan and delegated to him the prerogatives that Islamic law accords to the caliph: the interests of Muslims, and custody of religion.[70] It is in this sense that Mamlūk sultans were entitled, among other things, *qasīm amīr al-mu'minīn*, almost a 'partner' of the caliph.[71] Charge of the law and of devotions were important functions of the caliphate, but were delegated to the sultan, the representative of natural kingship, who is effectively in charge of it,[72] and in Mamlūk times legislation was even theoretically recognised to have consisted of two classes, that deriving from politics, and that belonging to *shar'*[73] — a matter which was to become much more explicitly pronounced under the Ottoman empire. In all cases, the class of *'ulamā'*, arbitrated these matters and provided the ideological guardians of *shar'* utopia.

Yet this must not prompt us to adhere to the standard position of scholarship on this matter, which has it that the matters just described were an attempt to reconcile the moribund reality of the caliphate with its ideal.[74] The caliphate did not undergo, not even in theory, an adjustment. The caliphal utopia has been a remarkably lasting one, and if an utopia were to be constantly disabused and its codes violated, this does not cause it to cease being a utopia, venerated, striven towards, cited. The 'reconciliation' story of modern scholarship is a subtle change in the pitch of reality which results in a gross distortion. For reconciliation was never attempted as such, the classical theory of the caliphate was unaltered, and the provision for obedience to the powers of the day could legally — and the theory of the caliphate was a legal theory — be accommodated in terms of *force majeure*, without this altering the original parameters of the caliphal topic. And whereas modern scholarship has seen this admission of *force majeure* to be a displacement, in law, of the bases of state legitimacy, this is not in fact the case, and the theory of the caliphate was never a theory of legitimacy, nor a theory of the state. The culmination of this trend was the *Siyāsa shar'iyya* of Ibn Taimiyya, which attempted to inject a lawful orientation (and I will not say content) to *siyāsa*, politics as such, which was never part of the theoretical or semantic fields of the caliphate, but was concerned with human husbandry, as it were.[75] Without any reference whatever to the caliphate, which was thus deliberately invested with utopian and silently eschatological value, Ibn Taimiyya wrote what we might well describe as a *Fürstenspiegel* whose content is legal. In it, and on the assumption that 60 years under an unjust *imām* are better than one single night without a king, he elaborates ways in which the sovereign, any sovereign, could rule in a manner which might best approximate the requirements of *shar'*.[76] For rule by purely profane standards, he wanted to substitute rule no less profane, but informed by the minima of religion. In all this, the absence of the caliphate did not imply its abolition as an utopian ideal, but its irrelevance for the immediate present.

The pure and true caliphate, and the pure and unadulterated legal system emanating from it, are therefore utopian ideas sustained by, and delegating legitimacy to, the *'ulamā'*. They are ideas based on a conception of an erstwhile fulfillment and realisation in the past, the first four Caliphs (for the Sunnites) having been the model along with previous anticipations, such as the rule of the Jewish Patriarchs before the Kings, in addition to manifestations of proto-Islamic moments in the divine history of mankind, both antedeluvian and post-deluvian.[77] Utopia is therefore a matter already accomplished in the past at various times when God chose to intervene directly and break the absurdity of dynastic succession with the infusion of moments that belong to him only. Correlatively, this order of divine rectitude is also a utopia still to be fulfilled, for the main theme in Islamic eschatology is the revival, amidst calamities such as the wars of Gog and Magog and the advent of the Antichrist (*al-dajjāl*), of rule according to the will of God. The agency of this is variously said to be the *Mahdī* (especially by the Shī'ites and mystics) and 'Īsā b. Mariam, Jesus Christ, who will, however, be thoroughly Islamised, having descended unto earth at the White Minaret of the Umayyad mosque in Damascus, having married an Arab woman of the Azd tribe and having definitively transcended his Christianity by breaking the cross and exterminating swine.[78] Only then will the world again be filled with justice as it is filled with iniquity, and only then will the perfection of the Beginning again be attained. The Beginning is God's primordial will and plan, disturbed by Satan in the Garden of Eden, thus precipitating History, whose yearning is to transcend History and enter the world of eternity and divinity, eschewing the remains of History — the damned — and relegating them to the absurdity of Hell, and preserving those elements of History which are in accordance with God's will in Heaven. But in the interregnum dividing the present from definitive fulfillment in the Apocalypse, the functions and duties that were Muḥammad's and which are, by law, the caliph's, devolve upon the *'ulamā'*: it is they who are the preserves of the Community, being the preservers of its sciences,[79] and amongst their numbers the judges especially are seen as the guardians and custodians of Muḥammad's message, for judges are third in the ladder that begins with prophets and goes on to caliphs.[80] In this interregnum — and this interregnum remains beyond the pale of science, for the natural state is not the object of a science, only a practical situation that has to be negotiated in the best way possible[81] — the *'ulamā'* (rather, the prominent and influential class of *'ulamā'* who arrogate to themselves the prerogative of speaking on behalf of this fictitious and utopian collectivity) represent the divine moment in history under thoroughly natural, inauspicious circumstances. That is why it is quite accurate to describe their general attitude as a mixture of social opportunism and of profound utopianism[82] — they are the representatives of culture in nature, of divinity amongst humanity, of spirituality in carnality, and their world is severely cleft between the call of God and the calling of the world, in which the will of God, or such of it as is not entirely ineffable, has to be fulfilled *in partibus infidelium*, where that which is God's is out of God's element.

Official Knowledge and Social Catholicity

The ideological collectivity of *'ulamā'* as well as the concept of *'ulamā'*, are equally utopian collectivities and utopian concepts. This utopia was not particular to this utopian group, but was general, held by sovereigns, and held in sometimes very interesting cadences by the popular masses. Yet this group carried knowledge, and its members were the producers, preservers and distributors of knowledge. It is in this capacity that they ought to be regarded in connection with studying the relationship of science to the socio-political order. And since our task is to suggest some points of relevance relating to the epistemic economy of Arabic-Islamic culture, we must first indicate that sciences were disseminated through scientific activity, and not only didactically. Science was present in the social system through its presence in law. It was present in polity through its presence in astrology. It is present in ideology through its action in eschatological and other contents of devotional incantatory statement and the statements of the Qur'ān and *ḥadīth*. In each of these and other locations, science was present in both a learned manner and in one concordant with popular cultures — it should never be forgotten that Arabic thought dwelt in very different cultures and times, and that it engendered a learned *esprit de corps* which did not necessarily effect the popular masses, especially not the rural masses, who did not speak Arabic in most cases, though the majority by the beginning of the fourth/tenth century had embraced Islam with different proportions in different Islamic lands, the briskest rates of conversion having been in Iran, with slower rates in Iraq and Syria.[83] Islamisation was really the redefinition of local situations as Islamic.

In this situation of rigorous imperfection — diversity and severe localism and parochialism of rural cultures in an age when communications were so difficult, along with attenuated but equally parochial urban cultures, the demands of natural kingship and general illiteracy — knowledge and the utopian vocation of a very important sector of knowledge, that based on divine statements, had to locate its practical tasks (legislation, education, etc.) as well as its manners of diffusion and self-perpetuation. This is why Arabic-Islamic high culture appears to us today to have been so vastly catholic, its mainstream so thoroughly irenical, its general disposition so tolerant in practice, as long as the Islamic authority, no matter how nominal, was maintained and the sacred utterances of Islam were not bent. This is also why Islamic law had provisions for and was capable of absorbing so many varieties of legislation by means we have already explored. Indeed, the maintenance of utopianism amid unrelenting imperfection is premised on tolerance within the bounds of the name of Islam, on a minimalist definition of Islam as a religion based upon the *shahāda*, the public and explicit profession of faith, and of Islamic institutions as those upheld, no matter how nominally, in the name of Islam and with due respect to its explicit discourse, the Qur'ān and its cognates. Beyond this minimalism stretches a spectrum of historical possibilities, all of which are in evidence, bounded by the limitless possibilities of casuistry on the one hand, and the rigourism of, say, some *ībaḍī* communities on the other, or of intellectuals like Ibn Ḥazm and Ibn Taimiyya.[84] The rigourism of an institution such as Catholic Inquisition is unthinkable in a truly catholic situation like that of medieval Arab-Islamic culture, and was indissolubly connected with the attempt to break localisms and to homogenise disparate societies under the aegis of a proto-nationalist royal absolutism.

High culture, literate culture, of which science is a form, was restricted to very small sections of the population, and whatever of it that happened to filter down, and this in itself was circumscribed, was inevitably adulterated. Some of it was irrelevant, a most important example of which is the legal prescription, directly based on Qur'ānic authority, that women should inherit, though half the share of a male — this illustrates an instance of the practical relation of scientific knowledge to society. In patrilocal societies based on patrimony in land and livestock, such as rural (settled or otherwise) societies in the Near and Middle East, this was a most unnatural proposition as it would have destabilised society. Thus it is not at all surprising to find that beduins, for instance, simply disinherited females, it appears simply by not marrying them according to the legal contracts stipulated by the *shar'*,[85] much as women in the rural Maghreb today were disinherited by the simple expedient of families turning their patrimonies into *awqāf* — paradoxically, the letter of the Qur'ānic inheritance legislation is adhered to only by the partly matriarchal Tuareg of Ahaggar.[86] Doubtless the proliferation of *awqāf* in the cities of Islamdom was at least partly the result of a similar impulse, and a careful study of positive Islamic law and of local practices will certainly reveal a great many similar matters.

Mystical orders are another case in point, although all of them built for themselves shaikhly and saintly genealogical lines going back to 'Alī and the first four caliphs — with the exception of 'Uthmān, who figures in only one such *silsila*.[87] Incorporations into the body of things Islamic was thus accomplished, despite outstanding questions of doctrine, some of which have already been discussed, and the outcome of which, with few exceptions, scholars did not seek definitely to establish. More germane for the present purpose is a category of mystics and mystical orders which did not benefit from such a genealogy of legitimate initiation. Lone mystics of this type are termed *majdhūb* (literally, a theoleptic, pl. *majādhīb*), which in popular usage denotes a holy fool in whom people have fervent belief, and which technically denotes a freelance mystic who had not been properly taught and initiated by a recognised shaikh.[88] Some appear to have been quite genuinely mad, others antinomian, and yet others deliberately malevolent,[89] all in competitive wonder-working — Shaikh Aḥmad al-Badawī (d. 675/1276), founder of one of the greatest orders, was notorious for the amount of harm he is said to have brought to people.[90] Some *majādhīb* were the voice of popular resentment, such as a certain Shaikh Sha'bān (d. after 900/1494) of Cairo, who would sit in smaller mosques reciting imitations of the Qur'ān he had composed himself, the combination of nonsense designed to emulate the holy rhythms and of rebellious content: 'And in believing Hūd you shall not be truthful. And God has sent unto us people who with things of untruth beat us and take our money away, yet we have no succour'.[91] For reasons the investigation of which could be the subject of an interesting study, vocal and organised antinomianism grew more pronounced with the course of the Mamlūk empire, at more or less the same time as 'maraboutic' movements based on local cults started their famous course in the Maghreb; but these were met with strong resistance, not least on the part of Ibn Taimiyya.[92] Yet it appears that, contrary to the sanitised, learned mysticism of Baghdad and the great cities of Khurāsān, and to the esoteric intellectualism of the Ibn 'Arabī tradition, illiterate ecstatics seem to have been particularly cultivated by Mamlūk grandees and sultans. Baibars himself seems to have had his Rasputin,[93] and many Mamlūks had a predilection for the antinomian Qalandariyya who practised such outlandish devotions as perforating their penises in a mark of abstinence[94] — although members of this order were at times ordered by the sultan to adhere to norms established according to the sunna,[95] in effect ordering them to become *malāmatiyya*, i.e. *qalandariyya* without appearing to be so. Indeed, illiterate antinomian ecstatics were as often represented by the Mamlūks under local pressure as they were encouraged;[96] but what is incontrovertible is that the Mamlūks held them in devotional esteem, especially as they seem to have mostly come from Ḥanafite parts of central Asia and eastern Anatolia,[97] and if they could be deployed in the cities as a troublesome mass which could be used in urban political settings which involved great masses of lumpen elements. Such appear to have been the *Ḥarāfīsh*, an organised order of troublesome mendicants whose leader seems to have risen to high office.[98] Ḥanafites, one could surmise, were probably mostly of foreign origin, and as such might have acted as a counterweight to the predominantly Shāfi'ite Arab establishment of Cairo and Damascus.

Wayward mystics represent unofficial knowledge, knowledge which is not subject to the monopoly of production and distribution held by the scientific establishment and its institutions. Indeed, what general knowledge the illiterate population had was so dismal that Abū Ya'lā, who belonged to the Ḥanbalite school which, we suggested, was markedly populist in comparison to other schools of law, stated that it was sufficient for the populace to know that they are indeed subject to an *imām*, without necessarily having to know who that person is.[99] What scientifically grounded knowledge the populace are required to know consists, as we saw, of a number of elementary dogmatic and legal statements which could be supplied by local prayer leaders. The division that we encountered more than once in the foregoing chapters between the *khāṣṣa* and the *'āmma*, the 'initiates' and the akousmatics, is not only one of the epistemological, but also of the sociological order. And in terms of this latter order it does not only apply to senior members of secret esoteric societies, but applies to the whole mass of the learned personnel of exoteric science, the *'ulamā'*, and is also applied to distinguish senior from junior members of this mass. The distinction is applied to bar the mass of people from involvement in the production and distribution of official knowledge, an involvement which, as we saw, scholars thought would only lead to unbelief.[100] And indeed, they were right; if we were to look at Ibn Tūmart and the title of *mahdī* he adopted, we can find plentiful evidence to suggest that, rather than carrying a doctrinally crypto-Shī'ite connotation, the title was interpreted by his Berber *montagnards* in a decidedly thaumaturgic and eschatological sense[101] which legists in Fez, for instance, would never have considered admissible. Similarly, there are saintly and magical qualities attributed to the caliphate,[102] qualities which could probably be construed along lines already studied with respect to medieval European kingship in terms of christological exemplarism[103] and of popular thaumaturgy,[104] which bear serious study and scrutiny from the perspective of the distinction between official and unofficial knowledge.

The devotional establishment was the means through which official, legitimate knowledge was disseminated in the lower rungs of the social order. For, in addition to the possibility that some members of these orders may have had access to the elementary instruction in the text of the Qur'ān and sometimes in reading and writing as well as was obtainable in the local *kuttāb*,[105] the popular masses were a mix of uprooted peasants, lumpen elements verging on criminality, foreign wanderers, in addition to the local artisanal classes, who could not have been much better off than the others.[106] They had access only to some mystical instruction as might have been available on street corners, as well as the entertainment afforded by shadow plays (*khayāl al-ẓill*) for those who could bear the cost of attendance.[107] Both this last and, more important, the popular sagas such as *sīrat 'Antar* and the stories of the Thousand and One Nights, contain not only themes extolling popular and knightly virtues, but are replete with conceptions of history and of polity which accord with official theories of absolute kingship, of the centrality of Islam and the justice of the order of which they are the pillars. This appears not only implicitly, but we can see in the Thousand and One Nights a multitude of passages that sound like the simplified version of standard scholarly positions.[108] Additionally, popular city culture as was contained in such works utilised much material of scientific provenance, material from history, *fiqh*, exegesis and other sciences.

But the devotional establishment, the main avenue through which official knowledge was distributed amidst the urban and (to a lesser extent) rural masses, obviously had no monopoly over knowledge dissemination, nor consequently of its contents. It appears that the lower echelons of the devotional establishment, the lower preachers (*wu''āẓ, quṣṣās, mudhakkirūn*), somewhat merged with similar persons, popular preachers, of no formal training, or at least without the cover of establishmentarian appurtenance. Ibn al-Jawzī, the preacher *par excellence*, recorded many iniquities of popular preachers: self-flagellation, the tearing of clothes in shows of ecstasy, inaccuracy in the rendition of *ḥadīth* and invention of *ḥadīths*, praise of Ḥallāj and other matters.[109] There is doubtless a merger here between popular preaching and street-corner mysticism, and Islamic divines everywhere warned against unofficial and uncontrollable preaching of this type. But the responsibility of a preacher is a grave one, for preachers are asked about a variety of things and ought to be particularly learned and erudite,[110] and ignorant ones cannot be distinguished by their audience from learned ones, for their audience consists of 'ignorant commoners who are animals'.[111] Thus some divines sought to control preaching by banning preachers from relating matters pertaining to the Prophet and by limiting their topical concern to sagely stories culled from the histories[112] — in which case narratives whose veracity is not fully ascertained could well be related, as such narratives are exemplary.[113] Others were less severe, and sought to restrict the common preachers' competence by banning only the voicing of opinions on dogmatics, especially matters related to divine attributes.[114] There were works which were considered particularly suitable for public delivery to these commoners, some written specifically for this task: Ghazālī's *Iḥyā'* (The Revivication of Religious Sciences), works by Nawawī and, naturally enough, books and manuals by Ibn-Jawzī.[115] It was only thus that preaching could be done in a manner whose content was controlled and whose pedigree was recognisable, unlike one young Damascene preacher who always spoke tearfully in a rhymed prose akin to that of soothsayers and claimed it was inspired by the *jinn*.[116] Very much unlike this profane inspiration was the substance of Nawawī's popular work, recommended by Subkī for preaching to commoners: this contained only *ḥadīth* narratives culled from canonical works, along with legal details and devotional methods[117] — totally devoid of frivolity, but above all, utterly bereft of profanation. That Nawawī declared all Muslims competent to relay his work is an index not only of its popular character, but of its total belonging to the sphere of official knowledge, duly certified by Nawawī's *barnāmaj*, itself transmitted as an *ijāza* to all Muslims.[118]

Of course, by the very nature of things, not even official preaching could realistically afford to be bookish and sober. The very paragon of preachers, Ibn al-Jawzī, gloried in the comprehension of his audience only when they had been enraptured by his words.[119] In all cases, the dissemination of knowledge outside specialist circles is not meant to engender expertise; it is not a discursive knowledge that is transmitted, not one that is designed to be practically wielded, in acts of legislation for example. It is not scientific and other knowledge as technique that is transmitted outside the body of scientific establishments, but knowledge as the repository of what anthropologists might understand by the term 'symbolic power', knowledge as a location for the exercise of hegemony based upon the acceptance of a common apodicticity whose custodians are a particular class of people — in this case, the upper echelons of the *'ulamā'*. And such knowledge is the collection and multiplication of what we have already seen to have been paradigmatic statements to which allegiance is made without any further ado. Theoretically, such knowledge is apodictic. Practically, it is exemplary. And the *ḥadīth* and other contents of popular knowledge — exhortatory, sententious — does not go beyond this and constitute theoretical knowledge, which might be further used to produce more and further knowledge, or to pass on as knowledge. All knowledge that is imparted and immediately consumed in the process of its use is knowledge designed for immediate effect; it can elevate, caution, frighten or promise. It never instructs.[120]

Rapture, like that obtained by Ibn al-Jawzī, is an aesthetic comment on the substance of what is said and the manner in which it was said. It is a suitable form of comment, indicating assent with statements said, and attesting their overwhelming authority, along with that of the speaker, not as discursive act, but as the instance of authority. The rectitude of the statement is a matter not of the statement, but of its authority, irrespective of its content, although dogmatic statements are fastidious about their letter, for, being arbitrary and authoritative by virtue of their custodian, their fixity visibly underlines their authority. But imparting official knowledge to the masses, or to the kings, and in general to all who are not professional scholars, is not a means of controlling imperfection of belief and utterance indifferent as to its mode and tenor. On the contrary, it is very specific as to these matters, and this is a direct effect of the form of statements in question, a form whose paradigm is the primary apodictic statements of all sciences which are, as we saw, held by authoritative compulsion and not necessarily on any intrinsic merit. Like the apodictic beginnings of science, and indeed the dogmatic fundamentals of belief, they consist of two formal classes: performative statements of exhortation, command, advertence, execration, interdiction and the like on the one hand, and narrative statement of fact, both facts relating past events and facts relating happenings to come. The text of the Qur'ān, as well as that of *ḥadīth* and of history, consist exclusively of these two forms of discourse. But unlike the apodictic beginnings of science, this extra-scholarly knowledge as is imparted to the masses and the sultans is not a fund of fundamentals liable to discursive development, but is a quarry of exemplarism, to guide people to salvation by prescribing particular courses of conduct, to lead them to success by means of special prayers and ritual or talismanic observances, and to attain for the sovereigns the glory that can be had and maintained by heeding the example of past kings as the histories preserve and the *Fürstenspiegel* collect.

Exemplarism is a reminder of perfection and a prescription for its attainment. With regard to the perfection that is touched with divinity, the exemplarism contained in religious command and prohibition as well as in moral stories of prophets and kings of yore is a preparation for attaining as much of perfection as is possible in an imperfect world before the End recapitulates the purity of creation. As for profane perfection, this can only be brought about by the technique of the world. What some authors have termed 'Islamic political theory' is in fact, as we have seen earlier, a collection of exemplary anecdotes culled from historical works which are invested with paradigmatic value that, almost talismanically, is supposed to ward off ill fortune and lead to the attainment and preservation of stately glory. Indeed, one of the main components of *adab* is the knowledge and purveyance of historical anecdotes fit for the attention of kings even to the extent that one king with a literary bent, Ibn Khaldūn's one-time employer and king of Tlemcen, Abū Ḥammū, wrote a *Fürstenspiegel* for the instruction and edification of his son and heir, which is a collection of historical cautionary anecdotes and sententious reflections on the conduct of the state which, incidentally, contained invaluable information on the latter concern.[121] For the *Fürstenspiegel*, one main subdivision of historical writing, is exactly what its name denotes: a mirror for princes.[122]

It was quite natural for the public dissemination of official knowledge to have taken the exemplary form. This dissemination was not literate; it was undertaken by oral delivery, whether in court or on a street corner and in many intermediate stations, to an audience which was largely illiterate, an audience which, in the case of many sovereigns of Arab lands, often had at best an imperfect grasp of Arabic. It has been remarked that, in oral culture, a tale takes the place of what for the scientific specialist would have been a schema.[123] It has also been suggested, with regard to Iliad and the Odyssey, that they constituted a 'Homeric encyclopedia', a repertory of rules of conduct, rites and the like, preserved in a paradigmatic tribal epic, and used 'poetic *paideia*',[124] a means for the dissemination of the rules of conduct. It appears eminently possible to construct a repertory of *ḥadīth* and other texts, profane and otherwise which perform the same function in lands where Arabic culture was paramount, though these would also involve linguistic problems which are irrelevant in the Homeric text which was only current in a more or less linguistically uniform area. And indeed, study of medieval European rural religious instruction and propaganda by the Cathars indicates the primacy of the repetition of *exempla* for the dissemination of myth.[125]

Exemplarism, Authority and the Best of All Possible Worlds

Exemplarism ratifies the authority of those who provide example, as well as that of the authority in the name of which and for the sake of whom the paradigm is prescribed and, in the case of God, by the very author of the paradigm. Herein lies the present use of myths of origin. When exemplarism is religious in content, it becomes a form of devotion, though not quite a litany. It is a beholding of a sacred original presence in the form of language but which indicates the presence of the preacher or teacher who is, in effect, the representative for the specific purpose at hand of the authority behind this presence. The authority which induces knowledge is never anonymous. We have seen how scientific knowledge is inextricably tied to its proximate and distant pedigrees through the institution of *ijāza* and *riwāya*, and that mystical organisations attribute to themselves initiatory pedigrees. Indeed, the Mu'tazilites, for instance and in varying circumstances traced their pedigree through Ḥasan and Ḥusain to Ibn 'Abbās and Abū Bakr,[126] or through 'Umar b. 'Abd al-'Azīz to the first four caliphs;[127] and the Ash'arites, for their part, saw fit to see Ash'arī prefigured in sayings of Muḥammad,[128] whereas philosophers saw the prophets themselves as the pedigree of their wisdom.[129] What applies to dogmatics and philosophy, not to speak of exegesis, linguistic sciences, history and *ḥadīth*, applies equally well to dynastic genealogies. These were legion, and dynasts always sought to ascertain their genealogies by means which historians considered to be suspect but inevitable. Historians and others were acutely aware of the fact that genealogies are telescoped, shifted, reconstructed and overhauled by exigencies of the present, and that dynasties often sought to give themselves superior pedigrees, usually Arab and Quraishaite.[130] But these genealogies, and disputes over them, as the particularly elaborate one over the authenticity of the Fatimids,[131] were political struggles, disputes over legitimacy with a particular physiognomy: appurtenance to a line that carries, in terms of its time, the highest degree of compulsion to obey, so that a Berber dynasty, for instance, might have a local lineage in its place of origin, and an Arab lineage in its capital city. That is why history, as we saw, appears not one of development, of fulfillment, or of oriented movement, but one in which origins and beginnings, which had initially been complete, are recapitulated: prophecies recapitulate one another, and Islam recapitulates and transcends them all by recapitulating the beginning of all beginnings which was the creation and the Adamic order. Eschatology recapitulates this very beginning by recapitulating Muḥammad's order. A dynast recapitulates his real or (more usually) spurious eponym, as a Shī'ite dynast might recapitulate 'Alī, and as Muḥammad himself recapitulated everyone's eponym, Adam, and through him, the original order of creation. Similarly, the proper use of language recapitulates its original and first use, just as the proper interpretation of divine and all other discourse seeks to unravel the original intent, and just as the object of knowledge in general is to recapitulate its object in another medium, and the object of legislation is to recapitulate and thus recover the original purpose of God, in so far as it is ascertainable. The apodictic premisses of all sciences fall in the same category of origins, of inaugural events.

Exempla and the genealogical call of dynasties and sciences are therefore based, not on a prefiguration which is realised in the course of time, as modern historicism would have it to the exclusion of all premodern thought, but on the recapitulation of an original event. Indeed,[132] Arabic historical literature is replete with descriptions of inaugural events, from the inauguration of humanity, to that of peoples like the Semites, descendants of Shem, and their Arab, Israelite, Persian and other subdivisions, on to that of particular dynasties, not to speak of the origins of particular institutions and techniques, like religions, beliefs, swords, tortue and others. Devotions were invariably portrayed, with fine anthropological sense, as the repetition of events, like the circumambulation of the Ka'ba by Abraham and, to some, by Adam himself. There is a special literary genre in Arabic (and other languages, including Chinese) termed *awā'il*, a register of first occurrences, such as the first instance when a particular style of dress was worn or the first time when a man fornicated with his own mother. But all this is not history. All genealogies obey a positional logic,[133] a compulsion to recapitulate, not an inaugural event, but the present in the guise of an inaugural event. Lucid Arabic thinkers, especially those attuned to the ways of the world, were aware of this. Ibn al-Khaṭīb declared that the grandfathers of two persons are related according to the relation of their grandchildren,[134] for such is the logic of genealogy, in the contradistinction to the logic of history, which starts properly speaking with the anterior event.[135] The disjunction in real terms that we have seen between the apodictic premisses of a science, and the theses of the science, runs parallel to this. Like it, it is based on a supposed beginning, a beginning which is nominal in fact, but incontrovertible in explicit terms; the two are combined by an external compulsion which decrees the combination: the schools, the paradigm, the genealogist backed by the king in search of an origin to match that of other kings. To convince, this combination has to be enforced. That is the purpose of the institution, the guardian of the cultural arbitrary. The combination in question is the linkage between the present — proposition, king, topic — and the tradition — premiss, origin, object. But tradition is only deliberately so, being the present in the guise of the past. It is the token of every present, just as philosophy is a token of irreligion. The standard is the present: it is the *telos* of all, for it is always the best of all possible worlds, not least because it compels assent to the linkage of present with origin. Yet never is this present disembodied. It is always manifested in the voice of the present and harbinger — and continuation — of origins: the manufacturers of tradition and its guardians, the *'ulamā'* as an ideological unit and their wider bearing, the world of things called Islamic.

It thus appears that Arabic culture fashions myth out of the science of history. The apodictic origins of science, and the inaugural events of history, are not real beginnings, but paradigms which compel explicit assent to their authority. The beginnings of science are constructed on the basis of the present, as are those of a dynasty, of humanity and as are the *exempla* of the commoners and of the kings. And if sciences presume a deductive relation, this does not necessarily have to imply that such a relationship exists, but what is far more likely and more in keeping with the nature of things is that they are retrospective constructs in the guise of apodictic premisses. In this way, the past is not the progenitor of the present, but is at best its paradigm in the realm of fantasy. Yet such fantasy as is infused in these myths of origin under discussion constitutes absolute points of reference which common sense and public spirit shield from close scrutiny, as we saw with reference to *ḥadīth* criticism. They are points of reference which are present as if all new events — kings, special points of law — recapitulated them, repeated them, doubled up into them. They are points infused with unassailable authority, possessing absolute and unassailable normative precedence present as if it were historical and ontological anteriority.

What makes the arbitrariness of scientific premisses and imaginary origins of a dynasty irrelevant is apparent self-evidence born of a compulsion congenital to a cultural system. What makes a statement upon which a present event is ostensibly based incontrovertible, and indeed what makes its contrary unthinkable, is the symbolic power with which it is invested by the powers that maintain the social order through the political, social, educational and devotional systems. That the real disjunction between origin and present is invariably presented as a real filiation is a means of assuring the absolute authority of the former in the fantastic faculty. It is a means of maintaining an hierarchy based on the cultural appropriation of a particular class of utterances, and simultaneously a means of maintaining the epistemic and political hierarchy at the apex of which stands the learned establishment and the state, in close alliance. The authority of an apodictic event, be it a text or a supposed occurrence, testifies to the authority of its consequent, and thus mediates the authority of whatever class of persons is charged with establishing this connection with specialised knowledge specifically devoted to the recapitulation and maintenance of connections with origins, of which *qiyās* is perhaps the paradigm. This hierarchy inside knowledge is in fact sultanic: it is absolute, and structured by an absolute normative distinction in which only the origin is positive. The apex of all epistemic activities of use in law, in dynastic history, in lexicography is this primacy of the beginning. Apodicticity is the discursive avatar of the sultan.[136]

The past, text or event, is thus constructed in the image of the present, or at the very least under its *leitmotiv*. Even when the inferiority of today in comparison with olden times is lamented, this is but a variation of the myth we have been discussing, of an accomplished past and the promise of its recapitulation in the future. Awareness of spurious origins, and the explicitness of supposed assumptions, is absolutely essential in Arabic culture; and the elision of origins that is seen to characterise modern ideologies as goes under the name of reification and its cognates is uncalled for. Indeed, explicitness of beginnings is a myth of origin of the greatest consequence. The myth of origin construes the origin in the image of the result, in which foundation and accomplishment are coterminous, and draws the past as an inevitable — because existent — present. This is tantamount not only to the presentation of the present as if it were eternal, having been inaugurated at its beginning and having in the medium of time done nothing but recapitulate this inaugural event. It amounts in fact to an effective deification of the present. For if the present were ever-present in the intention of God, and if the ultimate ground of positive law be the divine text, of a king the founder of the dynasty, of a word its posited sense and of the world and of all else,

God, then origin becomes not only the ultimate explanatory principle of everything, but in fact all things become a mere repetition of origin. This origin is the principle which explains that which has no explanation and for which no explanation is attempted; it is an explanatory principle which is posited and which is arbitrary in the sense indicated. In effect, therefore, explanation of the present — a king, a law — is undertaken in terms of this very present, but presented as if it were the result of something anterior — an eponymous king, a Qur'ānic text, or God himself. Explanatory paradigms, and God is the ultimate one, which also especially explain creation, merely restate what they are meant to explain, indicate them, elicit them out of themselves, without begetting them, and consequently do not explain them as much as simulate such an explanation. Events not being in fact explained, they become explainable only in terms of themselves, their real explanatory principle being their very existence. And indeed, as we saw, the present is composed of things each of which is the most apposite of its kind, or at least should aspire to be so: musical melodies, languages, laws. For this is indeed, the best of all possible worlds, in which the present is based upon the best of all possible origins, and these origins could not but beget the best of all possible results. The genealogy of knowledge, as of society, is a hyper-positivist register of knowledge and society of the day.

This is precisely what is meant by the deification of the present: that which is positively given is absolutely given, and its supposed antecedent and paradigm is only nominally so. This is why the past appears inevitable, and that is equally why we have found entelechy-related concepts such as *al-aṣlaḥ* and *maqāsid al-shar'*, to be less an expression of the meaning of these terms than statements of practice. This is also why analogy is almost always valid, for its presupposes its result in the beginning. This is the inexhaustible fund of casuistry: the primacy of that which exists, which is given and which therefore is idolised with reference to a supposed origin. But this origin is spurious, and thus only nominal. That which is Islamic is so in the sense that it is nominally Islamic, and that which is not accepted as such is rejected not through intrinsic criteria, but at the discretion of authorities whose task it is to differentiate the Islamic from the non-Islamic, and these have changed in time and place. Like other religions, Islam can mean all things to all people within the bounds of the minimalist definition suggested above, and has in fact been many things in different historical settings. What decides Islamic legitimacy is not theoretical definitions, but the capacity of defining agencies to enforce the bounds they consider legitimate. Heresies are always considered as transgressions of the inaugural or intermediate authorities: Muḥammad, the *ḥadīth*, the history of prophecy. With these inaugural authorities recognised, heresy is impossible to ascertain, just as loyalty to a dynasty might mitigate sedition directed against one particular king. The inclusion or exclusion of a group, or an idea, from appurtenance to the great nominal unity which is Islam, is exclusively the right of such authority as can claim such appurtenance and enforce this claim.

* * *

Power — whichever power — is therefore correlative with the popular as well as the scientific modes of knowledge. Just as God stands at the apex of the universe and the king at the apex of the body politic in manners that have been described in some detail, so the apodictic premiss of knowledge stands in respect to the statements of knowledge. The parallelism of epistemological, dynastic and metaphysical genealogies is clear. But such analogies of hierarchy are not an explanation of these hierarchies, but their *modus operandi*. They are the indices of systematic closure of each, so that they constitute high-cultural principles which could run correlatively with a variety of political and social systems, as long as the nominal unity is preserved. These analogies each define a sliding continuum of power distribution, much like the political systems appropriate for the tributary modes of production[137] where Arabic thought prevailed, animated by these hierarchies. Indeed, the situation appears much like certain features of medieval Europe, where the various orders of existence are unified by being presented as emanations of a unity principle, that of divine will.[138] A transcendental perspective such as that evinced in this medieval unification of things, as well as in scientific disciplines, is necessary for the preservation of authority.[139] The correlation between knowledge and power, in Arabic as well as with respect to Latin thought, is not open to question. What remains to be investigated is the relevance of questions of causality: whether, on the one hand, one engenders or represents the other in the Durkheimian sense which, to the present author, is not invalid yet not quite adequate in principle, although it has led to some very fecund investigation into such matters as Greek philosophy[140] and Indo-European 'ideology';[141] or whether the matter has to do with cultural repertoires of symbols, institutions and other artefacts, that were appropriated by Arabic thought in its correlative political spheres. But this is the task of an independent study.

Notes

1. K. Mannheim, *Ideology and Utopia* (London, 1966), pp. 49 ff.

2. I.M. Lapidus, *Muslim Cities in the Later Middle Ages* (Cambridge, Mass., 1967), p. 108.

3. See the cautionary factual comments against this view by J.E. Mandaville, 'The Muslim Judiciary of Damascus in the Late Mamluk Period', unpublished Ph. D. dissertation, Princeton University, 1969, pp. iii ff.

4. See the comments of A. Al-Azmeh, 'What is the Islamic City?', in *Rev. of Middle Eastern Studies*, 2 (1976), pp. 8–9.

5. See the informative but not very useful article by H.I. Cohen, 'The Economic Background and Secular Occupations of Muslim Jurisprudents and Traditionists in the Classical Period of Islam', in *JESHO*, 13 (1970), pp. 6–61.

6. Gilbert, *The Ulama of Damascus*, pp. 71, 139 ff., 59, 69, 78 and *passim*.

7. See Mandaville, *The Muslim Judiciary of Damascus*, pp. 68 ff. and C.F. Petry, *The Civilian Elite of Cairo in the Later Middle Ages* (Princeton, 1981), pp. 220 ff., 246 ff., 316 and *passim*. An idea of salaries is given by Lapidus, *Muslim Cities*, pp. 138 f.

8. A detailed discussion is given by Qalqashandī, *Ṣubḥ*, vol. 4, pp. 41–3. For a Baghdad example, see Yāqūt, *Irshād*, vol. 1, pp. 234–5. In Mamlūk times, this division was jealously guarded. See, for instance, Maqrīzī, *Sulūk*, vol. 2, p. 664.

9. Subkī, *Mu'īd*, pp. 94 ff.

10. Bulliett, *The Patricians of Nishapur*, pp. 54 ff.

11. Mandaville, *The Muslim Judiciary*, pp. 8, 41 and Petry, *The Civilian Elite*, pp. 226, 229.

12. Mandaville, *The Muslim Judiciary*, pp. 13–14 and *passim*.

13. W.M. Brinner, 'The Banū Ṣaṣrā: A Study in the Transmission of a Scholarly Tradition', in *Arabica*, 7 (1960), pp. 167–95.

14. Laoust, 'Le Hanbalisme sous les Mamlouks', pp. 38 ff.

15. K.S. Salibi, 'The Banū Jamā'a. A Dynasty of Shāfi'īte Jurists in the Mamluk Period', in *SI*, 9 (1958), pp. 97–109.

16. See the article by M. Hadi-Sadok in *EI*, vol. 3, pp. 865–8.

17. Ibn Khallikān, *Wafayāt*, vol. 4, pp. 68 ff.

18. Ibn Rajab, *Dhail*, vol. 2, pp. 258–9. So illustrious and rich was this family that they were able to establish a college in Damascus former students of which often attained the office of Ḥanbalite judge — Nu'aimī, *Dāris*, vol. 2, p. 33.

19. Ibn Farḥūn, *Dībāj*, p. 92.

20. Suyūṭī, *Muḥaḍara*, vol. 1, p. 422.

21. Mandaville, *The Muslim Judiciary*, pp. 108 ff.

22. For instance, Ibn Khallikān, *Wafayāt*, vol. 7, p. 89 and Ghubrīnī, *'Unwān*, p. 185.

23. Ibn Khaldūn, *Prolégomènes*, vol. 2, p. 300.

24. Maqrīzī, *Sulūk*, vol. 1, p. 465. On control of *awqāf* and accruing incomes see Makdisi, *The Rise of the Colleges*, pp. 44 ff., 52 ff., 57 ff.

25. Nu'aimī, *Dāris*, vol. 2, p. 156 and see Maqrīzī, *Sulūk*, vol. 1, pp. 771, 809, 828, 901, 924, 927, 929; vol. 2, p. 337.

26. Maqrīzī, *Sulūk*, vol. 1, p. 773.

27. Ibn Khallikān, *Wafayāt*, vol. 3, p. 168.

28. There was increasing venality and sales of office after the disturbances of 806/1403–4, which had been preceded by successive depredations of the plague, and which shook the Mamlūk empire and ushered in a century of almost perpetual disturbance. This situation must have worsened the lot of the legal hierarchy, whose actual income from formal emoluments does not seem to have increased throughout Ayyubid and Mamlūk times, and having thus fallen in terms of purchasing power. See E. Ashtor, 'Salaires dans l'Orient musulman médiéval à la base-époque', in *REI*, 39 (1971), pp. 113–14 and Maqrīzī, *Sulūk*, vol. 3, p. 324 and *passim*.

29. See, for instance, Nu'aimī, *Dāris*, vol. 1, p. 57 and for the existence or otherwise of emoluments, Mandaville, *The Muslim Judiciary*, pp. 105 ff. and compare Leo Africanus, *Description de l'Afrique*, tr. A. Epaulard (Paris, 1956), vol. 1, p. 206.
30. Bulliett, *The Patricians of Nishapur*, p. 25.
31. See Salibi, 'The Banū Jamā'a', p. 101.
32. For instance, Maqrīzī, *Khiṭaṭ*, vol. 2, pp. 370–1; Nu'aimī, *Dāris*, vol. 1, pp. 193, 198, 253–4 and *passim*, and, on Ghazālī's brother taking over the Niẓāmiyya from his famous brother while the latter devoted himself to God before returning to his position, Ibn Khallikān, *Wafayāt*, vol. 4, p. 217.
33. Nu'aimī, *Dāris*, vol. 1, pp. 363–4.
34. Maqrīzī, *Sulūk*, vol. 1, pp. 678–9.
35. Qalqashandī, *Ṣubḥ*, vol. 1, p. 39.
36. For instance, *ibid.*, pp. 184, 191 and Maqrīzī, *Sulūk*, vol. 1, p. 689 and vol. 3, p. 225. See also 'Īsā, *Bīmāristānāt*, pp. 22, 126–7, 130.
37. Lapidus, *Muslim Cities*, pp. 73–4.
38. Qalqashandī, *Ṣubḥ*, vol. 4, p. 39.
39. *Ibid.*, p. 193.
40. On this and related matters, see Maqrīzī, *Khiṭaṭ*, vol. 2, pp. 296, 392, 402–3 and Nu'aimī, *Dāris*, vol. 1, pp. 359, 491.
41. Maqrīzī, *Sulūk*, vol. 2, p. 362.
42. *Ibid.*, pp. 442–3 and Nu'aimī, *Dāris*, vol. 2, pp. 47, 51.
43. Maqrīzī, *Sulūk*, vol. 1, pp. 741–2; vol. 2, p. 126.
44. Ibn Rajab, *Dhail*, vol. 2, p. 390.
45. *Ibid.*, pp. 332–3.
46. Maqrīzī, *Sulūk*, vol. 3, p. 170.
47. For instance, Ibn 'Abd al-Barr, *Jāmi'*, vol. 1, pp. 170 ff.
48. For this corporation, see Sakhāwī, *I'lān*, p. 57. See Subkī, *Mu'īd*, p. 94.
49. Qalqashandī, *Ṣubḥ*, vol. 4, p. 194.
50. Maqqarī, *Nafḥ*, vol. 2, p. 223.
51. Ibn Khallikān, *Wafayāt*, vol. 2, p. 78 and Yāqūt, *Irshād*, vol. 3, pp. 84, 85, 87.
52. For one such exception, see Suyūṭī, *Bughya*, vol. 1, pp. 48–9.
53. Elgood, *Medical History*, pp. 267 ff.
54. Ibn Abī Uṣaibi'a, *'Uyūn*, p. 648.
55. *Ibid.*, p. 740.
56. 'Īsā, *Bīmaristānāt*, pp. 73, 162, 195, 217.
57. For instance, Ibn Khallikān, *Wafayāt*, vol. 2, p. 129 (on Niẓām al-Mulk) and Ibn al-Aḥmar, *Rawḍa*, pp. 27–8 (on Abū 'Inān).
58. Ibn Ṭabāṭabā, *Fakhrī*, p. 16.
59. R. Blachère, 'Quelques refléxions sur les formes de l'encyclopédisme en Egypte et en Syrie du VIII/XIVe siècle à la fin du IX/XVe siècle', in *BEO*, 23 (1970), pp. 19 and *passim*.
60. See the comments of Yāqūt, *Irshād*, vol. 1, p. 13.
61. *Ibid.*, vol. 4, p. 51.
62. Ibn Taghrī Birdī, *Manhal*, vol. 1, pp. 153 ff. and Sakhāwī, *Ḍaw'*, vol. 1, pp. 130 ff.
63. Al-Azmeh, *Ibn Khaldūn: An Essay*, p. 6.
64. Ibn Khaldūn, *Tārīkh*, vol. 6, p. 187 and see also A. Laroui, *History of the Maghreb*, tr. R. Manheim (Princeton, 1977), p. 167.
65. Ibn Qunfudh, *Fārisiyya*, p. 120.
66. See the account of E. Tyan, *Histoire de l'organization judiciarie en pays d'Islam*, 2nd edn (Leiden, 1960), pp. 17 ff., 100 ff.
67. On this office, which emerged with the emergence of the *khānqāh* under Saladin, see Maqrīzī, *Khiṭaṭ*, vol. 2, p. 415; Qalqashandī, *Ṣubḥ*, vol. 4, pp. 38, 193, 221 and Suyūṭī, *Muḥāḍara*, vol. 2, p. 260.
68. The best sketch of the classical theory of the caliphate is by Qalqashandī, *Khilāfa*,

vol. 1, pp. 8 ff. and Ibn Khaldūn is the most consummate analyst of the caliphate and kingship, on which see Al-Azmeh, *Ibn Khaldūn: An Essay*, pp. 84 ff.

69. Ḥajji Khalīfa, *Kashf*, col. 19. The crux of Māwardī's argument is to be found in his *Aḥkām*, pp. 54–7.

70. Qalqashandī, *Khilāfa*, vol. 2, pp. 241 ff. For historical examples, see Maqrīzī, *Sulūk*, vol. 1, pp. 60, 242, 247 and *passim*.

71. Ibn Khaldūn, *Ta'rīf*, p. 250.

72. Qalqashandī, *Khilāfa*, vol. 1, p. 80.

73. Maqrīzī, *Khiṭaṭ*, vol. 2, p. 220.

74. The standard work is that of E.I.J. Rosenthal, *Political Thought in Medieval Islam* (Cambridge, 1958).

75. See, for instance, the definitions of Ibn Khaldūn, *Prolégomènes*, vol. 1, p. 344.

76. Ibn Taimiyya, *Siyāsa*, pp. 77 and *passim*.

77. On these and related matters, see 'Aẓma, *Al-Kitāba at-tārīkhiyya*, pp. 117 ff. and *passim*.

78. *Ibid.*, pp. 113–14.

79. For instance, Ibn Khaldūn, *Ta'rīf*, p. 281 and Ghubrīnī, *'Unwān*, p. 19.

80. For instance, Nubāhī, *Tārīkh*, p. 2. Not unnaturally, mystics believe saints to be vicars of prophecy — for instance, Sulamī, *Ṭabaqāt*, p. 2.

81. Aẓma, 'Al-Siyāsa wa al-lā Siyāsa', *passim* and see 'A. 'Arwī, *Mafhūm ad-dawla* (Casablanca, 1981), p. 123.

82. 'A. 'Arwī, 'Ishkālīyat ad-dawla al-'Arabiyya al-Islāmīyya' in *Al-Mashrū'* (October, 1980), p. 25.

83. R.W. Bulliett, *Conversion to Islam in the Medieval Period* (Cambridge, Mass. and London), 1979, graphs no. 5, 15, 17, and 19. Arabic overtook all other local languages in the official fields of learning and the state. Though in Iran for instance, Persian started coming back into literary use at the start of the fifth/eleventh century, and especially under the Samanids (see Browne, *Literary History*, vol. 1, *passim*), when an attempt was made to substitute Persian for Arabic in the Samanid chanellery this was thwarted, having been considered an inexcusable barbarism (see G.E. von Grunebaum, 'Firdausī's Concept of History', in *Fuad Köprülü Armağani* (Istanbul, 1953), p. 185 n. 2). With Christian writers, Arabic was universally adopted except for some strictly ecclesiatical writings; much of even the ecclesistical output itself comprised translations into Arabic from Greek, Syriac and Coptic (see Graf, *Geschichte*, vol. 1, p. 3) and, in Spain, from Latin, although treatises in canon law and other matters were written in Spain in Arabic (C.-E. Dufourcq, *La vie quotidienne dans l'Europe mediévale sous la domination Arabe* (Paris, 1978), p. 141). This linguistic state of affairs was not absolute, of course, as there were also Muslim works written in Persian as of the second half of the fourth/tenth century (see, for instance, Browne, *Literary History*, vol. 1, pp. 477–8). In any case, learning and new books travelled remarkably fast; Rāzī's works from eastern Khurāsān reached Mesopotamia and the Maghreb during his life, or at the latest very shortly afterwards (Ibn Khallikān, *Wafayāt*, vol. 5, p. 312 and Ibn Farḥūn, *Dībāj*, p. 99). This learned unity was the correlate of a great economic and cultural unity, in which trade (see M. Lombard, *The Golden Age of Islam*, tr. J. Spencer (Amsterdam and Oxford, 1975), part 2, *passim*) went hand in hand with pilgrimage, scholarship and that sure but silent index of systematic linkage, the diffusion of crops (A.M. Watson, *Agricultural Innovation in the Early Islamic World. The Diffusion of Crops and Farming Techniques* (Cambridge, 1983), ch. 18).

84. An excellent review of the connection in a different context between folklore and high culture is given by J. Le Goff, *Times, Work, and Culture in the Middle Ages*, tr. A. Goldhammer (Chicago and London, 1982), p. 157.

85. Subkī, *Mu'īd*, p. 76.

86. G. Tillion, *The Republic of Cousins*, tr. Q. Hoare (London, 1983), pp. 139–47.

87. See J.S. Trimingham, *The Sufi Orders in Islam* (Oxford, 1971), p. 149 and ch. 2 and 3,*passim*.

88. Maqrīzī, *Khiṭaṭ*, vol. 2, p. 435; Nu'aimī, *Dāris*, vol. 1, p. 213 and Ibn Khallikān, *Wafayāt*, vol. 7, p. 256.

89. For instance, Sha'rānī, *Ṭabaqāt*, vol. 2, pp. 66, 85, 140, 142.

90. Suyūṭī, *Muḥāḍara*, vol. 1, p. 522.

91. Sha'rānī, *Ṭabaqāt*, vol. 2, pp. 185–6. Hūd was a prophet and the name of the Qur'ānic chapter. 'Things of untruth' is a possible translation of *mu'tafikāt*, from the root a-f-k, which occurs in the Qur'ān.

92. Maqrīzī, *Sulūk*, vol. 2, p. 16. See the study and translation M.U. Memon, *'Ibn Taimīya's Struggle against Popular Religion* (The Hague-Paris, 1976).

93. Maqrīzī, *Khiṭaṭ*, vol. 2, pp. 430–1.

94. *Ibid.*, p. 433 and Trimingham, *Sufi Orders*, p. 268.

95. Maqrīzī, *Khiṭaṭ*, vol. 2, p. 433.

96. For instance, Maqrīzī, *Sulūk*, vol. 2, pp. 494, 516 and Nu'aimī, *Dāris*, vol. 2, pp. 198–9.

97. For instance, Maqrīzī, *Sulūk*, vol. 2, pp. 767–8; Sakhāwī, *Ḍaw'*, vol. 2, p. 215 and Ibn Ḥajar, *Durar*, vol. 2, p. 107.

98. See W.M. Brinner, 'The Significance of the Ḥarāfīsh and their "Sultan" ', in *JESHO*, 6 (1963), pp. 190–215.

99. Abū Ya'lā, *Mu'tamad*, para. 450.

100. For instance, Ghazālī, *Iljām*, p. 4.

101. Marrakishī, *Mu'jib*, pp. 247, 255–6; Ibn Khaldūn, *Prolégomènes*, vol. 2, p. 51 and Ibn Khaldūn, *'Ibar*, vol. 6, p. 562, and se Urvoy, 'La pensée d'Ibn Tūmart', pp. 38–9. Qalqashandī (*Khilāfa*, vol. 1, p. 25) proffered a simple and curious interpretation: that Mahdī was simply his caliphal title, adopted as other caliphs always adopted titles.

102. See the undeveloped sketch by A. Abel, 'Le Khalife. Préscence sacré', in *SI*, 7 (1957), pp. 29–45.

103. E.H. Kantorowicz, *The King's Two Bodies. A Study in Medieval Political Theology* (Princeton, 1957), esp. pp. 16, 19, 47–8, 87–9. Compare the parallelism between the king's *character angelicus* (*ibid.*, p. 8 n., and *passim*) with similar pronouncements by Ibn Khaldūn (*Prolégomènes*, vol. 1, p. 259). Both seem to be informed by the special place of the king on the chain of being.

104. M. Bloch, *The Royal Touch: Sacred Monarchy and Scrofula in England and France*, tr. J.E. Anderson (London, 1973).

105. See Subkī, *Mu'īd*, p. 185 and Ibn Khaldūn, *Prolégomènes*, vol. 3, pp. 261–2.

106. The social structure and composition of cities in question has been the topic of largely unsuccessful studies. More rewarding than modern scholarship is scrutiny of Maqrīzī's division of classes of people (*Ighātha*, pp. 111 ff.). Maqrīzī placed ordinary students on a par with ordinary soldiers, and this might explain the exhortation (Sam'ānī, *Imla'*), p. 108) to students to distinguish themselves from the ordinary commoners.

107. For a study of this and some texts, see 'A. Abū Shanab, *Masraḥ 'Arabī qadīm: Karākūz* (Damascus, n.d.).

108. This matter still awaits study. See for instance *Alf Laila wa laila*, vol. 1, p. 173.

109. Ibn al-Jawzī, *Quṣṣās*, pp. 93 ff., 117. See pp. 9–11 for the various categories and functions of preachers.

110. *Ibid.*, p. 24 and Ibn al-Ukhuwwa, *Ḥisba*, pp. 179 ff.

111. Ibn al-Jawzī, *Quṣṣās*, p. 108.

112. Ibn 'Abd al-Ra'ūf, *Ḥisba*, p. 113.

113. Kāfiyajī, *Mukhtaṣar*, p. 556.

114. Ibn al-Jawzī, *Quṣṣās*, p. 142 and Subkī, *Mu'īd*, p. 162.

115. Subkī, *Mu'īd*, p. 163.

116. Ibn Taghrī Birdī, *Manhal*, vol. 1, p. 93.

117. Nawawī, *Adhkār*, pp. 4–5.

118. *Ibid.*, p. 369. The custodians of official knowledge were not infrequently looked upon with cynical suspicion by the common masses, and were the butt of irreverent

lampoons. See the lines of 'an impudent poet' quoted by Subkī, *Mu'īd*, p. 146 and those quoted in Ibn Khallikān, *Wafayāt*, vol. 7, p. 45.

119. Maqqarī, *Nafḥ*, vol. 5, p. 162.

120. Knowledge can also symbolically and magically be used to bless, even by means of its dregs: Ibn al-Jawzī stipulated that, upon his death, his corpse should be washed, in preparation for meeting his maker, with water heated by burning the flakes accumulated from the pens he sharpened in order to write *ḥadīth*, and this was done — Ibn Khallikān, *Wafayāt*, vol. 3, p. 141.

121. Abū Ḥammū, *Wasīṭa, passim.*

122. The reader is reminded that Arabic historical literature is quite consciously an attempt to gather practical precedents for legislation in its early phase, and that this function of exemplarism was later generalised to cover all aspects of royal conduct, hence the existence of the term *'ibra, exemplum*, and cognate terms in the titles and prefatory discourses of very many historical works, not least that of Ibn Khaldūn. See 'Aẓma, *Al-Kitābā at-tārīkhiyya*, pp. 134 ff.

123. Serres, *Hermes*, p. 88.

124. E.A. Havelock, *Preface to Plato* (Oxford, 1963), pp. 124, 140, and ch. 4, *passim*.

125. E. Le Roy Ladurie, *Montaillou*, tr. B. Bray (Harmondsworth, 1980), p. 344.

126. 'Abd al-Jabbār, *Faḍl*, p. 214.

127. Ibn al-Murtaḍā, *Ṭabaqāt*, pp. 5, 9 ff.

128. Ibn 'Asākir, *Tabyīn*, pp. 45 ff.

129. For instance, Ibn Rushd, *Tahāfut*, pp. 864 ff.

130. See Al-Azmeh, *Ibn Khaldūn: An Essay, passim.*

131. P.H. Mamour, *Polemics on the Origin of the Fatimi Caliphs* (London, 1934).

132. For what follows, see 'Aẓma, *Al-Kitāba at-tārīkhiyya*, pp. 99 ff.

133. P. Bourdieu, *Esquisee d'une théorie de la pratique* (Geneva, 1972), p. 88.

134. Maqqarī, *Nafḥ*, vol. 5, p. 121.

135. J. Caro Baroja, *Estudios Mogrebies* (Madrid, 1957), p. 30. [I am grateful to J. Esteban for help with the Spanish text.]

136. Most particularly, of course, when the sultan himself is placed inside knowledge as its agency and the custodian of every certainty, as in epistemic functions that devolve to the imām in Shī'ism, most particularly the esoteric variety: see R. Brunschvig, 'Argument fatimide contre le raisonnement par analogie', in *Recherches d'islamologie. Recueil d'articles offerts a G. Anawati et L. Gardet par leurs collègues et amis* (Louvain, 1977), pp. 75–84.

137. E. Wolf, *Europe and the People Without History* (Berkeley and Los Angeles, 1983), pp. 80, 83.

138. J. Huizinga, *The Waning of the Middle Ages*, tr. F. Hopman (Harmondsworth, 1972), p. 55.

139. See N. Frye, *The Great Code*, p. 12.

140. Especially J.-P. Vernant, *The Origins of Greek Thought* (London, 1982), pp. 42 ff.

141. For concise statements, see G. Dumézil, *L'Idéologie tripartie des Indo-Européens* (Brussels, 1958), I.16, I.26, II.9 and the sociological refinements by R. Dumont, *Homo Hierarchicus*, tr. M. Sainsbury (London, 1970).

Arabic Sources

More than one edition of some books is listed below. Unless otherwise indicated, the first of the editions listed is always referred to in the notes.

'Abd al-Jabbār, Al-Qāḍī al-Astarābādī, *Kitāb Faḍl al-I'tizāl wa ṭabaqāt al-Mu'tazila*, ed. F. Sayyid (Tunis, 1974)

——— *Sharḥ al-uṣūl al-khamsa*, ed. 'A. 'Uthmān (Cairo, 1965)

Abū Ḥammū, Al-Malik, *Wasīṭat as-sulūk fī siyāsat al-mulūk* (Tunis, A.H. 1279)

Abū Ya'lā, Ibn al-Farrā' al-Ḥanbalī, *Kitāb al-Mu'tamad fī uṣūl ad-dīn*, ed. W.Z. Ḥaddād (Beirut, 1974)

Aḥmad Bābā, al-Tunbuktī, *Nayl al-ibtihāj bi-taṭrīz ad-dībāj*, on the margin of Ibn Farḥūn listed below

Alf Laila wa laila, 4 vols. (Būlāq, A.H. 1279)

Āmidī, *Al-Iḥkām fī uṣūl al-aḥkām*, 4 vols. (Cairo, 1914)

Anbārī, *Luma' al-adilla fī uṣūl an-naḥw*, ed. A. Amer (Stockholm [1963] Acta Universitatis Stockholmiensis — Stockholm Oriental Studies, III)

Anṣārī, *Awḍaḥ al-masālik ilā alfiyyat Ibn Mālik*, 2nd edn (Cairo, 1950)

A'sam, 'A. (ed.), *Tārīkh Ibn al-Rīwandī al-mulḥid. Nuṣūs wa wathā'iq min al-maṣādir al-'arabiyya khilāl alf 'ām* (Beirut, 1975)

Ash'arī, *Al-Ibāna 'an uṣūl ad-diyāna* (Cairo, n.d.)

——— *Kitāb al-luma' fir-radd 'alā ahl az-zīgh wal-bida'*, ed. Ḥ. Gharāba (Cairo, 1955)

——— *Al-Luma' fir-radd 'alā ahl az-zīgh wal-bida'*, in R.J. McCarthy (ed.) *The Theology of Al-Ash'arī* (Beirut, 1953)

——— *Maqālāt al-islāmiyyīn wa ikhtilāf al-muṣallīn*, ed. M.M.'Abd al-Ḥamīd, 2 vols. (Cairo, 1950–4) [this appears to be a pirated edition of H. Ritter's edition, Istanbul 1929–30]

'Askarī, Abū Hilāl, *Kitāb aṣ-ṣinā'atain*, ed. 'A.M. Bijāwī and M.A. Ibrāhīm, 2nd edn (Cairo, [1971])

Avicenna, *De Anima (Arabic Text), Being the Phychological Part of Kitāb al-Shifa'*, ed. F. Rahman (London, 1959)

Baghdādī, 'Abd al-Qāhir, *Kitāb uṣūl ad-dīn* (Istanbul, 1928)

Baghdādī, Abul-Barakāt b. Malkā, *Al-Mu'tabar fil-ḥikma*, 3 vols. (Hyderabad, A.H. 1357–8)

Baghdādī, al-Khaṭīb, *Al-Kifāya fī 'ilm ar-riwāya* (Hyderabad, A.H. 1357)

Baiḍāwī, *Minhāj al-wuṣūl ilā 'ilm al-uṣūl* (Cairo, A.H. 1326)

Bājī, *Kitāb al-minhāj fī tartīb al-ḥijāj*, ed. A. Turki (Paris, 1978) Publications du Departement d'Islamologie de l'Université de Paris-Sorbonne, VII

Balkhī, Abul-Qāsim, *Bāb dhikr al Mu'tazila*, text in 'Abd al Jabbār, *Faḍl*, cited above

Bāqillānī, *I'jāz al-Qur'ān*, ed. S.A. Ṣaqr (Cairo, 1963)

——— *Kitāb al-bayān 'an al-farq bain al-mu'jizāt wal-karāmāt wal-ḥiyal wal-kahāna wassiḥr wan-nārinjāt*, ed. R.J. McCarthy (Beirut, 1958) Manshūrāt jāmi'at al-ḥikma fī Baghdād, silsilat 'ilm al-kalām, 2

——— *Kitāb at-tamhīd*, ed. R.J.McCarthy (Beirut, 1957) Manshūrāt jāmi'at al-ḥikma fī Baghdād, silsilat 'ilm al-kalām, 1
Baṣrī, Abul-Ḥusain, *Kitāb al-mu'tamad fī uṣūl al-fiqh*, ed. M. Ḥamidullāh *et al.*, 2 vols. (Damascus, 1964–5)
Baṭlayūsī, 'Mas'alat al-munāẓara ma 'Abī Bakr Ibn al-Ṣā'igh', ed. A.J. Elamrani-Jamal in *Arabica*, 26(1979), pp. 78–83
Bīrūnī, *Al-Āthār al-bāqiya 'an al-qurūn al-khāliya*, ed. C.E. Sachau (Leipzig, 1923)
——— *Taḥqīq mā lil-Hind min maqūla maqbūla fil-'aql aw mardhūla* (Hyderabad, 1958) [revised version of the Sachau edition, London, 1887]
Būnī, *Sharḥ al-jaljalūtiyya al-kubrā*, in Būnī, *Manba' uṣūl al-ḥikma* (Cairo, 1951)
——— *Al-Uṣūl waḍ-ḍawābiṭ al-muḥkama*, in Būnī, *Manba' uṣūl al-ḥikma*
Dhahābī, *Al-'Ibar fī khabar man ghabar*, ed. S. Munajjid (Kuwait, 1960ff.)
——— *Al-Mughnī fiḍ-ḍu'afā'*, ed. N. 'Itr, 2 vols. (Aleppo, 1971)
Fārābī, *'Arā' Ahl al-madīna al-fāḍila* (Cairo, 1368/1948)
——— *Fuṣūl al-Madanī*, ed. D.M. Dunlop (Cambridge, 1961)
——— *Iḥṣā' al-'ulūm*, ed. A. Gonzalez Palencia (Madrid, 1932)
——— *Iḥṣā' al-'ulūm*, ed. 'U. Amīn, 3rd edn (Cairo, 1968)
——— *Kitāb al-ḥurūf*, ed. M. Mahdi (Beirut, 1970)
——— *Kitāb al-milla*, ed. M. Mahdi (Beirut, 1968)
——— *Risāla fī 'arā' ahl al-madīna al-fāḍila*, ed. F. Dieterici (Leiden, 1895)
Ghazālī, *Faḍā'iḥ al-Bāṭiniyya*, ed. 'A. Badawī (Cairo, 1964)
——— *Faiṣal at-tafriqa bain al-Islām wal-zandaqa*, ed. S. Dunyā (Cairo, 1961)
——— *Iḥyā' 'ulūm ad-dīn*, 4 vols. (Cairo, 1939)
——— *Iljām al-'awām 'an 'ilm al-kalām* (Cairo, A.H. 1351)
——— *Al-Iqtiṣād fil-i'tiqād*, ed. I.A. Çubukçu and H. Atay (Ankara, 1962)
——— *Maqāṣid al-falāsifa*, ed. S. Dunyā (Cairo, 1961)
——— *Miḥakk an-naẓar fil-manṭiq*, ed. B. Na'sānī and M. Qabbanī (Cairo, n.d.)
——— *Mishkāt al-anwār*, ed. A. 'Afīfī (Cairo, 1964)
——— *Mi'yār al-'ilm*, ed. S. Dunyā (Cairo, 1961)
——— *Mīzān al-'amal*, ed. S. Dunyā (Cairo, 1964)
——— *Al-Munqidh min al-ḍalāl wal-mūṣil ilā dhil-'izzati wal-jalāl*, ed. J. Ṣalība and K. 'Ayyād, 7th edn (Beirut, 1967)
——— *Al-Mustaṣfā min 'ilm uṣūl al-fiqh*, 2 vols. (Cairo, A.H. 1356)
——— 'Al-Radd al-jamīl li-ilāhiyyat 'Īsā bi-ṣarīḥ al-Injīl', Arabic text in R. Chidiac, *Al-Gazali. Réfutation Excellente de la divinité de Jesus-Christ d'après les Evangiles* (Paris, 1939) Bibliothèque de l'école des Hautes Etudes, vol. 54
——— *Tahāfut al-falāsifa*, ed. S. Dunyā (Cairo, 1955; 4th edn, 1966)
Ghubrīnī, *'Unwān ad-dirāya fī man 'urifa min al-'ulamā' fil-mi'a as-sābi'a bi-Bijāya*, ed. 'A. Nuwaihiḍ (Beirut, 1969) [this edition is based on that of M. Bencheneb, Algiers, A.H. 1328]
Ḥajjī Khalīfa, *Kashf aẓ-ẓunūn 'an asāmī al-kutub wal-funūn*, ed. Ş. Yaltakaya and R. Bilge (Istanbul, 1942)
——— *Kashf aẓ-ẓunūn*, ed. G. Flügel (Leipzig, 1865 ff.)
Ḥayy Ibn Yaqẓān, ed. A. Amīn (Cairo, 1958)
Ibn al-Abbār, *Al-Takmila li-kitāb aṣ-ṣila*, ed. 'I.'A. Ḥusainī, 2 vols. (Cairo and Baghdad, 1955–6)
Ibn 'Abd al-Barr, *Jāmi' bayān al-'ilm wa faḍlih wa mā yanbaghī fī riwāyatihi wa ḥamlih*, 2 vols. (Cairo, A.H. 1346)
Ibn 'Abd al-Ra'ūf, text in *Trois traités hispaniques de ḥisba* (Cairo, 1955), Documents arabes inédits sur la vie sociale et économique en Occident musulman au Môyen Age, 1e série
Ibn Abī Uṣaibi'a, *'Uyūn al-inbā' fī akhbār al-aṭibbā'*, ed. N. Riḍā (Beirut, 1965)
Ibn Abī Ya'lā, *Ṭabaqāt al-Ḥanābila*, ed. M.H. Faqī, 2 vols. (Cairo, 1952)
Ibn al-Aḥmar, *Rawḍat an-nisrīn fī dawlat Banī Marīn*, ed. 'A. Bin Manṣūr (Rabat, 1962)

Ibn 'Aqīl, *Kitāb al-jadal 'alā ṭarīqat al-fuqahā'*, ed. G. Makdisi, in *BEO*, 20(1967), pp. 119–206
——— *Al-Ta'līqāt al-musammāt kitāb al-funūn*, ed. G. Makdisi, 2 vols. (Beirut, 1970–1)
Ibn 'Arabī, 'Fihrist mu'allafāt Muḥyī ad-dīn Ibn 'Arabī, ed. K. 'Awwād, in *Majallat al-majma' al-'ilmī al-'arabī*, 29(1954), pp. 345–59, 527–36
——— *Kitāb inshā' ad-dawā'ir*, in Ibn Arabī, *Kleinere Schriften*, ed. H.S. Nyberg (Leiden, 1919)
——— *Al-Tadbīrāt al-ilāhiyya fī iṣlāḥ al-mamlaka al-insāniyya*, in *Kleinere Schriften*
——— *Tanazzul al-amlāk min 'ālam al-arwāḥ ilā 'ālam al-aflāk, aw laṭā'if al-asrār*, ed. A.Z. 'Aṭiyya and Ṭ. 'A. Surūr (Cairo, 1961)
——— *'Uqlat al-mustawfiz*, in *Kleinere Schriften*
Ibn al-'Arīf, *Maḥāsin al-majālis*, facsimile reproduction with translation by W. Elliott and A. Abdulla (Avebury, 1980)
Ibn 'Asākir, *Tabyīn kadhib al-muftarī fī mā nusiba ilā al-imām Abil-Ḥasan al-Ash'arī*, ed. Ḥ. Qudsī (Beirut, 1979)
Ibn al-Azraq, *Badā'i' as-silk fī ṭabā'i' al-mulk*, ed. 'A.S. Nashshār (Baghdad, 1977)
Ibn Bāja, 'Ittiṣāl al-'aql bil-insān', in M. Fakhry (ed.), *Rasā'il Ibn Bāja al-ilāhiyya* (Beirut, 1968)
——— *Tadbīr al-mutawaḥḥid*, in *Rasā'il Ibn Bāja*
Ibn Farḥūn, *Al-Dībāj al-mudhahhab fī ma'rifat a'yān 'ulamā' al-madhhab* (Cairo, A.H. 1351)
Ibn Fūrak, *Kitāb mushkil al-ḥadīth*, ed. M.'A. Khan (Hyderabad, 1970)
Ibn Ḥajar, *Al-Durar al-kāmina fī a'yān al-mi' a al-thāmina* (Hyderabad, A.H. 1348)
Ibn al-Ḥājib, *Al-Kāfiya*, in *Majmū'a fin-naḥw* (Istanbul, A.H. 1302)
——— *Mukhtaṣar al-muntahā al-uṣūlī* (Cairo, A.H. 1326)
Ibn Ḥazm, *Al-Iḥkām fī uṣūl al-aḥkām*, ed. A. Shākir, 8 vols. (Cairo, n.d.)
——— *Kitāb al-fiṣal fil-milal wal-ahwā' wan-niḥal*, 5 vols. (Cairo, A.H. 1317)
——— *Mulakhkhaṣ ibṭāl al-ra'ī wal-qiyās wal-istiḥsān wat-taqlīd wat-ta'līl*, ed. S. Afghānī (Damascus, 1960)
——— *Risālat at-tawqīf 'alā shāri' an-najāt*, in I. 'Abbās (ed.), *Rasā'il Ibn Ḥazm al-Andalusī* (Beirut, 1982) vol. 3
——— *Al-Taqrīb li ḥadd al-manṭiq bil-alfāẓ al-'āmmiyya wal-amthila al-fiqhiyya*, ed. I. 'Abbās (Beirut, 1959)
——— *Ṭawq al-ḥamāma fil-ilfa wal-'i'tilāf*, ed. Ḥ.K. Ṣairafī (Cairo, 1950)
Ibn al-'Imād, *Shadharāt al-dhahab fī akhbār man dhahab*, 8 vols. (Cairo, A.H. 1351)
Ibn al-Jawzī, *Kitāb al-quṣṣāṣ wal-mudhakkirīn*, ed. M.S. Swartz (Beirut, n.d.)
——— *Al-Muntaẓam fī tārīkh al-mulūk wal-umam*, ed. Krenkow, 10 vols. (Hyderabad, A.H. 1357–8)
——— *Talbīs Iblīs* (Beirut, n.d.) [after the edition of Cairo, A.H. 1368]
Ibn Jinnī, *Al-Khaṣā'iṣ*, ed. M.'A. Najjār, 3 vols (Cairo, 1952–6)
——— *Al-Luma' fil-'arabiyya*, ed. F. Fāris (Kuwait, n.d.)
Ibn Kathīr, *Al-Bidāya wan-nihāya*, 14 vols (Cairo, 1932)
Ibn Khaldūn, *Lubāb al-muḥaṣṣal fī uṣūl ad-dīn*, ed. L. Rubio (Tetouan, 1952)
——— *Muqaddimat al-'allāma Ibn Khaldūn* (Beirut, 1900) [vocalised edition]
——— *Les Prolégomènes d'Ebn Khaldoun*, ed. E. Quatremère, 3 vols (Paris, 1858)
——— *Shifā' as-sā'il li tahdhīb al-masā'il*, ed. M. Ṭanjī (Istanbul, 1958)
——— *Shifā' as-sā'il*, ed. I.A. Khalifé (Beirut, 1959)
——— *Al-Ta'rīf bi Ibn Khaldūn wa riḥlatuhu gharban wa sharqan*, ed. M. Ṭanjī (Cairo, 1951)
——— *Tārīkh al-'allāma Ibn Khaldūn. Kitāb al-'Ibar*, ed. Y.A. Daghir, 7 vols (Beirut, 1956 ff.)
Ibn Khallikān, *Wafayāt al-a'yān*, ed. I. 'Abbās, 8 vols (Beirut, 1970)
Ibn al-Khaṭīb, *Al-Iḥāṭa fī akhbār Gharnāṭa*, ed. M.'A. 'Inān, vol. 1 (Cairo, 1955)
——— *Kitāb a'māl al-a'lām*, pt. 2, ed. E. Lévi-Provencal (Rabat, 1934) Institut des Hautes

Etudes Marocaines, Collection des textes arabes, III
——— *Rawḍat at-ta'rīf bil-ḥubb ash-sharīf*, ed. 'A.A. 'Aṭā (Cairo, [1967])
Ibn Maḍā', *Kitāb ar-radd 'alā an-nuḥāt*, ed. Sh. Ḍaif (Cairo, 1947)
Ibn Manẓūr, *Lisān al-'Arab*, 20 vols (Būlāq, A.H. 1300 ff.)
Ibn Maryam, *Al-Bustān fī dhikr al-awliyā' wal-'ulamā' bi-Tilimsān*, ed. M. Bencheneb (Algiers, 1326/1908)
Ibn Marzūq, *Al-Musnad aṣ-ṣaḥīḥ al-ḥasan fī ma'āthir mawlānā Abil-Ḥasan*, ed. E. Lévi-Provencal, in *Hespéris*, 5/4 (1925), pp. 1–24
Ibn al-Murtaḍā, *Ṭabaqāt al-Mu'tazila*, ed. S. Diwald-Wilzer (Beirut, 1961). Bibliotheca Islamica, 21
Ibn al-Nafīs, *Al-Risāla al-kāmiliyya fis-sīra an-nabawiyya*, ed. M. Meyerhof and J. Schacht under the title *The Theologus Autodidactus of Ibn al-Nafīs* (Oxford, 1968)
Ibn Qayyim al-Jawziyya, *Hidāyat al-ḥayārā fī ajwibat al-Yahūd wan-Naṣārā* (Beirut, n.d.)
——— *Miftāḥ dār as-sa'āda wa manshūr wilāyat al-'ilm wal-irāda*, 2 vols (Cairo, A.H. 1341)
——— *Al-Ṭibb an-nabawī*, ed. 'A. 'Abd al-Khāliq (Beirut, n.d.)
Ibn Qudāma, *Taḥrīm an-naẓar fī kutub ahl al-kalām*, ed. G. Makdisi (London, 1962)
Ibn Qunfudh, *Al-Fārisiyya fī mabādi' ad-dawla al-Ḥafṣiyya*, ed. M.Sh. Nīfar and 'A. Turkī (Tunis, 1968)
Ibn Qutaiba, *Ta'wīl mushkil al-Qur'ān*, ed. S.A. Ṣaqr (Cairo, n.d.)
Ibn Quṭlūbughā, *Tāj al-tarājim fī ṭabaqāt al-Ḥanafiyya* (Baghdad, 1962)
Ibn Rajab, *Al-Dhail 'alā ṭabaqāt al-Ḥanābila*, ed. M.Ḥ. Faqī, 2 vols (Cairo, 1952)
Ibn al-Rīwandī, *Faḍīḥat al-Mu'tazila*, edition of the reconstructed text by 'A. A'sam, *Kitāb Faḍīḥat al-Mu'tazilah. Analytical Study of Ibn ar-Riwandi's Method in his Criticism of the Rational Foundation of Polemics in Islam* (Beirut-Paris, 1975–7), pp. 105–67
Ibn Rushd, al-Jadd (the philosopher's grandfather), *Al-Muqaddimāt al-mumahhidāt li-bayān mā iqtaḍathu rusūm al-Mudawwana min al-aḥkām al-shar'iyyāt* . . . (Cairo, n.d.)
Ibn Rushd, al-Ḥafīd, *Al-Āthār al-'ulwiyya*, in *Rasā'il Ibn Rushd* (Hyderabad, 1947)
——— *Bidāyat al-mujtahid wa nihāyat al-muqtaṣid*, 4 vols (Beirut, n.d.) [after the undated Cairo edition of 'A. Maḥmūd and 'A.Ḥ. Maḥmūd]
——— *Faṣl al-maqāl*, ed. M. 'Amāra (Beirut, 1981)
——— *Al-Kawn wal-fasād*, in *Rasā'il Ibn Rushd*
——— *Kitāb faṣl al-maqāl wa taqrīr mā bain ash-sharī'a wal-ḥikma min ittiṣāl*, ed. G.F. Hourani (Leiden, 1959)
——— *Mā ba'd aṭ-ṭabī'a*, in *Rasā'il Ibn Rushd*
——— *Manāhij al-adilla fī 'aqā'id al-milla*, ed. M. Qāsim, 2nd edn (Cairo, 1964)
——— *Al-Nafs*, in *Rasā'il Ibn Rushd*
——— *Rasā'il Ibn Rushd* (Hyderabad, 1947)
——— *Al-Samā' wal-'ālam*, in *Rasā'il Ibn Rushd*
——— *Al-Samā' aṭ-tabī'ī* in *Rasā'il Ibn Rushd*
——— *Tahāfut at-tahāfut*, ed. S. Dunyā, 2 vols (Cairo, 1965)
——— *Talkhīṣ kitāb Arisṭūṭālīs fish-shi'r*, ed. M.S. Sālim (Cairo, 1971)
——— *Talkhīṣ as-safsaṭa*, ed. M.S. Sālim (Cairo, 1973)
Ibn Sab'īn, *Budd al-'ārif*, ed. J. Kattūra (Beirut, 1978)
Ibn al-Ṣalāḥ, *'Ulūm al-ḥadīth*, ed. N. 'Itr (Medina, A.H. 1386)
Ibn Sīnā — see also Avicenna
——— *Aqsām al-'ulūm al-'aqliyya*, in *idem.*, *Tis' rasā'il* (Istanbul, A.H. 1298)
——— *Ḥayy bin Yaqẓān*, in Amin ed., *Ḥayy bin Yaqẓān*
——— *Al-Ḥudūd* in *Tis' rasā'il*
——— *Ithbāt an-nubuwwāt*, ed. M. Marmūra (Beirut, 1968)
——— *Al-Najāt* (Cairo, A.H. 1331; 2nd ed., 1357/1938)
——— *Al-Qānūn fiṭ-ṭibb*, 3 vols. (Būlāq, A.H. 1294)
——— *Al-Risāla an-nairūziyya*, in *Tis' rasā'il*
——— *Al-Shifā (Ṭabī'iyyāt, 2, 3, and 4)*, ed. M. Qāsim (Cairo, 1969)

——— *Al-Shifā' (Mantiq, 4: Al-Qiyās)*, ed. S. Ziyāda (Cairo, 1964)
——— *Tis' rasā'il (Istanbul, A.H. 1298)*
——— *'A Unique Treatise on the Interpretation of Dreams by Ibn Sina', ed. A.M. Khan in Avicenna Commemoration Volume* (Calcutta, 1956)
——— *Al-Urjūza fiṭ-ṭibb*, ed. H. Jahiers and A. Noureddine (Paris, 1956)
Ibn Sīrīn, *Muntakhab al-kalām fī tafsīr al-aḥlām*, on the margin of Nābulsī's *Ta'ṭīr*, listed below [The author was in fact Abū Sa'd or Abū Sa'īd al-Wā'iẓ, whose dates are unknown. See M. Steinschneider in *ZDMG*, 17 (1863), pp. 227 ff. and Brockelmann, *Geschichte der arabischen Literatur*, Supplement, vol. 2, p. 165]
Ibn Ṭabāṭabā, also known as Ibn al-Ṭiqṭaqā, *Al-Fakhrī fil-ādāb as-sulṭāniyya wad-duwal al-islāmiyya* (Cairo, 1962)
Ibn Taghrī Birdī, *Al-Manhal aṣ-ṣāfī wal-mustawfī ba'd al-wāfī*, ed. A.Y. Najātī (Cairo, 1956), vol. 1
Ibn Taimiyya, *Muwāfaqat ṣaḥīḥ al-manqūl li-ṣarīḥ al-ma'qūl*, ed. M.M. 'Abd al-Ḥamīd and M.Ḥ. Faqī, 3 vols (Cairo, 1950–1)
——— *Naqḍ al-manṭiq*, ed. M. Ḥamza, M. Faqī and S. Ṣanī' (Cairo, 1370/1951)
——— *Al-Radd 'alā al-manṭiqiyyīn* (Lahore, 1978)
——— *Al-Siyāsa ash-shar'iyya fī iṣlāḥ ar-rā'ī war-ra'iyya* (Cairo, A.H. 1322)
Ibn Ṭufail, *Risālat Ḥayy bin Yaqẓān*, in Amin ed., *Ḥayy bin Yaqẓān*
Ibn al-Ukhuwwa, *Ma'ālim al-qurba fī aḥkām al-ḥisba*, ed. R. Levy (London, 1938), E.J.W. Gibb Memorial Series, XII
Ījī, *Tuḥfat al-faqīr*, translated by F. Rosenthal, *A History of Muslim Historiography*, 2nd edn (Leiden, 1969)
Ikhwān al-Ṣafā', *Rasā'il*, 4 vols (Beirut, n.d.)
Isfarā'īnī, *Al-Tabṣīr fid-dīn, wa tamyīz al-firaq an-nājiya 'an al-firaq al-hālikīn*, ed. M.Z. Kawtharī (Cairo and Baghdad, 1955)
Jābir b. Ḥayyān, *Kitāb Ikhrāj mā fī al-quwwa ilā al-fi'l*, in P. Kraus (ed.), *Mukhtār rasā'il Jābir bin Ḥayyān* (Cairo, A.H. 1354)
Jurjānī, 'Abd al-Qāhir, *Asrār al-balāgha*, ed. M.R. Riḍā, 2nd edn (Beirut, 1978)
——— *Dalā'il al-i'jāz fī 'ilm al-ma'ānī*, ed. M. 'Abdu, M.R. Riḍā and M. Shinqīṭī (Cairo, 1961) [after the impression of Cairo, A.H. 1330]
Jurjānī, al-Sharīf, *Kitāb al-ta'rīfāt*, ed. G. Flügel (Leipzig, 1845)
Juwainī, *Kitāb al-irshād ilā qawāṭi' al-adilla fī uṣūl al-i'tiqād*, ed. 'A.'A. 'Abd al-Ḥamīd and M.Y. Mūsā (Cairo, 1950)
Kāfiyajī, *Al-Mukhtaṣar fī 'ilm at-tarīkh*, ed. and tr. F. Rosenthal in *A History of Islamic Historiography*, 2nd edn (Leiden, 1968)
Kalābādhī, *Al-Ta'arruf ilā madhhab ahl al-taṣawwuf*, ed. M.A. Nawāwī (Cairo, 1969)
Khayyāṭ, Abul-Ḥusain, *Kitāb al-intiṣār war-radd 'alā Ibn ar-Rāwandī al-mulḥid*, ed. S. Nyberg (Beirut, 1957)
Khūnajī, *Al-Jumal fil-manṭiq*, in S. Ghurāb (ed.), *Risālatān fil-manṭiq* (Tunis, n.d.)
Khwārizmī, *Mafātīḥ al-'ulūm*, ed. G. Van Vloten [1895] (Leiden, 1968)
Lisān al-'Arab, see Ibn Manẓūr
Maqdisī, al-Muṭahhar b. Ṭāhir, *Kitāb al-bad' wat-tārīkh*, ed. C. Huart and attributed to Balkhī (Paris, 1899 ff.)
Maqqarī, *Nafḥ aṭ-ṭīb min ghuṣn al-Andalus ar-raṭīb*, ed. I. 'Abbās, 8 vols (Beirut, 1968)
Maqrīzī, *Ighāthat al-umma bi-kashf al-ghimma* (Beirut, 1980) [after the edition of M.M. Ziyāda and J. Shayyāl, 2nd edn (Cairo, 1957)]
——— *Al-Mawā'iẓ wal-i'tibār bi-dhikr al-khiṭaṭ wal-'athār*, 2 vols (Būlāq, A.H. 1270)
——— *Kitāb as-sulūk li-ma'rifat duwal al-mulūk*, ed. S.'A. 'Āshūr and M.M. Ziyāda, 3 vols (Cairo, 1956–71)
Marrakishī, 'Abd al-Wāḥid, *Al-Mu'jib fī talkhīṣ akhbār al-Maghrib*, ed. M.S. 'Aryān (Cairo, 1963), Book 3
Mas'ūdī, *Kitāb at-tanbīh wal-ishrāf*, ed. M.J. de Goeje (Leiden, 1894) Bibliotheca Geographorum Arabicorum, 8

——— *Murūj adh-dhahab wa ma'ādin al-jawhar*, ed. C. Barbier de Meynard and Pavet de Courteille, 9 vols (Paris, 1861 ff.)
——— *Murūj adh-dhahab*, above edition revised by C. Pellat (Beirut, 1965)
Māturīdī, *Kitāb at-tawḥīd*, ed. F. Khulaif (Beirut, 1970)
Māwardī, *Al-Aḥkām aṣ-sulṭāniyya*, ed. M. Enger (Bonn, 1853)
Miskawaih, *al-Hawāmil wash-shawāmil* [answers to questions by Abū Ḥayyān at-Tawḥīdī], ed. A. Amīn and S.A. Ṣaqr (Cairo, 1951)
——— *Maqāla lil-Ustādh Abī 'Alī Miskawaih fin-nafs wal-'aql*, ed. M. Arkoun, in *BEO*, 17 (1961–2), pp. 20–65
——— *Tahdhīb al-akhlāq*, ed. Q. Zuraiq (Beirut, 1966)
——— *Tajārib al-umam*, ed. H.F. Amedroz, 3 vols (Cairo, 1914–16)
Muqaddasī, *Aḥsan at-taqāsīm fī ma'rifat al-aqālīm*, ed. M.J. de Goeje, 2nd ed. (Leiden, 1906)
Nābulsī, *Ta'ṭīr al-anām fī ta'bīr al-manām*, 2 vols (Cairo, n.d.)
Nawawī, *Fatāwī al-Imām an-Nawawī al-mussamāt bil-masā'il al-manthūra*, ed. M. Ḥajjār, 2nd edn (Aleppo, A.H. 1398)
——— *Al-Adhkār al-muntakhaba min kalām Sayyid al-Abrār*, Beurit, 1973
Nu'aimī, *Al-Dāris fī tārīkh al-madāris*, ed. J. Ḥasanī, 2 vols (Damascus, 1948)
Nubāhī, *Tārīkh quḍāt al-Andalus* (Beirut, n.d.)
Nuwairī, *Nihāyat al-arab fī funūn al-adab*, 18 vols (Cairo, 1923 ff.)
Pazdawī, *Kanz al-wuṣūl*, printed on the margin of *Kashf al-Asrār 'alā uṣūl al-Bazdawī*, by 'Abd al-'Azīz al-Bukhārī (Istanbul, A.H. 1307)
Pseudo-Ibn Sīrīn — see Ibn Sīrīn
Pseudo-Qudāma — see Qudāma b. Ja'far
Pseudo-Sijistānī — see Sijistānī, Abū Sulaimān
Al-Qāḍī al-Nu'mān, *Kitāb al-majālis wal-musāyarāt*, ed. Ḥ. Faqī, I. Shabbūḥ and M. Ya'lāwī (Tunis, 1978)
Qalqashandī, *Ma'āthir al-ināfa fī ma'ālim al-khilāfa*, ed. 'A.A. Farrāj, 3 vols (Kuwait, 1964)
——— *Ṣubḥ al-a'shā fī ṣinā'at al-inshā*, 14 vols (Cairo, 1333/1915)
Qarāfī, *Sharḥ tanqīḥ al-uṣūl fil-uṣūl* (Cairo, A.H. 1306)
Qazwīnī, *'Ajā'ib al-makhlūqāt wa gharā'ib al-mawjūdāt*, ed. F. Sa'd [after F. Wüstenfeld] (Beirut, 1977)
Qifṭī, *Tārīkh al-ḥukamā'*, ed. J. Lippert (Leipzig, 1903)
Qudāma b. Ja'far, *Kitāb naqd an-nathr*, ed. Ṭ. Ḥusain and 'A. 'Abādī (Cairo, 1933) [on the authorship, see S.A. Bonebakker, *The Kitab Naqd al-Ši'r of Qudāma b. Ğa'far* (Leiden, 1956), pp. 3 ff., 15 f.]
Qushairī, *Al-Risāla al-Qushairiyya*, ed. 'A. Maḥmūd and M. Bin al-Sharīf, 2 vols (Cairo, 1972–4)
Rāzī, Fakhr al-Dīn Ibn al-Khaṭīb, *Kitāb asās at-taqdīs* (Cairo, A.H. 1328)
——— *Kitāb al-firāsa*, ed. Y. Mourad (Paris, 1939)
——— *Lubāb al-ishārāt* (Cairo, A.H. 1326)
——— *Al-Mabāḥith al-mashriqiyya fī 'ilm al-ilāhiyyāt waṭ-ṭabī'iyyāt*, 2 vols (Hyderabad, A.H. 1343)
——— *Muḥaṣṣal afkār al-mutaqaddimīn wal-muta'akhkhirīn min al-'ulamā' wal-ḥukamā' wal-mutakallimīn* (Cairo, A.H. 1323)
——— *Munāẓarāt*, text in F. Kholeif, *A Study of Fakhr al-Dīn al-Rāzī and his Controversies in Transoxiania* (Beirut, 1966)
Rāzī, Abū Bakr Muḥammad b. Zakariyyā, *Rasā'il falsafiyya*, ed. P. Kraus (Cairo, 1939)
Sakhāwī, *Al-Ḍaw' al-lāmi' li-ahl al-qarn at-tāsi'*, 6 vols (Cairo, A.H. 1353)
——— *Al-I'lān bit-tawbīkh li man dhamma at-tārīkh* (Damascus, A.H. 1349)
Sakkākī, *Miftāḥ al-'ulūm* (Cairo, 1937)
Sam'ānī, *Adab al-imlā' wal-istimlā'*, ed. M. Weisweiler (Leiden, 1952)
Sarrāj, *Al-Luma'*, ed. 'A. Maḥmūd and Ṭ.'A. Surūr (Cairo and Baghdad, 1960)
Shahrastānī, *Al-Milal wan-niḥal* (Beirut, 1981)

Shahrastānī, *Kitāb al-milal wan-niḥal*, ed. W. Cureton (London, 1846)
——— *Muṣāra'at al-falāsifa*, ed. S.M. Mukhtār (Cairo, 1976)
Sha'rānī, *Al-Ṭabaqāt al-kubrā al-musammāt bi-lāwaḥiq al-anwār fī ṭabaqāt al-akhyār*, 2 vols (Cairo, 1954)
Shāṭibī, *Al-Muwāfaqāt fī uṣūl al-aḥkām*, ed. M. Munīr, 4 vols (Cairo, A.H. 1341)
Shawkānī, *Irshād al-fuḥūl ilā taḥqīq al-ḥaqq min 'ilm al-uṣūl* (Cairo, 1937)
Sijistānī, Abū Sulaimān, *Ṣiwān al-ḥikma wa thalāth rasā'il*, ed. 'A. Badawī (Tehran, 1974) [On the authenticity of attributing *Ṣiwān al-ḥikma* to this author, see W. Qadi, '*Kitāb Ṣiwān al-Ḥikma*: Structure, Composition, Authorship, and Sources', in *Der Islam*, 58 (1981), pp. 87–124, where it is maintained that the author was in fact one Abū al-Qāsim, *Ghulām* of Abul-Ḥasan al-'Āmirī.]
——— 'Fī anna al-ajrām al-'ulwiyya dhawāt nafs nāṭiqa', in *Ṣiwān al-Ḥikma*
——— 'Fī al-kamāl al-khāṣṣ bi-naw' al-insānī', in *Ṣiwān al-Ḥikma*
——— 'Fī al-muḥarrik al-awwal', in *Ṣiwān al-Ḥikma*
Subkī, Tāj al-Dīn, *Mu'īd an-ni'am wa mubīd an-niqam*, ed. D.W. Myhrman (London, 1908)
——— *Ṭabaqāt ash-Shāfi'iyya al-kubrā*, ed. 'A. Ḥilū and M.M. Ṭanāḥī, 6 vols (Cairo, 1964 ff.)
Suhrawardī, *Ḥayy b. Yaqẓān*, in *Ḥayy b. Yaqẓān*, cited above
——— *Kitāb al-lamaḥāt*, ed. I. Ma'lūf (Beirut, 1969)
——— *Opera Metaphysica et Mystica*, ed. H. Corbin (Tehran-Paris, 1952), vol. 2
Sukūnī, *'Uyūn al-munāẓarāt*, ed. S. Ghurāb (Tunis, 1976)
Sulāmī, *Ṭabaqāt aṣ-ṣūfiyya*, ed. N. Shuraiba, 2nd edn (Cairo, 1969)
Suyūṭī, *Bughyat al-ruwāt fī ṭābaqāt al-lughawiyyīn wan-nuḥāt*, ed. M.A. Ibrahīm, 2 vols (Cairo, 1964–5)
——— *Al-Ḥāwī lil-fatāwī*, 2 vols (Beirut, 1975) [after the edition of Cairo, A.H. 1325]
——— *Ḥusn al-muḥāḍara fī tārīkh Miṣr wal-Qāhira*, ed. M.A. Ibrāhīm, 2 vols (Cairo, 1967)
——— *Al-Itqān fī 'ulūm al-Qur'ān*, 2 vols (Cairo, A.H. 1368)
——— *Kitāb al-iqtirāḥ fī 'ilm uṣūl an-naḥw*, ed. A.M. Qāsim (Cairo, 1976)
——— *Al-Muzhir fī 'ulūm al-lugha wa anwā'ihā*, ed. M.A. Jād al-Mawlā, M.'A. Bijāwī and M.A. Ibrāhīm, 2 vols (Cairo, n.d.)
——— *Naẓm al-'iqyān fī a'yān al-a'yān*, ed. P. Hitti (New York, 1927)
——— *Ṣawn al-manṭiq wal-kalām 'an fann al-manṭiq wal-kalām*, ed. 'A.S. Nashshār (Cairo, [1947])
Ṭabarī, Abul-Ḥusain b. Sahl b. Rabban, *Firdaws al-ḥikma*, ed. M.Z. Ṣiddīqī (Berlin, 1928)
Ṭabarī, Abū Ja'far b. Jarīr, *Min kitāb ikhtilāf al-fuqahā'*, ed. J. Schacht (Leiden, 1933)
——— *Tafsīr aṭ-Ṭabarī: Jāmi' al-bayān 'an ta'wīl al-Qur'ān*, ed. M.M. Shākir, 15 vols (Cairo, [1960])
——— *Tārīkh ar-rusul wal-mulūk*, ed. M.J. de Goeje, 12 vols (Leiden, 1879 ff.)
Taftāzānī, *Sharḥ al-'aqā'id an-Nasafiyya* (Cairo, A.H. 1335)
Tahānawī, *Kashshāf iṣṭilāḥāt al-funūn*, ed. G. Kadir, W. Nassau Lees, A. Sprenger and M. Wajih, 2 vols (Calcutta, 1854 ff.)
Ṭāshköprüzāde, *Miftāḥ as-sa'āda wa miṣbāḥ as-siyāda fī mawḍū'āt al-'ulūm*, ed. K.K. Bakrī and 'A. Abū al-Nūr, 4 vols (Cairo, n.d.)
——— *Risāla fī ādāb al-baḥth*, in M.H. Āl Yāsīn (ed.), *Nafā'is al-makhṭūṭāt, al-majmū'a ar-rābi'a* (Baghdad, 1955)
Tawḥīdī, Abū Ḥayyān, *Kitāb al-imtā' wal-mu'ānasa*, ed. A. Amīn and A. Zain, 3 vols (Cairo, 1953)
——— *Al-Muqābasāt*, ed. M.T. Ḥusain (Baghdad, 1970)
——— *Risāla fil-'ulūm*, ed. M. Bergé, in *BEO*, 18 (1963–4), pp. 241–98
Thalāth wathā'iq fī muḥārabat al-ahwā' wal-bida' fil-Andalus, ed. M.'A. Khallāf (Cairo, 1981)
Ṭurṭūshī, *Sirāj al-mulūk* (Cairo, A.H. 1319)
'Umarī, Shihāb ad-Dīn b. Yaḥyā, *Wasf Ifrīqiya wal-Andalus* [extract from *Masālik al-*

abṣār] ed. Ḥ.Ḥ. 'Abd al-Wahhāb (Tunis, n.d.)
'Uqbānī, *Kitāb tuḥfat an-nāẓir wa ghunyat adh-dhākir fī ḥifẓ ash-sha'ā'ir wa taghyīr al-manākir*, ed. 'A. Shanūfī ([Damascus], n.d.)
Yaḥyā b. 'Adī, 'Maqāla fī tabyīn al-faṣl bayna ṣinā'at al-mantiq al-falsafī wan-naḥw al-'arabī', ed. G. Enders, in *Majallat tārīkh al-'ulūm al-'arabiyya*, 2/1 (1978), pp. 38–50
——— *Tahdhīb al-akhlāq*, text in N. Takriti, *Yahya Ibn 'Adi. A Critical Edition and Study of his Tahdhib al-Akhlaq* (Beirut-Paris, 1978)
——— 'Un traité de Yahyā Ben 'Adī. Défense du dogme de la Trinité contre les objections d'al-Kindī', ed. A. Périer in *Revue de l'Orient Chrétien*, 22 (1920–1), pp. 4–14
Ya'qūbī, *Tārīkh*, 2 vols (Beirut, 1960) [on the basis of the edition of C. Huart]
Yāqūt, *Irshād al-arīb ilā ma'rifat al-adīb*, ed. D.S. Margoliouth, 7 vols, 2nd edn (London, 1923–35)
Zajjājī, *Al-Īḍāḥ fī 'ilal an-naḥw*, ed. M. Mubārak (Cairo, 1959)
Zarkashī, *Al-Burhān fī 'ulūm al-Qur'ān*, ed. M.A. Ibrāhīm, 4 vols, 2nd edn (Cairo, [1971])
Zarnūjī, *Kitāb ta'līm al-muta'allim ṭarīq at-ta'allum*, ed. M. Qabbānī (Beirut, 1981)

Index

Abbasids 220, 257
'Abd al-Jabbār, al-Qāḍī 60–1, 122, 171, 223
abrogation 126, 129, 160, 164–5, 170
Abū Bishr Mattā b. Yūnus 107
Abū Ḥammū, ruler of Tlemcen 267
Abū Ḥanīfa 164, 174, 221–2
Abū Hāshim 67
Abū Muslim, al-Khurāsānī 220
Abū Ya'lā 127, 216–17, 263
Abū Yūsuf 221
accidents 18–20, 22
action 12, 14, 207
adab 255, 267
aḍdād 34
'Ādiliyya College 253, 254–5
adultery 89
aesthetics 40–1
Aghlabids 221
Aḥmad b. Ḥanbal 217, 222
Aḥmadiyya 203
alchemy
  criticism of 12–13, 199, 203–4
  four elements in 22
  Ibn Sīnā on ii, 26–7
  Majrīṭī on 28
  origins 135
  principles 184
Aleppo 224
Alf lail wa laila see Thousand and One Nights
algebra 185
'Alī b. Abī Ṭālib 123, 131
allegory 126–35
Almeria 204
Almohads 205, 209–11, 256–7
Almoravids 210, 256
alphabet *see* letters, esoteric
'amal muṭlaq 176
Āmidī, Abūl-Ḥasan 14
analogy 87–94, 148–9, 158, 168, 176, 180
angels 2, 34, 57
anthropomorphism 64–8, 70, 91, 119, 122, 215, 217
Anti-Christ 259
antinomianism 179, 202, 204, 262–3
apodicticity 177–82, 184–6, 238, 266–72
aporiai 150–4, 159, 183
apostasy 201, 203
apprehension 147–9, 178
'aqā'id 215
arabic iv, 118, 167–8, 227, 260–1, 267
a'rāḍ 18–20, 22
arithmetic 150, 185
artifice 12, 14, 24
'aṣabiyya 11, 19
asbāb al-nuzūl 124, 126
Ash'arī, Abūl-Ḥasan 177, 217, 212, 232
  on body and soul 20
  on *i'jāz* 137
  on substance 18
Ash'arites 157, 210, 213–22, 225, 268
  on creation 177
  — divine attributes 64–8, 122
  — figurative language 125
  — free will 82–6
  — human activity 81
  — *jawhar* 16, 19
  — nature ii, 10
  — *sawiyya* 9, 20
Ashrafiyya College 225
asmā' al-ḥusnā 68, 72, 95, 170
astrology 72–3, 76–9, 195, 199, 203, 223, 260
astronomy 149, 185, 204
atomism 17–18, 208
attributes, divine 64–8, 70, 122, 215, 216–19
awā'il 269
awqāf 253–4, 262
Awzā'ites 221
Ayyubids 223

Baalbeck 216
Badawī, Shaikh Aḥmad 262
badī' 40, 119, 123
Baghdad 202, 214–22, 223–5, 231, 236, 255, 257, 263

Baghdādī, Abul-Barakāt 12, 17n127, 64, 184
Baihaqiyya College 223
Bājī 175
Balkh 223
balāgha 119, 169
Banū 'Abbād 256
Banū Ḥammād b. Zaid 252–3
Banū Jamā'a 252
Banū Marzūq 252
Banū Munajjā 252
Banū Qudāma 252
Banū Ṣaṣrā 252
Banū Shahrazūrī 252
Bāqillānī 14, 24, 60, 71, 152, 217
Basra 213, 220, 223
Baṣrī, Abul-Ḥusain 172
bāṭin 127–35
Bāṭiniyya 203, 213
beatific names 68, 72, 95, 170
beauty 40–1
being 109
belief 198–9, 207
bid'a 201–2
bimāristānāt 236, 237
biographical dictionaries 217, 254
Bīrūnī 117, 122, 161, 220
Bishr b. al-Mu'tamir 220
Bisṭāmī 204
blasphemy 112–13
body 3, 8, 15–16, 20, 27
Bukhārī 162, 163, 164
Bukhārī, Ṣadr al-Sharī'a 178
Bukhtīshū' (family) 236
Bulqīnī 227
Būyids 214, 216, 220

Cairo 215, 223–5, 232, 252–4, 262–3
caliphate 218, 257–9, 264
categories 151, 185
Cathars 268
causality 5, 14–15, 73, 80
celestial spheres 3, 6, 11, 24, 32, 78
certification 230–3, 235–6, 252, 265, 268
chain of being 1–9, 42n2, 55–6, 63, 69–70, 149
Christians iv, 111, 128–9, 152, 204, 208, 259
cities 251, 264
colleges
  ijāza 230–3, 235–6, 252, 265, 268
  location 223–5
  organisation 224, 226–7
  syllabus 224–5
  teaching 226–30, 251–5
  transmission of texts 230–8
commoners 122–3, 264
composites 14–16, 21, 32
consensus 87, 165, 203, 210
contingency 5
contrariety *see* opposition
conversion 259–60
coptic 261n83
Cordoba 209, 211, 225
corruption *see* generation and corruption
cosmology 62–3, 122, 183
creation 1–9, 122, 219
  Ash'arites on 177
  Māturīdī on 177
  Mu'tazilites on 14, 21, 85–6
cryptography 135

Dajjāl 259
Damascus 202, 214–15, 221, 224–5, 231, 236, 252–5, 263, 265
Dār al-Ḥikma 223
Dār al-'Ilm 223
Dārikī 222
definition 148
demonstration 150–2
Dhahabī 225
dhimma 203
dīwān al-qurrā' 254
dreams 61–2, 73–5, 184
dualism 152

economics 36, 39
education *see* colleges, *madāris*
elixirs 27–8
eloquence 119, 169
endowments 253–4, 262
epilepsy 78–9
eschatology 132, 216, 218, 259–60, 264, 269
essence 151
eternity 1, 4
etymology 116n72
evil 1, 6, 82, 176
examinations 200, 202, 209, 215, 237
exegesis 87–8, 94, 123–35, 137, 170, 234
exemplarism 264, 267–9

Fairūzābādī 167
fahrasa 232
falsehood 110–11, 162
Fārābī 3, 19, 111, 156, 159, 181, 184
  on being 109
  — hierarchies 63
  — *jinn* 208
  — logic 116
  — medicine 21
  — the Mu'tazilites 208
  — the soul 206
  — truth 5
Fatimids 223, 225, 268
felicity 206
Fez 253, 264
final cause 5
first intellect 2, 6
fiqh see law
form 16–22, 29
four elements 7, 15–16, 29–31
  Ibn Sīnā on 11, 58
  medical concept of 21–2, 184
  qualities of 23–6
  Rāzī on 11
fuqahā' 226
Fürstenspiegel 180–1, 259, 267
furū' 87–90, 94, 171, 174, 179

genealogy 160, 262, 268–72
generation and corruption 2, 17n127, 28, 31, 34, 132
geometry 150, 185
Ghazālī 153, 157, 204, 223, 226, 237, 265–6
  on classification of sciences 156
  — correspondence 110
  — esoteric letters 203
  — *ḥadīth* 163
  — Ibn Sīnā 112
  — justice 35, 38, 214
  — law 173
  — logic 158
  — matter 18
  — numerology 71
  — philosophy 208
  — the psyche 122
  — theology 171–2, 212
Ghaznavids 220
Ghulām Ẓuhal 76
gnosticism 109, 112–13, 178
good 1, 176
God
  and chain of being 1–9
  and history 271–2
  and order 41
  attributes of 64–8, 70, 122, 215, 216–19
  beatific names 68, 72, 95, 170
  Ibn 'Arabī on 16
  ma'rifa 113, 178–9
  Mu'tazilites on 21
  omnipotence 22, 95
  transcendence 68–9
  unity of 40
  will 81–6, 91
Gospels 128
grammar 107–8, 116–17, 153, 167–9, 214, 224, 235, 254–5
  parts of speech 4, 115–16, 118
greek 223, 261n83

ḥadīth 153–4, 162–7, 169, 224–8, 231–4, 253, 265
Ḥallāj 202, 204–5, 265
Ḥamā 252
Ḥanafites 213–15, 218, 221–2, 257, 263
Ḥanbalites 65–8, 199, 202, 213–22, 252
ḥarāfish 263
Ḥarīrī 135
Ḥarrān 216
Ḥāshiya 234
Ḥayy b. Yaqẓan cycle 28, 133
heavenly spheres *see* celestial spheres
hebrew iv
Herat 216, 223, 231
heresy 201–7, 209, 214, 264
hermeticism 70, 99n102, 131, 134, 183
hierarchy 1–9, 38–40, 55–6, 63, 69–70, 80–1, 272
ḥikma 159, 182
Hishāmiyya 64
history v–viii, 131, 180–1, 250, 259, 267–72
hospitals 236, 237
humanity 8, 56, 63, 81–6, 92, 167
humours 29–31, 71–2, 185

Ibāḍiyya 261
Ibn 'Abd al-Barr 22
Ibn 'Aqīl 127, 202–3, 216–17

Ibn 'Arabī 198, 262
on dreams 73
— exegesis 130
— God 16
— knowledge 179
— proof 173
— sainthood 204–5
— symbolism 134
Ibn al-'Arīf 199
Ibn 'Asākir 225, 231
Ibn Bāja 205–6
Ibn Bint al-A'azz 253
Ibn Bishrūn 25
Ibn Daqīq al-'Īd 214, 253–4
Ibn al-Fāriḍ 205
Ibn Fūrak 217
Ibn al-Ḥājib 153
Ibn Ḥazm
on analogy 87, 180
— classification of sciences 156–7
— consensus 210
— definition 148
— epilepsy 78–9
— exegesis 127
— *ḥadīth* 163
— language 125
— logic 107, 158
— miracles 60
— nature 10
— religious statements 69
— *taḥrīf* 111
— terminology 18, 20
Ibn Hubaira 216
Ibn Jamā'a, Badr al-Dīn 253
Ibn al-Jawzī 22, 111, 216, 252, 265–6
Ibn Jinnī 4, 89, 168–9
Ibn Kathīr 163, 225
Ibn Khaldūn 256
on action 12
— alchemy 27, 199, 203–4
— the Arabs 13
— *'aṣabiyya* 11, 19
— astrology 76–8
— civilisation 4, 84, 151
— colleges 227, 230, 233–4
— dreams 74
— esoteric letters 134
— *kasb* 36
— *khabar* 161, 163
— *mutashābihāt* 177
— nature 12
— philosophy 199, 206
— prophecy 33
— and Shāṭibī 153
— the state 15, 37, 39
— texts 136
— the *zā'irja* 203
Ibn Khallikān 253
Ibn al-Khaṭīb 269
Ibn Mālik 235, 254–5
Ibn al-Mu'ammil 254
Ibn al-Mu'tazz 40
Ibn Qāsī 203
Ibn al-Qāsim 174, 210
Ibn Qayyim al-Jawziyya 22
Ibn Qudāma al-Maqdisī 66, 217
Ibn Qutaiba 34
Ibn al-Rāwandī 202
Ibn Rushd (Averroes) 159, 209, 211
on astrology 77–8
— celestial spheres 3
— classification of texts 128
— commoners 123
— composites 32
— eternity 4
— figurative language 121
— Holy Scripture 129
— legal theory 210
— magnetism 79
— nature 12
— positive science 176
— theology 208, 210
— truth 128
Ibn Rushd, Abul-Walīd 174, 209
Ibn Sab'īn 134, 256
Ibn al-Ṣalāḥ 205, 225
Ibn Sīnā Avicenna 139, 199, 208, 237
on alchemy ii, 26–7
— astrology 78–9
— celestial spheres 3
— composites 32
— creation 4
— esoteric letters 134
— four elements 58
— humidity 23
— medicine 151, 236
— philosophy 151, 160, 186, 206
— prophecy 62, 186, 206
— the soul 20, 57–8
— theology 112, 207
Ibn Taimiyya 199, 214–16, 254
on Ash'arites 219
— commoners 123
— definition 148

— divine attributes 66
— four elements 21
— *kufr* 201, 203, 206
— law 173
— logic 13, 114, 157
— mysticism 262
— nature 10
— philosophy 183, 206
— politics 258–9
— positive science 161
Ibn Ṭufail 205–6, 209
Ibn Tūmart 176, 210, 264
Ibn Zuqā'a 256
idolatry 122
i'jāz 60–1, 137
ijāza 230–3, 235–6, 252, 265, 268
ijmā' 87, 165, 203, 210
ijtihād 175–6, 201, 210, 227
Ikhwān aṣ-Ṣafā'
and Isma'ilism 43n38
on astrology 78
— eschatology 132
— four elements 25
— hierarchy 7
— magnetism 79
— numerology 71, 184
— regularity 10
'ilal 89, 92, 146, 168
'ilm see knowledge
imām 210, 252–3, 263
imamate 131, 177, 202, 219–20, 270n136
imārat al-istīlā' 258
imāla 140n75
imlā' 232
imtiḥān 200, 202, 209, 215, 237
induction 147–8
inheritance 261–2
Inquisition 261
intuition 148
Isfahan 216, 223, 231
Isfarā'īnī, Abul Muẓaffar 67, 212
Isfarā'īnī, Abū Isḥāq 119, 214, 217, 232
ism al-a'ẓam 95–6
Ismā'īlīs iv, 213, 223
on astrology 76
— exegesis 130
— political theory 205
— reincarnation 7
— transcendence of God 68–9
istikhlāf 69, 81, 85
Jābir b. Ḥayyān 25, 27
Jāḥiẓ 208
Jamā'īlī, Taqī al-Dīn 215
Jarīriyya 221
jawhar 16–22, 63
Jerusalem 252
Jesus 128, 259
Jews iv, 111
jinn 25, 127, 208, 265
Jubbā'ī 232
judgement 147–9
judges 221, 252–4, 257
Jurjānī, 'Abd al-'Azīz 40
Jurjānī, 'Abd al-Qāhir 120, 137, 169
justice 35–40, 214
Juwainī, Imām al-Ḥaramain 223, 226, 232, 253
and Ash'arites 218–19
— divine attributes 67
— four elements 25

kasb 36, 83, 208
Kalīlawa Dimna 135
Kundurī, Abbasid vizir 218
karāma 59–61, 264
kātib al-ghaiba 226
khabar 130, 161–7
khānqāh 225
Khaṭīb al-Baghdādī 222
khayāl al-ẓill 264
khilāf 175, 221, 224
Khūnajī 184
Khwārizm-Shāhs 220
Khwārizmī 217
Kindī 70
kingship 38–40, 84, 96, 257–9, 261, 264, 267
knowledge
and God 178
and humanity 167
and science 227–31
and signification 136
classes of 146–7, 212
Ibn 'Arabī on 179
theory of 106–15
transmission 223, 250–5, 264–72
unofficial 263–4
Kufa 214
kufr 201–7, 209, 214, 264
Kullābiyya 213
kuttāb 252, 264

Laithī, Yaḥyā b. Yaḥyā 221
language
  aḍdād 34
  and orientalism v–viii
  and science 161
  etymology 116n72
  figurative 92–4, 117–23, 125–35, 170
  grammar 107–8, 116–17, 153, 167–9, 214, 224, 235, 254–5; parts of speech 4, 115–16, 118
  lexicography 167–8
  phonetics 111, 116
  synonymy 118n91
latin 168n168
law
  concepts: *'amal muṭlaq* 176; *bid'a* 201–2; *furū'* 87–90, 94, 171, 174, 179; *ijmā'* 87, 165, 203, 210; *ijtihād* 175–6, 201, 210, 227; *'ilal* 89–92, 146, 168; *khilāf* 175, 221, 224; *kufr* 201–7, 209, 214, 264; *maṣāliḥ mursala* 173; *qiyās* 87–94, 158, 176; *ratio legis* 90–1, 173; *shar'* 87–90, 178–9, 258–9, 262; *taklīf* 166; *uṣūl al-fiqh* 86–91, 94, 162–6, 171–6, 179, 235, 260
  maintenance of 260
  officials: *imām* 210, 252–3, 263; judge 221, 252–4, 257; *muftī* 213; *muḥtasib* 236–7; *mujtahid* 166, 226–7
  schools: Awza'ī 221; Ibāḍī 261; Ḥanafī 213–15, 218, 221–2, 257, 263; Ḥanbalī 65–8, 199, 202, 213–22, 252; Mālikī 204, 209–12, 221–2, 225, 253; Shāfi'ī 213–14, 218–19, 221–2, 225, 252, 257, 263; Shī'ī 175, 213–14, 220; Ẓāhirī 87, 91, 165, 168, 199, 209–10, 221–2; Zaidī 220
  teaching 223–5, 227, 232, 236
letters, esoteric 70–3, 94, 124, 134, 203
lexicography 167–8
libraries i, 225, 230, 236
logic 182
  and grammar 107–8, 116
  and the mind 149
  and science 154
  Ibn Taimiyya on 13, 114, 157
  place in Arabic thought 158, 184–6
  Suyūṭī on 205

Ma'arrī, Abul-'Alā' 202
madāris
  ijāza 230–3, 235–6, 252, 265, 268
  location 223–5
  organisation 224, 226–7
  syllabus 224–5
  teaching 226–30, 251–5
  transmission of texts 230–8
magic 60, 185n196, 200, 203, 264
magnetism 74, 79
Mahdī 129, 131, 259, 264
majādhib 113, 262
majāz 92–4, 117–23, 125–35, 170
Majrīṭī, Maslama 28
Malāmatiyya 263
Mālik b. Anas 232
Mālikites 204, 209–12, 221–2, 225, 253
Mamlūks 214, 252–4, 257, 262–3
ma'nā 116–17, 119–21
Manichaeans 152
Manṣūriyya College 224
Maqrīzī 36, 224
ma'rifa 113, 178–9
Marrakesh 209
maṣāliḥ mursala 173
mathematics 150, 152, 185
matter 16–22
Māturīdī 14, 82–4, 126, 177, 214, 220
Māwardī 258
medicine 151
  and four elements 21–2, 184
  and nature 207
  and physics 150
  and treatment of illness 30–1
  teaching of 224, 236, 254–5
memory 112, 233–5
Merv 223
Messiah *see Mahdī*
metals 25–6, 36
metaphor 92–4
metaphysics 8, 182–4, 185–6
metonymy 92–4
minerals 25–6
miracles 59–61, 264
Miskawaih 39
Mizzī 225

money 35–6, 39
Mongols 219, 252, 255
monism 6, 64, 204–5
mosque 224, 252–3, 259
Mosul 216, 223
movement 11, 24, 78
Mu'āwiya 215
mudarrisūn 226
mudhakkirūn 264–5
muftī 213
Mughīra b. Sa'd 70
muḥkam 124
muḥtasib 236–7
mu'īdūn 226
mujtahid 116, 226–7
muqaddimāt 146–9, 157, 160, 166, 180, 184–6, 198
muqallid 226
Muqaddasī 71
music 35, 71n110
Muslim b. al-Ḥajjāj 164
mustamlī 232
Mutanabbī 169
mutashābih 124, 177
Mu'tazilites 176, 208, 212–22, 256, 268
  on the caliphate 218
  — creation 14, 21, 85–6
  — divine attributions 65–8, 215
  — exegesis 170
  — free will 82–6
  — justice 214
  — *khabar* 161
  — law 88, 171–2
  — *naskh* 170
mysticism
  and defence of *shaṭḥ* 112–13
  and Shāfi'ites 213
  and truth 108
  development 178
  nature of 58–63, 262–4
  position in Islam 204, 219

Nābulsī, 'Abd al-Ghanī 75
naḥw see grammar
nairanjāt 74
naqīb al-fuqahā' 226
Nasafī 235
naskh 126, 129, 160, 164–5, 170
naṣṣ 126, 129
nature ii, 9–13, 21, 44–5n65, 207, 219
Nawawī 225, 265
Nawshajānī 17, 76
naẓar 149
Naẓẓām, Ibrāhīm b. Sayyār 20, 87
Nīṣābūrī, Abū Rashīd 154
Nīshāpūr 213, 216–19, 223, 231, 253
Niẓām al-Mulk 218–20, 223
Niẓāmiyya College 216, 223–4
Nu'aymī 224, 236
numerology 70–3, 184
Nuṣairites 131n188, 202

opposition 9, 33–4
orality 160, 232–5, 267
orientalism v–viii

pantheism 6, 64, 204–5
parts of speech 4, 115–16, 118
Perfect Man 63–4
Persian iv, 260n83
Persians 152, 255
pharmacology 185
philosophy 151, 159–60, 183–4, 186–7, 205–11
phonology 111, 116
physics 150
plagiarism 120n106, 121n119
plays 264
poetics 40, 119, 123, 235
political thought 38–40, 84–5, 180–1, 257–61, 267
preachers 252–3, 264–5
premisses 146–9, 157, 160, 166, 180, 184–6, 198
profession of faith 215, 261
prophecy 33, 39, 56–62, 82n196, 129, 186, 206
proportion 15
psyche 115, 122
pythagoreanism 184

Qabbāb 153
qābil 17
Qadariyya 213
qāḍī (*quḍāh*) *see* judges
Qāḍī 'Abd al-Jabbār 60–1, 122, 171, 223
Qāḍī al-Nu'mān 132–3
Qalandariyya 263
Qarmaṭism 213
Qarṭājinnī 169
qirā'a 232, 237

qiyās 87–94, 158, 176
Qur'ān
  ambiguous verses in 124, 177
  and orientalism vi
  divine attributes in 215
  inimitability 60–1, 137
  interpretation 87–8, 95, 123–35, 137, 170, 234
  recitation 234
  sciences of 170
  variant readings 235
Qushairī, Abū Naṣr 218
Qushairī, Abul-Qāsim 179, 204, 215
quṣṣāṣ 264–5

ratio legis 90–1, 173
Rāzī, Fakhr al-Dīn 170, 183, 214
  on alchemy 27
  on Bukhārī 164
  — celestial spheres 11
  — good and evil 1
  — *kufr* 203
  — law 179
  — occult science 203
  — philosophy 186
  — proportion 15
  — the Qur'ān 137
  — teaching 232
Rāzī, Muḥammad b. Zakariyyā 21, 31, 158, 184, 208
reason 198–9, 207
reincarnation 7, 132, 202, 220
Rummānī 153
Ruwāḥiyya College 224

sa'āda 206
Sabeans iv, 70
Saḥnūn 174, 210
sainthood 58–62, 204–5, 262–4
Sakkākī 107
Saljūqs 214, 216, 218, 223, 257
salvation 206
samā' 232, 237
Sam'ānī 228
Ṣarghatmushiyya College 232
Satan 57, 61, 257, 259
sawiyya 9–13, 20
scepticism 146
scholarship 226–7, 251–7, 259–60, 263–4, 266, 270
science
  classification of 155–9, 182
  legitimacy 199–200, 206
  nature of 146–54, 184–6, 198, 250–1, 260
  transmission 227–31, 233
  typology 160–76, 203; islamic 167–76, 203; positive 160–6, 203
sempiternity 1
Seven Bodies 25–6
Sha'bān, Shaikh 262
Shādhilī 233
shadow plays 264
Shāfi'ī 126, 222, 232
Shāfi'ites 213–14, 218–19, 221–2, 225, 252, 257, 263
shahāda 261
Shahrastānī 184, 212
shaikh al-shuyūkh 252–4, 257
shar' 87–90, 178–9, 258–9, 262
shaṭḥ 112–13
Shāṭibī, Abul-Qāsim 235
Shāṭibī, Ibrāhīm b. Mūsā 153, 165
  on law 88, 90–1, 173–4, 212
  — the Qur'ān 137
Shī'ites iv, 202
  conflict with Ḥanbalites 213–14, 216, 218–20
  on eschatology 216
  — history 131
  — law 175, 213–14, 220
  — *ta'wīl* 164
shuyūkh al-riwāya 226
signification 115–23, 136, 146
Sijistānī 160, 184, 208–9
  on evil 1
  — generation and corruption 31
  — grammar 116–17
  — kingship 39
  — nature 9, 12
  — potencies 56
  — theology 122
Sinān b. Thābit b. Qurra 237
Sīrāfī 9, 107, 116, 255
Sīrat 'Antar 264
soothsaying 33, 57, 61n42, 265
sorcery 203
soul
  and chain of being 8
  and elixirs 27–8
  and prophecy 61–2
  and temper 29
  and virtue 34

Ash'arī on 20
faculties of 3
Ibn Sīnā on 20, 57–8
Ibn Ṭufail on 206
Ikhwān aṣ-Ṣafā' on 132
potencies of 34
Tawḥīdī on 63
transmigration 7, 132, 201, 220
Stoics 21–2, 44–5n65, 70, 77, 109
students 226–7, 264n106
Subkī 6, 135, 212–14, 218–21, 226, 265
substance 16–22, 63
ṣūfism see mysticism
Sufyān al-Thawrī 221
Suhrawardī 22, 57, 82n196, 133, 184, 204
sultanate 218–19, 258
sunna 165
Suyūṭī iii
on grammar 153, 169
— *ijtihād* 227
— Māwardī 258
— philosophy 205
— women 178
syllogism 107, 110, 148, 181, 185, 208
symbolism 134–5
synonymy 118n91
syriac iv, 223, 261n83

Ṭabarī, Abul-Ḥusain b. Rabban 21
Ṭabarī, Muḥammad b. Jarīr 170, 221–2
tafsīr see exegesis, *ta'wīl*
Ṭaḥāwī 215
taḥrīf 111
ṭailasān 199
taklīf 166
ṭalaba 226–7, 264n106
ta'līqa 234
talismans 27, 72–4, 185n196, 200, 203
taqiyya 131
taqlīd 166, 175
taṣawwuf see mysticism
taṣawwur 147–9, 178
taṣdīq 147–9
Tawḥīdī 1, 12, 63
ta'wīl 126–8, 130, 164
temper 29–32, 37
terminology 9, 18, 20, 34, 153, 168n168
texts, transmission of 230–8
Thābit b. Qurra 70
theolepsy 113, 262
theology 112, 122, 208, 210
and human action 207
development 211–20
logic in 153–4, 158
nature of 176–8
primacy of 171–2
teaching 224, 232
Thousand and One Nights 41, 264
Tlemcen 267
translation 115, 223, 261n83
Tripoli (Lebanon) 202
truth 108, 110, 181
and *khabar* 162–6
and law 166
accessibility 124, 128
attainment of 105
empirical 147
Fārābī on 5
invariant 160
knowledge of 131
Tuareg 262
Ṭughrā'ī ii, 26–7, 255
Ṭurṭūshī 175, 256

'ulamā' 226–7, 251–7, 259–60, 263–4, 266, 270
Umayyads 225
unbelief 201–7, 209, 214, 264
uṣūl al-fiqh 86–91, 94, 162–6, 171–6, 179, 235, 260
utopia 257–61

virtue 34–40, 89

waḍ' 115–16, 118–19, 124, 129, 132, 134–5, 159, 167, 174
warrāqūn 230
will 81–6, 91
wine 93, 253
women 178, 261–2
wu''āẓ 264–5

Yaḥyā b. 'Adī 108, 159, 184, 208

ẓāhir 125–31
Ẓāhirites 87, 91, 165, 168, 199, 209–10, 221–2
Zaidiyya 220
zā'irja 72, 203
Zajjājī 169
Zamakhsharī 170
Zangids 223
Zarnūjī 228
Zoroastrians 220

For Product Safety Concerns and Information please contact our EU
representative GPSR@taylorandfrancis.com
Taylor & Francis Verlag GmbH, Kaufingerstraße 24, 80331 München, Germany

www.ingramcontent.com/pod-product-compliance
Lightning Source LLC
Chambersburg PA
CBHW052149300426
44115CB00011B/1589
* 9 7 8 1 1 3 8 9 1 2 5 3 3 *